Acting Up and Getting Down

D1065749

SOUTHWESTERN WRITERS COLLECTION SERIES

The Wittliff Collections at Texas State University
Steven L. Davis, Editor

Acting Up
& Getting
Down

PLAYS BY AFRICAN AMERICAN TEXANS

Edited and
with introductions
by Sandra M. Mayo
and Elvin Holt

University
of Texas Press
Austin

THE SOUTHWESTERN WRITERS COLLECTION SERIES
originates from the Wittliff Collections, a repository of literature, film, music, and southwestern and Mexican photography established at Texas State University.

Requests for permission to reproduce material from this work should be sent to:
    Permissions
    University of Texas Press
    P.O. Box 7819
    Austin, TX 78713-7819
    http://utpress.utexas.edu/index.php/rp-form

♾ The paper used in this book meets the minimum requirements of ANSI/NISO Z39.48-1992 (R1997) (Permanence of Paper).

Library of Congress Cataloging-in-Publication Data
Acting up and getting down : plays by African American Texans / edited and with introductions by Sandra Mayo and Elvin Holt. — First edition.
    pages   cm. — (Southwestern writers collection series)
    Includes bibliographical references.
    ISBN 978-0-292-75479-9 (cloth : alk. paper) — ISBN 978-0-292-75480-5 (pbk. : alk. paper)
    1. American drama—African American authors. 2. American drama—Texas. 3. American drama—20th century. 4. American drama—21st century. 5. African Americans—Drama. I. Mayo, Sandra Marie, editor of compilation. II. Holt, Elvin, editor of compilation.
    PS628.N4A28 2014
    812'.54080896073—dc23
                            2013030264
doi:10.7560/754799

CONTENTS

Acknowledgments vii

Introduction: Definition of Black Theatre 1

Camp Logan Celeste Bedford Walker 19

Johnny B. Goode Thomas Meloncon 95

Killingsworth Eugene Lee 157

Driving Wheel Sterling Houston 203

Br'er Rabbit Adapted by George Hawkins 229

When the Ancestors Call Elizabeth Brown-Guillory 249

Ancestors Ted Shine 295

APPENDIX A Chronology 333

APPENDIX B Playwrights' Canon 343

Publications by Black Texas Playwrights 353

Author Photo Credits 354

··

ACKNOWLEDGMENTS

Center for Multicultural and Gender Studies Staff:
  Luann Walker
  Ashley Cureton
  Stacey Wilson
  Mary Gibson
  Sophia Joseph
  Treena Herington
  Felix Adam
  C. Francis Blackchild
  Alana King
  Crystal Brown
  Sixto-Juan Zavala
  Danielle Antonetti
  Amanda Benoist

Jubilee Theatre, Fort Worth, Texas
The Black Academy of Arts and Letters, Dallas, Texas
The Renaissance Guild, San Antonio, Texas
Hornsby Entertainment Theatre, San Antonio, Texas
Encore Theatre, Houston, Texas
The Ensemble Theatre, Houston, Texas
Pro-Arts Collective, Austin, Texas
Austin History Center
University of Texas, Harry Ransom Research Center
Texas Southern University, Robert J. Terry Library
Prairie View A&M University, John B. Coleman Library

St. Philip's College Library
Texas State University, Alkek Library
Myra Davis Hemmings Resource Center, Delta Sigma Theta Sorority
University of Texas at San Antonio, Institute of Texan Cultures

Acting Up and Getting Down

Introduction

....

In "Note on Commercial Theatre," Langston Hughes, poet, novelist, editor, and playwright, predicts the emergence of a cadre of black playwrights dedicated to writing plays that explore the complexities and nuances of black life. Hughes asserts:

> You put me in Macbeth and Carmen Jones
> And all kinds of Swing Mikados
> And in everything but what's about me—
> But someday somebody'll
> Stand up and talk about me,
> And write about me—
> Black and beautiful—
> And sing about me,
> And put on plays about me!
>
> I reckon it'll be
> Me myself!
>
> Yes, it'll be me.[1]

Like the speaker in Hughes' poem, playwrights featured in *Acting Up and Getting Down: Plays by African American Texans* have accepted the challenge to write for a black theatre. One might ask: What is black theatre? According to W. E. B. Du Bois, eminent social scientist, historian, editor, author, and co-founder of the Krigwa Players, black theatre must be

1. About us. That is, they [plays] must have plots which reveal Negro life as it is.
2. By us. That is, they must be written by Negro authors who understand from birth and continual association just what it means to be a Negro . . . .

3. For us. That is, the theatre must cater primarily to Negro audiences and be supported and sustained by their entertainment and approval.
4. Near us. The theatre must be in a Negro neighborhood near the mass of ordinary Negro people.[2]

In the introduction to their *Black Drama Anthology*, editors Woodie King and Ron Milner insist that black theatre "must be housed in, sustained and judged by, and be a usable projection of and to a black community!"[3] Moreover, Willis Richardson, author of the first African American non-musical drama on Broadway, *The Chip Woman's Fortune*, explains: "When I say Negro plays, I do not mean merely plays with Negro characters, but dramas portraying the soul of a people."[4] While black theatre focuses mainly on works written by blacks about black life, it may also encompass works written by non-blacks about black life featuring black characters and actors—for example, *Green Pastures* by Marc Connelly or Eugene O'Neill's *Emperor Jones*. Typically, black theatres/artistic directors have adapted plays from other cultures and traditions, such as plays by Shakespeare, Euripides, and Tennessee Williams. Black theatre may also include all-black casts in productions of *A Streetcar Named Desire*, presented by Austin's Pro Arts Collective, or *Crimes of the Heart* and *Steel Magnolias*, produced by San Antonio's Renaissance Guild.

The plays in this collection probe the "soul of a people" while enriching and expanding the Texas theatrical canon. Historically, well-crafted plays by African American Texans have been denied a place in the canon, as anthologies like William Martin's *Texas Plays* attest. In a chapter in *Loose Canons: Notes on the Culture Wars* entitled "The Master's Pieces: On Canon Formation and the African American Tradition," Henry Louis Gates, Jr., discusses efforts to define the African American canon, mainly by editing anthologies of African American literature and citing anthologies dating from 1845 to the present.[5] In "Cultural Valorization and African American Literary History: Reconstructing the Canon," Sarah Corse and Monica Griffin envision the process of canon formation as a "field of contestation featuring struggles among diverse groups that propose, support, and contest specific canonical tests as a way of enhancing their own social standing." Corse and Griffin suggest, "One example of this contest for canonical authority was the struggle to include African American and other minority literatures in the American canon."[6] As Harry Elam, Jr., indicates in the anthology *The Fire This Time*, new writers extend the "definitions of what a black play is and what black theatre should be."[7]

The Vibrancy of Black Theatre in Texas

Black theatre in Texas dates from the rise of the minstrel troupes of the nineteenth century. The black theatre movement in Texas included early musicals, the Negro Little Theatre Movement of the 1920s and 1930s, theatre companies and productions organized at historically black colleges and universities in Texas as early as the 1920s, and the development of theatre companies as part of the Black Arts Movement of the sixties and seventies. This history of black theatre now serves as a foundation and source of inspiration for contemporary black theatre companies in Texas. Although scholarship focusing on black theatre in America began to appear shortly after the Civil War, serious research into the history and development of black theatre in Texas dates from 1981, when Sue Dauphin included a chapter on the history of black theatre in Houston in *Houston by Stages*.[8] Bernard L. Peterson chronicles black theatre in Texas in his 1997 book, *The African American Theatre Directory, 1816–1960: A Comprehensive Guide to Early Theatre Organizations, Companies, Theatres, and Performing Groups*.[9] In addition, Annemarie Bean's *Sourcebook of African Performances: Plays, People, Movements* includes a chapter by James V. Hatch, "Theatre in Historically Black Colleges: A Survey of 100 Years," that offers insight into theatre in historically black colleges and universities in Texas.[10] Dawn McGhee, founder and director of Dallas-based Artists for ArtSake, highlights the history of her father, Bill McGhee, who, in the early 1950s, broke through the barriers of race and racism and became the first African American to make a professional mainstream debut on the Dallas stage. A growing body of scholarship documents the long history of black theatre in Texas.[11]

In metropolitan Austin, Dallas, Fort Worth, Houston, and San Antonio, black theatre served as the cornerstone of arts activity prior to the twentieth century in community centers, churches, and historically black colleges. Because theatre often brings together a variety of performing arts, including dance, music (vocal and instrumental), and design, as well as acting, black theatre has served as an outlet for artistic expression in the black community. Notable theatre groups that performed before the 1950s include the Thespian Society for "Cullud genman" in Houston (1866), the Phyllis [sic] Wheatley Dramatic Guild Players in San Antonio (beginning ca. 1920), the Log Cabin Players at Wiley College in Marshall, Texas (1925), and the Charles Gilpin Players at Prairie View Normal and Industrial College, Prairie View, Texas (1929). Inspired by the Black Arts Movement of the 1960s, many more black theatre organizations emerged in the United States, and the black Texas theatre community participated in this historic flowering of artistic expression, or new Black Renaissance, with the establishment of the Urban Theatre in Houston (1969), the Black Arts Alliance in Austin (1970s), and the Sojourner Truth Players in Fort Worth (1972), among others.

Today, several successful black theatre groups in Texas maintain active production schedules; these groups include the Ensemble Theatre in Houston, the Black Academy of Arts and Letters in Dallas, and the Jubilee Theatre in Fort Worth (all with over thirty years of well-documented growth and development), in addition to the Encore Theatre in Houston, Pro Arts Collective in Austin, and Hornsby Entertainment Theatre Company and the Renaissance Guild in San Antonio. Black theatres are crucial for the nurturing of black playwrights. Whereas mainstream theatres typically produce one play a year by a black or minority playwright in conjunction with their "diversity initiatives," black theatres build their entire seasons on works by black playwrights. Therefore, the production of the seven plays at the center of this study by black Texas theatres not only offers diverse audiences enlightenment and entertainment but also provides opportunities for black Texas playwrights, directors, and technical staff to refine their craft and gain invaluable experience.

Black theatre documents the cultural legacy of black Texans, particularly during the sociopolitical upheaval that marked the period between 1930 and 1954.[12] For example, during the celebration of the Texas Centennial Exposition in 1936, the Harlem Unit of the Works Project Administration's Theatre Project of New York City presented *Macbeth* in an open amphitheatre in Dallas before a capacity audience of two thousand black and white spectators.[13] However, amateur theatrical productions also gained popularity among black Texans in the 1930s. Organized in 1931, the Houston Negro Little Theatre opened with three short plays: *White Dresses* and *No 'Count Boy* by Paul Green and *The Slave*, written by Elizabeth Yates, a member of a prominent African American family in Houston.[14] In 1940, the Department of Recreation sponsored a drama tournament at Emancipation Park for the three playgrounds in Houston. The competition presented one-act plays judged by representatives of the Houston Negro Little Theatre.[15] In 1953, the Houston Negro Little Theatre performed Tennessee Williams' *Glass Menagerie* before an enthusiastic audience. Several months later, the theatre presented Sophocles' *Antigone*, using contemporary costumes. The success of the Negro Little Theatre in Houston inspired similar efforts in Dallas.[16]

While the Negro Little Theatre Movement was limited to large urban communities, it nurtured and sustained black cultural expression when few other outlets existed: "If nothing else, the Little Theatres marked a period of self-expression and self-revelation among the black people of the state."[17] It was a time when "black culture in Texas was conceived by black artists within the black urban community for black audiences,"[18] in keeping with Du Bois' theory of Black Arts. Black playwrights in Texas began to emerge in the 1960s, entertaining and enlightening audiences with original comedies, domestic dramas, and thought-provoking history plays.

The Identification of African American Texas Playwrights

In assembling this collection of plays by black Texas playwrights, our first challenge involved defining the black Texas playwright. Because William Martin, editor of the anthology *Texas Plays*, encountered a similar challenge, we adapted his approach to defining the "Texas" play and the Texas playwright. Martin writes:

> In compiling this anthology, I have made no attempt to rigorously define Texas play or to balance choices of writers or works to fit a plan. Not all of the nine authors represented are native Texans, and [the] majority make their homes in either New York or California. Those who are not natives, however, have studied and lived in Texas long enough for it to constitute a significant influence. All have given serious attention to the distinctive characteristics of life in Texas and are represented by works that contribute to its greater appreciation and understanding. Also, of course, they have dealt with the "problems of the human heart in conflict with itself" and with the universal struggles for knowledge, ease, and love that transcend boundaries.[19]

Represented in our collection are not only black writers who were born in Texas but also those who have lived and worked in Texas for decades, even though they were born elsewhere. Like the writers featured in Martin's book, our black Texas playwrights' artistic sensibilities were fundamentally informed by their long-term exposure to black Texas culture and history. Four of the seven plays in the collection are set in Texas. All of the playwrights in the collection have had one or more of their plays produced in Texas by a theatre group or at an institution committed to the development of the black theatre canon in Texas. Of the black playwrights featured in *Acting Up and Getting Down*, four received undergraduate degrees at Texas universities—Eugene Lee, Thomas Meloncon, George Hawkins, and Celeste Bedford Walker. Six of the seven playwrights attended public schools in Texas. Although Elizabeth Brown-Guillory attended public schools in Louisiana, she has been a professor in Texas for the last twenty-five years and currently serves as distinguished professor of theatre, associate provost, and associate vice president for academic affairs at Texas Southern University in Houston. Others in the collection who have taught at Texas universities or colleges include Ted Shine and Thomas Meloncon. Eugene Lee, artist-in-residence at Texas State University—his alma mater—is also the founder and artistic director for the state of Texas' annual Black and Latino Playwrights Conference.

Accolades for African American Texas Playwrights

Although the playwrights represented in *Acting Up and Getting Down* are essentially regional writers, they have garnered significant regional, national, and international recognitions and awards. For example, Ted Shine, author of over thirty plays, including many comedies and serious dramas as well as a history play, received the Brooks-Hines Award for playwriting in 1970 and the Texas Playwrights Award from Houston's Ensemble Theatre in 2007. He studied playwriting with the noted playwright Owen Dodson. Shines' *Contribution*, written in 1969, is one of the most frequently produced plays in the African American theatrical canon. He is co-editor (with James V. Hatch) of *Black Theatre U.S.A.*, the standard anthology of plays by black authors.[20] His papers now reside in the prestigious Hatch-Billops Collection in New York City. Another highly successful black playwright in Texas is Thomas Meloncon, author of more than thirty plays. A native Houstonian, Meloncon has taught in the Department of Communications and in the Fine Arts Department at Texas Southern University. He has received many awards and honors, including the Outstanding Texan Award from the Texas Legislative Black Caucus for his contributions to the arts, a creative writing award from the Houston Chapter of the National Association of Black Journalists, and an achievement award from the Texas Southern Program Council. He was among the writers honored in the Salute to Texas Playwrights by the Ensemble Theatre of Houston.

Like Ted Shine and Thomas Meloncon, Eugene Lee, Sterling Houston, and George Hawkins are key figures in the development of black theatre in Texas. Eugene Lee—artist-in-residence at Texas State University and founder and artistic director of the annual Black and Latino Playwrights Conference, which is hosted by the Texas State Department of Theatre and Dance—has seen his plays produced at the Jubilee Theatre in Fort Worth, Texas, the Joseph Papp Public Theatre in New York City, the Royal Court Theatre in London, England, and several other venues. Lee was one of the writers honored during the Salute to Texas Playwrights by the Ensemble Theatre of Houston. The late George Hawkins, the multi-talented founder and artistic director for Houston's Ensemble Theatre, wrote and directed six plays, including *Br'er Rabbit*, a popular children's play. Adapted from the classic folktale, *Br'er Rabbit* is produced annually by the Ensemble's Children's Theatre. Hawkins also wrote and directed a humorous murder-mystery entitled *Who Killed Hazel Patton?*—a box-office hit that is revived periodically. Although Hawkins died before his full potential as a writer could be realized, he is still remembered fondly at the Ensemble, where one of its performance spaces is named in his honor.

Another Black Texas playwright who died in his prime was Sterling Houston, the former artistic director and writer-in-residence for the Jump-Start Performance Company and author of thirty-three plays. Houston received a New Forms Regional Initiative Grant funded by the Rockefeller Foundation, the Andy Warhol Foundation, and the National Endowment for the Arts. Houston's play *Black Lily and White Lily* was selected to open the Cleveland Public Theatre's Festival of New Plays in 1996, and in 1997, the Texas legislature honored Houston with a citation for his invaluable contributions to the cultural life of Texas. As further evidence of the high esteem in which he was held in the San Antonio artistic community, Jump-Start renamed its performance space the Sterling Houston Theatre in 2009.

The women playwrights represented in the anthology have also received notable honors and recognitions. Celeste Bedford Walker, one of the most prolific black Texas playwrights, has written nearly forty plays. Her celebrated historical drama *Camp Logan* (a National Association for the Advancement of Colored People Image Awards winner) has been performed in major venues across the country, including the John F. Kennedy Center for the Performing Arts. She was a finalist for the Susan Smith Blackburn Prize, given to an outstanding female playwright, and she was among the writers honored in the Salute to Texas Playwrights by the Ensemble Theatre of Houston. Walker has also served as resident playwright for the Ensemble Theatre. Like Shine and Meloncon, Walker has received numerous commissions to write plays for theatres and other groups.

Another outstanding Houston playwright is Elizabeth Brown-Guillory; she has held playwright residencies in Illinois, Wisconsin, and New York. Her work was showcased recently in Houston at the Ensemble Theatre's "Heart of the Theatre" series. Brown-Guillory was named distinguished scholar/artist-in-residence at the University of Wisconsin at Eau Claire. She was also winner of Denver's Eden Theatrical Playwriting Award, as well as Danny Glover's Robey Theatre Playwriting Award. The playwrights represented in this anthology are experienced, prolific, and highly regarded writers whose work deserves a wider audience.

The Importance and Uniqueness of This Anthology

This anthology makes plays by black Texas writers accessible to theatre professionals around the world. One of the greatest challenges facing emerging playwrights is getting their work into the hands of artistic directors and other theatre professionals. Playwrights make their plays accessible to readers by circulating their work in manuscript form, thereby risking copyright infringement, or they seek public readings at venues such as the National Black Theatre Festival, which is held in Winston-Salem, North Carolina, every two years. They engage in networking at theatre conferences, or they host public readings of their work. The well-known and widely produced playwright Pearl Cleage, author of *Flyin' West* and *Blues for an Alabama Sky*, used these strategies to bring her work to the stage.

Once playwrights garner major awards—such as a Tony, Obie, Lorraine Hansberry Award, a Theodore Ward Prize, or a Pulitzer Prize—publishers are more likely to accept their manuscripts. But even when playwrights are fortunate enough to get their work accepted, they are often published in a script form that is not reviewed or catalogued in libraries, resulting in limited access for general readers and theatre professionals. This limited access is even more problematic, as recent scholarship indicates that African American drama is performed by international and transracial theatre companies when scripts are available.[21] Two cases in point are Lorraine Hansberry's *Raisin in the Sun*, which has been translated into more than thirty languages and staged in Poland as well as other international venues,[22] and black Texas playwright Eugene Lee's *East Texas Hot Links*,[23] which was mounted at Britain's Royal Court Theatre, a theatre noted for its production of international plays.

Our anthology not only gives a voice to black Texas playwrights but also highlights the importance of regional theatre in Texas. Although New York City remains the Mecca of American theatre, regional theatres offer opportunities to new playwrights. African American playwrights, who rarely get a chance to showcase their work on Broadway, depend upon regional theatres to stage their plays. In Texas, these theatres include Houston's Ensemble Theatre, Fort Worth's Jubilee Theatre, Dallas' Black Academy of Arts and Letters, and Austin's Pro Arts Collective.

While African American Texas playwrights have enjoyed success in the regional theatres, their work remains virtually unknown to the mainstream theatre establishment. This anthology privileges writers who would be invisible without it. William Martin's 1990 anthology, *Texas Plays*, includes no plays by black Texas playwrights, suggesting that none exist. *Acting Up and Getting Down* corrects this misperception.

Typically, plays are published individually as scripts, but publishers are also producing a wide variety of play anthologies that present plays as literary texts. Anthology models for *Acting Up and Getting Down* include *The Longman Anthology of Modern and Contemporary Drama, The National Black Drama Anthology, The Lorraine Hansberry Playwriting Award: An Anthology of Prize-Winning Plays, Asian American Drama: 9 Plays from the Multiethnic Landscape, The Pain of the Macho and Other Plays*, and *American Gipsy: Six Native American Plays*.[24]

Just as black Texans have made and continue to make a unique contribution to Texas music, black Texas playwrights' singular contributions foreground a marginalized community whose history and culture are often neglected, devalued, and/or ignored. While Texas theatre aficionados would most likely recognize the names of Texas playwrights such as Horton Foote, Ramsey Yelvington, and Oliver Hailey, few, if any, are familiar with Black Texas playwrights Ted Shine, Celeste Bedford Walker, Eugene Lee, or Thomas Meloncon. This anthology bridges the gap between the two groups and complements earlier texts such as William Martin's *Texas Plays* (1990) while celebrating the state's cultural diversity and unique Texas "brand."

The Texas "Brand"

As Leigh Clemons notes in *Branding Texas*, African American Texans and other ethnic minorities are engaged in a struggle for the control of Texas history and, by extension, the maintenance of Texas cultural identity.[25] The Texas "brand," or Texas cultural identity, encompasses much more than the iconic cowboys and oil wells. Clemons describes the uniqueness of the Texas cultural identity, which derives from a "whitewashed" discourse that relegates people of color to the margins, with white males dominating the cultural center.[26] Although the construction of the Texas cultural identity remains a highly contested process, it is often represented in "violence as romanticized spectacle" grounded in revolution and performed in reenactments.[27] According to Clemons, "Historical plays serve as a form of ritual sacrifice presented as if for all Texans, but, in fact, they operate within the Anglo/Mexican binary."[28]

Although white male experience dominates the construction of Texas cultural identity, other groups—Mexican Americans, African Americans, and women—strive to ensure that their own representations are included. Clemons argues that "Texans can be created through historical plays."[29] The two historical plays in this anthology, *Ancestors* by Ted Shine and *Camp Logan* by Celeste Bedford Walker, also promote the impulse to construct a more diverse Texas cultural identity. In the dominant narrative featuring white males, African Americans are relegated to the periphery of the action, defined as objects rather than subjects with agency. However, African American playwrights refocus the traditional narratives, situating African Americans at the center of the action. Clemons suggests that "Blacks and American Indians, long excluded but with many historical ties to the state, struggle even to be acknowledged as part of the historical narrative other than as footnotes."[30] In *Ancestors*, a play commissioned for the Texas Sesquicentennial Celebration, Shine focuses on the Battle of San Jacinto, the decisive battle of the Texas Revolution. Bose Ikhart, a slave, and Greenbury Logan, a former slave, participate in the battle. One of the most important facets of white male Texas culture is a selfless courage in the face of danger. By fighting in the battle, Bose Ikhart displays a type of bravery not typically attributed to slaves, yet he hopes that performing this act of courage will prompt his white master to find him worthy of his freedom. Similar gestures toward the development of Texas cultural identity are highlighted in Celeste Bedford Walker's historical drama, *Camp Logan*, as well as in the family dramas set in Texas.

The Black Aesthetic

Plays in *Acting Up and Getting Down* can be profitably studied and evaluated through the lens of the black aesthetic. In the introduction to *The Black Aesthetic*, Addison Gayle asserts that Black Art, a "unique art derived from unique cultural experiences[,] mandates unique critical tools for evaluation."[31] Therefore, when we refer to the black aesthetic, we call attention to critical tools that take into account culturally specific techniques such as call and response, repetition, oral tradition, folklore, and jazz and blues motifs used by writers like Langston Hughes and August Wilson. In an essay entitled "The Development of African American Dramatic Theory," Mikell Pinkney traces theoretical writings on the black aesthetic from W. E. B. Du Bois in the 1920s to August Wilson in the 1990s, citing five fundamental aesthetic principles and seven periods of black aesthetic thought in America.[32] The aesthetic principles or elements encompass protest, revolt, assertion, music, and spirituality. The periods of development include (1) Plantation or Slavery, (2) American Minstrelsy (slavery, end of slavery through the turn of the century), (3) New Negro Renaissance, or Harlem Renaissance (1917 through the 1920s; W. E. B. Du Bois, Montgomery Gregory, Alain Locke), (4) Assimilation (1930s through the 1950s; the Federal Theatre, the American Negro Theatre, Lorraine Hansberry), (5) Black Power/Black Arts and Black Aesthetic/Black Revolutionary Era (beginning mid-1960s to mid-1970s; Amiri Baraka, Ed Bullins, Larry Neal), (6) Revolutionary Afrocentric Era (beginning mid-1970s through 1980s; Paul Carter Harrison, Barbara Ann Teer), and (7) New Age Post-revolutionary Era (1990s to present; postmodern intellectual spiritualism and prophetic pragmatism, including Ntozake Shange, Suzan-Lori Parks, August Wilson, Cornel West).[33]

For more than eighty years, black scholars and literary theorists have engaged in a continuing dialogue about the nature and function of the black aesthetic. The concept of the black aesthetic was at the center of the influential Black Arts Movement of the 1970s, whose theorists reject the prevailing "Eurocentric criticism that judges the literature's merit based on its appropriation of European literary genres, languages, and aesthetics."[34]

The Black Aesthetic and the Regional Theatre Movement

The black aesthetic informs the work of the black regional theatres in Texas. The regional theatres are absolutely indispensable to fledgling playwrights struggling against great odds to bring their plays to the stage. While mainstream regional theatres may produce one play annually in their "diversity slot," black regional theatres—for example, Houston's Ensemble Theatre, Fort Worth's Jubilee Theatre, and Austin's Pro Arts Collective—build their seasons around plays by black playwrights, nurturing and promoting black Texas playwrights. The black Texas regional theatre movement is part of a larger national regional theatre movement in the United States. For example, the League of Resident Theatres consists of professional (paid-staff) non-profit companies that function outside of New York's commercial theatre. The league's member theatres frequently produce new plays, experimental work, and plays by unknown playwrights. Black Texas regional theatres also provide training and employment for black theatre professionals; involve local communities via churches, city arts councils, and local news media; engender community pride; and establish successful arts education programs for youth. The regional theatres are the lifeblood of professional theatre in Texas.

Universality

The plays in this collection explore enduring universal themes and issues involving father/son conflicts and search for identity (*Johnny B. Goode*), sibling rivalry and the influence of the past on the present (*When the Ancestors Call*), the quest for self-fulfillment (*Driving Wheel*), the pain of injustice (*Camp Logan*), the importance of family unity (*Killingsworth*), the importance of honoring history (*Ancestors*), and the importance of living by your wits (*Br'er Rabbit*). These plays probe "the connections between the social, political, and the metaphysical."[35] We use the term "universal" to suggest themes, ideas, and experiences that apply to human beings regardless of race, ethnicity, gender, or social class.[36]

The Pulitzer Prize–winning playwright August Wilson comments on the universal in theatre, writing that

> theatre asserts that all of human life is universal. Love, Honor, Duty, Betrayal belong and pertain to every culture and every race. The way they

are acted out on the playing field may be different, but betrayal is betrayal whether you are a South Sea Islander, a Mississippi farmer or an English baron. All human life is universal, and it is theatre that illuminates and confers upon the universal the ability to speak for all men.[37]

The plays in this collection speak eloquently to all audiences.

Organization, Genres, and Style

Since our forthcoming companion volume to this anthology documents the history of black theatre in Texas, it seems logical that we open and close the book with strong history plays. Between them we include a dramatized folktale, realistic dramas, domestic dramas, an autobiographical memory piece, and plays that blend realism and magical realism. As well as following the traditional structure of a well-made play, the authors of the four two-act plays and three one-act plays create interesting characters involved in compelling situations that demand our attention. As previously noted, Ted Shine began writing plays during the 1950s, the period identified with assimilation; however, four of the black Texas playwrights in this anthology are products of the black intellectual aesthetic that gained prominence in the 1970s—the period identified as the Revolutionary Afrocentric Era, dating from the mid-1970s through the 1980s (George Hawkins, *Br'er Rabbit*; Ted Shine, *Ancestors*; Eugene Lee, *Killingsworth*; and Celeste Bedford Walker, *Camp Logan*). Three of the playwrights developed their plays here during the seventh period, the New Age Post-revolutionary Era (Sterling Houston, *Driving Wheel*; Thomas Meloncon, *Johnny B. Goode*; and Elizabeth Brown-Guillory, *When the Ancestors Call*).[38]

Play Selection

After consulting with artistic directors and others familiar with black theatre in Texas, we identified more than a dozen black Texas playwrights who submitted twenty-seven manuscripts for review. For each play, we created a matrix covering plot, characters, themes, setting, central message, and production history. We wanted intellectually challenging plays that examine timeless, universal ideas, plays that illuminate the black experience in Texas. Assisted by C. Francis Blackchild, a doctoral student conducting independent research on black theatre under the direction of co-editor Sandra M. Mayo, we evaluated each manuscript carefully in weekly roundtable discussions. To make the book useful to artistic directors looking for scripts, we selected stage-worthy plays with a documented stage life. Our goal was to showcase well-written and (with one exception) unpublished one- or two-act, multi-character plays by black Texans, women and men, veteran and emerging playwrights.[39]

Although we discovered several talented black playwrights/performance artists in major Texas cities, their work, in some instances, did not fit our play selection criteria. For example, Austin's Zell Miller, a noted hip-hop theatre artist, has received many awards for his one-man shows, and Austin writer/performer Naomi Mitchell Carrier has written an impressive collection of brief dramatic pieces meant to be performed outdoors at sites such as the George Ranch Historical Park. These writers continue to make valuable contributions to black theatre in Texas. Other worthy plays came to our attention that could not be included in this collection because of space limitations. The seven plays featured in this anthology are representative of the outstanding body of work that black Texas playwrights have produced.

The Audience

This collection will appeal to students and scholars of theatre and performance history and readers interested in cultural, ethnic, African American, and Southwestern studies. In addition to introducing new plays and playwrights to a wide readership, we have included appendices of the playwrights and their published and unpublished plays, an overview of significant developments in black theatre in Texas and the national black theatre movement, and related black historical events. These appendices further underscore the contributions of black Texas playwrights.

Conclusion

Plays by African American Texans probe the complex dynamics of African American family life, entertain and enlighten children via the legacy of black folklore, and interrogate Texas history that is typically forgotten, ignored, and/or misrepresented. As a companion to our historical study of black theatre in Texas (forthcoming from the University of Texas Press), this collection enriches the cultural heritage of blacks in Texas. In the introduction to *"La Voz Latina,"* an anthology of contemporary plays by Latinas, the editors state that "this anthology contributes to an understanding of the cultural contributions of Latinas/Latinos to U.S. and world culture."[40] We feel confident that *Acting Up and Getting Down* accomplishes the same goal for blacks in the Lone Star State.

Playwright Celeste Bedford Walker's insightful critique of her own plays aptly applies to the canon of black Texas playwrights; she asserts that they "embrace the sacred and the mundane, the serious and the comic[,] but what they all have in common is a delight in the wisdom and witlessness of the human condition."[41] Echoing the words of Langston Hughes, we find that black Texas playwrights have accepted the call to stand up and tell their stories. They have placed black characters in black stories about black issues celebrating what is black and challenging and inspirational:

> . . . someday somebody'll
> Stand up and talk about me,
> And write about me—
> Black and beautiful—
> And sing about me,
> And put on plays about me!
> I reckon it'll be
> Me myself!
> Yes, it'll be me.[42]

NOTES

1. Langston Hughes, *Selected Poems of Langston Hughes* (New York: Vintage Books, 1990), 190.

2. W. E. B. DuBois, "Krigwa Players Little Negro Theatre," *Crisis* 32, no. 3 (July 1926): 134.

3. Woodie King and Ron Milner, eds., *Black Drama Anthology* (New York: Signet, 1971), ix.

4. Willis Richardson, "The Hope of Negro Drama," *Crisis* 19, no. 1 (November 1919): 338.

5. Henry Louis Gates, "The Master's Pieces: On Canon Formation and the African American Tradition," in his *Loose Canons: Notes on the Culture Wars* (New York: Oxford University Press, 1993), 24–31.

6. Sarah Corse and Monica Griffin, "Cultural Valorization and African American

Literary History: Reconstructing the Canon." *Sociological Forum* 12, no. 2 (June 1997): 173–283; quotes on 175.

7. Harry Elam, Jr., "Getting the Spirit: An Introduction," in *The Fire This Time*, ed. Harry Elam, Jr., and Robert Alexander (New York: Theatre Communications Group, 2002), xiii.

8. Sue Dauphin, *Houston by Stages: A History of Theatre in Houston* (Austin, TX: Eakin Press, 1981).

9. Bernard L. Peterson, *The African American Theatre Directory, 1816–1960: A Comprehensive Guide to Early Theatre Organizations, Companies, Theatres, and Performing Groups* (Westport, CT: Greenwood Press, 1997).

10. James V. Hatch, "Theatre in Historically Black Colleges: A Survey of 100 Years," in *A Sourcebook of African American Performances: Plays, People, Movements*, ed. Annemarie Bean (London: Routledge Press, 1999).

11. "Bill McGhee, Pioneer Actor: Biography," n.d., http://dawnmcghee.net/uploads/Biography_of_Dad.pdf; Dawn McGhee, interview by Sandra M. Mayo, August 8, 2011.

12. Neil Sapper, "Black Culture in Urban Texas: A Lone Star Renaissance," in *The African American Experience in Texas*, ed. Bruce A. Glasrud and James M. Smallwood (Lubbock: Texas Tech University Press, 2007), 232.

13. Ibid., 235.

14. Ibid., 248.

15. Ibid., 249.

16. Ibid., 250.

17. Ibid.

18. Ibid., 251.

19. William Martin, "Preface," in *Texas Plays*, ed. William Martin (Dallas, TX: Southern Methodist University Press, 1990), xi.

20. James V. Hatch and Ted Shine, *Black Theatre U.S.A.: Forty-five Plays by Black Americans, 1847–1974* (New York: Free Press, 1974; revised and expanded to two volumes, 1996).

21. For example, see Katarzyna Jakubiak, "The Black Body in Translation: Polish Productions of Lorraine Hansberry's *A Raisin in the Sun* in the 1960s," *Theatre Journal* 63 (2011): 541.

22. Ibid.

23. Eugene Lee, *East Texas Hot Links: A Drama* (New York: Samuel French, 1994).

24. Michael Greenwald et al., eds., *The Longman Anthology of Modern and Contemporary Drama: A Global Perspective* (New York: Pearson Longman, 2004); Woodie King, Jr., ed., *The National Black Drama Anthology: Eleven Plays from America's Leading African-American Theaters* (New York: Applause, 1995); *The Lorraine Hansberry Playwriting Award: An Anthology of Prize-Winning Plays* (Topeka, KS: Clark Publishing Co., 1996); Brian Nelson, ed., *Asian American Drama: 9 Plays from the Multiethnic Landscape* (New York: Applause, 1997); Rick Najera, ed., *The Pain of the Macho and Other Plays* (Houston, TX: Arte Público Press, 1997); and Diane Glancy, ed., *American Gipsy: Six Native American Plays* (Norman: University of Oklahoma Press, 2002).

25. Leigh Clemons, *Branding Texas: Performing Culture in the Lone Star State* (Austin: University of Texas Press, 2008), 11.

26. Ibid., 10.

27. Ibid., 8.

28. Ibid., 27.

29. Ibid., 7.

30. Ibid., 9.

31. Addison Gayle, Jr., *The Black Aesthetic* (New York: Doubleday, 1971).

32. Mikell Pinkney, "The Development of African American Dramatic Theory: W. E. B. DuBois to August Wilson," in *August Wilson and Black Aesthetics*, ed. Dana Williams and Sandra Shannon (New York: Palgrave Macmillan, 2004).

33. Ibid.

34. Ibid.

35. Elam, "Getting the Spirit," xiv.

36. We are aware of the ongoing discussion about the use of the term "universal" in describing great works. For example, Charles Larson makes an interesting point in "Heroic Ethnocentrism: The Idea of Universality in Literature" when he argues that "the term universal has been grossly misused when it has been applied to non-Western literature, because it has been so often used in a way that ignores the multiplicity of cultural experiences. Usually when we try to force the concept of universality on someone who is not Western, I think we are implying that our own culture should be the standard of measurement." See Charles Larson, "Heroic Ethnocentrism: The Idea of Universality in Literature," in Chapter 12 of *Postcolonial Studies Reader* by Bill Ashcroft, Gareth Griffiths, and Helen Tiffin (New York: Taylor & Francis, 2006), 78. However, though great literature comes most often from a particular culture, if it is widely read or performed, has stood the test of time, and is translated into many languages—as is the work of many African American writers (e.g., Langston Hughes, Lorraine Hansberry, and other black writers)—a description as universal is not without support.

37. August Wilson, *The Ground on Which I Stand* (New York: Theatre Communications Group, 1996), 45.

38. Pinkney, "The Development of African American Dramatic Theory."

39. Sterling Houston's *Driving Wheel* is the only previously published work. Because Houston's unpublished work does not reflect his best achievement as a writer, we opted for one of his strongest published plays.

40. Elizabeth C. Ramirez and Catherine Casiano, *"La Voz Latina": Contemporary Plays and Performance Pieces by Latinas* (Urbana and Chicago: University of Illinois Press, 2011).

41. Celeste Bedford Walker, http://celestebedfordwalker.net/.

42. Hughes, "Note on Commercial Theatre."

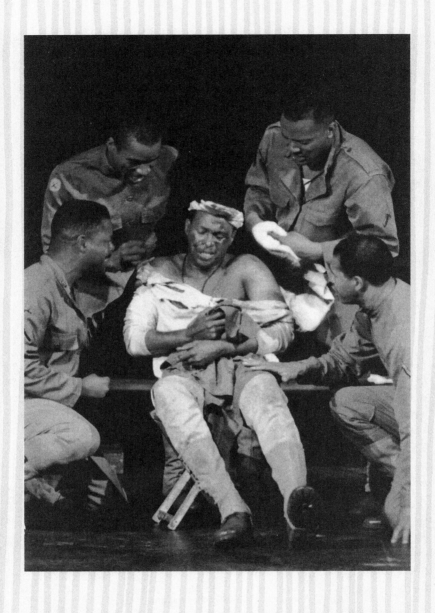

Camp Logan. (*Left to right*) Lawrence Evans, Timothy Dickson (*top*), André Minkins (*center*), Marvin Wright-Bey, and Michael Green. Photo by Jessica Katz.

Camp Logan

CELESTE BEDFORD WALKER

Celeste Bedford Walker received the August Wilson Playwright Award in 2009 at the National Black Theatre Festival in Winston-Salem, North Carolina. Her canon includes approximately thirty-seven plays. Her celebrated historical drama, *Camp Logan* (National Association for the Advancement of Colored People [NAACP] Image Award winner), has been performed in major venues across the country, including the Kennedy Center for the Performing Arts. Not only has she been honored by the NAACP Image Award for positive portrayal of African Americans in the media, but she has also received New York City's AUDELCO Award for best play and the Heart of Theatre Salute to Texas Playwrights by the Ensemble Theatre in Houston. She was selected as a finalist for the international Susan Smith Blackburn Prize for outstanding work by a female playwright in the English-speaking theater. In addition, Walker has received numerous commissions, grants from the National Endowment for the Arts and the National Endowment for the Humanities, and cultural arts grants to write dramas, comedies, musicals, and children's shows for theaters, schools, museums, and organizations. In 2003, Walker received a Recognition of Excellence from the ABC TV Talent Development Program for screen writing. Houston's Cultural Arts Council awarded her a fellowship to complete the play *Sassafras Girls*. She was featured by organizers of the thirtieth anniversary celebration of the Susan Smith Blackburn Prize as part of their "Women in Theatre: Houston Voices" theme. In 2008, the Alley Theatre in Houston commissioned her to write the historical drama for young people, *I, Barbara Jordan*.

Walker is a Texan who has been involved with theatre in Houston for over thirty years. She was born and raised in Houston. She attended Jack Yates Senior High and received a BA from Texas Southern University in Houston, where she majored in English. She worked as a data processor for many years before turning to writing plays full-time. She has been able to focus on her writing because of the many fellowships, commissions, and grants she has received, but she also has a supportive husband. She has always loved literature and thought she might write novels like Toni Morrison, but she soon discovered that she was more interested in dialogue. She admired the work of many playwrights when she began writing, especially the comic work of Neil Simon and the serious drama of Lorraine Hansberry. Involvement with a theatre group in the seventies, the Black Arts Center in the Fifth Ward, sparked her writing career. The actress Loretta Devine came out of this group. Walker met a group of writers and with them formed Writers Clinic, Inc., led by Alma Carriere. She worked with the Writers Clinic in the seventies for about five years, and her first play and first produced work, *Sister, Sister*, was the result.

Walker has not only written full-length and one-act plays for adults but also for youth and children. The most acclaimed of the full-length plays are *Distant Voices* (Susan Smith Blackburn Prize finalist), *Once in a Wife Time* (formerly *Sister, Sister*, NAACP Image Award winner), *Reunion in Bartersville* (NAACP Image Award nomination, AUDELCO Award winner), *Over Forty* (AUDELCO Award winner), and *Praise the Lord and Raise the Roof* (a 1999 Olympics Cultural Arts Festival selection). *Sassy Mamas* (2008), produced by the Hansberry-Sands Theatre in Milwaukee, Wisconsin, is one of the full-length works. Ten of her thirteen one-act plays have also been produced. They include *Noble Lofton*; *Buffalo Soldier*; *Adam and Eve, Revisited*; *Spirits*; *Smokes Bayou*; *The Boule*; *Jack Yates*; *Blacks in the Methodist Church*; *Hip Hoppin' the Dream*; *Reparations Day*; and *The History of Wheeler Baptist Church*. Some of her children's shows, performed before thousands of students over the years, include *Freedom Train*, *The African Talking Drum*, *Where My Girls At?*, *Giants in the Land*, *Fabulous African Fables*, and *Black Diamonds*.

Walker grew up hearing about the Camp Logan riot and interviewed Houstonians who had relatives caught up in the event. Although she studied the documents on the event in the Robert J. Terry Library of Texas Southern University and in the Black History Section of the downtown Houston Public Library, as well as consulted Robert Haynes' *Night of Vio-*

lence (Baton Rouge: Louisiana State University Press, 1976), she found the oral history she collected a rich source for the emotional and personal stories of the soldiers.

As You Read *Camp Logan*

Camp Logan is a two-act tragedy in eight scenes, with a prologue and epilogue, based on the 1917 riot by black soldiers at Camp Logan. The play is a faithful re-telling of the historical events leading up to the riot, the carnage resulting from the riot, and the sentences meted out to the black soldiers. The action revolves around a male cast of six soldiers and their white captain. The six black soldiers are a composite of the group immersed in the tumultuous event. Walker brings to life their humanity through their camaraderie in the barracks and the stories of home, women, and brushes with discrimination and white hatred. The drama juxtaposes the soldiers' attempts at normalcy with the hostile events in the environment in which they are placed. The humiliation is offstage, but it is under constant discussion in the private space of the barracks. The style combines presentational (direct address to the audience) with representational (slice-of-life) scenes to immerse the readers and audience in the action, but it also allows them to step back from the action and see it in a different perspective— though always through the eyes of the soldiers caught up in the tragedy.

The events of *Camp Logan* and the play's grounding in the civil rights struggles of blacks throw into relief the price that had to be paid for dignity. This play is reminiscent of other plays about the struggles of black soldiers, including *Aftermath* (1919) by Mary P. Burrill, *A Medal for Willie* (1951) by William Branch, and *A Soldier's Play* (1981) by Charles Fuller. It is also akin to the contemporary movies *Glory* (1989) and *Tuskegee Airmen* (1995) in chronicling the stories of blacks in the U.S. military.

Representative Production History

Kuumba House, Houston, Texas, 1987
Carver Community Center, San Antonio, Texas, 1990
Billie Holiday Theater, Brooklyn, New York, 1991
Kennedy Center for the Performing Arts, Texas Festival, Washington, DC, 1991
Victoria Five Theatre, New York, New York, 1994
McKenna Auditorium, Claremont McKenna College, Claremont, California, 1993

McClintock Theatre, University of Southern California, Los Angeles, 1995

Shades of Truth Theatre, Kumble Theater for the Performing Arts, New York, New York, 2008

African American Performing Arts Community Center, Albuquerque, New Mexico, 2011

Robey Theatre Company, Los Angeles Theatre Center, Los Angeles, California, 2012

Characters

SGT. MC KINNEY: Spit and polish career officer. Twenty-two years of army service. Kentuckian, forty years old.

GWEELY BROWN: Twelve years of army service. Texan, thirty years old.

JOE MOSES: Ten years of army service. New Yorker, thirty years old.

JACQUES "BUGALOOSA" HONORÉ: Louisianan, twenty-five years old.

ROBERT FRANCISCUS: Chicagoan, twenty-five years old.

CHARLES HARDIN: Six months of army service. Minnesotan, nineteen years old.

CAPT. ZUELKE: White Kentuckian, thirty-five years old.

THE SOLDIERS OF THE COMPANY

A TOWNSMAN

ANNOUNCER

Setting

Time: Summer 1917

Place: Outside the army camp, Camp Logan, Houston, Texas

PROLOGUE

(AT RISE: *It's a rainy morning, around 6 a.m. In the blackout, we hear the sound of a train engine coming to a halt, delivering the soldiers to the camp. Off Stage we hear the Camp Logan Quartet (consisting of the members of the cast who can sing) singing an a capella rendition of "Buffalo Soldier" (by Bob Marley and Noel G. "King Sporty" Williams). On Stage we see slides from the Camp Logan Photo Exhibit (the author drew on her personal collection of Camp Logan photos, but exhibit photos are available at the Buffalo Soldier National Museum in Houston and the Houston Public Library in the Texas Room).* CAPT. ZUELKE *enters, dressed in an army-issue rain slicker. He salutes and addresses the audience as the townspeople of Houston. As he talks, slides from the Camp Logan Exhibit may continue to be shown.*)

CAPT. ZUELKE: Good evening folks, I'm Captain Harris Zuelke of the 24th Infantry, Company "I." Now that Colonel Gentry has briefed you on the battalion in general, I'm glad to get the opportunity to tell you something about my men in "I" Company in particular. For the past eleven months, these boys have been stationed in the desert of Columbus, New Mexico, chasing Pancho Villa. And let me tell ya something, after being out there in that desert, we're mighty happy to be here in this good ol' Houston rain. (*Beat.*) This battalion has a fine record. We've pulled duty out West in the Indian Wars, served in the Philippines, and in the Yellow Fever camps in Siboney, Cuba, and went up San Juan Hill with Teddy Roosevelt. These boys are bearcat fighters and I'm proud to serve with them! Sergeants!

(SGT. MC KINNEY *marches* THE SOLDIERS *of* THE COMPANY *On Stage to cadence.*)

SGT. MC KINNEY: Ten-hut!

(THE COMPANY *is brought to order.* CAPT. ZUELKE *inspects the troops.*)

CAPT. ZUELKE: Parade!

SGT. MC KINNEY: Parade!

CAPT. ZUELKE: Rest!

SGT. MC KINNEY: Rest!

(*The men of* THE COMPANY *stand at parade rest.*)

CAPT. ZUELKE: I know the idea of 654 colored troops being stationed near your town has got some of you white citizens of this town worried. But let me assure you, no need for alarm with these boys. I ought to know, I've served with colored soldiers all of the fifteen years I've been in the army, and I can truthfully say that these boys are the best of their race—they're intelligent, hardworking, and as disciplined as any white soldiers I've seen. (*Beat.*) Now, I understand that some of you still remember the Brownsville, Texas, incident a few years back. But that was just an isolated incident. There are some ten thousand colored soldiers in the regular army, and for the most part they're happy, cheerful, easygoing fellows who aren't looking to do any violence against white citizens. (*Beat.*) But to help soothe some of your fears about any violence occurring here, let me give you the rules and regulations of the camp. First, only sentries on duty will carry firearms, and they won't be allowed to *load* those weapons except in case of an emergency, such as somebody trying to break into camp or somebody trying to steal supplies. And of course no white folks'll be doin' that. The soldiers are divided into four grades, and only the first three grades will be allowed to leave camp. So, set your minds at ease folks, you don't have to worry about any hotheads walking among the civilians, only soldiers with good conduct will be allowed into town. And you men of the press will get your chance at the soldiers, but first I want the citizens to observe the well-organized way these boys put up camp. They'll have the latrines dug, grass cut, tents up, in record time! Thank you for coming out, and we look forward to a pleasant stay here in Houston.

(A TOWNSMAN *planted in the audience, jumps up, shouting hate-filled remarks.*)

TOWNSMAN: Put those monkeys back on the train!

CAPT. ZUELKE: Sergeants!

SGT. MC KINNEY: Ten-hut!

(THE SOLDIERS *snap to attention, eyes straight ahead.*)

SGT. MC KINNEY: (*Continued.*) Your left, your left, your left, right, ha!

THE SOLDIERS: (*Singing.*) Oh here we go, oh here we go, we're at it again, we're at it again, we're movin' out, we're movin' in!

SGT. MC KINNEY: Your left, your left, your left, right, left . . . (*Etc.*)

TOWNSMAN: They touch our women, it'll be a lynchin'!

SGT. MC KINNEY: Your left, your left, your left, right!

TOWNSMAN: Remember Brownsville!

THE SOLDIERS: Oh here we go, we're at it again . . . !

TOWNSMAN: You niggers better not come into town!

THE SOLDIERS: (*Eyes straight ahead.*) We're movin' out, we're movin' in!

(SGT. MC KINNEY *leads the men Off Stage.*)

END OF PROLOGUE

ACT ONE

Scene 1

(SETTING: *A giant U.S. flag on SCRIM provides the backdrop of the tent barracks set of "I" Company. The living accommodations consist of a bunk bed Upstage Center for* SGT. MC KINNEY *and* FRANCISCUS. FRANCISCUS *on lower berth. A wooden set of shelves, with water basins, ladle, water bucket, towels, and other prop items is on one side of the stage. The stacked rifles are on the opposite side. The U.S. flag and the yellow 24th Infantry blockhouse flag are prominently displayed. Four cots, two to the right, two to the left, with footlockers and duffle bags for* GWEELY, MOSES, BUGALOOSA, *and* HARDIN, *are Downstage. A colorful Mexican blanket is placed at the foot of* MOSES' *cot. Next to* BUGALOOSA's *cot is a crude altar to the Virgin Mary and his cornet.*

(AT RISE: *A few minutes later. The lights fade up to the sound of a steady rain and clap of thunder. Hot, tired, and wet, the men run in from the rain.* MOSES *gets a wash basin from the shelf and begins washing up. He's quickly followed in by* BUGALOOSA, *who immediately drops to his knees before his altar, and* FRANCISCUS, *who's trying to get egg stains off his shirt. As* HARDIN *puts away his belongings, he's dismayed to discover that the tent is leaking over his cot.*)

MOSES: (*Running in.*) These southern crackers acting up already!

FRANCISCUS: (*Taking off his shirt.*) Damn rednecks. Look at this, eggs all over my uniform!

BUGALOOSA: Welcome to the South boys.

FRANCISCUS: I finally get a uniform with just the right fit and now—I'm sure glad Priscilla wasn't out there to see this.

MOSES: They better be glad they didn't hit me.

BUGALOOSA: (*Getting whiskey bottle.*) They say we better not come into town tonight.

MOSES: Hell, I'm going into town!

(GWEELY *runs into the barracks, shaking out his rain slicker.*)

GWEELY: Well, at least we got camp up 'fore that downpour come.

BUGALOOSA: Yeah, I think we broke our record this time.

MOSES: Rain and nothing else gonna keep me in camp tonight. I can't wait to see what old Houston town's got to offer. Gweely, you sure they have plenty colored girls here?

GWEELY: Do a snake crawl?

MOSES: Well, how come we didn't see any out there then? You and Bugaloosa swore up and down they were gonna swamp us.

GWEELY: They is, they is. But ain't no colored gal gon' be out 'fore day in the moanin', in the rain.

FRANCISCUS: No decent one anyway.

BUGALOOSA: Yeah, ain't none of 'em that patriotic.

FRANCISCUS: Priscilla and some of her church friends were planning to meet us, but since they sneaked us in here in the dead of night—

MOSES: Like we're criminals or something.

FRANCISCUS: But that's all right. Priscilla sent me this colored newspaper, and listen to what it has to say about us. (*Reading.*) "Although the white populace is experiencing some consternation about colored troops being stationed here in town, we at the Texas Freedman's Press hail these fine young men as a credit to our race. When the white soldiers from the 5th Infantry came to town, there was a big hoopla, and flags flew from every post. Let's give the 24th the same honor. Wake up Houston! This is 1917!"

GWEELY: That's right, Houston, this is 1917!

BUGALOOSA: Wake up!

MOSES: 'Cause the "Deuce-Four" is here!

HARDIN: (*Looking up.*) Do you fellows realize that it's leaking in here? (*They notice* HARDIN *for the first time.*)

BUGALOOSA: (*Good-naturedly.*) Oh, that'll stop when the rain stops. (*The men laugh.* HARDIN *wipes raindrops from his face.*)

HARDIN: These tents need mending.

GWEELY: Where you say you from, boy?

HARDIN: Minnesota.

GWEELY: Min-ne-sota? Hear that place so cold, it freeze the balls off a brass monkey.

HARDIN: Well, yes sir, it does get pretty cold at home.

GWEELY: Didn't even know they had no colored in Minnesota.

HARDIN: Not many like they have here in the South, sir. In my hometown there were only two colored families—the Nesbits and us Hardins.

MOSES: Still ain't figured out why they'd throw a draftee like you in with reg'lars.

HARDIN: (*Peeved.*) I'm not a draftee, I volunteered. I quit college to join up, and I've been in the army six whole months now and I—

BUGALOOSA: Y'all hear that? Six months he say. Well now, I reckon that make him a real soldier all right.

(*They laugh.*)

GWEELY: Tell you one thang boy, you lucky to be in the 24th, 'specially "I" company. We'll learn you how to be a soldier.

FRANCISCUS: So, you quit college to join up huh?

HARDIN: Oh yes. It was quite obvious to me from newspaper articles that this country was going to have to go to war, so I joined up to be ready.

FRANCISCUS: I went to college at home in Chicago for a while.

HARDIN: Then you quit to join the war effort too?

FRANCISCUS: (*Laughing.*) Hell naw. I quit to join the *Franciscus* effort. When my pa got sick, I took over his job at the slaughterhouse. But I got tired of looking at those bloody sides of beef, and decided to hitch up about five years ago.

HARDIN: (*Fervently.*) Yes well, my conscience dictated that I put my education on hold, because I feel that any man, colored or white, who is not willing to fight and die for this country, is not worth his weight in salt!

GWEELY: (*Rolling a cigarette.*) Speak boy, speak!

HARDIN: (*Sheepishly.*) Well . . . I guess I do feel rather strongly about this war, sir, but I—

MOSES: Will you stop calling him "sir."

GWEELY: Shut up, Moses. Let the boy show some respect if he want to.

HARDIN: Well, I feel as William Burghardt Du Bois feels, he says that—

GWEELY: Who??

FRANCISCUS: W. E. B. Du Bois.

GWEELY: Oh yeah, I remember now, that's the fella you be tellin' us about, 'Ciscus.

HARDIN: (*Passionately.*) Du Bois says that this war is "an end and also a beginning." He says, "Never again will the darker people of this world occupy just the place we have before . . . "

(MOSES *crosses the tent to throw out dirty water.*)

HARDIN: (*Continued.*) ". . . and after we have proved ourselves worthy by fighting and dying for this country, a grateful nation will gladly give us the recognition and respect that the white man now enjoys!"

GWEELY: (*Impressed.*) Boy, you sound like a professor.

(*A clap of thunder as* MOSES *rushes back in.*)

MOSES: It's coming down in buckets out there.

BUGALOOSA: (*Shining his cornet.*) Hope it slacken up 'fore we get out tonight.

MOSES: I don't care if it's raining horse mess; I'm going into town tonight.

GWEELY: Me too, if I gotta paddle a canoe.

MOSES: Anyway, this rain looks good, after being stuck out there in the desert, chasing Pancho Villa's behind.

HARDIN: You chased Pancho Villa?

MOSES: Yeah, me and Gweely were in Pershing's special guard for a time.

GWEELY: But I'm the one almost caught him. I come that close . . . (*Snaps fingers.*) . . . that close to catching Ol' Pancho single-handed . . .

BUGALOOSA: You believe that lie, you believe anything.

GWEELY: Hell, I did, you don't know. (*Arm around* HARDIN.) It was evenin', boy, 'long about dusk dark, and I was out patrollin' . . .

ALL: . . . all by myself!

(*They laugh, as* GWEELY *waves them off.*)

FRANCISCUS: Gweely wasn't the only one out there that evening.

MOSES: We had Ol' Pancho right in our sights— (*Holding up his rifle.*)

GWEELY: (*Lovingly caressing his rifle.*) With these new Springfield rifles. Ain't she a beaut? Thirty ought caliber, battle sights, ladder sights up to a thousand yards . . .

FRANCISCUS: Zuelke had told McKinney to take a few of his best shooters out to scout for Mexican Federales. But he said don't shoot any Mexicans this time, though. 'Cause we're at war with the Germans now.

MOSES: He just wanted us to fire a few rounds and leave our empty brass, so their German advisors could see what they were up against.

GWEELY: So we went into this little Mexican village to talk to this colored Seminole scout sittin' under a tree. So we asked him if he knowed anythang. But he was part colored and part Indian, and didn't speak nothin' but Spanish.

FRANCISCUS: "Dónde están los oficiales alemanes y los federales?"

GWEELY: (*Translating.*) "Where the German officers with the Federales at?"

FRANCISCUS: Then the scout said, "Yo te llevo. Siento bien haciendo poquito trabajo." (*Translating.*) "I will take you to them. It will be good to do a little work."

MOSES: So we find their camp. A Federale and a German are each holding maps, discussing strategy. We laying up on a hill in the grass, watchin 'em with binoculars. We get in position—McKinney is holding binoculars to spot for me—

GWEELY: Franciscus spottin' for me.

(GWEELY *and* MOSES *enact the scene.*)

MOSES: I'm trained on the Federale—

GWEELY: Got my sights on that godless German hun—

FRANCISCUS: McKinney gives the word . . .

GWEELY/MOSES: We fire!

FRANCISCUS: Almost simultaneously. Maps start flying, officers hit the dirt . . .

GWEELY: (*Laughing.*) Thankin' they was dead. . . . But all we done was shoot the maps out they hands—

MOSES: Orders were—don't kill 'em—

GWEELY: —Jest let 'em know we'd been there. (*Plants a big kiss on his rifle.*) Sweet Jesus! What a weapon!

FRANCISCUS: Yeah well, I'm glad to be shed of Columbus, New Mexico.

GWEELY: Place wasn't so bad—them senoritas was nice.

FRANCISCUS: Yeah, but eleven months of nothing but rock and sagebush was starting to get to me. I'd forgot what a tree looked like.

BUGALOOSA: Damn a tree, I forgot what a colored gal looked like.

MOSES: Me too. I got so sick of looking at Mexican faces and hearing talk I didn't half understand. Tonight I'm gonna get my hands on a colored girl, the *blackest* one I can find!

BUGALOOSA: That Selena sho' was crazy about you, though. She couldn't say nothin' in English but "I love Joe Moses too much; I love Joe Moses *too* much."

MOSES: I taught her how to say that.

GWEELY: Useta wear me out with that mess. Hell, I met her first, don't know what she seen in you—you ugly and you sho' don't part with no pesos.

MOSES: (*Smugly.*) I'll have to tell you my secret one day, Gweely.

FRANCISCUS: (*Shining his boots.*) Ol' Selena's probably hooked up with some other soldier by now.

GWEELY: Sho is.

MOSES: Say Franciscus, you still writing that cross-eyed pen pal of yours?

FRANCISCUS: (*Good-naturedly.*) Yeah, and she's not cross-eyed, either.

MOSES: (*Winking at* GWEELY.) How would you know, you ain't never seen her.

FRANCISCUS: Gonna see her tonight.

MOSES: Me, I couldn't write a woman all this time without knowing what she look like.

GWEELY: Me neither. But Moses, we got to remember, Franciscus ain't innerested in what a gal look like—all he innerested in is how much book learnin' she got.

BUGALOOSA: And how much money her folks got.

FRANCISCUS: Aw, you two just jealous because those pen pals you had in 'Frisco turned out so bad.

BUGLOOSA: Didn't they tho.

MOSES/GWEELY: (*Waving them off.*) Aw man, forget that, don't nobody want to hear about that . . . (*Etc.*)

FRANCISCUS: Hardin wants to hear it; don't you Hardin?

HARDIN: Yes, yes I would like to hear about their exploits.

BUGALOOSA: Y'all hear that—ex-ploits?

FRANCISCUS: Well Hardin, my boy, they finally met these two sisters they'd been writing to in San Francisco. Twins they were . . .

BUGALOOSA: O-ra and Do-ra.

(*MOSES and GWEELY groan in remembrance.*)

FRANCISCUS: Well, Ora turned out to be cross-eyed—

BUGALOOSA: And Dora was big as a bale of cotton!

(*Laughing, BUGALOOSA spreads his arms and lumbers across the tent.*)

GWEELY: Well, I jest might put all these women down over here, and marry up with one of them Franch senoritas.

MOSES: Let you tell it, you always gonna "marry up" with somebody.

FRANCISCUS: Yeah, remember he said the same thing in the Philippines.

GWEELY: But I ain't shuckin' and jivin' this time though. Bugaloosa even much been learnin' me some of that Franch lingo. (*Takes a deep breath.*) Pol-ly Vouse Frances? Comin' Alice too?

BUGALOOSA: Man, they ain't gonna understand a word you saying. Permittez-moi de presenter. J'ai m'pelle Jacques Honoré. Comment-allez vous?

GWEELY: Oo-wee, listen at how that trip offen his tongue! Be glad when I learns how to whisper it like that in them Franch senoritas' ears.

BUGALOOSA: (*Disgustedly.*) "Mademoiselles," man, "mademoiselles." How many times I got to tell you, you call French women "mademoiselles"?

GWEELY: Yeah, well, me and you got to get together on that stuff. Yep, after the war I just might settle overseas. They say a colored man get treated with respect overseas.

HARDIN: We're going to be treated with respect right here in America after the war.

MOSES: Yeah, things'll be different when we get back.

BUGALOOSA: If we get back.

FRANCISCUS: If we don't get back, then our children'll get the respect.

GWEELY: Yeah, that's right.

FRANCISCUS: Black Jack Pershing here we come! Finally gonna see some action!

MOSES: (*Sourly.*) You call guarding this campsite action?

FRANCISCUS: We're not going to be here long, Moses—this is just a stopover. Sergeant McKinney says we'll be shipping out for the war zone as soon as they finish the construction here.

MOSES: We better. All this outfit's been pulling is garrison duty. White boys see all the action.

GWEELY: Yeah, but pretty soon we gon' be over there in the foxholes with the rest of 'em.

BUGALOOSA: But what about that stuff you be reading in that N-A-A-C-P magazine, Franciscus? About the gov'ment using colored soldiers to grow food for the army? What about that?

MOSES: I'd like to see the first son of a gun tell me about growing some vegetables! Hell, I ain't no plowboy, I'm a soldier!

FRANCISCUS: Calm down Moses. They don't mean reg'lars like us. They're talking about draftees, like Hardin here, who don't know which end is up on a musket. (*He playfully throws a towel at* HARDIN.)

HARDIN: (*Unamused.*) Look, I know which end is up on a musket! And I didn't join up to be a plowboy either! (*He throws the towel back.*)

FRANCISCUS: You'll do what they tell you to do. (*Throwing the towel back again.*)

HARDIN: (*Stubbornly.*) I'm not going to a farm. I'm going overseas and fight.

BUGALOOSA: Next he'll be giving orders to Old Black Jack hisself.

HARDIN: (*Smugly.*) Not to him. But maybe to all of you.

MOSES: What?

HARDIN: They've just opened up a colored officer's training school in Des Moines, Iowa, and I plan to sign up for it.

MOSES: Officer training? For a colored man? Ain't no such thing.

FRANCISCUS: Yeah, it is, Moses. They just opened it up last month. (*Looking pointedly at* BUGALOOSA.) Remember that article I read to you about the N-A-A-C-P putting pressure on the War Department to have colored officers? Well, they just started the school.

MOSES: (*To* HARDIN.) What makes you think you could be a officer, you cocky little son of a b—

GWEELY: How old you say you is boy?

HARDIN: Nineteen. (*The others groan.*) But I've always made top honors in R.O.T.C. (*Another groan.*) And I've always been a leader in all school activities and—

MOSES: School? Who the shit talking about school, boy? This the army. I

been in ten years and ain't no boy like you gonna give me no orders, I
don't care how much "schoolin'" you got.

GWEELY: (*Grinning.*) Boy got plenty of gumption, don't he?

MOSES: I don't know what he got, but I know where he's gonna be—over
there in the trenches with the rest of us.

BUGALOOSA: Or growing squash.

MOSES: (*Laughing.*) Hey, tell him Frenchy. Nigger talking about being a
officer . . .

FRANCISCUS: Ten-hut!

(*The men snap to attention as* SGT. MC KINNEY *strides in. He's holding a burlap
sack and a tin cup. He puts these items on the shelf.*)

SGT. MC KINNEY: As you were. All right, all right, listen up!

(*All the men, except* HARDIN, *resume what they're doing.* HARDIN *continues to
stand at ramrod attention.*)

SGT. MC KINNEY: (*Continued.*) Ok. We in a Southern town now. And a colored soldier can run into a lot of trouble in a Southern town if he ain't
careful. Houston ain't like some of the other places we been stationed
in, where they lets colored come and go like they please. It ain't like
that here. They got a lotta rules for colored here. Got signs all over the
place, tellin' colored where to eat, where to sleep, where to get on the
trolley, where to get off. (*Pause.*) Ok. Some of these rules might be a
bit irksome to some of ya, but I expect ya to go by 'em, 'cause they the
law here. You men from the South unnerstand all this, but some of you
boys from the North might have some problems wit' it, but I don't aim
to have no problems. (*He stops in front of* MOSES.) So, anybody got any
questions, best speak 'em now.

MOSES: Now, I just wanna make sure *I* understand. Now—if I catch a trolley
car and all the seats in the colored section are all filled up, but it's plenty
empty ones in the white section, you saying I still have to stand up?

SGT. MC KINNEY: That's what I'm saying.

MOSES: Don't make no sense.

SGT. MC KINNEY: Ain't got to make no sense, they the rules. You just follow
'em. It don't need to be a whole lotta traffickin' on them trolley cars no
how. Walk—you need the exercise.

MOSES: I hear a colored man can't hardly walk the streets because of the
white police.

SGT. MC KINNEY: You soldiers ain't got to worry 'bout the city police (*Amid
murmurs of approval.*), you answer to you own MP's like you always do.

And while we here, we gon' put on some extra MP's. Franciscus! You one of 'em.

FRANCISCUS: Yes sir.

SGT. MC KINNEY: And you can start your duty by taking this here sack . . . (*Throws it to* FRANCISCUS.) . . . and goin' 'round collectin' all that whiskey y'all snuck in from New Mexico.

THE MEN: (*Trying to sound innocent.*) Whiskey? What whiskey? We ain't got no whiskey . . . (*Etc.*)

SGT. MC KINNEY: In the sack.

BUGALOOSA: (*Pained.*) Lord have mercy, Sarge.

(FRANCISCUS *goes around to* MOSES *and* GWEELY *with the sack. They grudgingly give up a bottle each.* HARDIN, *of course, has nothing. Throughout the collection,* SGT. MC KINNEY *holds forth on the evils of liquor.*)

SGT. MC KINNEY: I can't unnerstand what make a colored man drank liquor. Let the white man drank hisself to hell. He get drunk, go out, do somethin' foolish, no harm done. But don't you fools know a colored man can't 'ford to get all liquored up! Next moanin' he find hisself swangin' from a tree.

(*At this point,* FRANCISCUS *is at* BUGALOOSA's *cot.* BUGALOOSA *is pulling out bottle after bottle after bottle from his footlocker.* SGT. MC KINNEY *is unaware of what's going on at* BUGALOOSA's *cot.*)

SGT. MC KINNEY: (*Continued.*) I ain't gon' bide no drankin' in this comp'ny—either in barracks or in public. We gon' leave a real good impression on these white folks. Ain't gon' be no congregatin' on the street corners, no cussin' or spittin' in public, and no *drunkenness* in "I" Comp'ny. Nothin' look worser to white folks than a drunk—(*Suddenly aware of the constant "clink" of bottles coming from* BUGALOOSA's *direction, he whirls around to see Bugaloosa sadly putting a final bottle in the sack.*) —loud cussin' nigger!

HARDIN: Yes sir!

SGT. MC KINNEY: Sit down, Hardin.

(HARDIN *sits.* FRANCISCUS *exits with the sack.*)

SGT. MC KINNEY: (*Continued.*) Now to cut down on a lot of goin' back and forwards into town, the white folks done give up some of their own buildings right close to camp and turned it into a dance hall for y'all soldiers. Somewhere over on Washington Street, they say.

GWEELY: (*Doing a little jig.*) Hoo-ray! Just point me in the direction, Sarge, 'cause I got my dancin' shoes ready.

SGT. MC KINNEY: Just hold your horses, Brown. 'Fore y'all go out and blow your pay on some gal, I wants your money for your liberty bonds. (*He gets the tin cup from the shelf, while the men go in their pockets.*) And dig deep. Them bums in "M" comp'ny beat us out last time.

(*SGT. MC KINNEY goes around with the cup, stopping at GWEELY first.*)

SGT. MC KINNEY: (*Continued.*) I'm takin' up money for the folks in East St. Louis too.

GWEELY: I sho' aims to give to that. I hear some of them folks ain't got the money to bury they dead.

SGT. MC KINNEY: That's what some of this here money's for.

GWEELY: What they do to them white National Guards?

SGT. MC KINNEY: Nothin'.

BUGALOOSA: Got clean away with murder.

SGT. MC KINNEY: (*Sharply.*) You watch yo' choice of words, Honoré. You talkin' 'bout men in uniform.

BUGALOOSA: I know, Sarge, but those colored folks wasn't nothin' but civilians, didn't have nothin' to fight with but rocks and sticks.

HARDIN: Sergeant McKinney? What do you think started that riot, sir?

SGT. MC KINNEY: Ain't got no time to waste speculatin'. I wasn't there, don't know the straight of it.

(*SGT. MC KINNEY rattles his cup before BUGALOOSA. BUGALOOSA drops in two coins.*)

SGT. MC KINNEY: (*Continued.*) (*Disgustedly.*) Is that all you givin' Honoré?

BUGALOOSA: (*Shrugging.*) Tha's all I got—deux sous.

SGT. MC KINNEY: Two pennies?

BUGALOOSA: That's all I got, Sarge. I just bought a new cornet, don'tcha know, and I'm a little short.

SGT. MC KINNEY: You *always* a little short. (*To HARDIN.*) Boy!

HARDIN: Yes sir!

SGT. MC KINNEY: Kin you count money?

HARDIN: Yes sir, I can count!

SGT. MC KINNEY: (*Giving him the cup.*) Count this. (*Back to the men.*) One mo' thang. The colored folk in town is got it planned to treat y'all like you some kinda heroes or somethin'—got all kinda festivities planned for ya. But don't none of y'all get the big head about this. And Colonel Gentry figured it would be good for morale to throw the camp open, and let y'all have visitors from thirteen hundred hours to right 'fore curfew . . . (*He holds up a restraining hand at the men's approval.*) as long as you men not on duty and done finished all assignments. (*Pause.*) Now, they say some Eye-talian woman, name—a—uh—Miss Step-nu-chi or somethin'—she live cross the way and she say you soldiers is welcome to use her telephone . . .

THE MEN: (*Excitedly.*) Telephone?! We can use a telephone . . .! (*Etc.*)

SGT. MC KINNEY: . . . but I don't want none of y'all troopin' in and outta that white woman's house, I don't care what they say. (*Pause.*) Now, y'all all know how Colonel Gentry always want to be the one give out the good news, and leave it to us non-coms to give out the bad. So, when he call 'sembly at eighteen hundred hours this evenin', act like y'all ain't heard none of this.

GWEELY: Sarge? Then visitors? That mean womens too, don't it?

SGT. MC KINNEY: (*Dryly.*) Yeah Brown, that mean womens. (*At* GWEELY's *big grin.*) But let me tell you somethin', Gweely Brown: I got my first time to catch a female in barracks and ain't gon' be no mo' women visitors for "I" Comp'ny period. Unnerstand?

GWEELY: Oh yeah, sure, I unnerstand that.

SGT. MC KINNEY: You done countin' that money, boy?

HARDIN: Yes sir! Five dollars and thirty . . . (*Looks pointedly at* BUGALOOSA.) . . . *two* cents, Sergeant McKinney, sir.

SGT. MC KINNEY: Humph. Curfew same as usual. And any soldier out pass that time got me to deal with.

(SGT. MC KINNEY *strides out of the tent.*)

GWEELY: (*Imitating McKinney.*) And any soldier out past that time, got me to deal with—

SGT. MC KINNEY: (*Re-enters.*) And remember this here . . .

(GWEELY *jumps to attention, as the men cut short their laughter.*)

SGT. MC KINNEY: You soldiers of the United States Army, and if some of these white folks don't respect yo' color, they bound to respect that uniform. So, compote yo'selves at all times so's you don't brang no dishonor on that uniform.

THE MEN: (*Solemnly.*) Yes sir.

SGT. MC KINNEY: Ok, that's it.

(SGT. MC KINNEY *exits.* GWEELY *makes a point to be sure that* SGT. MC KINNEY *is gone before he speaks this time.*)

GWEELY: Yeah, and I bet he'll be standin' guard too, makin' sho' every man is in at curfew.

BUGALOOSA: Much as I plan to do, curfew need to be at sunrise.

GWEELY: Wish he was like some of the other non-coms around here. The boys in "M" Comp'ny have to cover for Murphy all the time.

BUGALOOSA: Yeah, he be goin' AWOL, whorin' and drinkin' with the best of us.

(BUGALOOSA *takes another whiskey bottle from his footlocker.*)

MOSES: McKinney ought to get him a woman. I ain't never seen him with no woman.

GWEELY: Last woman he was with was in 1907.

MOSES: (*Laughing.*) Man, how you know that?

GWEELY: I was with him. Tried to hook him up with this little gal, but he runned her off, same way he run all his women off—treatin 'em like boots—(*Demonstrates on* BUGALOOSA.) Straighten up that spine! Throw back them shoulders, pull in that gut! (*They laugh.*) I ain't lyin', he run 'em all off like that, so I quit tryin' to hook him up y'know, and then after he made sergeant, we just kinda went our diff'rent ways.

(GWEELY *starts looking for Franciscus' hair pomade and mirror, finds it, and takes it back to his cot.*)

HARDIN: You've been in the army as long as Sergeant McKinney?

GWEELY: Damn near. Been in longer than any of these fellers.

HARDIN: You could be a sergeant, maybe even an officer.

GWEELY: (*Flattered.*) Oh, they done come to me 'bout it, but I don't want to be in charge of no nigger but me.

(FRANCISCUS *re-enters, puts the empty sack back on the shelf.*)

BUGALOOSA: You didn't get rid of all of it, didcha?

FRANCISCUS: (*Breezily.*) Those were my orders. (*Beat.*) And guess who came out to help me get rid of the contraband?

BUGALOOSA: (*Disgusted.*) Cap'n Zuelke.

FRANCISCUS: Down his gullet. (*Looking through his belongings, puzzled.*)

BUGALOOSA: (*Heatedly.*) That drunk bum! (*MOSES laughs.*) Hey man, that ain't funny, no! That was some good liquor all gone to waste. Bon je senyé!

GWEELY: That's all right, Boog, we ain't gon' cry over spilt whiskey, plenty mo' where that come from.

FRANCISCUS: (*Absently, as he searches.*) I guess Zuelke figured we owe him. He's the one who told Colonel Gentry it would be good for morale to open up the camp. But Gentry'll come in here and take all the credit.

GWEELY: McKinney beat him to it this time.

MOSES: Now we'll have to hear that same speech all over again.

(BUGALOOSA *starts to play on his cornet the song "Over There." All join in as they put finishing touches on their uniforms.*)

GWEELY: (*Concluding the song.*) Hey! Way I figure it, we'll go by this dance hall on Washington Street first, see what the house got there, then . . .

(*At this point,* FRANCISCUS *spies his pomade, starts over to* GWEELY'S *cot.*)

GWEELY: (*Continued.*) . . . then we'll mosey on into town, check out the juke joints there.

MOSES: All right by me.

FRANCISCUS: (*Snatching pomade.*) You're welcome!

GWEELY: Oh yeah—thanks. Got to buy me some of that stuff one day.

FRANCISCUS: You been saying that ever since I met you.

GWEELY: (*Looking in the mirror.*) Look-a-there, make my hair look kinda wavy, don't it? (FRANCISCUS *takes the mirror.*) You gon' paint the town with us, Franciscus?

FRANCISCUS: Not tonight. Tonight I'm going to meet Pris-cil-la.

GWEELY: Well, have fun with yo' preacher gal, but preacher gal ain't exactly what I'm lookin' for tonight.

BUGALOOSA: Me neither.

FRANCISCUS: She may be a preacher's daughter, but her letters sound mighty lively.

GWEELY: What about you, boy? Wanna come with us?

(HARDIN'S *been lounging on his cot, reading pamphlets. He eagerly sits up.*)

HARDIN: Well, what do you fellows have planned to do?

GWEELY: Find some women and get drunk.

HARDIN: Oh—well—I was just planning to go sightseeing.

(*The men try to keep a straight face.* HARDIN *runs over to them with a pamphlet.*)

HARDIN: (*Continues.*) I have this little pamphlet here on Houston, and they have these two skyscrapers I'd really like to see—the Carter Building, which is sixteen stories high, and the Rice Hotel, with twenty-two stories.

GWEELY: Colored 'lowed in 'em?

HARDIN: Well—uh—I don't know, I was just planning to stand outside and look up at them.

(*The men burst out laughing.*)

MOSES: Boy really know how to have a good time, don't he?

GWEELY: Come on boy, we gon' break you in tonight. You can see a tall building any time, but bet you ain't never had no poontain.

HARDIN: (*Afraid to ask.*) Uh . . . exactly what is that?

(*Roar of laughter from the men.*)

GWEELY: (*Slapping him on back.*) Naw, you ain't never had none. Come on, boy, you goin' with us tonight.

HARDIN: Ok, if you fellows really want me.

(HARDIN *heads for his cot,* BUGALOOSA *cuts him off, pulls him aside.*)

BUGALOOSA: You got any money?

HARDIN: (*Reaching into his pocket.*) Well yes, as a matter of fact, I do, my mother just sent me—

GWEELY: Don't worry Bugaloosa, me and Moses got plenty money, we take care of you.

MOSES: Hey nigger, don't be loaning out my money. He ain't got no money, let him stay in camp.

(*The call for assembly sounds.*)

FRANCISCUS: (*Snapping to attention.*) As-sem-bly! Look smart, men, look smart!

(*The men snap to attention. By this time they are sleek and sharp in their uniforms, except* HARDIN. BUGALOOSA *starts playing "Over There," and the men join in.*)

THE MEN: (*Singing.*) Over there, over there, tell the men to beware over there, 'cause the Yanks are comin', the Yanks are comin' and we won't stop marchin' 'til it's over, over there . . .

(*They dance a little jig on out the tent.* HARDIN *scurries after them, tucking in his shirt tail.*)

(*Fade out.*)

Scene 2

(AT RISE: *Two days later. The Barracks of "I" Company.* MOSES *is sitting on his cot, holding a crudely painted sign.* GWEELY *is sitting on his cot, playing with a colorful parasol. He has a loopy grin on his face.* FRANCISCUS *flips through a magazine;* BUGALOOSA *is losing a hand of solitaire to himself.*)

MOSES: (*Reading the sign.*) "No Negroes or Dogs Allowed." I don't believe this shit! (*Turns the sign around.*) We don't take no stuff like this up North!

GWEELY: (*Twirling the parasol.*) That's the way it is in the South.

MOSES: (*Pacing.*) And these white conductors act like they're giving a colored man a free ride. This little ol' conductor last night, got mad 'cause some of us was sitting in the white section. He stopped the trolley, went and got the police. I started to throw that thing off the tracks. Hell, we pay our fare, we ought to be able to sit anywhere we want to!

GWEELY: Aw, you make too big a deal out of it. Don't matter where I sit, strap me on top, so long's I'm ridin'.

MOSES: Comparing us to dogs! How the colored here take this?

BUGALOOSA: Way of life here. They used to it.

FRANCISCUS: Bound to respect the uniform, huh? (*Closes the magazine.*) These whites here don't act like they're bound to respect anything that belongs to the colored man.

BUGALOOSA: A bunch of them tried to run me off the sidewalk last night. They better be glad I didn't have my sidearm.

(*MOSES takes another sign from under his cot.*)

MOSES: And look at this one here, fellers. Got it off the trolley car . . . (*Reads.*) "No Colored Seated beyond This Point."

FRANCISCUS: (*Coming after MOSES.*) No wonder we have so many complaints about missing signs!

MOSES: (*Dodging FRANCISCUS.*) Gonna keep these as souvenirs. (*Puts them in his footlocker.*) When I show 'em to my buddies in New York, they ain't gonna believe this. (*Beat.*) I kept inching up and inching up behind that conductor until I was breathing down his white neck.

FRANCISCUS: All right, Moses, these white folks here take those trolley cars real serious. You gonna find yourself in stockade, or worse, in the city jail. And if I catch you confiscating any more of those signs, Moses, I'm gonna have to report you.

MOSES: (*Drops to his knees.*) Oh please, Mr. Corporal Franciscus, Mister MP, suh! Can I just keep those signs suh! I want to show 'em to my son when he grows up, so he'll know how it was for us, Mr. Corporal Franciscus, suh?

FRANCISCUS: Get away from me. You ain't gonna make me feel bad about doing my job. If I don't do my job, I get in trouble with the Sarge and Zuelke.

MOSES: You always worried about getting in trouble.

GWEELY: (*Blowing smoke.*) Ain't he though? Don't you know we don't get in trouble in the 24th? We kicks trouble's behind.

MOSES: (*Lying on his cot.*) Yeah, we lead a charmed life, don't you know? They loved us in Manila, they loved us in San Fran.

GWEELY: In Manila they gave the deuce-four the keys to the city. Told us we was welcome back any time. And the same thang gon' happen here, Franciscus. We gon' win these white folks over too. All we got to do is grin.

BUGALOOSA: (*Not looking up from his cards.*) And don't look at the white women.

MOSES: Damn these crackers. They ain't got to like me. The colored here sure treating us right.

GWEELY: Ain't they though? (*Twirling the parasol.*) I got to return this here parasol to a pretty little gal I met yesterday.

BUGALOOSA: Man, I'm still full from that picnic yesterday. I never seen that much food in my life.

FRANCISCUS: Me either. Tubs full of rice and potato salad . . .

BUGALOOSA: All different kind of cakes and cookies. And creole food almost as good as Grandmere used to cook.

MOSES: It seemed like all the colored in the world was there . . . (*Overlapping.*)

FRANCISCUS: Young folks, old folks—

GWEELY: Women.

BUGALOOSA: Preachers, teachers—

GWEELY: Women.

MOSES: An army of black faces, spread all over the grounds—

GWEELY: Women. (*Smacks a kiss to the air.*) I coulda just hugged and kissed 'em—

FRANCISCUS: Church choirs singing—

BUGALOOSA: Preachers preachin'—

GWEELY: In they pretty little parasols and dresses.

MOSES: They were following after us, trying to touch us, just like we was Jesus or somebody.

GWEELY: Just like bein' in a candy sto'.

BUGALOOSA: Little boys runnin' up to us, wantin' to shake our hands—

FRANCISCUS: Old men calling us soldiers of freedom.

MOSES: I believe they would've done anything we told 'em to do that day. I believe they would have followed us right straight into the future.

FRANCISCUS: Yeah . . . it was something all right . . . I'll never forget that day . . .

ALL: Yeah . . . (*Beat.*)

FRANCISCUS: Hey, what you fellows think of Priscilla?

(*They make a "so-so" gesture with their hands and a sound that says they're unimpressed.*)

GWEELY: I guess she ain't bad for a preacher's daughter. But what was all that crazy talk she was talkin' and them papers she was passin' out?

FRANCISCUS: (*Proudly.*) Priscilla's what you call a suffragette.

THE MEN: A what?

FRANCISCUS: A suffragette. She thinks white women ought to have the right to vote.

MOSES: What she care about white women getting the vote, when a colored man can't even vote.

FRANCISCUS: Well, she's in this group that figures if white women get the vote, maybe then it'll come on down to the rest of us.

MOSES: How's a bunch of colored gals gonna get us the vote? When we win this fight overseas, that's when we gonna get the vote.

FRANCISCUS: Hey fellers, let me tell you what you have to see: You have to see her father's house. It's a palace, I tell ya, a real live palace!

(*He eagerly waits for them to ask for further details; they don't.*)

BUGALOOSA: (*Finally looking up from his solitaire.*) So, what's it look like, Franciscus?

FRANCISCUS: It's got *electric* lights.

THE MEN: (*Impressed, despite themselves.*) Electric . . . ?

FRANCISCUS: And *inside* bathrooms—

THE MEN: Naw, for real? (*Etc.*)

FRANCISCUS: Two of 'em! Five bedrooms, a library—everything!

GWEELY: (*Rolling a cigarette.*) He must really be passin' 'round the collectin' plate.

FRANCISCUS: He pastors a mighty big church all right, mighty big. Priscilla says all of the best colored families attend there.

GWEELY: Boy you steppin' in high cotton now.

FRANCISCUS: I told her father the Camp Logan quartet would sing at his church next Sunday.

GWEELY: Next Sunday? Man, next Sunday I plans to be wakin' up 'side of the most prettiest gal in the world. Mavis. Work at the dance hall. Beautiful. Ain't she Moses?

MOSES: (*Shrugging.*) She all right.

GWEELY: Pretty woman like that can have all my money.

MOSES: She did.

GWEELY: (*Ignoring Moses.*) She tall, Franciscus, big-hipped, like I like 'em, y'know, and she got this smooth brown skin, and kinda slanted-like eyes, and—oh Lawd—I gits weak 'bout the knees just thankin' about her.

MOSES: (*Beat.*) They say she belongs to the meanest white policeman in town—name of O'Reilly. They say he just came off suspension for killing two colored civilians.

GWEELY: (*Unperturbed.*) She ain't mentioned no O'Reilly to me.

FRANCISCUS: O'Reilly? Yeah, he's with the Mounted Police. We met him last night when the city police briefed us. Tall, red-haired peckerwood, mean as a hornet. They say he rides a big black horse called "Nigger." Say he'll go up side a colored man's head as soon as look at him.

GWEELY: (*Unperturbed.*) I'm goin' 'round to her house tonight.

BUGALOOSA: Bet not let that cracker catch you.

GWEELY: (*Breezily.*) He don't bother me; I won't bother him.

MOSES: Man, she ain't worth it.

GWEELY: (*Sharply.*) How you know what she worth? You just jealous 'cause Selena showed up and plucked that sweet black berry out yo' hand.

MOSES: Selena don't stop me from nothing!

GWEELY: (*Laughing.*) Tell her that, not me.

MOSES: (*Frustrated.*) She don't understand no English, dammit!

FRANCISCUS: I still can't believe she followed you here.

MOSES: Well, she did. I don't know how she did, but that crazy Mexican did.

GWEELY: He'd met this pretty little colored gal too, Franciscus. And she was buying him beer by the barrel—matter fact, the whole house was buying us soldiers' beer—

BUGALOOSA: Didn't have to spend a nickel. I won ten dollars off those civilians too—

MOSES: I came that close—(*Snaps fingers.*)—that close to taking that little colored gal in the back room—

(*MOSES is unaware that GWEELY has sneaked up behind him. GWEELY slips MOSES' Mexican blanket off MOSES' cot and wraps it around his shoulders.*)

MOSES: (*Continued.*)—when out of the blue—man I thought I was hearing things—

GWEELY: (*A coquettish Spanish voice.*) Joe! Joe Moses? Joe Moses? (*Minces around the tent, batting his eyelashes.*) I just love Joe Moses too much. I just love Joe Moses *too* much!

(*MOSES holds his head in anguish, as the men roll on their cots with laughter.*)

GWEELY: (*Continued.*) You coulda bought Joe Moses with a penny. (*He throws the blanket over* MOSES *head.*)

BUGALOOSA: (*Winking at* FRANCISCUS.) Hey Mose! Guess who got that little colored gal of yourn?

MOSES: Who!

GWEELY: (*Gleefully.*) Hardin.

MOSES: Hardin?!

GWEELY: Well, he coulda had her, but he didn't know what to do with her.

BUGALOOSA: She started battin' her eyes at him, but he just sit there—

GWEELY: Lookin' like a scared rabbit, ready to bolt.

(SET UP BY PLAYWRIGHT: *All black 24th Infantry Regiment soldiers stationed in Houston during World War I, before being shipped overseas to fight in France, suffered constant harassment by the white police officers and the conductors of the trolley cars.*)

(*In this scene the hot-tempered Joe Moses, from up North, is being reprimanded by his sergeant for not following the senseless Jim Crow rules of this Southern town.*)

SGT. MC KINNEY: (*Off Stage.*) Mo-ses!

MOSES: (*Under breath.*) Damn.

(FRANCISCUS *exits, as* SGT. MC KINNEY *enters, and crosses to* MOSES' *cot.*)

SGT. MC KINNEY: Moses. Heard you threatened to turn over the Franklin Street trolley last night.

MOSES: (*At attention.*) Turn over a trolley?

SGT. MC KINNEY: You heard me, you heard me. I'm sho' you wasn't the onliest one in on it . . . (*Looks around at the others.*) . . . but the conductor 'members hearin' yo' name loud and clear.

MOSES: (*Trying to bluff.*) A trolley car? I don't know nothing about turning over no trolley car. I just know it was the last trolley running back to camp before curfew, and a lot of us kinda pile on—

SGT. MC KINNEY: —rambunctious like, and spilt over into the white section of the car.

MOSES: (*Decides to come clean.*) Look Sarge, it wasn't but a few white men sitting in the white section of the bus that time of night, and I figured—

SGT. MC KINNEY: Oh, you figured—?

MOSES: Yeah. It didn't make sense to me that we couldn't sit in those empty seats. It didn't make sense to me for half of us to have to get off the bus, and be late for curfew, when we was already on a trolley full of empty seats.

SGT. MC KINNEY: Look, I toldt you not to try to make no sense outta these rules. I toldt you, you just follow'em, you stay outta trouble, and that's all you do.

MOSES: But we don't take no stuff like this up North. Look at this sign I got outta one of the store windows, Sarge. (*Reading.*) "No Negroes or Dogs Allowed."

SGT. MC KINNEY: You the one been stealing all those signs.

MOSES: Yeah, I'm gonna take 'em back home as a souvenir. The boys back home ain't gon' believe this shit.

SGT. MC KINNEY: The next time I catch you wit' one of them signs, I'm gon' have to report ya. These white folks in Houston take those signs mighty serious.

MOSES: Yeah, they have signs for colored people all over the place: tellin 'em where to eat, where to sleep, where to get on the trolley, where to get off.

SGT. MC KINNEY: (*Sternly.*) And I expect ya to go by 'em, 'cause they law here. (*Beat.*) You boys from up North might have some problems wit' this, but I don't aim to have no problems. You understand that?

MOSES: (*Long sullen stare.*) Yeah . . . I understand.

SGT. MC KINNEY: (*In* MOSES' *face.*) Don't you be buckin' me, boy! I'll break you down to the lowest tin can of a buck private, I'll have you on dirty detail 'til the day you die!

(*Reluctantly,* MOSES *averts his gaze.* SGT. MC KINNEY *walks toward the other men.*)

SGT. MC KINNEY: (*Continued.*) Ain't had no displi'nary problems in this comp'ny, ain't gon' have none now, even if I got to keep half of ya locked up in stockade. Wonder how y'all 'pect to hold up under fire in France, if you loses yo' head with a conductor on a trolley car. We soldiers! Our fight ain't here in this muddy bayou town with these civilians, it's overseas with them godless huns! (*Beat. Walking toward* MOSES.) Maybe I had you pegged wrong, Moses. Maybe I had all y'all pegged wrong, maybe I needs to weed through this comp'ny, and see who ready to fight with the white boys in France and who ain't.

MOSES: You know I'm ready for France and anything else they throw at us, but if you'd heard the way that conductor *talked* to us—

SGT. MC KINNEY: Oh! So you didn't like the way he *talked* to you, that it? (*Circling* MOSES.) Well, how you likes to be talked to Moses . . . huh . . . ? (*Mocking, feminine voice.*) Words got to be poured over you like blackstrap molasses, all so-o-o-ft and swe-e-e-t, like a gal?

MOSES: (*Squirming with anger.*) Now Sarge, you know it ain't like that, but we're getting ready to lay our lives down for this country, and we deserve respect!

SGT. MC KINNEY: Respect. (*Patriotic fervor.*) We bring back the vic'try from overseas, then this country is bound to give us our glory and respect. (*Beat, then lays it on thick, as others snicker.*) You know Moses, they's got a-plenty of them German huns just dyin' to sweet-talk a colored boy like you right on over to they side. Yeah, that's how come the gov'ment scared to send colored troops overseas, you know that? They's scared that when them sneaky huns gets through tellin' ya what a hard time you got over here, you jest might turn your gun on your own officers! That's what they scared of, Moses. And maybe they got good reason to be scared, 'cause I'm wonderin' what you gon' do when one of them godless huns slides up in yo' face wit' all that sweet talk. (*In his face.*) What you gon' do, Moses? (*Disgustedly.*) You gon' follow 'em like a lamb to the slaughter. (*Turns on his heels and starts for exit.*)

MOSES: (*Calls after him.*) Naw. (*Beat.*) I'm gonna mow them white son of a guns down like a boweevil going through cotton!

(SGT. MC KINNEY *calmly strides back.*)

SGT. MC KINNEY: Oh yeah? (*Smirking.*) Well . . . we'll see, Moses . . . we'll see. Double guard duty for you, starting . . . (*Pulls chain watch out of his pocket.*) right now!

(*Black out.*)

Scene 3

(SETTING: *The small office of* CAPT. ZUELKE. *The office consists of an old beat-up desk, two chairs, and an American flag. The desk is cluttered with stacks of paperwork, coffee cups, old food, etc.*)

(AT RISE: *Mid-morning, and already hot.* CAPT. ZUELKE *is seated at his desk, fanning himself as he shuffles paperwork. He's florid and sloppy from the heat and too much whiskey.* SGT. MC KINNEY *stands at ease before him, all spit and polish. These two, both loners, have worked together for years—unwillingly united in the command and discipline of the men.*)

CAPT. ZUELKE: Another note from that damn Harris County Patriotic League. Blast that group to hell! I believe they'd report their own mothers for "seditious" and "traitorous" behavior.

SGT. MC KINNEY: What they sayin' now, Capt. Zuelke?

CAPT. ZUELKE: That the soldiers in this company are consortin' with Mexican spies.

SGT. MC KINNEY: (*Snorts.*) Mexican spies?

CAPT. ZUELKE: I know, a bunch of hogwash, but we can't just ignore these folks, we have to give 'em some kind of report.

SGT. MC KINNEY: Well, we was in Mexico so long, a lotta the soldiers picked up that Mexican lingo. Reckon that's what they talkin' about.

CAPT. ZUELKE: Maybe—but spy around into it. You never know what these boys might let themselves get talked into.

SGT. MC KINNEY: Yessuh.

CAPT. ZUELKE: Now, this trouble between the white construction workers and the soldiers is goin' from bad to worse. Construction workers say they're gonna walk if the attitude of some of the soldiers don't change. You know the ones I'm talking about in "I" Company.

SGT. MC KINNEY: Well suh, from what I kin see, it's them construction workers causin' all the trouble—

CAPT. ZUELKE: Wait a minute, McKinney. We gotta try to be fair about this.

SGT. MC KINNEY: Well suh, I figure I'm bein' fair. I'm in camp all the time and I see—

CAPT. ZUELKE: Wait a minute, McKinney. You tryin' to say I'm not in camp long enough to know what's going on with my men?

SGT. MC KINNEY: Naw suh, I ain't sayin' that. I know *you* in camp all the time, suh, but well—Colonel Gentry and some of the other off'cers—

CAPT. ZUELKE: (*Reprimandingly.*)—are away from camp a lot, yes. But an officer's got more to do than just run camp, McKinney. He's got to keep good relations with the folks of a town, and sometimes, yes, that might mean goin' to dinner or playing a game of bill-yards. (*Taking a sip of coffee.*) All in the line of duty.

SGT. MC KINNEY: Yessuh.

CAPT. ZUELKE: Now. The construction workers say that some of your boys take every chance they get to act insolent to 'em.

SGT. MC KINNEY: Insolent?

CAPT. ZUELKE: Yeah, insolent, you know—hos-tile. They say the soldiers keep on insistin' on being called colored.

SGT. MC KINNEY: Insteada nigger.

(*A beat as* CAPT. ZUELKE *tries to assess if* SGT. MC KINNEY *is being insolent or not.*)

CAPT. ZUELKE: I know the men ain't used to being called names. But they've got to try to understand that these people don't mean no harm, that's just what they're used to callin' their colored here.

SGT. MC KINNEY: I don't reckon the soldiers mean no harm, neither, Cap'n, they jest tryin' to let them workers know they don't cotton to bein' called nigger.

CAPT. ZUELKE: (*Beat.*) 'Course they don't. But I understand that it's the tone of voice the men use with the white workers that's upsetting 'em.

SGT. MC KINNEY: (*Dryly.*) Well, I'll speak to the mens about the *tone* of they voices.

(*Catching the sarcasm this time,* CAPT. ZUELKE *gives him a hard look, forcing* SGT. MC KINNEY *to add*—)

SGT. MC KINNEY: Suh.

CAPT. ZUELKE: (*Jumps up from his desk.*) And *your* tone is pretty damn close to insubordination, boy! (*A beat, then he resumes good-naturedly.*) Aw hell McKinney, we're both from Kentucky. You know how it is in the South. Little things—tone of voice, expression on your face, can set off a riot. And we don't want another East St. Louis on our hands, do we?

SGT. MC KINNEY: (*Ready to appease.*) Naw suh, we don't.

CAPT. ZUELKE: Well, the soldiers are gonna have to get off their high horses in this town. They're gonna have to realize that they're colored first in this town, and soldiers second. (*Sits, resumes shuffling papers.*) Now, Colonel Gentry says that the white citizens have even been com-plainin' that since the soldiers come to town, the colored civilians have started acting funny toward the white folks.

SGT. MC KINNEY: "Funny"?

CAPT. ZUELKE: Yeah—funny. Disrespectful. Like they think the soldiers are gonna back up anything they do. Why, Colonel Gentry even says that a socialite friend of his complained that her domestics have been acting mighty sassy since the soldiers arrived.

SGT. MC KINNEY: (*Holding back a smile.*) Well suh, what you 'spect me to do 'bout that? I ain't got no control over nobody's sassy maid.

(CAPT. ZUELKE *is up from his desk like a shot, in* SGT. MC KINNEY's *face.*)

CAPT. ZUELKE: I expect *you* as the so-called leader of that outfit over there to be aware of such things!

SGT. MC KINNEY: Yes suh!

CAPT. ZUELKE: And if any of the boys in this company are encouraging misbehavior among the colored civilians, I expect *you* to put an end to it, that's what I expect *you* to do! Is that clear!

SGT. MC KINNEY: Yes suh!

CAPT. ZUELKE: (*Fussing with things on his desk.*) Thought being in town with so many of their own kind would be good for morale, but looks like all this hero worship's just givin' them the swelled head.

SGT. MC KINNEY: Most of 'em adjustin' just fine, Cap'n. It's just a few of 'em actin' up, and I'll straighten them out.

CAPT. ZUELKE: See that you do. Or else I've got a good mind to suspend this company's privileges. (*Shuffling papers.*) And another thing—why in the Sam Hill are so many of our boys bein' thrown in the city jail? Where the hell are the MPs?

SGT. MC KINNEY: (*Plaintively.*) They right out there, Cap'n, tryin' to do they job, but the civil police won't let 'em. If a soldier get into trouble on the street, the civil police hauls him off to jail, and if the MP complain 'bout it, they throw him in jail right along with the wrongdoer.

CAPT. ZUELKE: (*Hoping to give the impression he has influence with the Colonel.*) Well, Colonel Gentry is having dinner with Chief Brock tonight. I'll have him bring the matter up.

SGT. MC KINNEY: Oh? You mean they invited you? To supper?

CAPT. ZUELKE: (*Testily.*) I'm sure I *will* be invited, McKinney.

SGT. MC KINNEY: (*Beat.*) Well, if you *do* get to go, Cap'n, kin you tell 'em the MPs need to be able to carry they sidearms, like they always do?

CAPT. ZUELKE: Outta the question, and you know it. Colonel Gentry assured the townspeople that the soldiers wouldn't be allowed to walk the streets with weapons.

SGT. MC KINNEY: But this the military police. How kin they keep the peace when they ain't got nothin' to keep the peace with?

CAPT. ZUELKE: (*Dismissively.*) Those are the colonel's orders, nothing I can do about it. (*Big sigh.*) And about these dadburn water barrels. The workers say they've caught the soldiers drinking outta the barrel clearly marked "white."

SGT. MC KINNEY: (*Carefully.*) That's 'cause for "some reason" the colored barrels keep runnin' dry.

CAPT. ZUELKE: (*Just as carefully.*) You think the construction workers are emptyin' water outta the colored barrel?

SGT. MC KINNEY: It's crossed my mind.

CAPT. ZUELKE: Still—the soldiers gotta follow the regulations. So tell 'em to leave that white water barrel alone.

SGT. MC KINNEY: (*Holding in rising anger.*) And what the men gon' do for water?

CAPT. ZUELKE: I'll tell the foreman to keep a better eye on his workers—

SGT. MC KINNEY: Been told that before, didn't do no good.

CAPT. ZUELKE: I guarantee you there'll be water in the soldiers' barrel, if I have to stand out there with my rifle and guard it myself.

SGT. MC KINNEY: Thank you, suh.

CAPT. ZUELKE: Now, let's see here . . . one of the townspeople has made a complaint against Moses and—

SGT. MC KINNEY: I know 'bout that, Cap'n, and to my way of thankin', Moses was in the right this time, he was—

CAPT. ZUELKE: This ain't a matter of right or wrong, it's simply a matter of keepin' things runnin' smooth.

SGT. MC KINNEY: But all Moses done was ask to see the civilian's pass, it's the sentry's duty to ask to see the pass each and every time for security—

CAPT. ZUELKE: Don't you quote the regulations to me, dammit! I know the regulations, I'm the officer in this outfit! (*As though explaining to an idiot.*) But the *white* men coming in and out of here on business ain't used to having to identify themselves to a *colored* man. A lot of them are city officials, get it, friends of Colonel Gentry's, and they've complained about the procedure. So, from now on, white visitors don't have to show their passes to the colored soldiers, only to the white gatekeeper. After all he's the one who's actually supposed to check the passes anyway, the soldiers are just there to guard the construction.

SGT. MC KINNEY: (*Pushing it.*) All right, I'll tell 'em, but the men already feel like they can't half do they job, they already feel—

CAPT. ZUELKE: (*Slams fist on desk.*) Dammit McKinney! Don't you make no federal case outta this! I always thought you ruled them boys with a iron hand, but all I hear outta you lately is—(*Whining voice.*)—the men don't like this, the men don't like that. You got to stop mollycoddling them! They're soldiers, dammit, and they have got to bear up under pressure just like any white soldier. (*Takes a few steps toward SGT. MC KINNEY.*) You know the government is scared to send colored troops overseas, and you know why. Well, now is a chance to test that, to see what a colored boy is really made out of. But if they can't take a little hasslin' from the local yokels, how in the Sam Hill do they expect to perform on a real battlefield?

SGT. MC KINNEY: (*Quietly.*) I unnerstand all that, suh. I just thought you'd like to hear the soldiers' side of it, so's you have all the facts.

CAPT. ZUELKE: (*Shaking papers in* SGT. MC KINNEY's *face.*) I have all the facts. I have more doggone facts than I know what to do with! But the fact of the matter is, the battle is not here in this muddy bayou town, it's in France against them godless huns!

(CAPT. ZUELKE *takes a few deep breaths, wiping his hand across his lips. He needs a drink badly. He takes a liquor flask out of the drawer, pours himself a large drink, takes a deep swallow.*)

CAPT. ZUELKE: (*Continued.*) (*Cordially.*) Sit down, McKinney, sit down.

(SGT. MC KINNEY *sighs. He can see he's about to be invited to one of Zuelke's pity parties, wishes he could decline, but he can't. Reluctantly he lowers himself to the edge of his chair.*)

CAPT. ZUELKE: (*Continued.*) (*Expansively.*) Relax yourself. That's what's wrong with you, you don't know how to relax. (*Extending the flask.*) Have one?

SGT. MC KINNEY: (*Self-righteously.*) Naw suh, you know I don't drank.

CAPT. ZUELKE: (*A beat, as he decides to respond good-naturedly.*) Bad habit, not drinkin'. Granddaddy always said never trust a feller who won't take a nip every now and agin. (*Confidentially.*) But I can trust you, can't I, McKinney?

SGT. MC KINNEY: Yessuh. I just don't like the taste of the stuff, is all.

CAPT. ZUELKE: You don't drink it for taste, dummy.

SGT. MC KINNEY: (*Standing.*) Well suh, if that's it, I'll just—

CAPT. ZUELKE: This here's about the only little pleasure I get outta life, McKinney, a quiet little drink every now and agin.

(*Trapped,* SGT. MC KINNEY *sits back down. He pulls out his pocket watch and sneaks glances throughout* CAPT. ZUELKE's *whining.*)

CAPT. ZUELKE: (*Continued.*) I don't rate getting invited to their dinner parties and such, like the other shiny new officers in this outfit. But I'm the one they call on when they need their little amusements from you boys. Tell Gweely, I want him to get up that minstrel show for the Chamber of Commerce next week.

SGT. MC KINNEY: (*Rising.*) Yessuh, I'll get right on it—

CAPT. ZUELKE: Naw, I'm not like the other officers in this outfit . . . especially those high and mighty lieutenants from West Point.

(*SGT. MC KINNEY sits back down.*)

CAPT. ZUELKE: (*Continued.*) (*Bitterly.*) Damn apple polishers, flittin' around the brass like fireflies.

(*CAPT. ZUELKE takes a deep drink, lost in bitter thoughts. SGT. MC KINNEY slowly rises.*)

CAPT. ZUELKE: (*Continued.*) Naw . . .

(*SGT. MC KINNEY sits back down.*)

CAPT. ZUELKE: (*Continued.*) I ain't never gonna get no higher than I am right now. I never went to West Point, I clawed my way up through the non-com ranks, like you. But the looies in this outfit got their bright young futures ahead of them. And this here battalion's just practice until they get a commission over white troops.

(*FRANCISCUS enters, and tries to get SGT. MC KINNEY's attention, without attracting ZUELKE's. MC KINNEY is divided between trying to figure out what FRANCISCUS wants and giving the appearance of listening to his superior.*)

SGT. MC KINNEY: (*Distractedly.*) Well—uh—who know, Cap'n? You might get a white commission one day.

CAPT. ZUELKE: I don't want it! They couldn't hand it to me on a silver platter! I don't want no white troops, I like things just the way they are, me and the colored boys. (*Raises his glass in a toast.*) That's why "I" Company's got to bear up, so I can show 'em.

SGT. MC KINNEY: Uh—don't worry, Cap'n, uh—we ain't gon' let you down.

CAPT. ZUELKE: (*Warmly.*) I know you ain't McKinney, y'all some good boys. You saved my life in the Philippines, I never will forget that. (*Takes a drink.*) But the first one of ya turn tail and run, I'll have lined up and shot. (*Suddenly spotting FRANCISCUS.*) What the hell you want, Franciscus?

FRANCISCUS: (*Steps forward, snapping to attention.*) Uh—sir! Uh—yes sir, we—uh—

CAPT. ZUELKE: Speak up, boy, speak up!

FRANCISCUS: Well—uh—we need to see the sarge outside right away—

CAPT. ZUELKE: What the hell for?

FRANCISCUS: Well—uh—

CAPT. ZUELKE: Speak up, speak up!

SGT. MC KINNEY: (*Standing.*) Trouble?

FRANCISCUS: One of the white laborers turned over the colored water barrels—again. And now one of the soldiers is threatening to run him through with his bayonet.

CAPT. ZUELKE: Damn, who the hell is it—Moses?

FRANCISCUS: No sir, Gweely.

CAPT. ZUELKE/SGT. MC KINNEY: Gweely?

(SGT. MC KINNEY *starts for the exit,* CAPT. ZUELKE *pushes past him.*)

CAPT. ZUELKE: I'll handle this.

(*As a minstrel tune starts to play, they exit, with* CAPT. ZUELKE *leading, and* FRANCISCUS *and* SGT. MC KINNEY *following, whispering and gesticulating together. Fade out.*)

Scene 4

(*The barracks of "I" Company.*)

(AT RISE: *It's evening, about a week later. In the BLACKOUT, as the minstrel tune plays, we hear the SOUND OF COINS being dropped into a tin cup. The LIGHTS SLOWLY FADE UP on* GWEELY *and* BUGALOOSA *sitting on their cots. They have just returned from performing a minstrel show, and are still in BLACKFACE.* GWEELY *was released from stockade to do the show only hours earlier. Under his comical face, he's stiff with anger.* BUGALOOSA *is gleefully counting the change he made for doing the show.* HARDIN *lies on his cot, reading his Bible.*)

BUGALOOSA: (*Dropping the coins.*) Man, I'm sure glad Zuelke sprung you outta stockade in time to do the show.

(GWEELY *is holding a mirror, looking at his blackfaced image.*)

GWEELY: (*Sullenly.*) Yeah.

BUGALOOSA: I was broke as a skunk and, man, them white folks paid off. Stay your butt outta lockup, so we can make some more money.

GWEELY: (*Rigid with anger.*) I don't know what come over me. I know I don't let these Southern crackers get next to me, but all of a sudden I seen blood in my eyes. (*Pause, as he relives the moment.*) Good thang Sarge come out there when he did, else I'da been in a heap of trouble. And the bad thang about it was, I thought he was a pretty good ol' white boy, y'know. We'd been passin' the time, playin' cards, shootin' craps, he was even talkin' about us maybe doin' the show at his lodge. Then later on, I heard him and this other worker laughin' and jokin' 'bout it cost twenty-five dollars to kill a buzzard in Texas and five dollars to kill a nigger. I didn't say nothin'. Then after that, I seen him and this other cracker empty the water outta the colored barrel, I turnt my head, let it go. Then this po' hot colored worker come to git him a dip of water, barrel was dry. I still ain't said nothin'. But then this cracker spits in the barrel and tells the colored feller, drink that, nigger. Well—when I come to myself, I was in stockade.

BUGALOOSA: (*Getting angry.*) Gimme something to take this mess off my face.

GWEELY: Here.

(*GWEELY throws him a jar of cleansing cream.*)

HARDIN: Why do you have to wear that stuff?

GWEELY: (*Sarcasm.*) Got to put yo' blackface on.

HARDIN: You already have a blackface.

GWEELY: White folk jest don't like a colored man to entertain 'em in his own face. They jest don't get no kick out of it.

BUGALOOSA: That's how come I hate to do these minstrel shows—you got to look like a clown. It ain't like that in New Orleans, playing the jazz houses. Wish I was in New Orleans right now . . . if I was I'd be in the section called Back o' Town, catchin' a set at Ponce's or maybe sitting in with the boys at Matranga's. My brother writes me they got a boy play at Matranga's now—Dipper Armstrong—say he got fire in his horn. Say he may even take the crown away from Joe Oliver. But I don't believe that. Oliver is the king.

HARDIN: The king? The king of what?

BUGALOOSA: (*Impatiently.*) You know, the blues, the Dixieland, the king.

HARDIN: Can he play as good as you?

BUGALOOSA: (*Flattered.*) Well—yeah. Hell, I'm good, true enough, but Oliver, well, he got the chops, yeah. He's the king. Yeah . . . in New Orleans the white folks would pack in to hear us, and all we had to do was play the music, didn't have to put nothin' on our faces. (*Continues taking off the makeup.*)

GWEELY: Well, in New Orleans you was playin' real music. (*He jumps to his feet, shaking off depression.*) Minstrel show ain't nothin' but clownin' around. (*Grinning, he hops up on HARDIN's footlocker.*) Fox had his eye on this here turkey a-top a tree. The fox called up to the turkey. Hey Br'er Turkey, is you heard 'bout the new law? (*BUGALOOSA jumps up on his locker, flapping his arms and gobbling.*) The new law say foxes can't eat no mo' turkeys, and hounds can't chase no mo' foxes. So, come on down from that tree, Br'er Turkey, and let's jest talk about it for a while.

BUGALOOSA: Gobble, gobble, gobble . . .

GWEELY: Br'er Turkey say, nothin' doin', Br'er Fox, I'm stayin' right up here in this tree, where I is, we kin talk about it right where we is. All of a sudden Br'er Fox heard some hounds comin' over the hill . . . (*BUGALOOSA starts barking.*) Well, I guess I'll be runnin' along, said Br'er Fox. Br'er Turkey said, I thought you said the new law say hounds can't chase you foxes no mo'? And Br'er Fox hollered back over his shoulder, that's right, that's what the law say, but them hounds'll run right over that law!

(*HARDIN falls on his cot laughing.*)

HARDIN: Did you sing any blues, Gweely?

GWEELY: Do a hog love slop?

BUGALOOSA: We gave 'em a little Beale Street Blues and St. James Infirmary.

(*BUGALOOSA and GWEELY do a song and dance to "St. Louis Blues."*)

HARDIN: (*After the song.*) I'll bet they liked you fellows.

GWEELY: (*Getting the cold cream.*) Liked us? Boy, them white folks loved us.

BUGALOOSA: Picked up a nice piece of change too. Hey Hinky!

GWEELY: Yeah Dinky?

BUGALOOSA: Parlez-vous Francais?

GWEELY: You don't leave my woman alone, I'm gon' polly yo' francis! Then we give 'em a little Ballin' the Jack. (*Sings "Ballin' the Jack" as he dances.*) Come on, boy, get up from there, and ball that jack! Come on, boy, ball that jack!

HARDIN: I told you I can't dance . . .

GWEELY: (*Pulling him up.*) Yes you kin, all niggers kin dance! Come on boy . . .

(*HARDIN stiffly tries to imitate GWEELY's movement.*)

GWEELY: That's right, that's right, move boy . . . !

(*HARDIN gets into the spirit of the thing.*)

HARDIN: (*Singing, as he concludes.*) "And that's what I call ballin' the jack"!

GWEELY: Yeah, there you go, I knew you had it in ya. (*Gets a towel from his cot.*) Then we closed the show out, marchin' 'cross the stage, wavin' Old Glory.

(*Singing, GWEELY marches across the stage, waving the towel like it's a flag. BUGALOOSA joins in.*)

GWEELY/BUGALOOSA: (*Singing.*) "Over there, over there, 'cause the Yanks are comin', the Yanks are comin', and we'll all meet ya over there. . . . "

BUGALOOSA: Them bigshot white folks ate that up.

HARDIN: Wish I could have seen the show.

GWEELY: (*Stops in his tracks.*) Hell boy, you jest seen the show—for free.

HARDIN: Gee, I did, didn't I?

GWEELY: Yeah. And we gon' put it on for the rest of the colored folks at the watermelon fest. (*He finishes taking off his makeup.*)

BUGALOOSA: You know "M" Company gonna play those Buffs durin' the fest?

GWEELY: "M" Comp'ny can't play no ball. We beat the socks off 'em in New Mexico.

BUGALOOSA: That's why I got four bits ridin' on the Buffs.

(*Enter* MOSES *and* FRANCISCUS.)

MOSES: That's the last time, the last time! I ain't standing for this shit no more!

FRANCISCUS: Calm down, Moses, calm down—

MOSES: Don't tell me to calm down! I'm sick of this! I'm a soldier of the United States Army, and, dammit, I aim to be treated like one.

GWEELY: What happened?

FRANCISCUS: White civilian flashed a blank piece of paper at him, and walked right on in camp.

GWEELY: (*Shrugs.*) They done flashed all kinda fake stuff at me, one time or 'nother—baseball passes, tickets—

MOSES: Then he stood there grinning at me, like I was some kinda dummy or something!

FRANCISCUS: Zuelke say we're not supposed to worry about checking their ID anymore, so I just ignore 'em—

MOSES: I ain't ignoring nothing no more! The next one pull a trick like that on me is gonna get a bullet!

BUGALOOSA: Fool around and get yourself court-martialed.

FRANCISCUS: Look who's talking. You tried to make a white National Guardsman salute you last night.

BUGALOOSA: (*Jumps up.*) Tried! Hell, I made him salute! (*Salutes.*) Next thing I knew I was hauled off to the city jail. Soldier ain't supposed to go to the city jail, the MPs supposed to handle us.

FRANCISCUS: Yeah well, I *was* "handling" it, but you kept running off at the mouth, so I *let* them take you down.

MOSES: (*Pacing.*) Then they bring us back to camp in those damn paddy wagons. The MPs supposed to bring us back! (*Disgustedly.*) But the MPs ain't worth their weight in cat mess in this town.

GWEELY: Hey, be quiet Moses—

FRANCISCUS: Let him talk! Let the nigger talk. That's all he's good for anyway is running off at the mouth!

MOSES: (*Charging.*) I'll show you what I'm good for!

FRANCISCUS: Come on then, come on—!

(GWEELY *and* BUGALOOSA *struggle to keep the two men apart.* FRANCISCUS *breaks away, paces.*)

FRANCISCUS: (*Pacing.*) Look, we do the best we can out there with no weapons and no respect! Damned if we do, damned if we don't!

(*Pause. All of the men look at each other, then down at the floor.*)

FRANCISCUS: (*Continued.*) I can't even pack a weapon to handle military business, but Zuelke and McKinney just got through bawling me out because I didn't stop some colored civilian from jumping a white man! And I'm supposed to do that with my bare hands! Then I got to come back to barracks and hear you niggers run off at the mouth! Damned if I do, damned if I don't!

(FRANCISCUS *looks around for something to kick, slams his foot into* BUGA-LOOSA's *locker. Bugaloosa hurries to it, praying that none of his whiskey bottles are broken.*)

MOSES: (*Grudging apology.*) Yeah . . . yeah, I know . . . it's just this town, man . . . it's just this hot, Southern town. . . . (*Accusingly.*) Gweely, I thought you said this town was ok.

GWEELY: (*Rolling a cigarette.*) It is ok. Plenty of colored here.

MOSES: Yeah, but they all act like slaves. (*Beat.*) I saw this old colored man downtown today. He was standing in the middle of the street, with tears running down his face, getting cussed out by some young white gal. She was talking to him like he had a tail, 'cause he'd dropped some packages he was carrying for her.

GWEELY: Well Mavis say since we hit town, the colored done started speakin' up some for theyselves.

MOSES: They need to do something.

GWEELY: Well, I hope I ain't here next weekend. Put in for a three-day pass to my home. Hey Mose, why don't you grab Selena, since she *still* in town, and come go with me and Mavis?

MOSES: Naw. I got my fill of Texas.

GWEELY: I ain't gon' be up there long, just wanna see my baby sister, and walk 'round the old homestead. Ain't nobody livin' up to the old place no mo'. Used to be eight of us chil'ren—two boys and six girls, but they done all died off with that TB. Then Baby Sister moved into town after Mama . . . Mama gave me this here watch 'fore she died, said it would brang me good luck.

FRANCISCUS: This place is worse than Stamps, Arkansas. I used to visit my grandparents there every summer, and I thought that place was bad. A colored man couldn't walk the road there. He see a white man coming, he'd have to step in the ditch. But Houston—it's worse.

BUGALOOSA: Bogalusa, Louisiana, man. You don't never want to go there. They lynch a colored man as soon as look at him. (*Rubs the ugly scar on his neck.*) I guess I'll die with this scar.

(*HARDIN crosses over to BUGALOOSA.*)

HARDIN: (*Fascinated.*) How did you get that?

BUGALOOSA: Lynchin'.

HARDIN: But—but you're still alive.

BUGALOOSA: Somethin' distracted 'em and Grandmere and my brother came and cut me down, revived me.

HARDIN: (*Accusingly.*) Why did they lynch you? What did you do?

BUGALOOSA: (*Sarcastically.*) What else . . . raped a white woman.

HARDIN: (*Repulsed.*) You did that?

BUGALOOSA: That's what they *say* I did. (*Beat.*) I used to play at this café, white feller owned it. And he had this little yellow-haired gal, who loved the way I made—music. (*Plays a riff on his cornet.*) Well, the owner and her brothers got it into their heads it was somethin' going on between us, and got up a lynch mob.

GWEELY: Why sho' boy, don't you know? Us colored mens jest can't keep our hands off them "pretty" white women. They all jest so "pretty," don'tcha know? Why, it jest ain't no such thang as a ugly white woman, naw suh, you jest can't find one. (*Beat.*) One thang I hope I live to see, is a pretty monkey and a ugly white woman.

(*They laugh.*)

BUGALOOSA: (*Rubbing the scar.*) Sometimes . . . I can still feel that rope around my neck . . . (*Speaks in Creole, as he loses control.*) Gro ché fee pátan . . . gro ché fee pátan . . . (*Etc.*)

GWEELY: (*Hand on his shoulder.*) Come on, soldier, get a grip, that's all behind you now . . .

BUGALOOSA: (*Trying to laugh it off . . .*) Yeah, yeah . . . they thought I was dead. To this day they think I'm in my grave, but the blessed Virgin Mary was with me. . . . (*Kisses the cross.*) Grandmere hid me out until I got better, then I snuck outta town.

FRANCISCUS: Consider yourself one lucky soldier.

BUGALOOSA: Yeah, I used to be an altar boy, so the Blessed Mother Mary protected me. After that I hitched up in the army. I figured it would be better for a colored man in here than out there, but now I don't know . . . after this war . . . I think I'm gonna get out and put me a band together . . .

MOSES: (*Rolling a cigarette.*) Well, ain't none of these peckerwoods gonna run me off, I don't let no peckerwood push me around, I don't care who he is, I get 'em all straight. Remember that time I had to set that little white corporal straight about those cakes, Gweely?

GWEELY: Yeah, that was in 'Frisco, after the quake.

MOSES: Me and Gweely was helping out in the white mess, so this little corporal came up to me and told me that the mess sergeant wanted me to cut up two big cakes and put 'em out, so I said ok, and I cut 'em up and put 'em out. Well, those greedy white boys went at 'em like hotcakes. So when this little corporal comes back later to get him a piece, cake is all gone. So he comes up to me and he says, (*Imitates Southern drawl when speaking as the Corporal.*) "Didn't I tell you Sergeant Driscoll said for you to cut up those cakes and put 'em out?" I said, "Yeah I already did that." He said, "You sure?" I said, "Yeah, I'm sure." Then he looked around and asked me again. "You *sure* you put those cakes out?" I said, "Yeah, I did." Then I could see he was getting ready to ask me that same question all over again, so I said, "Look! Don't ask me that no more! I already told you I put those cakes out. What you think, I ate 'em both up!"

GWEELY: (*Laughing.*) That boy turned beet red.

MOSES: He said I was insubordinate to him. I said he was insubordinate to me; I was a corporal just like he was—at the time. I said I may be colored, but I'm a man just like you. He looked at me, shook his head and walked off. After that, whenever he'd see me, he'd point and tell whoever he was with, "See that nigger there—he's crazy." But that's all right though, he didn't never ask me the same question twice no more.

(*The men laugh, regaining their confidence.*)

THE MEN: That's all right, Mose, tell it, you sure told him (*etc.*).

GWEELY: Yeah, we laffed 'bout that for time to come.

HARDIN: (*Smugly, after the laughter subsides.*) Well, so far, *I'm* not having any trouble with anybody. *I* just follow the rules. I think we have to prove to them that we're *intelligent* enough to follow the rules.

FRANCISCUS: And everything will be just fine and dandy huh?

HARDIN: Well—yes. I mean, I think if we just stop concentrating on the bad things and look for what's workable between the races, things will go smoother.

MOSES: For who?

HARDIN: Why for all concerned.

BUGALOOSA: Y'all hear that? This here boy ain't run up against the wall yet.

GWEELY: He live long enough, he will.

HARDIN: What wall?

BUGALOOSA: Y'all hear that? (*Mimics.*) "What wall?" (*In HARDIN's chest, forcing him to back up with each sentence.*) The white wall, boy. Ain't you ever seen it? It stretches all across this country. Colored man can't get over it, can't get around it, can't get under it. All he can do is butt his head up against it, 'til he bust his brains out.

GWEELY: (*Shining his boots.*) See—you been up there in Minnisota with all that white snow and all them white folks, and they treated you good, 'cause it was jest a few of ya—

MOSES: Like a little pet.

GWEELY: So you think everythang's jest hunky-dory. But that ain't the natural way of white toward colored. Every colored man come to learn that when he run slam up against that wall.

FRANCISCUS: He don't understand what you talking about.

HARDIN: (*Peeved.*) I understand what you're saying. You're talking about the wall of prejudice and ignorance that *some* white people put up toward the colored race. But not all white people are like that. I know, because I know some good white people, who are just as human as we are.

MOSES: Don't fool yourself boy. Every white man you meet, aim to keep his foot on your neck.

HARDIN: (*Exasperated.*) If you fellows don't have any hope for our country's future, what are you doing in the army?

FRANCISCUS: Hey boy, we're not talking about hope, and we're not talking about the future. We're talking about how things are right here and now. You need to face *that* before you can do anything about the future.

GWEELY: Yeah, get your head outta that snow.

HARDIN: So, what you're all saying is that the only way for the colored man to progress is to hate the white man?

MOSES: We're saying you better believe they hate you.

HARDIN: (*Stubbornly.*) Not all of them.

MOSES: The ones who don't hate you, don't count.

HARDIN: I think you have it backwards.

(*Fed up,* FRANCISCUS *strides over to* HARDIN.)

FRANCISCUS: All right boy, don't be arguing with us. You supposed to be so smart, why don't you learn when to shut up!

HARDIN: Why don't you make me shut up!

(FRANCISCUS *starts toward* HARDIN. BUGALOOSA *and* MOSES *intervene.* GWEELY *grabs* HARDIN. FRANCISCUS *fakes returning peacefully to his cot, then manages to tap* HARDIN *upside the head, and returns to his cot.*)

HARDIN: (*Struggling, but not too hard.*) Let me go, let me at him . . .! (*Etc.*)

GWEELY: Come on boy, come on now (*Etc.*) (*Getting pencil and paper.*) Now listen—calm down now boy, calm down—now listen, I been tryin' to call my woman all day, but she ain't been in. . . .

MOSES: (*Under breath.*) Probably with that red O'Reilly.

GWEELY: (*Sharply.*) What's that?

MOSES: Nothing.

GWEELY: (*A beat. Then back to* HARDIN.) I go on duty in a few minutes, and when I leave I want you to go 'round to Miss Stephanucci's and try to get a hold of Mavis agin.

(GWEELY *turns* HARDIN *around so that he can use* HARDIN'S *back as a desk to write down Mavis' phone number.*)

GWEELY: (*Continued.*) This is Mavis telephone number. I want you to call her and tell her don't she go nowhere tonight, 'cause I'm comin' 'round there after I get off duty. (*Puts paper in* HARDIN'S *hand.*) Got that?

HARDIN: I got it.

(HARDIN *returns to his cot, giving* FRANCISCUS *a wide berth.*)

BUGALOOSA: Hey, want me to go 'round to the house and tell her something?

GWEELY: I don't want you to do nothin', but keep your Franch eyeballs off my woman.

BUGALOOSA: (*Innocently.*) Aw man, you can trust me, yeah.

(GWEELY *gathers his things, preparing to go on duty.*)

GWEELY: I don't trust you no further than I can run my hand up a wet paper bag. I know 'bout you Louisiana men, you be done put some kinda hex on her.

BUGALOOSA: Not me. I ain't gonna mess with that woman, no. I ain't crazy like you, no, I ain't gonna have that white police after me.

FRANCISCUS: They say he already killed one colored man over that woman.

GWEELY: That peckerwood don't scare me none. Anyway, she gon' cut him loose jest as soon as she pick the right time to break the news.

MOSES: (*Winking at the others.*) Oh, I see, he ain't got the "news" yet. No wonder he's always dropping in the dance hall, hugging and squeezing on your woman.

GWEELY: That's all gon' come to a halt right soon.

MOSES: Man, you ought to leave that woman alone. They say she's been hooked up with that white boy for six years and ain't about to give him up for no nigger.

GWEELY: (*Unperturbed.*) That was in the past, 'fore she met up with Gweely Brown. And we done talked about why she took up with that white boy in the first place. It wasn't for love or nothin' like that, naw it was jest so's she'd have some help feedin' her chil'ren.

BUGALOOSA: Yeah well, that youngest one of hers got red hair.

MOSES: Man, you better be careful. That kinda gal'll get your neck stretched.

GWEELY: (*Getting angry.*) It's my neck.

MOSES: All right, all right.

BUGALOOSA: But seriously, Gweely, he's just sayin' you need to watch your back, that's all.

GWEELY: (*Pointedly.*) I'm always watching my back. 'Specially when I starts to git all this "brotherly" concern.

(*GWEELY eyes all of them with contempt, then goes to the stacked rifles, gets his. Humming "Amazing Grace," he breaks down the rifle. Awkward silence.*)

FRANCISCUS: Hey—uh—fellows, Priscilla told me to tell you she sure appreciated us singing at the church last night.

BUGALOOSA: Yeah, we killed 'em, didn't we? The ladies were shoutin' and wavin' their handkerchiefs at us—"Sing it, soldier boy, sing it. . . ."

(*The quartet consisting of the singers in the cast who can sing, harmonize on "It's Me Oh Lord." Still upset, GWEELY ignores them.*)

BUGALOOSA: (*Continued.*) (*Getting a bottle.*) Yeah, everything was all right, until them temperance people got to talkin'. Look like the more they talked about the evils of liquor, the thirstier I got. (*Takes a drink.*) But her papa's got a nice big church, though.

MOSES: Yeah, he ought to take in a big haul.

FRANCISCUS: (*Nervously.*) He does, he does. Uh—we—I mean, me—I mean, well—Priscilla and I, well, we're thinking about hitching up before I ship out.

MOSES: What? Married? See that Gweely, it's just like you said, we gotta watch these quiet ones. (*GWEELY won't be drawn in.*)

FRANCISCUS: And guess what? Her old man says that after I get out of the army, if we settle here in Houston, he'll build us our own house, just like the one they have on Heiner Street. (*His chest swells with pride.*)

MOSES: And I guess when the babies start coming, he'll give you the keys to the kingdom huh?

FRANCISCUS: (*Smugly.*) Well, I will be his son-in-law.

BUGALOOSA: Just what you always dreamed of being—a rich man's son-in-law.

FRANCISCUS: (*Defensively.*) Now look, her pa's money didn't have a thing to do with it—I don't care who's money it is—(*Catches himself.*) I mean, I'd marry her, even if she didn't have a cent—

MOSES: That's what you *say*, but I never knew you to spend much time with a woman who didn't have a little something.

FRANCISCUS: So, what's wrong with a man trying to pull up?

GWEELY: Yeah, what's wrong with that, Mr. Know-it-All?

MOSES: (*Going toward FRANCISCUS.*) Ain't nobody said nothing. . . .

FRANCISCUS: (*Turning away from MOSES.*) I'll treat her right. . . .

MOSES: (*Following FRANCISCUS.*) I ain't said nothing. . . .

FRANCISCUS: (*To the others.*) I'll be better to her than a lot of other fellows in this town. . . .

MOSES: (*With outstretched arms.*) What did I say?

FRANCISCUS: She could go farther and do a whole lot worse. . . .

MOSES: (*Going around in circle.*) He's just going on and on and I ain't said nothing. (*Plops down on his cot.*)

HARDIN: Congratulations, Mr. Franciscus.

FRANCISCUS: (*Gratefully.*) Thanks, Hardin.

BUGALOOSA: Hey, let me shake your hand too. I wish you luck, man. Shoots, wish I could meet me a gal with some money. Seem like all I meet is the whiskey heads.

GWEELY: Yeah, good luck, Franciscus. Who knows, I jest might come back here and marry up with Mavis. And ain't no man gon' have nothin' to say about it, colored or white.

MOSES: Hell, I don't want the woman if that's what you think. But you're ignorant when it comes to a woman, man, ignorant, and I just don't want to see you get hurt over no humbug, that's all.

GWEELY: I told you I ain't worried about no O'Reilly. He ain't no more'n me. (*Hoisting rifle.*) 'Cause this here rifle makes me jest as much man as he is.

(GWEELY *snatches up his rain poncho, exits in a huff. Lights fade out on a stanza from "Buffalo Soldier": "When will they call you a man?"*)

INTERMISSION

ACT TWO

Scene 1

(AT RISE: *In the blackout, we hear the mournful sound of taps. The lights slowly fade up on "I" barracks. Off Stage or behind* SCRIM *we see* BUGALOOSA *playing "Taps." Inside the barracks,* FRANCISCUS *has dozed off on his bunk, reading a magazine.* SGT. MC KINNEY *is shaving with a knife, peering into a broken mirror by lantern light. As the last notes of "Taps" fade, a* HOOT OWL *calls out in the night. Suddenly,* SGT. MC KINNEY *lets out a blood curdling scream.*)

SGT. MC KINNEY: (*Frantically wiping at his face.*) Aw-w-w! Aw-w-w!

FRANCISCUS: (*Running to* SGT. MC KINNEY.) Sarge, what is it! What's the matter?

SGT. MC KINNEY: Blood! Blood! All over my face, blood!

FRANCISCUS: Blood?

SGT. MC KINNEY: All over my face, all over my face—!

FRANCISCUS: But—but there's no blood on your face, Sarge, no blood at all. Look.

SGT. MC KINNEY: (*Peering into the mirror.*) But . . . but . . . I . . . was trimmin' my moustache in the glass here . . . when . . . when all of a sudden-like my face . . . I seen blood streamin' down my face. . . like rain . . . blood . . .

(SGT. MC KINNEY *wipes at his face with a towel, then looks hard into the mirror.*)

FRANCISCUS: See, no blood. You must have fell asleep. You had a nightmare.

SGT. MC KINNEY: Naw, I was awake, wide awake . . . I . . . (*Pauses, collecting himself.*) . . . maybe . . . maybe you right . . . maybe I jest . . . fell off . . .

FRANCISCUS: Yeah, that's what happened. We've all been having bad dreams lately. Bugaloosa had one the other night.

SGT. MC KINNEY: Yeah. . . . when my pap died, 'fore I even so much as heard a word that he'd went down in El Caney, I seen his face in this here lookin' glass. (*Pause.*) I was trimmin' my moustache then too, when Pap's face kinda jest appeared-like, lookin' over my shoulder, then it jest kinda faded away. Right after that, we got word, he'd went down in battle. (*He takes a small photograph from his pocket.*) This here's a picture of him.

FRANCISCUS: (*Respectfully.*) Looks like a tough old soldier.

SGT. MC KINNEY: (*Proudly.*) He was. A real army man, Pap. He were born a slave, though. But he runned off from his marster when he was fifteen, and joined up with the Union troops. Reckon that's why soldierin's so strong in my blood. I were born to the army. Even my mammy, she was a soldier. (*Chuckles at FRANCISCUS's look.*) Well—she was a cook for the Union troops.

FRANCISCUS: Is that right?

SGT. MC KINNEY: Oh yeah. They both used to tell me stories 'bout the battles durin' the Civil War.

(*SGT. MC KINNEY takes the U.S. flag from the stand.*)

SGT. MC KINNEY: (*Continued.*) They said the slave soldiers fought right 'longside the Union troops, and they held Old Glory high! (*Waving the flag above his head.*) They never let her touch the ground, never let her touch the ground! (*Fiercely.*) And we ain't gon' let her touch the ground neither, Franciscus! We gon' show 'em! This town ain't gon' make us forget our duty!

FRANCISCUS: Yes sir. Sarge? How long you been in the army?

SGT. MC KINNEY: Twenty-two years.

FRANCISCUS: That's a long time. Bet you seen a lot.

SGT. MC KINNEY: Seen all that's to be seen. You young fellers always gripin' 'bout how hard you got it. But colored soldier done come a long way. When I was trainin' in Newport News, Virginny, we slept out in the open, rain or shine, wasn't supplied with no eatin' utensils or nothin', had to eat with our hands, and we had to work, sick or well. Remember back in ninety-eight, a bunch of us from the 24th volunteered to care for the white soldiers in the yellow fever camps in Siboney, Cuba. We was forty days and forty nights nursin' them dyin' white boys. They said us colored boys had some kinda im-im-munity to the fever. (*Pause.*) But a lot of us colored boys died helpin' out. (*Beat.*) I almost died. Yep. I done seen all it is to be seen.

FRANCISCUS: Yeah, I guess you have . . . guess you have. You really think the colored troops gonna see any action?

SGT. MC KINNEY: We better. I ain't been a soldier all these years for a war to come, and I don't fight in it.

FRANCISCUS: *Crisis Magazine* says that they're not going to send us regulars overseas, because we might come back with fancy notions of equality. Du Bois says they're just planning to send the draftees overseas, because they'll be easier to handle and—

SGT. MC KINNEY: (*Disdainfully.*) Aw, that Du Boys feller don't know nothin' 'bout the military. He jest sit and spin them tall tales to sell that magazine of his, and you fool enough to buy 'em. Us reg'lars *is* goin' to France and we gon' fight for their freedom and ours too. Jest like President Wilson say, we gon' spread damocracy all over this world, even to the South. . . . That's what's gon' happen 'cause colored ain't gon' sit still for nothin' else to happen. Our chance done come.

FRANCISCUS: That's the same thing Du Bois is saying. He says there's a colored renaissance, a change coming for colored folks all over this country. And after the war when we come back heroes, the sky's gonna be the limit—!

(*GWEELY and MOSES rush in, out of breath. They spot SGT. MC KINNEY and stop in their tracks.*)

MOSES: Wait a minute, now Sarge—

GWEELY: Yeah, we gotta explain—

MOSES: Gotta tell ya—

GWEELY: What happened—

SGT. MC KINNEY: Y'all thirty-five minutes pass curfew.

GWEELY: Yeah, but it wasn't our fault, we had to walk all the way from town—

MOSES: That conductor, the one I had the run-in with—

GWEELY: Zipped right past us—

MOSES: With plenty of empty seats—

SGT. MC KINNEY: Franciscus?

FRANCISCUS: Yes sir?

SGT. MC KINNEY: Get my book there. Mark down Gweely Brown and Joe Moses out pass curfew.

FRANCISCUS: (*As he gets the book.*) I know the conductor they're talking about, though, Sarge. He's always passing up soldiers, especially at curfew.

GWEELY/MOSES: Tell him, uh-huh, that's right . . . (*Etc.*)

SGT. MC KINNEY: Hell, you can't get a ride back, don't go into town. You two was late last night. I let it pass. Give y'all a inch, you takes a mile. Mark 'em down. KP duty all next week.

(*SGT. MC KINNEY goes back to his bunk.* FRANCISCUS *writes in the book.*)

GWEELY: (*Pacing.*) It ain't right, it ain't right . . .

MOSES: That conductor needs him some chastising. And I'm just the one to do it. Next time I see him . . . (*Pounding his fist into his palm.*) I'm gonna beat him 'til his heart gets *right*!

(*Blackout.*)

Scene 2

(SETTING: CAPTAIN ZUELKE's *office.*)

(AT RISE: *Mid-morning. One week later.* SGT. MC KINNEY *sits in a chair, hat on his knees, pleading with* CAPT. ZUELKE. *A stone-faced* CAPT. ZUELKE *sits at his cluttered desk, rolling a cigarette.*)

SGT. MC KINNEY: It's this town, Cap'n. It's got the mens actin' like this. You know Franciscus ain't never been in no kinda trouble befo'.

CAPT. ZUELKE: And that Hardin boy too. They're corrupting him already—taken to the city jail for gambling. I bet that drunk Honoré was behind that.

SGT. MC KINNEY: Well Cap'n, I don't think—

CAPT. ZUELKE: No excuses. These men are soldiers, Franciscus an MP at that. He ought to be able to take a little pressure.

SGT. MC KINNEY: That's jest it. These men been soldiers too long to take this mistreatin' without a fight.

CAPT. ZUELKE: Sounds like you can't handle your men no more, McKinney.

SGT. MC KINNEY: I kin handle the men, suh, but I can't handle this town and them police, I can't—

CAPT. ZUELKE: If the men would try to follow the rules of this city with a little better spirit, I'm sure the town would meet 'em halfway. (*Looking through papers.*) So, Colonel Gentry's give out some more rules to try and keep some order in this place.

SGT. MC KINNEY: And that's another thang, Cap'n. Look like all these here rules jest make thangs worser. Like sendin' the mens back to camp in them paddy wagons after they spends a night in jail—it's bad for morale. The mens feel like they criminals—

CAPT. ZUELKE: Swinging on a civil police officer *is* a criminal act. Franciscus brought it on himself.

SGT. MC KINNEY: Yessuh, but it make the mens feel like the army's sidin' with the civil police.

CAPT. ZUELKE: Well, you know that ain't the truth.

SGT. MC KINNEY: Yessuh, I know that, but the mens, they—

CAPT. ZUELKE: (*Exasperated.*) So what the hell you want me to do, McKinney?

SGT. MC KINNEY: (*Desperate to get his point across he stands, leans into the desk.*) Well, Cap'n Zuelke, I been hearin' "talk" amongst the men, y'know grousin' and grumblin'. (*Desperate whisper.*) I know 'em, know what they can take, and I don't thank they can take much more of this without—I don't thank the mens ought to be let go into town no mo', no suh, and I don't thank the colored civilians ought to visit no mo'. 'Cause see, they got a hand in alla this too, y'know, they eggs the soldiers on, makes 'em do stuff they wouldn't ordinary do.

CAPT. ZUELKE: I don't hear none of the other non-coms whinin' about closing up camp.

SGT. MC KINNEY: Well that's jest how I feels about it, Cap'n, that's all. (*Sits back down.*)

CAPT. ZUELKE: (*Scratching his head.*) Hell man, I'm the one who suggested the colonel open up camp. I'm supposed to be the "expert" on you colored boys and now you want me to go tell him I made a mistake, that we officers can't handle the men?

SGT. MC KINNEY: It ain't you officers suh, it's the mens. (CAPT. ZUELKE *listens with pursed lips and steepled fingers.*) That's right, the mens can't handle theyselves out there. All this—this—freedom done gone to they heads.

CAPT. ZUELKE: (*Thoughtfully.*) Hum . . . I don't know . . . maybe you're right . . . (*Making a little joke.*) Give a nigger a inch, he'll take a mile.

SGT. MC KINNEY: Yeah. You sho' know how they is. (*Beat.*) And now this thang with Franciscus is got 'em all riled up. They figure the police ought to be done released Franciscus by now. They figure maybe somethin's done happened to him, they figure—

CAPT. ZUELKE: (*Absently searching desk.*) Franciscus is all right, nothing's happened to him.

SGT. MC KINNEY: Yessuh.

CAPT. ZUELKE: I want you to go in there and let the men know that.

SGT. MC KINNEY: Yessuh.

CAPT. ZUELKE: He'll be released when they get through processing him.

SGT. MC KINNEY: Yessuh.

CAPT. ZUELKE: Ah, here it is. This is the weekend pass Gweely wanted. (*He snatches it back, as* SGT. MC KINNEY *reaches for it.*) Ordinary I'd give it to him, just like that. But I got a good mind to deny it this time.

SGT. MC KINNEY: How come?

CAPT. ZUELKE: Don't like his attitude lately. Ain't you noticed? He used to be a pretty fair soldier. Now he's gettin' as bad as that dadblasted Moses. (*Pockets the pass.*) I want you to talk to him.

SGT. MC KINNEY: Yessuh.

CAPT. ZUELKE: And uh—I'll think on goin' to the colonel with what you said. Maybe it wouldn't hurt to close up camp for the remainder of the time.

SGT. MC KINNEY: I hopes you get on it real quick, Cap'n, 'cause I don't want these mens to do somethin' crazy and miss out on France where the real fight is. 'Cause they good men, they don't want no trouble over here, they wants to fight them heathens overseas, they wants to—

CAPT. ZUELKE: (*Conversation at an end, he stands up, stretching.*) So do we all, McKinney, so do we all. (*Beat. Carefully, watching for* SGT. MC KINNEY'S *reaction.*) But guardin' this campsite is every bit as important as being on the front lines in France. Or guardin' the borders, stateside. Everybody won't be going to France, y'know.

SGT. MC KINNEY: (*Unworried.*) I reckon they won't. But I know we goin', a good seasoned outfit like us, been waitin' for this all our lives, I know we goin'. (*Gets no response.*) Ain't we, Cap'n?

CAPT. ZUELKE: (*Walking away from* SGT. MC KINNEY'S *gaze.*) Border duty's just as important.

SGT. MC KINNEY: But we goin' to France, ain't we Cap'n Zuelke?

CAPT. ZUELKE: We'll go wherever the army sees fit to send us.

SGT. MC KINNEY: But the 24th? We goin' to France? Ain't we, Cap'n?

CAPT. ZUELKE: (*Without anger.*) Dammit McKinney, I got work to do, you do too. Oh yeah, that Hardin boy, I got transfer papers here for him.

SGT. MC KINNEY: (*Slowly rising from his chair.*) You tellin' me we ain't goin'. (CAPT. ZUELKE *takes his time putting out a cigarette.*)

CAPT. ZUELKE: (*Sighs regretfully.*) None of the four colored regiments are goin', McKinney. You're all stayin' stateside.

SGT. MC KINNEY: Stateside? How come?

CAPT. ZUELKE: A soldier don't ask why, he just do his duty.

SGT. MC KINNEY: So Franciscus was right. He said wasn't nobody but colored draftees goin', it ain't right, he said the army—

CAPT. ZUELKE: You tell Franciscus to keep his big mouth shut! He gonna question the brass? They know what they're doing. Why, you boys are the cream of the crop of your race. They want to keep you out of harm's way.

(SGT. MC KINNEY *stands like a stone statue.*)

CAPT. ZUELKE: (*Continued.*) (*Trying to win him over.*) Why, I hear they even got a colored officers training school somewhere in Iowa—can you believe that—and they're going to pull colored non-coms from the four regiments. A lot of you non-coms'll get promoted to officers . . . (*Chuckling.*) . . . can you believe that? I even hear Ol' Murphy's up, so who knows? I know you can't read or write, but depending on what I say about you, you might—

SGT. MC KINNEY: (*Sullenly.*) The war ain't in Iowa.

CAPT. ZUELKE: (*Getting angry.*) You arguing with your orders?

SGT. MC KINNEY: I ain't arguing with my orders. I jest don't know how the mens gon' take this, I jest—

CAPT. ZUELKE: (*In* SGT. MC KINNEY'S *face.*) You don't tell the men a thing, not a damn thing, until I give you official orders, is that understood!

SGT. MC KINNEY: Yessuh.

CAPT. ZUELKE: I had no business tellin' you yet. Don't know why I did, but well—I figure you kinda deserve to know, what with all the years you put in. . . . I just figured you ought to know.

SGT. MC KINNEY: Thank ya.

CAPT. ZUELKE: Aw hell, McKinney, I don't know why. It ain't no figurin' the brass, you know that. I thought you boys were going, I really did.

... (*Takes a folder from his drawer.*) But the War Department sent around this report on how the colored regiments are to be dealt with. (*He flips through it.*)

SGT. MC KINNEY: What that report say, Cap'n?

CAPT. ZUELKE: All it boils down to is—the 24th ain't going. (*Puts the report back.*)

SGT. MC KINNEY: Cap'n? Ain't it somethin' you can do about this?

(CAPT. ZUELKE *lights up another cigarette, shaking his head no.*)

SGT. MC KINNEY: (*Continued.*) I mean, these is good, seasoned men to go to waste—

CAPT. ZUELKE: (*Shrugging.*) I know it. Ain't a dadburn thing I can do about it. I'd rather be in the trenches with you boys. I know ya, know what you made out of, but these here white troops they're gonna give me—

SGT. MC KINNEY: White troops! You mean *you* goin'? You mean *you* got a command over *white* troops!

CAPT. ZUELKE: (*Chuckling, fit to bust.*) Damndest thing, ain't it? I finally got me a white command.

SGT. MC KINNEY: (*Devastated.*) But what about us?

CAPT. ZUELKE: I begged for you boys, you know I did.

SGT. MC KINNEY: Cap'n can't you go in there and talk to the colonel, again?

CAPT. ZUELKE: Ain't nothin' the colonel can do about this, these orders came straight from the top—

SGT. MC KINNEY: Tell him you got to fight with "I" Comp'ny, tell him we trained and ready, tell him we got a right to fight, we earned the right to fight—!

CAPT. ZUELKE: (*In SGT. MC KINNEY's face.*) You breathe a word of this to the colonel and I will break you down to the lowest tin can of a buck private. I will have you cleanin' latrines until the day you die! You understand that!

SGT. MC KINNEY: (*Snaps to attention.*) I understand it.

CAPT. ZUELKE: What you boys so all fired up to fight for, I don't know.

SGT. MC KINNEY: (*Eyes straight ahead.*) We jest wants a chance to die for this country, like any other soldier.

CAPT. ZUELKE: Nobody wants to die.

SGT. MC KINNEY: Naw suh, nobody want to die. We jest want to show we willin' to die for this country if we have to. We jest wants to do our part.

CAPT. ZUELKE: Well, you'll be doing your part—stateside. Now let's get outta here, I got a meeting to go to. (*Gets his hat, starts toward exit.*)

SGT. MC KINNEY: Cap'n?

CAPT. ZUELKE: What is it now, McKinney?

SGT. MC KINNEY: That bottle you keep? Reckon you could give me a little nip out of it?

CAPT. ZUELKE: (*Big grin of surprise.*) Why sure. Have at it. (*He takes it from his drawer, sets it on desk.*) Like I always say, nothin' wrong with a little nip now and again. Keeps a man from being so pent-up. Why, after a coupla minutes with that bottle, you'll be seeing things in a whole new light. Put the bottle back when you finish. (CAPT. ZUELKE *exits, shoulders thrown back, whistling a happy tune.* SGT. MC KINNEY *puts the bottle back, untouched. He takes out the report, puts it in his pocket and exits.*)

(*Lights fade.*)

Scene 3

(SETTING: *"I" Company barracks.*)

(AT RISE: *Later that same day. The men angrily pace the barracks. All are present, except* FRANCISCUS. *All are holding rifles, except* HARDIN, *who's holding his head in his hands.* SGT. MC KINNEY *is perched up on his bunk, surveying the chaos.*)

MOSES: We gotta do something—!

GWEELY: We ain't gon' sit still for this—!

BUGALOOSA: Them rednecks done tasted colored blood, and nothing'll stop 'em now—!

MOSES: They call us nigger when we walk down the street—

GWEELY: They throw us in jail at the drop of a hat—

MOSES: And now they've killed Franciscus! We gotta *do* something!

SGT. MC KINNEY: (*Jumps down from his bunk.*) Awright, keep yo' heads, calm down—!

BUGALOOSA: But they killed Franciscus—!

ALL: We ain't gon' stand for this. We gotta do somethin'. We gotta clean up this town . . .! (*Etc.*)

SGT. MC KINNEY: Calm down, I say! And put them rifles down!

GWEELY: But we gotta get out there and show 'em, we can't stay cooped up in here like cowards—!

MOSES: We ought to march down to that police station, and kill us some white policemen!

SGT. MC KINNEY: Ain't nobody marchin' nowhere. Nobody leavin' this camp tonight, unlessen I give the order. Now, the brass gon' handle this. If the police at fault, they gon' be punished.

GWEELY: Yeah, sho'.

BUGALOOSA: Sarge, you know Slim the shoe-shine boy? He say he was in Cap'n Zuelke's office, shining his boots and he heard Zuelke talkin' on the telephone to Chief Brock about a white mob comin' this way.

ALL: Yeah! What about that! (*Etc.*)

SGT. MC KINNEY: Shut up, alla ya! Squawkin' like a bunch of scared hens! That ain't nothin' but talk, ain't nobody crazy enough to march on a armed camp!

HARDIN: (*Speaking for the first time.*) Oh God! (*Hands over his face.*) I can't get the sight of Franciscus out of my mind! His head and face was covered with blood, just covered with it . . . !

SGT. MC KINNEY: (*Harshly.*) If you'da minded yo' own business, none of this woulda happened!

HARDIN: (*Almost crying.*) I know, I'm sorry, but I just couldn't stand by and watch that police officer beat up that colored woman.

SGT. MC KINNEY: She was a prostitute!

GWEELY: Don't matter what she was; she was colored, and they had no business puttin' they hands on her!

BUGALOOSA: All it was, Sarge, was a little crap game, yeah. Then outta the blue O'Reilly and his partner show up on their horses, aiming six-shooters at us. The civilians I was playin' with scattered—one went under this woman's house and I—well—I took off runnin' back to camp. Hardin, he jest stood there lookin' like a dummy, so they grabbed him . . .

HARDIN: (*Rapid fire delivery. Fighting to keep the tears and emotion out of his voice.*) I was going to go peacefully with them, Sgt. McKinney sir, but then O'Reilly started to hit this colored lady, Mrs. Travers, because she couldn't tell them where the other fellow had gone, and when I tried to help her, they started to hit me. At about this time Franciscus came along and inquired as to what was going on, and O'Reilly said: You want some of this too . . . (*Shudders at the word.*) . . . nigger! And he pulled his weapon and started firing at Franciscus. Well, Franciscus had to take off running down the street for his life . . . then O'Reilly and Daniels got on their horses and chased him down the street. I saw him in jail . . . after they'd beaten him and . . . and . . .

GWEELY: If Franciscus had been armed, none of this never woulda happened! These yeller crackers too scared to fight a colored man on equal terms!

SGT. MC KINNEY: A good man, kilt over a prostitute!

HARDIN: Sgt. McKinney, Mrs. Travers was not a prostitute. She was a decent, hardworking colored woman, but they treated her like a dog. She was in her house, ironing, but they dragged her out, barefooted and in her underclothes, and took her to jail. And when she asked if she could take her baby with her, they said no, and threw the baby on the grass.

MOSES: We're sick and tired of seeing our people done any kind of way in this town!

SGT. MC KINNEY: Civilians ain't none of our concern.

HARDIN: How can you say that? We're getting ready to put our lives on the line for the civilians of this country, colored and white and I think—

SGT. MC KINNEY: Don't be givin' me no speeches boy.

GWEELY: Hell, the war ain't over there; the war is over here! But we ain't gon' let 'em git away with killin' Franciscus; we ain't gon' let 'em git away with that!

SGT. MC KINNEY: Hardin, you sho' Franciscus was . . . ?

HARDIN: He was dead. I saw him. He wasn't moving, he wasn't breathing . . . he was just lying there. They beat him to death. (*Finally gives way to sobs.*)

SGT. MC KINNEY: (*Grabbing HARDIN's shoulder.*) Don't do that Hardin. Damn!

BUGALOOSA: (*Nervously trying to roll a cigarette.*) I just wish we was transferred outta here, that's all, just transferred outta here . . .

SGT. MC KINNEY: No need a-wishin' and a-hopin'. We gon' be right here 'til we gets orders to pull out. (*Pause.*) Ain't nothin' we kin do about Franciscus now. He's a soldier gone down.

(*Silence.*)

SGT. MC KINNEY: Hardin? You can read fancy writin', can't ya?

HARDIN: Yes sir, I can read.

SGT. MC KINNEY: (*Pulls report from pocket.*) Read this.

GWEELY: What's that Sarge?

SGT. MC KINNEY: Somethin' I got offa Zuelke's desk.

HARDIN: (*Reading.*) "The Disposal of the Colored Drafted Men."

BUGALOOSA: Disposal?

SGT. MC KINNEY: Shut up. (*Waves HARDIN on.*)

HARDIN: (*Reading.*) "At the present contemplated rate of calling the draft, we can count on approximately two hundred seventy thousand colored men being drafted. It is the policy to select colored men of the best physical stamina, highest education and mental development for combatant troops, and there is every reason to believe that these specially selected men, the cream of the colored draft, will be fully equal to the requirements and make first-class combatant troops. (*Murmurs of approval from the men.*) But—the mass of colored drafted men, the illiterate day-laborer class has not the mental stamina or moral sturdiness to put him in the line against opposing German troops . . . therefore it is recommended that these poorer-class backwoods Negros be organized into labor battalions. In this way, instead of laying around camp all day, they'll be kept out of trouble by doing useful work, plus the medical department can be working on them in the meanwhile, curing them of venereal diseases and putting them in shape. However—

SGT. MC KINNEY: That's a nuff.

GWEELY: Catchin' VD and doin' day labor?

BUGALOOSA: That's all they figure we good for.

MOSES: (*Holding up his rifle.*) I'll show 'em what I'm good for.

HARDIN: This report seems to be specifying newly inducted draftees.

SGT. MC KINNEY: That's how they feel about alla us.

BUGALOOSA: Yeah, they don't think us colored soldiers is worth nothin'.

MOSES: But we'll show 'em in France.

GWEELY: Like to git the peckerwood who wrote that in my line of fire, over yonder in France.

SGT. MC KINNEY: Well, you won't.

BUGALOOSA: Naw, you won't catch the brass in the trenches with the real men.

GWEELY: They'll be laid up with some German woman, while we po' "backwoods VD niggers" is takin' a snoutful of mustard gas.

MOSES: What's that report say about us regulars?

SGT. MC KINNEY: I can tell ya that. We ain't goin' to France.

THE MEN: (*Puzzled.*) What . . . ? Not going . . . ? What you mean not goin' . . . ? (*Etc.*)

SGT. MC KINNEY: Find it, Hardin, in that re-pote.

HARDIN: (*Flipping through the report.*) . . . it says here that "while the ten thousand regulars in the four colored regiments are the cream of the crop, well trained, and proven in service, it is in the interest of the United States' stability and security to keep these men stateside."

(*The stunned men are mute with betrayal.*)

HARDIN: (*Continued.*) (*Reading.*) "It is believed that the tractability of the colored draftee, under the leadership of white officers will be more suitable for the role the colored soldier will play in this war."

SGT. MC KINNEY: Ain't gon' be no fight in France for us.

MOSES: Not goin' to France . . . ?

BUGALOOSA: Why? What we do? Is it 'cause of the trouble here?

SGT. MC KINNEY: Naw, they wrote that out way 'fore we even come here. It's jest like Franciscus said, they ain't sendin' nobody but draftees. Hardin here, he might be goin'.

HARDIN: But I don't understand. Why aren't they sending you, you're the real soldiers, you're the regulars?

MOSES: (*Bitterly.*) They don't want us to prove ourselves. They're scared we'll go over there and come back heroes.

SGT. MC KINNEY: And they always wants to be the heroes, and us to be the cowards.

HARDIN: But that's not right.

SGT. MC KINNEY: Naw it ain't right, but that's the way it is. They always want to put the sorriest coloreds out front.

GWEELY: I don't believe this; I jest don't believe it. We the ones trained to fight; we the ones done give our blood and sweat for this outfit, and you tellin' me they gon' send a bunch of backwoods draftees in our place?

BUGALOOSA: Maybe that drunk Zuelke don't know what he talkin' about, maybe he—

SGT. MC KINNEY: He know what he talkin' 'bout, you jest heard the readin'.

BUGALOOSA: Well, let 'em keep their precious war, they all white anyway, let 'em kill each other.

SGT. MC KINNEY: Naw, they never meant for the colored soldier to fight in this here war. They don't want no colored fightin' men, all they want is colored clean-up mens—mend the roads, dig the graves, unload the supplies, cook the mess—Ten-hut!

(*All the men snap to attention as* CAPT. ZUELKE *enters with a short riding crop under his arm. He paces the ranks in disapproving silence.*)

CAPT. ZUELKE: I'm disappointed. Real disappointed in this company. I want you to know that. I went to bat for you boys with the colonel. I want you to know that. I told him he'd be doin' the whole camp a real favor if he let you mingle freely with your own kind. But it looks like the colored in this town is a bad influence on ya. So, since you boys can't seem to handle yourselves in town, from now on, for the duration of our stay, you will be confined to camp. No passes into town whatsoever. No visitors allowed in camp. Period.

GWEELY: What about my pass home suh?

CAPT. ZUELKE: (*Struts over to* GWEELY, *gets in his face.*) De-nied.

SGT. MC KINNEY: What about Franciscus?

CAPT. ZUELKE: (*Whirls around to* SGT. MC KINNEY.) What about Franciscus?

SGT. MC KINNEY: Hardin here says he seen the police beat him to death down the jailhouse.

CAPT. ZUELKE: (*Struts over to* HARDIN.) So, you're the one spreadin' them doggone rumors?

HARDIN: Well sir I—

CAPT. ZUELKE: (*Slams him on the arm with the riding crop.*) I didn't tell you to speak boy! (*He circles* HARDIN.) You saw Franciscus get roughed up a little bit, you overreacted. It's been a lot of that in this outfit lately, overreactin', and I've had just about enough of it. I ain't heard no report of no soldier being dead in this company. And believe me, I'd be the one to know about it and not Hardin here. I'm sure Franciscus will be back in camp in a short while, and I don't wanna hear no more of them dadburn rumors. Is that understood!

THE MEN: Yes sir!

CAPT. ZUELKE: (*Curtly to* SGT. MC KINNEY.) Step outside, I wanna speak to you a minute.

SGT. MC KINNEY: (*To the men as he exits.*) As you were.

(CAPT. ZUELKE *and* SGT. MC KINNEY *step Downstage out of the men's hearing. The lights dim on the men in barracks, as they huddle, grumbling. Spotlight on* CAPT. ZUELKE *and* SGT. MC KINNEY, *side by side, at parade rest, eyes straight ahead, speaking in rapid fire fashion.*)

CAPT. ZUELKE: Colonel wants all the rifles and ammo taken up tonight, locked in the equipment tent.

SGT. MC KINNEY: Take up the rifles? But why?

CAPT. ZUELKE: (*Testily.*) Just as a precaution. And don't mention this to the men until we get ready to take 'em up at roll call.

SGT. MC KINNEY: Expectin' trouble outta the mens tonight, Cap'n?

CAPT. ZUELKE: This ain't no disciplinary action against the men. (*Proudly.*) Some of us officers will be away from camp tonight at a symphony. We just want to make sure every weapon is accounted for, that's all. (*Beat.*) There's talk of a group of whites comin' this way tonight, and we're gonna take up the weapons, so's we don't come back to camp and find all hell's broke loose.

SGT. MC KINNEY: But I ain't understandin'. If we takes up the weapons, what the mens 'spose to do if a mob *do* come?

CAPT. ZUELKE: Who said anything about a mob? I'm talkin' about maybe a few young boys sowin' their wild oats.

SGT. MC KINNEY: What if they come "sowin' their wild oats" with weapons and my mens ain't got nothin'?

CAPT. ZUELKE: (*Catching the sarcasm.*) Look McKinney, we're just tryin' to nip this shit in the bud. We officers'll have our weapons, we'll keep the peace.

SGT. MC KINNEY: (*Under his breath.*) Jest said y'all won't be in camp . . . be out on the town . . .

CAPT. ZUELKE: How's that?

SGT. MC KINNEY: I say yessuh, I'll see the weapons git took up.

CAPT. ZUELKE: No. We officers have to see to that personal. I'll be back at 0600 for roll call and I want every weapon accounted for, every man in camp and answering for himself. And I ain't just talkin' a voice check either. I got to see the whites of their eyes.

SGT. MCKINEY: Yessuh.

(*CAPT. ZUELKE salutes, turns and exits. SGT. MC KINNEY follows suit. As the lights go up on the men in the barracks, they erupt into loud talk.*)

MOSES: You believe that lie about Franciscus?

GWEELY: Hell naw, that damn O'Reilly killed him.

BUGALOOSA: Yeah, Zuelke's just trying to throw us off. If Franciscus is all right, why ain't he back in barracks?

MOSES: 'Cause he's dead, that's why!

HARDIN: Maybe—maybe I was wrong. I mean, I don't think Captain Zuelke would lie, do you?

(*They groan at his naiveté.*)

ALL: Man . . . !

HARDIN: (*Hopefully.*) But—but maybe, somehow, Franciscus is alive, maybe—

GWEELY: (*In HARDIN's face.*) You know what you seen, don'tcha boy?

HARDIN: Well . . . I thought . . .

GWEELY: You thought! Don't you know what you seen!

HARDIN: Well, I—I—I—

GWEELY: Don'tcha!

HARDIN: Yes . . . yes! I know what I saw! I saw Franciscus—dead!

MOSES: (*Grabbing his rifle.*) That's enough for me.

GWEELY: (*Holding up rifle.*) Me too.

MOSES: Franciscus is dead and this town is gonna pay!

BUGALOOSA: I knew this place wasn't gonna be no good, ain't nowhere in the South no good. I just wish we was outta here, that's all, just outta here—!

MOSES: Well, we ain't, we're right here! And I'm ready for a fight. They ain't going to let us go overseas, right? Well ok, we might as well have our war right here.

GWEELY: I'm spoilin' to chastise me a white boy anyway. And the first one I'm gon' look for is O'Reilly.

BUGALOOSA: Yeah man, after what he did to you—made you get up from the table with your own woman.

GWEELY: If I'da had me a pistol I'da kilt that redneck right dead on the spot.

HARDIN: (*Obvious disappointment.*) Yeah Gweely, why *did* you get up from the table like that? Why didn't you just stand up to him and—?

(*Hurt by* HARDIN's *lack of understanding,* GWEELY *covers it with anger.*)

GWEELY: (*Grabs him by the collar.*) Boy, I ain't had nothin' on me but a pocket knife. He had a six-shooter on his hip—what was I supposed to do . . . ?

(*For a beat,* HARDIN *and* GWEELY *stare at each other, reliving the incident in their minds.* GWEELY *turns away.*)

GWEELY: (*Continued.*) . . . get my head blew off over some nappy-headed gal! (*Walking over to* MOSES.) You were right about that Mavis, man. Did you see how she jest laffed and grinned all up in that peckerwood's face? Jest like I didn't even much exist . . .

MOSES: What else you expect the woman to do, Gweely? He could've went upside her head with that six-shooter.

GWEELY: Yeah . . . maybe . . . but still, I don't know, seem like she coulda . . . I jest don't know about that gal no mo'. . .

HARDIN: Franciscus!

(FRANCISCUS *enters the barracks, very badly beaten, his pride as deeply wounded as his body. He's in a silent rage as the men eagerly gather around him, overlapping in their comments.*)

HARDIN: Franciscus! I thought you were dead!

(*The men put a stool under* FRANCISCUS.)

BUGALOOSA: Man, are we glad to see you! This here boy had us thinking you was dead—

HARDIN: Well, he looked dead—!

GWEELY: I thought I was seein' a ghost—!

MOSES: For once it's good to see your ugly face—!

GWEELY: You all right, soldier?

FRANCISCUS: (*Clenched teeth.*) I don't want to talk about it! I'm through talking!

GWEELY: O'Reilly—he was in on it, wasn't he?

FRANCISCUS: The ringleader.

GWEELY: Don't worry, he gon' get his.

MOSES: Yeah, and that conductor too.

SGT. MC KINNEY: Ten-hut!

(SGT. MC KINNEY *enters with* CAPT. ZUELKE. *The men jump to attention, helping* FRANCISCUS *up.*)

CAPT. ZUELKE: Well. I see ya got Franciscus back with ya?

SGT. MC KINNEY: (*Surprised and glad to see* FRANCISCUS.) Yessuh, yessuh, and mighty glad to have him back.

CAPT. ZUELKE: Yeah well, that'll teach you to monitor your mouth, Hardin.

HARDIN: Yes sir.

CAPT. ZUELKE: (*Very put upon.*) And now, as if I don't have enough to deal with, the city police have sent a detective to camp. It seems a soldier swiped a shoe-shine kit from some store, and we've got to search all the barracks.

MOSES: A shoe-shine kit—!

SGT. MC KINNEY: Shut up. Don't worry, Cap'n, if it's in here, of which I don't believe it is, I'll find it. (*To the men.*) All right, turn yo' stuff out.

CAPT. ZUELKE: (*Looking at his watch.*) And make it snappy.

(*Grumbling under their breath, the men throw open their footlockers, shake out their duffle bags, etc.* SGT. MC KINNEY *goes down the line, with* CAPT. ZUELKE *behind him.* SGT. MC KINNEY *stops in front of* GWEELY *and looks at a beat-up shoe-shine kit.*)

GWEELY: You know I been had that kit ever since I been in the army.

SGT. MC KINNEY: (*Putting it back.*) Yeah, I know.

CAPT. ZUELKE: Here, let me see that.

SGT. MC KINNEY: Oh, he been had this old raggedy thang, Cap'n.

(*CAPT. ZUELKE knows it's not the kit, but wants to assert his authority.*)

CAPT. ZUELKE: I *said* let me look at it. (*SGT. MC KINNEY lets it drop into CAPT. ZUELKE's hand.*) No, this can't be it, McKinney. I told you the one we're lookin' for is spank brand new.

SGT. MC KINNEY: Probably find it in "M" Comp'ny. You know how them boys is.

CAPT. ZUELKE: (*Chuckling.*) Yeah, they'll steal the wet outta water, and the stink outta . . . hey, what's this? (*At BUGALOOSA's cot, holding up a new kit.*)

BUGALOOSA: Suh, I didn't steal nothin'. It's spank brand new, yeah, but I paid for that kit, I bought it at some store in town, I'll take you to the store.

MOSES: I was with him when he bought that kit.

BUGALOOSA: Tell him, Moses, I ain't stole nothin'.

CAPT. ZUELKE: Maybe, maybe not. But I got to collect all new shoe-shine kits, and you got to come with me. (*Starts to lead BUGALOOSA away.*)

BUGALOOSA: But—but I ain't done nothin'.

SGT. MC KINNEY: What they gon' do to him, Cap'n?

CAPT. ZUELKE: If he didn't steal it, nothing'll happen to him. All the men with new kits have to be taken down to city jail where the store owner can look 'em over. If he's innocent, he'll be let go.

MOSES: You'll be back in a minute, Boog.

BUGALOOSA: (*Hopeless.*) Yeah.

CAPT. ZUELKE: (*To BUGALOOSA.*) Wait here a minute. (*He walks over to GWEELY.*) Damn good minstrel show you gave the other day Gweely. I want you to do it for the men in camp tonight.

GWEELY: I can't do the show without Bugaloosa, suh. Me and him does the show together.

CAPT. ZUELKE: Well—get Moses.

GWEELY: Suh, Moses can't dance or sing.

CAPT. ZUELKE: (*Looking at MOSES.*) Sure he can. (*To GWEELY.*) Do the show.

GWEELY: Yessuh.

CAPT. ZUELKE: (*Aside to SGT. MC KINNEY.*) Figure the show is a good way to keep 'em occupied tonight, you know what I mean? See it gets organized.

SGT. MC KINNEY: I'll get right on it.

CAPT. ZUELKE: Come on, Bugaloosa.

(*CAPT. ZUELKE and BUGALOOSA EXIT.*)

SGT. MC KINNEY: (*To the men.*) I'll be right back. Brown, get that show together. (*He exits.*)

MOSES: (*Slams lid on his footlocker.*) A shoe-shine kit! A damn shoe-shine kit!

GWEELY: A minstrel show!

MOSES: Can you believe that!

GWEELY: It be a minstrel show tonight; Zuelke'll be the one to do it.

HARDIN: I've never stolen anything in my life! And if I ever would, it sure wouldn't be a damn shoe-shine kit! (*Slams the lid of his footlocker.*)

GWEELY: Tell it boy.

HARDIN: And Moses, you told him you were with Bugaloosa when he bought that kit, and he still took him down.

MOSES: Hell, I don't know where Bugaloosa got that kit from, and I don't care. But they still ain't got no right to come in here on us like we're a bunch of criminals.

FRANCISCUS: This place just gets worse and worse. The jail and the infirmary were full of coloreds who'd been beat half to death by the police.

HARDIN: I know, I saw them.

FRANCISCUS: I heard O'Reilly and the mounted police making plans to come out here and put us "uppity" niggers in our place.

GWEELY: We heard the talk.

FRANCISCUS: (*Stands up, sights his rifle into the audience.*) Well, let 'em come.

MOSES: (*Sights his rifle into audience.*) Yeah, we'll be ready for 'em.

GWEELY: (*Sights his rifle into audience.*) Let 'em come.

(*Fade out.*)

Scene 4

(AT RISE: *Company "I" barracks. A few hours later. We hear the distant sound of thunder and a light drizzle. MOSES is skulking in an area outside the barracks; GWEELY paces with his rifle; FRANCISCUS tends his wounds; BUGALOOSA is on his knees at his altar. MOSES takes a final look around, then ducks into the barracks with an ammunition box.*)

MOSES: Hey fellows, I got some more ammo.

(*The men crowd around as* MOSES *puts the box on the floor and opens it.* SGT. MC KINNEY *quietly enters at one of the tent entrances and watches the men, who are unaware of him.*)

MOSES: (*Continued.*) I figure we can make a coupla more trips to the supply tent before eight o'clock tonight.

(MOSES *is on his knees passing out the ammo to the men, who stash it in their duffle bags, gun belts, etc.*)

BUGALOOSA: (*Hiding ammo.*) We gotta be able to get enough of the men to stand with us, though. That's the thing. If just one or two of us go out after that mob, we gonna get our butts court-martialed.

GWEELY: Stop worryin', I talked wit' the boys in "M" and "J"; they say they wit' us. They can't court-martial alla us; worse they kin do is kick us all out.

MOSES: Hell, I been court-martialed before, did three months hard labor.

FRANCISCUS: If they heard the talk I heard down at the jailhouse, everybody'd be with us.

MOSES: Yeah, even the uncle toms.

FRANCISCUS: In the jitney on the way back to camp, the looie they sent to pick me up tried to get me to come back here and try to smooth things over, told me not to mention anything I'd heard or seen at the jailhouse. Told me to keep you fellows "calm."

GWEELY: (*Small laugh.*) What'd you tell him?

FRANCISCUS: I told him ok. Give me some more of that ammo.

SGT. MC KINNEY: That all you men gon' do . . . ?

(*The surprised men jump to attention.*)

SGT. MC KINNEY: . . . sit around and grumble . . . ? I say, that all y'all gon' do—talk? Huh?

MOSES: (*Unsure.*) Well Sarge, what you want us to do?

BUGALOOSA: We can't just wait here like sitting ducks.

GWEELY: Yeah, we figure if trouble comin', we ought to meet it head-on.

SGT. MC KINNEY: Head-on huh? Wit' yo' bare hands?

GWEELY: (*Holding up his rifle.*) Bare hands?

SGT. MC KINNEY: (*Calmly.*) They plannin' to take up the rifles at roll call.

THE MEN: (*Outraged.*) What—? Take up the rifles! They can't do that! (*Etc.*)

SGT. MC KINNEY: Gentry's orders.

BUGALOOSA: What they tryin' to do, get us killed?

SGT. MC KINNEY: Say he don't want no trouble in camp tonight.

BUGALOOSA: Trouble? This town causing all the trouble.

FRANCISCUS: But the army don't care about us, so long's no white folks get hurt.

MOSES: So what are we supposed to be—target practice?

SGT. MC KINNEY: We ain't gon' be target practice for nobody.

FRANCISCUS: So, what do we do when they come for the rifles?

SGT. MC KINNEY: (*Sizes up the men.*) Soldier don't give up his rifle.

GWEELY: So, whatcha sayin' Sarge?

MOSES: Sounds like he saying we go down first! Well, I'm for that!

SGT. MC KINNEY: Oh you is, is ya? You got a lotta mouth Moses. Alla y'all got a lotta mouth this evenin'. But what I heard y'all plannin' take more'n mouth. It take guts. It take bein' ready to put everythang on the line. 'Cause if you buck this town, ain't no turnin' back. (*He looks them in the eyes one by one.*)

MOSES: I don't want to turn back.

FRANCISCUS: All I know is, no white man's gonna put his hands on me again, that's all I know.

GWEELY: I'm ready to put my rifle where my mouth is.

BUGALOOSA: We don't want no trouble, Sarge, but don't look like we got no choice—we can't sit here, waitin' for that mob to take us. We ain't got no choice.

SGT. MC KINNEY: You right, we ain't got no choice. This here town done took everythang we come in here wit'—our respect, our chance for glory in France, and now the army want us to give up our weapons so's they kin come in here and slaughter us. Well, if this be the only battle they let us fight, it ain't gon' be no slaughter!

MOSES: Damn sho' ain't!

GWEELY: We ain't givin' up our rifles!

FRANCISCUS: We'll go down first!

BUGALOOSA: We'll die like fightin' men!

SGT. MC KINNEY: All right! Y'all sound like the reg'lars you was trained to be, and I stand wit' ya! Yo' bootlickin' superiors done deserted ya; they ain't gon' protect ya. But y'all my men, and I'll go down wit' ya. I'm gon' round up the rest of the comp'ny, weed out the cowards from the mens. And all who ain't wit' us, is agin us. Understand?

THE MEN: (*Gripping their rifles.*) We understand.

(*HARDIN runs in, out of breath, with a shirt full of loose ammunition.*)

HARDIN: Hey fellows, I got some more ammo. Sorry it took so long but—

(*Spots* SGT. MC KINNEY.) Oh! Sarge! (*He jumps to attention, dropping the ammunition to the floor.*)

SGT. MC KINNEY: At ease boy, and pick up that ammo.

(HARDIN *scrambles to pick it up, looking to* GWEELY *for an explanation.*)

SGT. MC KINNEY: (*Continued.*) I stood out there 'bout half a hour watchin' you git up the nerve to go in the supply tent.

HARDIN: (*Gulps.*) You did?

SGT. MC KINNEY: It was clear as water what you was up to.

HARDIN: It was?

SGT. MC KINNEY: A looie was comin' yo' way; I had to head him off with some cockamamie story.

HARDIN: You did?

GWEELY: Relax, Sarge is wit' us.

HARDIN: He is?

SGT. MC KINNEY: Stash that ammo, boy. Zuelke'll be in here in a minute. And when he come in, everybody jest go 'long with whatsoever I do.

MOSES: What about when he ask for the weapons?

SGT. MC KINNEY: I said jest go 'long wit' whatsoever I do.

(*The men nod satisfied and continue hiding ammo in different items of equipment.*)

SGT. MC KINNEY: (*Continued.*) And while you stashin' that ammo, save a bullet for yourself.

(*The men stop, understanding what's really being said.*)

HARDIN: (*Puzzled.*) Sir?

SGT. MC KINNEY: This ain't no chillun's game we playin' tonight. We could swang for what we gon' do. Only a soldier don't die by the rope, criminals die by the rope. A soldier go down in battle. That's why I say, save a bullet for yo' self. (SGT. MC KINNEY *holds up a bullet, then puts it in his shirt pocket. The men do the same.*) You understand boy?

HARDIN: (*Solemnly.*) Yes sir.

SGT. MC KINNEY: You ready?

HARDIN: Count me in.

SGT. MC KINNEY: Ten-hut!

(*Enter* CAPT. ZUELKE, *holding a lantern, and wearing a sidearm for the first time.*)

CAPT. ZUELKE: All right, McKinney, fall the men in for roll call!

SGT. MC KINNEY: Y'all heard yo' Cap'n, fall in!

CAPT. ZUELKE: (*Handing the lantern to* SGT. MC KINNEY.) Hold this up to each man's face, as you call his name.

(*Holding up the lantern,* SGT. MC KINNEY *goes down the row.*)

SGT. MC KINNEY: Brown!

GWEELY: Here!

SGT. MC KINNEY: Hardin!

HARDIN: Here!

SGT. MC KINNEY: Honoré!

BUGALOOSA: Here!

SGT. MC KINNEY: Franciscus!

FRANCISCUS: Here!

SGT. MC KINNEY: Moses!

MOSES: Here!

CAPT. ZUELKE: (*With his back to* SGT. MC KINNEY.) All right, McKinney, you can take up the rifles now. (*Pause, as he waits for* SGT. MC KINNEY *to give the order.*) I said you—

(CAPT. ZUELKE *hears the sound of a rifle cocking. He whirls around to find himself looking down the barrel of* SGT. MC KINNEY's *weapon. The other men train their rifles on him too. Except* HARDIN, *who watches openmouthed.*)

CAPT. ZUELKE: What . . . ? What the hell . . . !

SGT. MC KINNEY: We ain't givin' up our rifles.

CAPT. ZUELKE: What is this? (*Takes a step.*)

SGT. MC KINNEY: Take another step and I'll bore ya. Gweely, get his weapon.

CAPT. ZUELKE: (*Upraised hands.*) What is this? What's behind this?

SGT. MC KINNEY: We ain't gon' let this town lynch us, that's what's behind it.

CAPT. ZUELKE: (*Angrily.*) I told you we would handle that.

MOSES: Yeah, we just bet you would—

CAPT. ZUELKE: Shut up Moses!

MOSES: You shut up!

CAPT. ZUELKE: McKinney—stop, think. You're puttin' your head in a noose. You're gonna throw twenty-two good years down the drain, and for what?

SGT. MC KINNEY: I done already throwed twenty-two "good" years down the drain, workin' and sweatin' with this outfit. And now the army tell me, me and my mens ain't good enough to fight with the white boys in France.

CAPT. ZUELKE: So that's what's behind this insurrection?

SGT. MC KINNEY: They takin' our chance at glory in France, but we gon' get that glory anyway.

CAPT. ZUELKE: Glory? Hell, you're crazy!

GWEELY: (*Poking* CAPT. ZUELKE *with his rifle.*) You keep talkin', we gon' sho you who crazy.

CAPT. ZUELKE: I can't believe this.

MOSES: You keep talking; you gonna believe a bullet in your gut.

CAPT. ZUELKE: Look, you boys—(*The men raise their rifles.*) I mean you men have been under a lot of pressure lately; I know that, and if you just put those weapons down, I'd be willin' to forget this whole thing.

SGT. MC KINNEY: Now you crazy.

CAPT. ZUELKE: (*Putting in his bluff.*) Listen to me and listen good, all of ya! If you don't put those rifles down, every last damn one of ya is gonna be court-martialed, and hanged!

BUGALOOSA: Ain't nobody gonna put a rope on me no more. (*Starts speaking in Creole.*)

CAPT. ZUELKE: Franciscus? I can't believe you're going along with this, you're an MP—

FRANCISCUS: That don't mean nothing in this town.

CAPT. ZUELKE: Franciscus! These men are disobeying an officer, I command you to arrest them!

FRANCISCUS: I take my orders from Sgt. McKinney.

SGT. MC KINNEY: That's right. These men is mine. Franciscus, check outside.

FRANCISCUS: Yes sir. (*He limps out.*)

CAPT. ZUELKE: Franciscus! Come back here! Arrest these men, I'll see it goes easy on ya!

SGT. MC KINNEY: You wastin' yo' breath—boy.

CAPT. ZUELKE: McKinney, we been through a lot together. As one career man to another—

SGT. MC KINNEY: One man to another? You ain't never really seen me as no man. You done showed me that in all kinda ways. All these years us colored soldiers done took seconds in everythang—food, uniforms, 'quipment, whiles you white boys got the best. But we taken it, 'cause we always figured the day was comin' when we'd git our chance to prove ourselves. (*Raises his rifle.*) Well, that day done come. We marchin' outta here tonight, and we gon' meet that mob head on!

THE MEN: Yeah!

MOSES: Finally gonna see some action! And the first one I wanna run into is that white conductor!

CAPT. ZUELKE: McKinney, you go marching these men outta here, looking to harm white civilians—

SGT. MC KINNEY: We ain't looking to harm no white civilians, we after them civil police who ain't give us nothin' but trouble since we come here.

CAPT. ZUELKE: You'll be finished in the army.

SGT. MC KINNEY: I'm already finished in this white man's army. Fed up! We all is. We gon' march through this town and teach colored how to stand up!

(FRANCISCUS re-enters.)

GWEELY: Let's head for that police station and wipe out all them no-good police!

BUGALOOSA: And let all the colored prisoners go free!

MOSES: I'm ready to go to town and get to work!

CAPT. ZUELKE: You'll never make it.

SGT. MC KINNEY: We'll make it.

CAPT. ZUELKE: (*Pleading.*) What about me? What about my career? You go marching these men outta here, what do you think the brass'll do to me?

(SGT. MC KINNEY paces around CAPT. ZUELKE, looking him up and down in disgust.)

SGT. MC KINNEY: (*Spitting out the words.*) Brass shoulda got rid of you long time ago. The other officers laugh at you behind your back. You drunk eighteen hours out the day, you sloppy and undisciplined—a disgrace to that uniform. And yet the army see fit to send the likes of you to France. (*He dismisses* CAPT. ZUELKE *with a wave of his hands, turns away.*)

CAPT. ZUELKE: (*Sarcasm.*) So, this is how you "prove" yourselves huh? You wouldn't catch white troops doing this. But then, I always knew you niggers wouldn't make the grade—!

THE MEN: (*Incensed.*) Let me kill him; you want us to kill him, Sarge. Let us mow this damn cracker down! (*Etc.*)

SGT. MC KINNEY: No! Tie him up.

(*Suddenly,* CAPT. ZUELKE *makes a dive for his gun.*)

GWEELY: He's goin' for his gun, he's goin' for his gun—!

(*The men wrestle with* CAPT. ZUELKE *for the gun, and in the struggle,* SGT. MC KINNEY *stabs* CAPT. ZUELKE.)

BUGALOOSA: Sweet mother of God . . .

(*Breathing hard,* SGT. MC KINNEY *takes a handkerchief from his pocket, and wipes the bloody knife.* HARDIN *is transfixed.*)

GWEELY: He brung it on hisself, Sarge; he brung it on hisself—

MOSES: Yeah, it wasn't your fault; he was going for his gun—

FRANCISCUS: You had to stop him; he was going to turn us all in—

BUGALOOSA: (*Going around in circles.*) Holy mother of God, holy mother of God, holy mother of God . . .

GWEELY: We gotta git outta here fast, we gotta—

SGT. MC KINNEY: Wait! Get a grip, don't lose your heads.

HARDIN: Sergeant . . . maybe—maybe you should just throw yourself on the mercy of Colonel Gentry, explain to him—

SGT. MC KINNEY: Mercy? Boy, I done kilt a officer—ain't no mercy, no mercy on this earth. (*Pause.*) And that goes for alla us—you too boy— we all in this together. Stand by your race.

HARDIN: Yes sir, yes sir.

SGT. MC KINNEY: All right. Get plenty of ammo. Make sho' you canteens full. From now on we gon' be on the move, so I'll say it now. You a good bunch of men, real soldiers, reg'lars, and I'm proud to serve wit' ya. (SGT. MC KINNEY *and the men salute each other.*) Moses you take the point.

MOSES: Sir! (*Gathering his equipment.*)

SGT. MC KINNEY: Gweely, you bring up the rear.

GWEELY: Suh!

SGT. MC KINNEY: And remember, any yeller coward who ain't wit' us is agin us.

(*The sound of gunfire.*)

BUGALOOSA: Sarge! Sarge! They're out there!

SGT. MC KINNEY: Get yo' guns! Shoot out the street lights as we go. And remember—save a bullet for yourself. All right, that's it, let's go. Right face! Forward march!

(*As the men file out,* GWEELY *stops* HARDIN. *They are the only two left in barracks, except for* CAPT. ZUELKE's *still body lying in the middle of the floor.*)

GWEELY: Where you goin', boy!

HARDIN: With the rest of you—!

GWEELY: Naw you ain't, you goin' to France—

HARDIN: (*Desperately trying to push past.*) No, I'm going with the company—!

GWEELY: It ain't too late for you. (*Takes Hardin's rifle away from him.*) You
run away from here boy!

HARDIN: (*Still struggling.*) No!

GWEELY: Run like the devil hisself is after you! Gone!

HARDIN: Let me go!

GWEELY: Run to some—some white person's house, yeah, run to Miss
Stephanucci's, ask her to hide you out—

HARDIN: But Gweely I don't want to hide out, I want to go—

(*The gunfire escalates.*)

GWEELY: Shut up! You got to do what I say!

HARDIN: But Gweely, Gweely . . .

GWEELY: (*Pleading.*) We at the end of the line, but you—you gotta go on
and fight for the 24th in France. (*He takes off his watch.*) Here, take this,
Hardin. And remember me in France. Run, Hardin! (*Gunfire.*) Run!

(*HARDIN runs a few steps, stops, turns. He and GWEELY exchange salutes, then
take off running in opposite directions. The lights dim to a bloody red glow.
Sounds of fighting, gunshots, shouts, horse neighs, etc. In the dimmed light
CAPT. ZUELKE rises weakly to his knees, coughing and gripping his side. He calls
for help, and stumbles Off Stage. Fade out.*)

EPILOGUE

(SETTING: *An auditorium.*)
(AT RISE: *Two years later, 1919.* HARDIN, *in an officer's uniform, with lieutenant insignia, stands behind a lectern, addressing the audience. His hat and
notes are on the lectern. The barracks behind* HARDIN *are in dimmed light or
behind closed curtain.*)

HARDIN: Good evening, folks, I'm Second Lieutenant Charles W. Hardin
of the 373rd Infantry Regiment, 92nd Division. I'd like to thank you for
inviting me to speak to you this evening about the incident in Houston,
Texas, back in 1917, and of my war experiences in France.
In this tumultuous "red" summer of 1919, colored civilians are rioting
out of frustration all across this nation. Many of us colored soldiers
have returned home from the war to be spat upon, ridiculed, and
even lynched. But schools and organizations like yours have chosen to
honor those of us in uniform, by having us speak of our experiences in

the war. I think it is good that we have these meetings, for it is the only way our race can gather a fair accounting of the colored soldier's role in the military.

After the incident in Houston, Texas, I was transferred to one of the few colored regiments that actually got a chance to fight overseas. A group of mostly Southern draftees, we weren't expected to amount to much, but we showed 'em, we got our chance at glory! We went through the enemy like boweevil going through cotton! The French army awarded our entire unit the Croix de Guerre with Palm for Bravery.

(*Briskly.*) In reference to the so-called Houston riots in 1917: On the night of August 23rd, some members of the 24th Infantry mutinied and marched into the city to take revenge on the civil police for various and repeated indignities perpetrated upon individual soldiers of the regiment. When that confrontation was over, some twenty whites lay dead or seriously wounded, including five police officers. The same night of the mutiny, Sergeant McKinney stood beside a Southern Pacific railroad track and executed himself with a gunshot wound to the head—with the bullet he'd "saved" for himself. Captain Zuelke, the officer of "I" Company, wounded during the uprising, later committed suicide, also with a gunshot wound to the head.

In a sensational trial, held in Fort Sam Houston, San Antonio, which lasted one month, sixty-three defendants were tried. None of the accused testified, all pleaded not guilty. When the trial was over, forty-one men were sentenced to hard labor for life, four to shorter prison sentences, five were acquitted, and thirteen were sentenced to be hanged by the neck until dead.

Four of those sentenced to be hanged were good friends of mine— Corporal Robert Franciscus; Private First Class Gweely Brown; Private First Class Joseph Moses; and Private First Class Jacques Honoré. Some hail these men as heroes; others say that they have irreparably damaged the colored soldier's reputation in the military. But whatever is said of these men, they met their deaths like soldiers. They had requested a military execution by firing squad, but they were hanged like criminals.

Strangely enough, we have an eyewitness account of the hanging in the words of a Northern white soldier, an Illinois guardsman of the all white 19th Infantry, Company "C." They were assigned to guard the prisoners during the trial and execution, and during that time these white soldiers became close to the doomed men. In a letter home to his mother, the Illinois guardsman writes:

(*Reading matter-of-factly to keep emotion at bay.*) Early on the next morning, Mother, the day of the execution, my post was at the front of the guardhouse. What a cheerless, miserable morning it was! Five o'clock and pitch dark—no trace of moon or a single star anywhere. The air was damp and cold, and a bleak wind blowing made it feel colder than zero. In the darkness, I could hear the jingle of the chains . . .

(*We hear the JINGLE OF CHAINS.*)

HARDIN: (*Continued.*) The men were coming to be placed in the trucks that would take them for their last ride . . . to the hanging site . . .

(*In eerie, indistinct light, we see* GWEELY, MOSES, BUGALOOSA *and* FRANCISCUS *shuffle On Stage in chains. Each stands ramrod straight at his cot.*)

HARDIN: (*Continued.*) What a horrible ride it was! The road was full of bumps and hollows. Before our gloomy procession reached its destination, the doomed men took off their watches and rings, and gave them to us white soldiers as keepsakes. Gweely Brown made a speech to us.

GWEELY: (*Voice coming out of the gloom.*) You soldiers in Company "C" didn't treat us like criminals, but you treated us like brothers. And if my thanks is worth anythang to you men, I want to give it to ya. If any of you fellers ever git to France . . . I want you to go through the enemy like boweevil goin' through cotton!

(*SGT. MC KINNEY appears On Stage.*)

HARDIN: (*Still reading.*) As the ropes were fastened about the men's necks, Gweely Brown suddenly broke into a hymn . . .

GWEELY: (*Singing.*) Comin' home, comin' home, never more to roam . . . (*Etc.*)

HARDIN: And the others joined him . . .

THE MEN: (*Harmonizing.*) Comin' home, comin' home, never more to roam. Open wide the arms of love. Lord, I'm comin' home . . . (*Etc.*)

HARDIN: When they'd finished, and after a prayer, a major spoke to the doomed men: "Just as soon as I give the command, 'At-ten-tion,' I want you men to stand up! Ten-hut!"

(*The men snap to attention.*)

THE MEN: (*Wearing a proud smile.*) Goodbye Company "C"!

(*SGT. MC KINNEY raises his handgun and fires at his head, simultaneously with the sound of the trap door. Each soldier simulates hanging by letting his head roll to his shoulder as though snapped—or—as director stages it.*)

HARDIN: (*Crisply.*) After the war, I returned to the States and resumed my education. For I strongly believe that the only way for me, as a colored man, to deal with the wall of prejudice that surrounds this country, is to take advantage of any opportunity that allows me to open a door that was once closed to my race. And I still remain confident that if the colored man continues to chip away at that wall whenever, wherever, and in whatever form he can, one day that wall must crumble to the ground. For if France can honor the colored soldier, can America, the greatest country on earth, do less?

(*HARDIN steps to the side of the lectern and puts on his hat. We observe for the first time that he has lost an arm.*)

HARDIN: (*Continued.*) And now to the men of the 24th, and for all the soldiers of every race, who have given their blood, sweat, and tears for this country—I, Second Lieutenant Charles W. Hardin, salute you!

(*HARDIN salutes the audience, turns sharply, and marches up through the barracks and on into the future. Opening cadence begins.*)

VOICES OF THE MEN: (*Off Stage.*) Oh here we go, oh here we go, we're at it again, we're at it again, we're movin' out, we're movin' out, we're movin' in! Your left, your left, your left, right, left!

(*At this point, an announcement is made.*)

ANNOUNCER: Out of respect for the tragedy that happened at Camp Logan, there will not be a curtain, but the men will meet the audience in the lobby.

(*The men, still in uniform, form a reception line in the lobby to greet the audience.*)

THE END

Johnny B. Goode. (*Left to right*) Lloyd W. L. Barnes, Jr., Juan A. Fernandez, and Robert L. Rouse, Jr. Photo by Buddy Myers.

Johnny B. Goode

THOMAS MELONCON

Thomas Meloncon, prolific and versatile play-wright and poet, graduated from Houston's Kash-mere Gardens High School in 1967, where he par-ticipated in drama and forensic competitions. An outstanding athlete, Meloncon received a basket-ball scholarship to South Texas Junior College, which later became the University of Houston–Downtown. He transferred to Texas Southern University, where he earned a bachelor's degree in jour-nalism and a master of arts in communication. A recipient of numerous awards for his writing, Meloncon serves as a professor in the Fine Arts Department at Texas Southern University, where he teaches courses in playwriting and introduction to theatre. He also held an appointment as playwright-in-residence at Houston's High School for the Performing Arts from 1989 to 2002.

Although Meloncon maintains a full-time job, he has produced an im-pressive body of work, including more than thirty plays and three pub-lished books of poetry. One of his best-known plays, *Diary of Black Men* (written 1978), was produced off-Broadway in 1982. Consequently, the play came to the attention of talk-show host Phil Donahue, who invited Mel-oncon to appear on his show in 1989. For more than twenty years, the play has toured throughout the United States, including performances at the Kennedy Center for the Performing Arts. Meloncon is noted for his radio drama series, *The Robeson Family Chronicles*, which aired weekly on KTSU radio for three years. He was also commissioned to write *Sarah and Joshua: A Juneteenth Musical* for Houston's Annual Juneteenth Celebration. Several of Meloncon's children's plays have been toured by Express Children's The-atre. His plays for adult audiences have been produced at Houston theatres such as the Main Street Theatre, which opened its 2002–2003 season with the world premiere of *The Laws of Storms*, a piece that examines the experiences of one family during the aftermath of the Galveston Storm of 1900.

Another facet of Meloncon's art reflects his social consciousness and commitment to educational theatre. He has written a series of plays that enlighten audiences on topics such as breast cancer, prenatal care, teen pregnancy, and male/female relationships. Moreover, agencies as diverse as the March of Dimes, the National Head Start Bureau, the University of Texas Health Science Center, and the Houston Area Women's Center have commissioned educational plays by Meloncon. He uses educational theatre to raise awareness and promote positive change within Houston's black community and beyond.

As You Read *Johnny B. Goode*

Johnny B. Goode, a domestic drama that merges realism with the supernatural, takes its title from the 1958 rock-and-roll classic written and performed by Chuck Berry. Set in Port Arthur, Texas, in 1955, the multi-faceted, richly nuanced play explores intergenerational conflicts between a father and his son, the tensions between older black musicians dedicated to traditional blues and the younger artists who favor the newer, more commercially viable rock and roll. Readers and theatre audiences might compare and contrast Meloncon's play with August Wilson's *Ma Rainey's Black Bottom*, a play in which proponents of old and emerging musical styles clash. Both writers call attention to the value of black music as a repository of black culture and a means of survival. Like Lorraine Hansberry's *A Raisin in the Sun*, *Johnny B. Goode* is a conventional work loosely modeled upon the structure of the well-made play. Meloncon's insightful development of character, imaginative, tightly controlled plot, keen ear for African American vernacular English, and his strong sense of history combine to make *Johnny B. Goode* a challenging, entertaining play that rewards close reading and attentive viewing. It also raises intriguing questions about African Americans and the uses of art.

Representative Production History

Ensemble Theatre, Houston, Texas, 1997–1998
Jubilee Theatre, Fort Worth, Texas, 1998–1999
Washington State University, Pullman, Washington, 2002–2003

Characters

JOHNNY A. GOODE: A man who has invested his life in preserving the blues and its legacy. What he wants is the past to stand still long enough for him to hold on. He is a man possessed by the bitter truth of his son's rejection of him and the reality of the changing world.

JOHNNY B. GOODE: The son of Johnny A. Goode. He is a liberated man who from childhood has been held hostage to his father's brutal ego. What he wants is to define his music and his life on his own terms. His father is both his mentor and his demon.

ELIZABETH GOODE: A woman who refuses to allow the past to strangle the future. She is a woman who appreciates the promise and the meaning of family. She is the moral glue and spirit that bind the loose ends of her family. She is armed with logic, humor, and love.

SLEEPY: The brother of Johnny B. The so-called black sheep of the family. He is his own worst enemy because he never learned to trust his own instincts and values. He is nervous when he speaks because he does not believe his own words.

RETHA C. GOODE: Sleepy's daughter. She contracts polio and employs this handicap as a tool to get what she wants from her father. She is womanish ("too grown" and too self-assured for her age) because her father is afraid to impose the discipline needed to raise her. But even though she is sassy, we see a beauty and a strength that transcend her handicap.

RED DOG: Childhood friend of Johnny A. He can sense trouble and avoids it by avoiding the truth. He is a conformist and wants no sign of change.

DUCE: A childhood friend of Red Dog. He speaks slowly, but slow speech does not indicate that his perceptions and intelligence are low. He wears his age gracefully and is more youthful looking than Red Dog and Johnny A.

Setting

There is a music that has risen out of troubled waters. Those waters that carried slave ships from the West Coast of Africa had inside their wooden bosom the seeds of Huddie "Lead Belly" Ledbetter, Lightnin' Hopkins, Ma Rainey, Muddy Waters, and Mamie Smith. Inside those dark corridors, lying in their waste, were the medicine men, witch doctors, and griots who, although chained and bound, stored inside their memory and genes the ancient ingredients for the blues. There is a music that rolled from the dry tongues of field slaves, who laid the economic foundation for white civilization.

In 1619, in Jamestown, Virginia, the first Africans arrived in America without their drums. The blues began. It began when Africans remembered how their forefathers used an elongated gourd containing five strings tied to a wooden stick, and how they sang songs with this in the village. These Africans brought this instrument to the American South and called it the "banjo." Later, the guitar became the dominant instrument for the blues.

The year is 1955, and the stingy summer of that year will not allow the wind to cool off the streets and back yards of Port Arthur, Texas. Port Arthur is a seaport town nestled between Beaumont and Houston. Many of the blacks of Port Arthur migrated from Louisiana, Mississippi, and Georgia, looking for jobs that would allow them and their children to live better lives. City life offers them promise and potential, a place where they can walk upright, not stooped and submissive. Just as their ancestors brought with them on those ships the basic ingredients for the blues, these rural blacks, who landed in Port Arthur in the early years of the century, brought with them the stories, songs, and hollers that added to the great legacy of the blues. It was a great and troubled era, where whites manufactured and distributed the coon, mammy, minstrel images of blacks. These whites both emulated and borrowed from the blues, yet its art was truly African and American, born from the chain gangs and cotton fields of American slavery. This so-called race music contained the stories, both sorrowful and beautiful, of a people uprooted. But in Port Arthur, as in many cities in the South, the blues had been labeled "dirty music" by whites who didn't profit from it and by middle-class blacks who rejected their culture.

The blues had been overhauled and given a "new beat," a new name, "rhythm and blues." From race music, to blues, to rhythm and blues, black people created it and played it, but did not control it.

There is a black man in Port Arthur named Johnny A. Goode, who has refused to surrender the legacy of the blues to white America. His father died because he refused to sell his songs. Now, Johnny A. Goode is struggling to pass on that same strength and legacy to his son, Johnny B. Goode.

Production Notes

(*Lights rise in Johnny A.'s café. The café was once a hot spot for popular country blues singers in the 1930s. It holds deep memories in its walls and chairs. Negro women dressed in red silk dresses and men in zoot suits, toe tapped and slow dragged to the raw mood of Mississippi and Texas blues. But it is now 1955, and only the ghosts of those blues singers sit drunkenly, trying to remember who left them there to ponder their uncertain destiny. The café feels and looks like it once contained great memories and occupants beside Johnny A., his two musician friends, and an occasional all-night blues session by traveling musicians. The café looks abandoned but functional enough for rehearsals. The main door for the café is Stage Right. The door always has a creaky sound when opening and closing, indicating its age and wear and tear. In a somewhat dark corner of the café, with a blown-out lightbulb covered with dust hanging over it, there are three small wooden card tables with chairs, each chair turned upside down on top of the tables. One senses that these chairs represent an end to a great era. Less action takes place here. The stage in the café is Upstage Center. It is small and made of wooden planks, some uneven, showing their rough construction. Three musicians can sit on the stage. There could be a slight dip in the middle, showing its usage over the years. Two stools are placed Downstage. There are four large pictures of early country blues singers, wrinkled and worn. Each picture has been signed by the artist. To the left of the stage is a small bar that holds five stools. The bar is ruggedly built and made of the cheap material of the 1930s. Behind the bar, on the wall, are soda and beer signs of that era, such as "Falstaff" and "Jax" beers and "Nehi" soda water. The cost of beer, soda, and small snacks should be on a crudely handwritten menu. Several feet from the bar is another table with three chairs. This table, the bar, and the stage are where most of the action takes place, but not the only place. There is a bathroom door at Stage Right of the café stage and a sign on the wall that says "Restroom." Blues songs are called out throughout the play; the director should choose which blues songs should be played where appropriate.*)

ACT ONE

Scene 1

(*Under blackout we hear the pre-show blues tune. As it dies, we immediately hear* SLEEPY *still under blackout trying to play* RED DOG's *guitar. It is obvious that he is not a musician. But we do hear him trying to play a specific blues*

*tune that his grandfather taught his father. We will hear the full tune later
at the end of Act Two. The lights rise.* SLEEPY *is wearing overalls and some
worn-down, unpolished brogans.* SLEEPY *is a man who is not concerned about
the challenge of tomorrow or the uncertainty of the distant future. Port Arthur,
Texas, is the beginning and end of his reality. His mission in life is to simply
rise each morning and see what happens.* ELIZABETH *enters as* SLEEPY *is on the
guitar.* ELIZABETH *wears her fifty-eight-year-old body with style and grace.
She knows her husband and his friends better than they know themselves. She
knows them because she has listened to each of their pains, even when they were
too busy to feel hers.* ELIZABETH *fills the empty space left by* JOHNNY A. *with
work. She waits for the moment when healing and forgiveness will bring her
family together again. She enters wearing a flowered dress and a hat. She has a
broom in her hand. She begins to sweep the floor.)*

ELIZABETH: Sleepy, you better get off Red Dog's guitar.
(He continues playing simple chords.)
SLEEPY: Hey mama, where you coming from dressed up?
ELIZABETH: I told you this morning before I left. Rev. Crowley had a
    service for Babycake.
SLEEPY: I still say Johnny B. shoulda took that spooky girl with him when
    he ran away. She mighta been alive today. *(SLEEPY hits a loud note on the
    guitar.)*
ELIZABETH: I know one thing, Red Dog walk up in here and catch you on
    his guitar, he gone spook you up.
SLEEPY: Come on mama, sing me one of them hoochie coochie songs. I
    don't know why you ain't never go on the road with daddy. I used to
    hear you.
ELIZABETH: 'Round the house, yea, but I told you a thousand times, mama
    and daddy was Holy Ghost people. We get caught singing the blues,
    they's make us chew a bar of borax soap and swallow it.
SLEEPY: Well, they been dead all these years. You been married to daddy
    forty years; you coulda been singing with him.
ELIZABETH: I ain't want to, one man singing the country blues for forty
    years in my life is enough for me. I don't need to sing my own blues.
*(SLEEPY stands up, props his foot on the bench, begins to play a blues song that
his father taught* JOHNNY B.)*
SLEEPY: Come on mama.
ELIZABETH: Go on, Sleepy now.

(SLEEPY *begins to sing as* ELIZABETH *sweeps the floor. She ignores him at first, then begins to remember the song.*)

ELIZABETH: That's the first song your daddy taught Johnny B. That's the one his daddy taught him.

(ELIZABETH *joins in the song slowly, then begins to sing with* SLEEPY. SLEEPY *then allows her to sing it alone; she then begins to move and groove. One senses that she has more talent than she admits, but she contains it. The song ends.* SLEEPY *dances toward his mother with the guitar as he plays simple chords.* ELIZABETH *continues to sing and dance.*)

SLEEPY: Go on, Mama. Look at Mama now!

(ELIZABETH *stops.*)

ELIZABETH: Let me stop. My mama and daddy look down from heaven and see me singing this stuff, they slap me. (*She walks behind the bar, noticing the empty beer chest.*) Sleepy, who drunk up all these beers?

SLEEPY: Daddy and them drunk 'em. You didn't hear all that noise in here last night?

ELIZABETH: I heard something. I looked out the window, saw two station wagons, went dead back to sleep.

SLEEPY: That was Lightnin' Hopkins and Texas Alexander's station wagons. You shoulda seen Texas' fingers. Nigger had diamonds on every finger except his thumb.

ELIZABETH: You better put Red Dog's guitar down before he walk up in here.

SLEEPY: Hell, Red Dog was here last night, him and Duce. He was too drunk to take his guitar, left it here.

ELIZABETH: He too old for that stuff, him and Duce.

SLEEPY: I told Lightnin' to sing "Short Haired Woman" for me; he tore it up. Then he sung one of Blind Lemon Jefferson's songs, had three women almost took they clothes off. Daddy joined the song.

ELIZABETH: What women?

SLEEPY: (*Puts* RED DOG'*s guitar back on stage.*) They got out the car with Texas Alexander. Had a fat one, a skinny one, and one with some gap teeth. You could run a baseball bat 'tween her teeth and still have room to hit a home run.

ELIZABETH: Hush up, Sleepy.

SLEEPY: She kept eyeing me, but I don't be talking to no gap-teeth women.

ELIZABETH: I heard somewhere them people in Africa say it's a sign of beauty for a woman to have gap teeth.

(SLEEPY *pulls out a large knife, shaped somewhat like a guitar. He pulls out a piece of old twisted wood that almost curves into a B. He begins to carve the wood over a trash can as he talks.*)

SLEEPY: Well, this ain't Africa, this Port Arthur and a gap-toothed woman can't do nothing for me but cover them teeth up.

ELIZABETH: You know Lightnin' used to play here when you and Johnnie B. wudn't but five or six years old.

SLEEPY: Yea, I remember Lightnin' Hopkins, Ida Mae Mack, William Mc-Coy. They all been on this here stage. Daddy had Johnny B. sitting right in front, listening to every song. That's why Johnny B. famous now.

ELIZABETH: That's when this place had life; it's dead now, ain't nothing but ghosts in here. Ghosts looking for somebody's soul to sing a song for.

SLEEPY: I don't know why Daddy won't close it down. Nobody come by here.

ELIZABETH: He hold on to it 'cause it got too many memories.

SLEEPY: Memories don't make no money; they just make tears.

ELIZABETH: If he let it go, he got to let Johnny B. go, too.

SLEEPY: All he do is rehearse here and now and sell beer to friends out of a ice chest.

ELIZABETH: (*Sweeping the floor.*) And have them all-night wild blues parties for those bands that come through here. (*Picks up some trash off the floor.*)

SLEEPY: He got to let go, one day.

ELIZABETH: (*To herself.*) He got to learn to let Johnny B. go.

SLEEPY: Yea, I could see Johnny B. now, on this stage. Johnny wudn't 'bout eight, had him singing the blues, once a week. Johnny B. was so good, them musicians wanted him to go on the road with them. Daddy wudn't let him.

ELIZABETH: I hope he taking care of himself.

SLEEPY: Johnny B. got three records out, he got money. When you got money, money take care of you.

ELIZABETH: Money ain't everything. It can be the root of evil.

SLEEPY: Naw Mama, I'll tell you what's evil, a broke nigger. Now that's evil. Now the white man can walk down the street broke, and he can still look like he own the world. But you see a broke nigger coming down the street in Port Arthur, you better get out the way 'cause somebody gone get cut. That's why I keep a switchblade. (*Throws the knife into the floor, and it sticks.*)

ELIZABETH: I still say money can be the root of all evil.

SLEEPY: (*Pulls out a large roll of money; the amount briefly catches Elizabeth's attention, but she makes no note of it.*) Mama, this is paper. This is power. Johnny B., he got power now, 'cause he got his. Now, how a piece of paper gone be evil?

ELIZABETH: It's what people do to get that paper.

SLEEPY: You do what you got to do to get it. Like Daddy always say, take what God gave you. Now, you take Johnny B. God gave Daddy a voice and right hand to sing the blues, then Daddy passed his voice and a right hand to Johnny B. Taught Johnny B. how to play the guitar before he was old enough to pee straight in the toilet. Now, what Daddy passed on to me? A hoe and a mule and led me to a crop of potatoes.

ELIZABETH: Your daddy tried to get you to play the guitar, but you had your mind on them twin girls, Ola and Jeanett, across the street.

SLEEPY: (*Pulls knife out the floor and puts it back in his pocket.*) Now, Mama, you know Daddy always favored Johnny B. on the musical end. He bring company over and have Johnny B. sitting in the living room, playing for them. Where he had me? Out cutting sugar cane, sun sitting on my head. That's why I'm so black now; Daddy turned me this black.

ELIZABETH: Hush up, Sleepy.

SLEEPY: I bet Retha was acting up at the church this morning.

ELIZABETH: Yea, she was. You let that girl get away with too much.

SLEEPY: I ain't got no wife, Mama. I try to teach her manners best I can.

ELIZABETH: You let her watch too much television, too. All she do is talk about Elvis Presley, like he everything.

SLEEPY: Mama, she like Elvis Presley. What you want me to do? Wup her 'cause she like Elvis Presley?

ELIZABETH: I know one thing you can do, stop telling her that one day that brace gone come off her leg.

SLEEPY: Ain't nothing wrong with that, mama. She my daughter, she ain't your daughter. I got to give her something that she can believe gone happen good to her one day.

ELIZABETH: And she come out the room with her hair half combed, dress on backwards and two left shoes.

SLEEPY: I told her she ain't had to go to that service. She scared of Babycake.

ELIZABETH: It wudn't nothing to be scared of. They didn't have no body, just some flowers. Her parents dead. Somebody had to say a prayer for her. Rev. Crowley was nice to buy her some flowers.

SLEEPY: I'm telling you that was Johnny B.'s fault. He shoulda took that girl way from here when he ran away several years ago.

ELIZABETH: People just came by the church and said a prayer for her.

SLEEPY: She was pretty, I tell you that. But crazy, too. Girl sitting up in a boarded house all them years waiting for Johnny B. to come back. If that ain't crazy, water ain't wet, and I just had a cup full. Some of them children playing around her house say they seen red eyes in the window at night, and blood running off the roof.

ELIZABETH: Them children ain't seen no red eyes. That's where Retha got that mess from.

SLEEPY: Why they got to lie about some red eyes? That girl was fourteen years old when Johnny B. left home. She turned into a witch, Mama.

ELIZABETH: Hush up, Sleepy. You thirty years old, talking about witches and red eyes.

SLEEPY: When they first moved here from Louisiana, they put a bunch of candles in they yard. That's all I needed to know.

ELIZABETH: Them people stayed to themselves; they ain't bothered nobody.

SLEEPY: Nobody hung around there except Johnny B.

ELIABETH: Him and Babycake had a crush on each other.

SLEEPY: Sneaked round there when Daddy was gone and played his guitar for her.

ELIZABETH: I knew he was over there. He ain't had no other friends.

SLEEPY: I say she spooked Johnny B. up. Probably another reason he ran away. Had that nigger zombified.

ELIZABETH: There you go, Sleepy. Sometimes God puts one person in your life to love you with all they heart. His heart was touched by her.

SLEEPY: Well, God sho' messed up with mine. Janie Lee Burkett told me she loved me with all of her heart. I married her, we had Retha. Two years later I walk upon her in our bedroom with Rev. Smith's son, and he sho' wasn't touching her heart! She jumped up talking 'bout they was praying. He had a handful of her prayer all right.

ELIZABETH: (*Laughing.*) Hush up, Sleepy. You say Duce and Red Dog were here last night?

SLEEPY: Yea, they was here. Daddy and Duce and Red Dog were here last night. Duce got mad, told him he wasn't gone cut his hair no more.

ELIZABETH: What they arguing 'bout, that rhythm and blues stuff?

SLEEPY: Yea. Duce just ask him again 'bout playing some R&B, a little dance music to get some customers back in here.

ELIZABETH: What Johnny say?

SLEEPY: He say he rather rent it to the devil himself than to play that coon music in his place.

ELIZABETH: Your daddy ain't interested in this being no club no more. When he first opened it, you couldn't get a seat. Had Big Joe Turner one night, Howlin' Wolf the next. Had Sonny Boy Williamson staying at our house, waiting to play on Saturday.

SLEEPY: Daddy a country blues man. He gone die a country blues man just like Grandpa did in Mississippi.

ELIZABETH: Johnny A. just happy to have a place where his old friends can stop by and practice. He just want to hold on to the past. He don't know the past got somewhere to go.

SLEEPY: That's all it's gone be now. Rusty's down the street, packing 'em in. They got a dance floor big as a cornfield, and a jukebox. Even had that boy Monty born with that short leg out there doing a jig.

ELIZABETH: Let them dance down there, and don't be talking about Rusty's to him, you know how he gets.

SLEEPY: I ain't said a word. I messed round and said T-Bone Walker's name, and his eyes looked straight through me, veins popped out of his forehead.

ELIZABETH: Where is he?

SLEEPY: He at Duce getting a haircut.

ELIZABETH: (*She walks to the counter, sees the fishing pole.*) You hurry up and get them. . . . (*Picks up pole.*) What this doing back here?

SLEEPY: I just bought it. You like it? I been trying the reel out. I'm going fishing in the river in the morning. Nowhere nears Lovers' Bridge, though.

ELIZABETH: You off tomorrow?

SLEEPY: Yea, I'm off. People say every since Babycake jumped off Lovers' Bridge in the river, they been catching catfish two feet long.

ELIZABETH: What that got to do with that girl?

SLEEPY: People say her soul floating in that river. They say Old Lady Ducanmore, that wear the wig, say her hair growing back.

ELIZABETH: Hush up, Sleepy. Here. (*Gives him several dollars.*) Go down to Butte's and get some beers before your daddy show up.

SLEEPY: (*Takes the money.*) That's what one of them Robey twins told me. I ain't seen her though.

ELIZABETH: That woman had burns on her scalp from that fire two years ago. She can't grow no hair.

SLEEPY: People say she washed her foot in the river. Her hair came back two days later. Couldna been another wig, though.

ELIZABETH: Gone outta here boy.

SLEEPY: I ain't putting my line down where she jumped off. My hair liable to fall off, my teeth turn gap, nuts fall too, while I'm talking. Excuse me, Mama.

(SLEEPY *about to exit.*)

ELIZABETH: (*She laughs.*) If you go by the house, tell Retha she better finish them ho cakes on the stove!

SLEEPY: She don't like no ho cakes.

(*As he is about to exit,* RED DOG *enters. He is a tall, red-freckled man with reddish hair and complexion.* RED DOG *is polite with a quiet sense of humor. He prefers to take the back road to conflict and tension. He has surrendered the fast world to the young and the restless. His loyalty is to truth and friendship.*)

RED DOG: Sleepy been on my guitar?

SLEEPY: I just looked at it.

ELIZABETH: Yea, he was.

RED DOG: I told you 'bout my guitar. That's a Gibson, that ain't second-hand. Where Johnny A.?

SLEEPY: He over at Duce, getting a haircut.

RED DOG: See, he always talking 'bout being on time. He show up late. We got that Beaumont gig tonight. Sleepy, you going fishing, huh?

SLEEPY: Yea, I'm off tomorrow, going fishing on the river.

RED DOG: Give me one of them Falstaffs, Elizabeth.

ELIZABETH: Ain't no more. Yawl drunk 'um up last night.

RED DOG: That wudn't me. I ain't had nothing but eight. That was Lightnin' drunk up all them beers. Hell, Johnny A. charged forty cents a can. Where you going fishing at? On the bridge?

SLEEPY: Naw, hell naw. I ain't throwing my line out where Babycake jumped off. I'm liable to pull up her dead body on my hook, knowing my luck.

RED DOG: That gull jumped off two days ago. Her body been gone, catfish and everything else done ate her up. Police couldn't find nothing.

SLEEPY: How catfish gone eat up a woman in two days, tell me that?

RED DOG: Hell nigger, I can eat up a woman in thirty minutes, won't be nothing left but the bedspread.

ELIZABETH: Don't be talking like that 'round me, Red Dog.

SLEEPY: (*Exiting.*) Red Dog, you something else . . . won't be nothing left. (*Laughing.*) You something else.

ELIZABETH: Sleepy, bring them beers, and don't muddy up my floor!

RED DOG: You sho' look nice in that dress.

ELIZABETH: Thank you. They had a little service for that girl. (*Begins to clean the beer chest.*)

RED DOG: Shame 'bout that gull. That woman that saw her jump off say she hollered Johnny B.'s name, smiled, then jumped two hundred feet, head first. Roger Justin was out there, say he seen a light in the water.

ELIZABETH: She couldn't take what happened to her, waiting for Johnny B. to come back, then getting raped. Too much for any woman.

RED DOG: Rev. Crowley tried to get that girl to come out after a month being in that house. Seven years in that house, waiting on Johnny B.

(ELIZABETH *discovers two beers left in the chest.*)

ELIZABETH: Look, had two beers left in the corner here.

RED DOG: Let me have them two beers. Put it on my tab.

ELIZABETH: You know Johnny count every beer in this box.

RED DOG: He ain't gone miss no two beers.

ELIZABETH: (*Gives him the two beers.*) I don't want to hear Johnny A.'s mouth 'bout them beers. You know how he is.

RED DOG: He ought to give us free beers. He don't pay me and Duce but six dollars a gig. Shit, we can make more on a chain gang.

ELIZABETH: Yawl ain't playing for the money no more. That was thirty years ago.

RED DOG: The hell you mean, ain't playing for no money? I need money. Johnny just tight. Tight as fish pussy.

ELIZABETH: (*Chuckles.*) Don't talk like that round me, Red Dog.

RED DOG: And that's waterproof.

ELIZABETH: (*Hides her smile. She continues cleaning the place.*) When I met Johnny, you, him, and Duce was making three dollars a show in them joints in New Orleans. That was round 1929.

RED DOG: Show you how you lying. Let's get the fact straight. Wasn't no 1929. Johnny A.'s daddy got killed in 1915. You met Johnny in New Orleans in 1930.

ELIZABETH: Johnny told me his daddy got killed in 1914.

RED DOG: Elizabeth, them crackers hung Johnny's daddy in 1915. Me and Duce grew up with the nigger in Mississippi. Johnny was twenty, I was nineteen, Duce was twenty-one after they buried Johnny's daddy. My Uncle Buddy and Duce's daddy say they wanted to move to New Orleans. That was in 1916, 'cause it be better opportunity for them to get jobs 'cause the Klansmen was getting hot. Plus we could play them joints. Johnny stayed with me and my uncle 'til May, 1917. He got a room at Mazola's. We started the Blues Masters in 1918. We played to house parties and whorehouses from 1918 to 1930. We got a weekend gig at the Hoochie Coochie Lounge and that's where Johnny met you. You was po' and hungry, waiting tables.

ELIZABETH: Don't be telling no lies like that. I wasn't no po' and hungry. I was single on my own. How much yawl make apiece at the Hoochie Coochie?

RED DOG: Three dollars. Johnny made five dollars.

ELIZABETH: That's what I thought.

RED DOG: Yea. That was 1916! That's why I'm telling you.

ELIZABETH: You still playing 'cause you love to play.

RED DOG: I'm still playing 'cause I love the nigger. I love him.

ELIZABETH: I love him, too. Even though he can drive me crazy.

RED DOG: We probably be rich today if we woulda stayed in New Orleans, playing them blues joints. Johnny A. says let's move to Port Arthur, open up our own blues club, and you listen to him, too.

ELIZABETH: Yea, I did. I wanted to see his dream come true, and it did. This place was jumping in thirty-three.

RED DOG: Well, at least Johnny B. done made it big. That boy ought to be a millionaire by now. You can't pick up a *Billboard* magazine without one of his records in the top fifteen R&B chart.

ELIZABETH: I bought two of them from the store, but I keep them hid. Johnny A. don't want them in the house.

RED DOG: I got a couple, too. I ain't mention it to Johnny A., though.

ELIZABETH: He left too soon. Thirteen is too young. He shoulda got his schooling. He can't read well.

RED DOG: Yea, he left young, but you just knew Johnny B. was gone be great. Boy wasn't six years old, Johnny A. hung a guitar round his neck, make him walk around with it. He'd be crying his ass off.

ELIZABETH: Every time he'd do it, I untie it, too.

RED DOG: Johnny ain't mean no harm. Just wanted Johnny B. to take up his name, like he took it from his daddy.

ELIZABETH: Didn't mean no harm, huh? Whip a eight-year-old boy with a ironing cord 'cause he play the wrong note. Make him go without supper 'til he sing the blues the way his daddy taught him to sing.

RED DOG: But look where it got him. He took him to that talent contest in Dallas when Johnny B. was ten years old, and T-Bone Walker was there. T-Bone Walker called him boy wonder on that guitar.

(RETHA, SLEEPY's *eight-year-old daughter, enters eating a popsicle. Her knee-length dress is dirty; she wears a brace on her left leg because of polio. She limps.*)

RETHA: Evening Mr. Red Dog.

RED DOG: Evening nothing, you better come hug me with your womanish self.

ELIZABETH: Retha, you finish them ho cakes? And don't get that popsicle on your dress.

RETHA: I don't like no ho cakes. (*Begins to sing a song; her voice is pretty, but unused.*)

ELIZABETH: You gonna finish them ho cakes.

RED DOG: That girl got a pretty voice. Why you ain't never got her singing?

ELIZABETH: I tried to get her to sing in church. She shame.

RED DOG: Come on over here and tell Red Dog what you wanna be when you grow up.

RETHA: (*Sits on his lap.*) I want to be beautiful like Babycake, and I want to sing like Uncle Johnny B., but I can't.

RED DOG: Why not?

RETHA: 'Cause I'm a cripple.

(ELIZABETH *walks slowly to* RETHA, *with a firm look.*)

ELIZABETH: Retha, don't you ever let those words come out of your mouth again. Do you hear me? You ain't no cripple. God gave you a brain. You can be anything you wanna be.

RETHA: That's what them children at the swimming pool call me.

ELIZABETH: I don't care what they call you. You can do whatever they can do.

RETHA: I can't walk like they walk.

(ELIZABETH *is lost for words. Suddenly,* SLEEPY *bursts through the door, breathing hard. He walks over to the window, carrying a case of beer.*)

SLEEPY: Tell me my eyes is right? (*Puts beer on the counter.* RED DOG *and* ELIZABETH *go over to the window.*)

ELIZABETH: (*At the window.*) Lord have mercy, they right.

RETHA: (*At window.*) Ooh! Is that Uncle Johnny B.? That's him?

SLEEPY: (*At window.*) Is my eyes lying?

RED DOG: They ain't lying. That's him.

SLEEPY: Now, tell me is that a Cadillac that nigger getting out of?

(RETHA *takes off running.*)

RETHA: Oooh! I ain't never rode in no real Cadillac! (*Exits.*)

SLEEPY: Retha, bring your narrow ass back here! (*Looks out the window.*)

ELIZABETH: (*Blankly.*) Babycake. Somebody told him about Babycake.

SLEEPY: Look, Retha girl ain't got no manners. Retha standing on top the man's hood. (*Walks angrily toward the door.*) Retha! (*Exits.*)

RED DOG: He can barely get out the car, people rushing him for autographs.

ELIZABETH: (*Tearfully.*) He's come home, thank God.

(JOHNNY B. *enters wearing a red suit with black alligator shoes. He is sporting a fabulous conk that runs to his neck.* RETHA *is holding his left hand. He is carrying his guitar in his right hand as he enters.* ELIZABETH *is speechless, her eyes studying him.* JOHNNY *is wordless as* RETHA *tinkers with his watch.*)

(ELIZABETH *embraces him deeply, then steps back and weeps.*)

SLEEPY: Johnny B., I bet you don't know who this girl is.

JOHNNY B.: Who is she?

RETHA: I'm your niece, Retha C. Goode. C. stands for "cutting up." But I don't be cutting up, though.

SLEEPY: I married Janie Lee Burnett, but we separated. Caught her butt naked in bed with Rev. Smith's son. First girl in the family. Ain't she pretty? Shake your famous uncle's hand and say hi. And don't be asking him for no money, just 'cause he rich.

RETHA: Hi, Uncle Johnny B. You got five dollars?

SLEEPY: Retha, where your manners? (*Johnny gives her a dollar.*)

ELIZABETH: Johnny, don't be giving that girl no money.

RED DOG: You gone live a long time, boy. I was just talking to Elizabeth about you. You the most famous person outta Port Arthur.

JOHNNY B.: Hello Mr. Red.

RED DOG: Mr. Red? You better call me Red Dog. Come back here with a California conk talking about Red. Red.

JOHNNY B.: (*They shake hands.*) Hello, Red Dog.

SLEEPY: That ain't no po' folk conk, neither! You use osh potatoes? I had a conk badder than James Brown. I messed round and got lye in my eyes. Shit, that was it for me.

RETHA: Them real alligator shoes, Uncle Johnny? (*Kneels down to the floor and rubs them.*)

SLEEPY: Get up from there, Retha, where your manners?

(*She remains.*)

JOHNNY B.: Yea, they real.

SLEEPY: What they cost, Johnny B.?

JOHNNY B.: I paid thirty-five dollars for them.

ELIZABETH: That's none of your business. Johnny B. you hungry? Look like you done lost some weight. You need some home cooking.

JOHNNY B.: No ma'am, I ain't had much appetite.

SLEEPY: Get up from there, Retha. I told you. (*She remains, tinkering with* JOHNNY B.'s *shoes.*) Where your manners?

JOHNNY B.: I miss yawl.

ELIZABETH: We missed you, too, Johnny B.

SLEEPY: I hate to tell you. Two days ago some hobos wandered into that house, where Baby was staying, found some bloody panties! They got the police. Police did some blood studying and found some man's life water. Same day she went up on Lovers' Bridge and jumped in the river. Police dragged the river couldn't find nothing. She stayed up in that old house for seven years crying 'cause you left. Hey, Johnny B. can I drive your Cadillac? I ain't gonna hurt it.

ELIZABETH: No, Sleepy. (*Separate thought.*) We sorry, Johnny B. They had a little service for her this morning.

JOHNNY B.: They found out who did it?

RED DOG: Naw. Probably some drifters raped that voodoo girl. His rod probably gone drop off.

ELIZABETH: Retha in here now.

SLEEPY: Johnny B. I ain't gone hurt the car.

(JOHNNY B. *hands him the keys.*)

JOHNNY B.: Where's Daddy?

RETHA: Oooh! Daddy, can I ride, too?

ELIZABETH: He's over at Duce's. He'll be here.

SLEEPY: Naw Retha, you stay here. You might dirty up Uncle Johnny's car. It's a Cadillac. You ain't custom to riding in no Cadillac. Maybe a truck.

ELIZABETH: Let that girl go.

(SLEEPY and RETHA exiting.)

SLEEPY: Don't you be acting no fool, you hear me?

(Both exit.)

ELIZABETH: You come to stay, Johnny B.?

JOHNNY B.: I don't know. We'll see.

RED DOG: That's all people ever talk about around here—is when Johnny B. coming home. 'Course, you can't get your daddy to say two words 'bout you. I been telling him that yawl ought to forgive and forget. That's what the Bible say.

ELIZABETH: We got a whole box of newspaper articles and pictures we saved about you. I still keep the one I took of you with T-Bone Walker when you was eight years old in Houston, on my dresser.

RED DOG: Yea, remember that day? Me, Duce, and your daddy opened the show for him at the Sugar Shack Lounge. Place was packed. Your daddy thought it be cute, play your guitar while he fixing his string. Shit, that little nigger tore the house down. T-Bone came out the dressing room. Couldn't believe his eyes.

(SLEEPY enters with two suitcases.)

SLEEPY: Johnny B., I brought your suitcases in. Damn, they heavy. You must got a good bunch of records in here. (RETHA is in the car, blowing the horn.) Stop blowing that horn. (She continues to blow it.) Im'ma drive around to Duce's, where Daddy is. He gone fall out when he see me.

(Exits.)

JOHNNY B.: Yawl still playing a lot?

RED DOG: Still playing? Hell yea! We just play to keep ourselves busy. Duce still got his barbershop over on Colored Avenue. I got two rent houses. Your daddy done paid for this place. Used to be packed 'til they opened that R&B lounge down the street. Now you can't pay some of these niggers to sit and listen to some real blues.

JOHNNY B.: What Sleepy been doing?

ELIZABETH: He work part-time at the dockyard. Him and Retha stay with us.

JOHNNY B.: I come back home to find out who raped Babycake and to get my money, eight thousand dollars.

ELIZABETH: (*Shocked.*) What on earth are you talking about Johnny B.? What money?

RED DOG: (*Stunned, sits. He needs a beer to take what he just heard.*) Give me a Falstaff, Elizabeth. Put it on my tab.

JOHNNY B.: I been sending my money to Babycake. She been keeping my money for me.

ELIZABETH: Babycake? Lord, Johnny B.

JOHNNY B.: That was money I saved from them three records I cut for RCA and cash I made on the road.

RED DOG: Johnny, I got that one you made last year call "Happy Feet Boogie." Hell, they still playing it over at Rusty's. But as far as Babycake, that girl died po' as a church mouse. Maybe that money in the river with her.

ELIZABETH: Johnny B., you been sending that girl money all these years?

RED DOG: Hell, you coulda been sending that money to your mama.

ELIZABETH: Naw, 'cause when Johnny B. was talking about running away, I told him I don't want nothing from him but to come back home. I want him and Johnny to sit down and talk, and smile at each other, and hold each other like a father and son supposed to.

RED DOG: I'd sho' like to see that day. See Johnny come hug Johnny B. Johnny B., what you make off them other two songs? The "Dance Hall Blues" and the other one . . . ?

JOHNNY B.: "Rocking Rhythm." They paid me cash for them songs.

RED DOG: Cash?

JOHNNY B.: Yessir.

RED DOG: You sign a contract?

ELIZABETH: Red, this ain't no time to be talking 'bout no contract. He just got home.

JOHNNY B.: I got some lawyer to read the contract for me, then I signed.

ELIZABETH: You want something to drink, Johnny B.?

RED DOG: You asked them what the contract say?

ELIZABETH: Red, I told you Johnny B. don't need to be thinking about all that stuff. He just shoulda got his schooling first, that's all.

RED DOG: Boy, they be playing your records all over Texas. I got a cousin up in College Station say they can't put 'em in the store fast enough. You better forget about Babycake and get on the road and make some more money.

JOHNNY B.: Sorry Red Dog, no man can forget about somebody like Babycake. I done had women in rows of cars following me from one state to the next. Some run out of gas and catch a bus. Some leave they husbands behind. None of them like Babycake. I don't even look at them.

ELIZABETH: Maybe you shoulda put your money in a bank?

JOHNNY B.: I ain't never stayed in one place long enough, Mama. For seven years, I been living on the road, town to town, dance hall to dance hall, motel to motel.

RED DOG: I say that girl put a hex on you. You need to see Rev. Crowley, get that hex off you and get back on the road.

JOHNNY B.: She ain't put no hex on me. (*Reflecting back.*) She helped me. After school, I would sneak away from Daddy, go down to the train station, play my guitar for people coming a going. Babycake would meet me down there. I would sit on an old tomato crate, play my music. Babycake would put her daddy's old hat on the sidewalk, and people would pitch pennies and nickels in there. I told her to keep my money for me. I was gone save it to buy me a electric guitar, like T-Bone Walker, Bo Diddley, and Chuck Berry. That's who I always wanted to be like. They got white people now buying they records. T-Bone took the blues from that Texas hollering, wailing back-alley sound, put a rhythm section to it, and now you got Pat Boone, Elvis Presley covering their songs.

ELIZABETH: That's enough, Johnny B., let's talk about something else.

RED DOG: Your daddy hear you say that, you'll be in that river with Babycake.

JOHNNY B.: Red Dog, you know it's true. This here is 1955. Country blues came to the city with Negroes coming out of Mississippi. Work gangs and plantations outta Texas prison farms. You got a new Negro out here now. I been out there, they wanna dance. I couldn't make it out there these seven years hollering no blues, you know that.

RED DOG: I smell trouble in your words.

ELIZABETH: Then let's talk about something else.

RED DOG: Elizabeth, let the man talk about where he been.

JOHNNY B.: I hopped a train, didn't care where it was going, as long as it left Port Arthur. Long as it put miles between me and my daddy.

ELIZABETH: Don't talk like that, Johnny B.

RED DOG: Where that train stopped?

JOHNNY B.: Went up through Lake Charles, Baton Rouge, crossed into Mississippi. I got off at Tugaloosa, slept in the bus station, made some change singing some country blues. A few people stopped and threw in some nickels, then some woman ask me to play some T-Bone Walker. The minute I started, people started dancing and shouting. I looked down in my hat and had twenty dollars. I got me a coke, a chili dog, and got on a bus ride to Atlanta. Got off at that bus station, started playing. This time dancing. Made me forty dollars.

RED DOG: Forty dollars!

JOHNNY B.: Got me a room, started playing at different clubs, made me one hundred dollars.

ELIZABETH: You sure you ain't hungry, Johnny B.?

RED DOG: Elizabeth, the man know if he hungry or not.

JOHNNY B.: Then I had to get out of Atlanta, fast.

RED DOG: Why? What happened?

JOHNNY B.: People found out Johnny A. was my daddy.

ELIZABETH: Johnny is your daddy.

JOHNNY B.: Club owner wanted me to sing one of daddy's song. I told him I don't sing no back-alley blues.

RED DOG: What he do?

JOHNNY B.: He ain't do nothing. I left the stage, walked right out the door, left one hundred people sitting there.

RED DOG: 'Cause the man asked you to sing one of your daddy's songs?

JOHNNY B.: I ain't Johnny A., I'm Johnny B.

RED DOG: Well, how you find out about Babycake?

JOHNNY B.: I was in Chicago. I opened for Chuck Berry at the Royal Theater. In the middle of my song, she called my name, Mama. She say she gone come take me to heaven with her.

RED DOG: When she called your name? When?

JOHNNY B.: Two days ago, Monday 'round 7:30, in the evening. She called my name, Mama.

RED DOG: Yea, that's when she jumped off, 7:30, but I know you ain't left a money gig 'cause you thought some woman called your name?

ELIZABETH: Johnny B., you just need some rest. You thought you heard something.

JOHNNY B.: Somebody got my money.

RED DOG: Any colored person walking around Port Arthur, Texas, with eight thousand dollars gone talk. It's colored folks nature to walk 'round, bragging about money, even if they ain't got shit in they pocket.

(DUCE *enters.* DUCE'*s speech is slow to the point of irritation sometimes.* DUCE *has a wonderful crop of gray hair, and he wears his age and spirit gracefully in his smile and the possibility of opportunity in his step.*)

DUCE: Damn! I thought Sleepy was lying. Johnny B. (*Shakes his hand.*) Come back here with a conk. You got a agent?

JOHNNY B.: How you doing, Mr. Duncan? No, I ain't got no agent.

DUCE: Damn! Don't even seem like seven years. You done got taller, boy.

RED DOG: Wudn't too long ago the little nigger was playing barefoot out in my front yard.

ELIZABETH: Johnny B. always wore shoes, Red Dog, now.

RED DOG: Nigger wearing alligators now! I bet his feet don't know how to act in them alligators.

DUCE: I just left the Barbecue Dog House over on Sally Street. They was playing your record.

JOHNNY B.: Mr. Lincoln still got the Dog House?

RED DOG: Yea, I just told him my cousin in College Station say they got people lined up to buy your records.

DUCE: Where you drove from, Chicago?

JOHNNY B.: Yessir.

DUCE: I thought that's where you been. Hell, I might just pack up and leave here with you. Every blues singer I know done gone up there. Howlin' Wolf, Muddy Waters . . .

RED DOG: You ain't going nowhere, Duce. You gone be buried right here in Port Arthur with me and Johnny A.

DUCE: You know where I'm going, Red Dog. I can play with Johnny B. It ain't nothing but the blues with a beat.

RED DOG: You ain't going nowhere. You seen Johnny B.'s Cadillac?

DUCE: Yea, I saw it. Sleepy stopped by in that red Cadillac, with Retha on top the hood, waving and grinning, talking 'bout it's his.

RED DOG: Boy ought to be rich by now, but messed 'round and mailed his money to Babycake.

DUCE: You talking about that witch girl jumped off Lovers' Bridge?

JOHNNY B.: She wasn't no witch!

ELIZABETH: I keep telling yawl that. It wasn't nothing wrong with that girl.

DUCE: How much you send that girl?

JOHNNY B.: Eight thousand dollars.

DUCE: Eight thousand? Damn Johnny, you been on dope?

RED DOG: Shit. I say she hexed him.

JOHNNY B.: She ain't hexed me.

DUCE: The police ain't found nothing in that house.

ELIZABETH: Johnny B. shoulda put that money in a bank.

DUCE: That's all you made, Johnny, since you been gone, eight thousand dollars?

ELIZABETH: So what, Duce? That's what he made. Gone in the house, Johnny B.

DUCE: You done cut three records. You came out with "Happy Feet" last year, and they had a line wrapped around the drugstore on Washington Street.

RED DOG: What kind of contract you got for them records?

ELIZABETH: That's his business. Now, why don't yawl get ready for practice? Come on Johnny B.

DUCE: I hope you ain't signed one of them contracts where you don't get no royalties. Did you Johnny B.?

JOHNNY B.: I ain't come here to talk about my contracts.

DUCE: Where is it? Let me see it.

JOHNNY B.: It's in my car.

DUCE: Well, when Sleepy get back here, let me see your contract.

RED DOG: That's if Sleepy get back. He liable to be somewhere near San Antonio in your car, with Retha on the hood.

DUCE: Johnny B. get your guitar out.

ELIZABETH: Naw, Johnny B. tired.

DUCE: He ain't too tired to play with us. I changed the nigger's diapers.

RED DOG: (*Irritated.*) Duce, where Johnny? We got to practice.

DUCE: I cut his hair, he left. I don't know where he is. Come on Johnny B.

ELIZABETH: I got some dirty rice and some boudain in there, Johnny B.

JOHNNY B.: I ain't hungry, mama.

DUCE: You too big time to play with us?

JOHNNY B.: Naw, I ain't never felt that way.

RED DOG: Johnny A. ought to come on. I got things to do.

(DUCE *pulls his harmonica out the case.*)

DUCE: Yea, big-time Johnny B. too big for us Port Arthur niggers.

RED DOG: Johnny A. always late.

ELIZABETH: He shoulda been here.

(DUCE *begins to play some down-home country blues tune.* RED DOG *gets his guitar and joins him.* JOHNNY B. *sits at the table.*)

ELIZABETH: You look tired, Johnny.

DUCE: Yea, he done rub elbows with them big-time record producers, been all up at the Apollo.

RED DOG: *Billboard* magazine.

(*JOHNNY B. gets his guitar from the case. DUCE begins to sing the blues tune. JOHNNY B. comes in strong with his blues chords, showing his ability to still play country blues the way his father taught him. We see that he never lost his touch. ELIZABETH listens, and although she enjoys his playing, there is still tension in her behavior. She looks toward the door during the song, anticipating JOHNNY A.'s entrance. One minute into the slow country blues, JOHNNY B. suddenly changes tempo and plays one of his recorded rhythm-and-blues tunes. RED DOG and DUCE look on, then DUCE joins in. RED DOG refuses to accompany. JOHNNY B. begins to dance on top of the table, benches, and chairs, with Chuck Berry's style of head-popping, body-twisting, knee-jerking moves. ELIZABETH enjoys this and begins to clap her hands. RED DOG looks on somberly. RETHA and SLEEPY enter and immediately begin to dance separately, then together. SLEEPY then grabs ELIZABETH and pulls her onto the dance floor, forcing her to dance.*)

ELIZABETH: (*Laughing.*) Stop Sleepy.

(*RETHA steps on the bar stool, gets on top of the bar and dances. She flicks her dress, and we get a better view of the brace on her leg. Her dancing also gives us a picture of her strength and her independence from all of those around her. JOHNNY A. enters. No one sees him but RED DOG, then SLEEPY, who stops dancing, with a look of guilt. JOHNNY A. stops at the door, his look is hateful and threatening.*)

SLEEPY: Hey Daddy, look who's here. Johnny B. here. He come home.

(*The music stops awkwardly. JOHNNY A. looks away from Johnny B., totally ignoring him. Retha remains standing on top of the bar. There is a nervous moment of tensed silence.*)

DUCE: He was playing that record he made, "Rocking Rhythm."

(*JOHNNY A. walks past JOHNNY B. to the bar.*)

SLEEPY: That's Johnny B. Cadillac out there. Got AM radio on it, too.

(*The tense silence still dominates the moment.*)

ELIZABETH: (*Nervously.*) He's here. Johnny B.'s come home.

JOHNNY A.: (*At the bar.*) Give me a Falstaff.

(*ELIZABETH gets it. JOHNNY B. remains standing like an unwanted bastard child, his guitar hung over his shoulder with his strap.*)

DUCE: He can still play the blues, Johnny A. He can still play.

JOHNNY A.: (*About to drink the beer.*) Get down from there, Retha.

SLEEPY: (*He gets her down.*) Retha, where your manners?

ELIZABETH: (*Trying to heal the tension.*) Johnny A., he's here.

(*JOHNNY A. turns the can of beer upside down and finishes it in one gulp, then slams the can on the bar.*)

DUCE: Hey, maybe Johnny B. can come with us tonight. He'll pack the place.

(*JOHNNY A. walks over to the stage.*)

JOHNNY A.: Motherfucker, are you gone practice or not? (*DUCE and RED DOG are frightened by JOHNNY A.'s shouting. DUCE gets his harmonica out again. RED DOG, with his guitar, sits on the stool. ELIZABETH looks on at JOHNNY B., who is frozen, looking lost, confused.*) Let's go over "Hoochie Coochie Blues."

(*They begin to play. JOHNNY B. walks slowly out the door. Lights fade as the blues tune plays. Others look at JOHNNY B. as he exits. FADE TO BLACK.*)

Scene 2

(*Later that night, the café is closed. JOHNNY A., DUCE, and RED DOG have returned from the Beaumont gig. They enter looking exhausted, laughing. They are all a little tipsy.*)

JOHNNY A.: (*All three laughing.*) You shouldna been driving that fast, Red Dog. You know how those redneck cops be. Wonder we ain't in jail.

RED DOG: I wudn't going no faster than thirty-five. You know that that old Studebaker couldn't do fifty when I bought it.

DUCE: (*Laughing hard.*) What you tell that cracker, Johnny? What you tell him when he stopped us?

RED DOG: Give me a beer Johnny A.

DUCE: What you tell him? (*Mimicking Johnny.*) Ah yessir, Mr. Police Officer, you see, we seen a car chasing us, the driver ain't had no head. He chased us from Beaumont to Port Arthur. That's why we was driving so fast. What that cracker do, Johnny? (*Laughs.*)

JOHNNY A.: He just looked at me, turned around got in his car. Guess he say if a nigger tell that type of story, they liable to carry guns.

RED DOG: Give me a beer, Johnny.

JOHNNY A.: That will be twenty cents, twenty-five with a cup.

RED DOG: Twenty cents! You supposed to pay me and Duce five dollars apiece tonight. You jump up with four dollars each 'cause half the people walked out.

DUCE: They walked out 'cause the man stood up and asked you if you could bring Johnny B. with you next trip, and you cussed him out.

JOHNNY A.: Yea, I cussed him out. If he want Johnny B., he right down there in Port Arthur.

DUCE: We kept playing Blind Lemon Jefferson's songs. That's why some of them walked out. They wanted some dance music, too.

JOHNNY A.: I ain't playing that Chuck Berry, Pat Boone watered-down shit. We play the blues, that's it.

DUCE: We saying we ought to mix it up a little, play some down-home with some of this new R&B.

JOHNNY A.: I tell you what, you go down to Rusty's, three blocks down from here, and play that fucking R&B. He got a jukebox and a band.

(RED DOG stubbornly goes into his pocket, pitches a quarter to JOHNNY A.)

RED DOG: Hell, Johnny, if you could get away with it, you'd have a lemonade stand at the gates of hell, charging niggers a dollar a glass.

JOHNNY A.: It'd be one dollar fifty, sugar done gone up. (All laugh.)

DUCE: You see them two women in the corner looking 'tween my legs when I started rolling with my harmonica? (He plays a note and does a pelvic roll.)

RED DOG: I saw 'em.

DUCE: One stuck her tongue out at me. I stuck mine back.

RED DOG: I saw that, too.

DUCE: Woman had the longest goddamned tongue I ever seen.

JOHNNY A.: Long as Southern Pacific.

RED DOG: You seen it too, Johnny?

JOHNNY A.: I saw it.

DUCE: Now, I could do something with a tongue like that.

RED DOG: Yea, both they eyes locked 'tween your legs, Duce.

DUCE: And smelling good.

RED DOG: Yea, they was smelling real good.

DUCE: I was trying to figure out why yawl wudn't checking 'em out. Yawl look the other way.

JOHNNY A.: 'Cause them was two men.

DUCE: Two men?!

RED DOG: That was Sugar Tank and Cherry Bottom.

JOHNNY A.: Yea, you was singing and blowing. (All laugh, DUCE looks dejected.)

DUCE: Don't tell me them was two men.

(JOHNNY A. *plays the song they were singing.* DUCE *laughs.* ELIZABETH *enters, the music stops.*)

ELIZABETH: Johnny, that boy is laying cramped up in the backseat of his car. Me and Sleepy been trying to get him to come in the house ever since yawl left here.

JOHNNY A.: Let him sleep in his car. Me and Duce done slept in cars, pickup trucks, and bus stations, 'cause it wudn't no colored hotels.

ELIZABETH: He's your son, Johnny.

JOHNNY A.: Did I tell him to sleep in his car? He drive up here in a Cadillac, seven years later, and he can't afford a cheap room. Lola Andres got rooms four dollars a night.

ELIZABETH: I know she got rooms. But he ain't got no money. He spent it all on gas driving here.

JOHNNY A.: You hear that, Red Dog? (*Laughs.*) The great Johnny B. Goode ain't got no money. The one that *Billboard* magazine say gone be the next T-Bone Walker. *Billboard* ain't said shit about Johnny A. Goode, did they, Red Dog? Ain't said nothing bout Johnny A. and the Blues Masters, baddest niggers to come outta New Orleans.

RED DOG: I didn't see nothing they say.

JOHNNY A.: But they interviewed Johnny B. and he ain't say a mumbling word 'bout who taught him.

RED DOG: You right about that.

JOHNNY A.: What you say 'bout that, Duce?

DUCE: I say he'd been good for our band. Putting you two together, hell we could clean up in every town in Texas.

JOHNNY A.: Is that what you say?

DUCE: The boy is good, Johnny.

JOHNNY A.: How do you feel about that, Red Dog?

RED DOG: Don't make no difference. I just wanna play.

JOHNNY A.: (*To* ELIZABETH.) How many newspaper articles you done collected on Johnny B.?

ELIZABETH: It's a dresser full, Johnny.

JOHNNY A.: How many them newspaper articles mention my name? (*She doesn't answer.*) I asked you a question. Any of them newspaper articles mention my name?

ELIZABETH: Just one or two, Johnny.

JOHNNY A.: (*Goes to guitar, holds it up.*) What name is this here on this guitar? And why you think I carry it on here?

RED DOG: Amos "Bad Boy" Goode, your daddy. Baddest blues singer to come outta Mississippi. He could play a banjo behind his head. People talking 'bout Chuck Berry. Shiiit. Chuck Berry ain't got shit on Bad Boy.

DUCE: What year was that?

RED DOG: Had to be around 1901. My uncle came to New Orleans from Mississippi. That's who taught me how to play guitar, Uncle Buddy. My daddy died when I was ten.

DUCE: Your uncle was twenty-one, Red Dog. You was living on Bay Street when Johnny A. moved from Mississippi in a rent house behind us. And you and your uncle, moved on Dyress Street next to the whore-house. I came up from Mississippi a year after you and Johnny A. come up here.

JOHNNY A.: Yawl talking about a whorehouse, and I'm trying to get Lizzy to see something. Why you think I been carrying my daddy's name on this guitar for forty years?

ELIZABETH: Everybody know why you carry your daddy's name on your guitar, Johnny. Everybody know that.

DUCE: 'Cause he took care of your ass, like mine did. You ain't never went hungry. Taught you the blues tongue. How to look at something that hurting your insides and make a song come of it.

JOHNNY A.: What I do when we formed the Blues Masters in thirty-one, in New Orleans and made that money on the road?

DUCE: You bought your daddy a big tombstone, put his banjo in the casket with him.

JOHNNY A.: When that white man killed my daddy over his songs, what happened?

DUCE: Had so many folks at the funeral, had to stand two hours in line to see his body. Big Mama Thornton, Lightnin' Hopkins, everybody was there. You told the folk at the funeral, you was gone pass the blues to little Johnny B. Just like your daddy passed it to you.

JOHNNY A.: Tell Johnny B. bring his ass here.

ELIZABETH: What you gone to do, Johnny A.? That boy ain't no child no more.

JOHNNY A.: You still in my face talking? I don't see that door opening. (ELIZABETH leaves.)

DUCE: Johnny A., you sixty-five years old. Johnny B. done got strong now. And I ain't in no shape to be pulling his ass off you.

JOHNNY A.: The day I let my son whip my ass, then he can have my house.

(JOHNNY B. *walks in with his guitar.* ELIZABETH *is beside him as if to protect him.*) Move back, Lizzy.

ELIZABETH: What you gone do, Johnny?

JOHNNY A.: Move back. (*She moves.*)

JOHNNY B.: I ain't no boy no more, Daddy. I ain't taking no licks from you. I'm twenty, I be twenty-one in January.

JOHNNY A.: How long you been gone?

JOHNNY B.: Seven years.

JOHNNY A.: Jump up one morning after I told you, you ain't playing no electric guitar in my house and walked out the door. I tried to call you back, you just kept walking, your mama sitting there crying.

JOHNNY B.: You know why I left.

JOHNNY A.: You left 'cause you hardheaded.

ELIZABETH: It's getting late, Johnny A., we can talk about this in the morning.

JOHNNY A.: Naw, we gone talk about this now. Why you just kept walking?

JOHNNY B.: 'Cause I was tired of you trying to make me what you failed to be.

JOHNNY A.: Boy, I ain't no failure. I ain't never been no failure. Where in the hell you get this shit about me being a failure? You hear this nigger, Duce?

DUCE: I hear him.

JOHNNY A.: A failure. You hear him, Elizabeth? He came back here with a conk and a red Cadillac, talking 'bout I'm a failure.

ELIZABETH: He didn't mean that. Tell him you didn't mean that, Johnny B.

JOHNNY B.: You tried to make me play what you wanted. Negro music is changing. This ain't the 1930s. People want dance music. They want rhythm and blues, rock and roll.

JOHNNY A.: Nigger, you said I was a failure. I heard those words come out your mouth. Did you hear 'em, Red Dog?

RED DOG: Sho' as I'm sitting here.

JOHNNY B.: I wanted to play my own music. Write my own music.

JOHNNY A.: Naw, you gone answer my question.

JOHNNY B.: If you don't want me to stay, I'll—

JOHNNY A.: (*Cuts him off.*) A man that can take what God gave him and make a living ain't no failure. God gave me a daddy that cared about his son. I ain't jumped up and left him after he taught me. I took what he passed to me—how to look at a woman's teardrops and pull out a song.

How to find notes on a guitar, and a holler from your throat that white folks can't put on a music sheet. I been making a living since I was thirteen years old. I done played with them all—Papa Charlie Jackson, Ida Mae Mack—they been on this floor.

RED DOG: John Lee Hooker.

JOHNNY A.: Gatemouth Brown.

DUCE: That ain't no lie.

JOHNNY A.: Everybody knew my daddy. They wouldn't pass through Mississippi without stopping by our house. Nobody got too big for they britches. I sat on Blind Lemon Jefferson's lap. Memphis Slim done ate at our table. B. B. King was born up the road in Indianola, Mississippi. He stopped by here three weeks ago to see me. You think he stopped by to see a failure?

JOHNNY B.: B. B. King changing, too. He playing up-tempo blues with a beat. He got horns and everything.

JOHNNY A.: Give me another beer, Lizzy. I don't care about the nigger playing R&B. You ain't no B. B. King, you Johnny B.

RED DOG: Give me one, too. (ELIZABETH *gets a beer for each of them.*)

JOHNNY A.: Twenty cents, Red Dog. You think you'd have that Cadillac out there, them alligator shoes, them clothes hanging off your black ass if your daddy was a failure? (RED DOG *pays* ELIZABETH.)

JOHNNY B.: (*Low.*) No sir.

JOHNNY A.: (*He guzzles the beer down.*) Speak up, boy I can't hear you.

JOHNNY B.: (*Louder.*) I said no sir.

JOHNNY A.: Why ain't you at T-Bone Walker house? He saw you and filled your goddamn head when you was a little boy. (*He tries to catch his breath.*)

ELIZABETH: Johnny, look at you, trying to breathe. You need to gone in the house.

RED DOG: She's right, Johnny.

JOHNNY B.: T-Bone ain't filled my head.

JOHNNY A.: Let me ask you a question: You think you big-time? You think you can whip my ass?

JOHNNY B.: I ain't come home to fight you, or see you. I came home to find my money.

JOHNNY A.: What money you talking 'bout? Lizzy, what this boy talking 'bout?

ELIZABETH: You ain't told him Duce?

DUCE: I told Red Dog to tell him.

RED DOG: Johnny was hotter than a dry radiator this evening. I wudn't gone tell him till he cool off.

ELIZABETH: (*Reluctantly.*) Johnny been sending money to Babycake.

JOHNNY A.: Babycake!

DUCE: Eight thousand dollars the way he tell it.

JOHNNY A.: Eight thousand dollars!

(*JOHNNY A. laughs as they talk.*)

RED DOG: I'm telling you that gull mind went bad. She went killed herself. Ain't no telling who got it.

ELIZABETH: Wudn't nothing wrong with her mind.

DUCE: Rev. Crowley tried to get that girl to come out. Had a choir on her porch one time, trying to sing her outta there. She ain't budge.

RED DOG: Even had the police checking up on her. That was before she got raped.

JOHNNY A.: (*Laughing.*) You been mailing cash in the mail to that gull?

JOHNNY B.: (*Distrustfully.*) She was the only one I could trust.

JOHNNY A.: (*Laughs.*) Eight thousand dollars?

RED DOG: A couple folks say she turned a witch after seven years locked up in that house.

ELIZABETH: That's voodoo talk.

DUCE: People from the church paid her utility bills.

RED DOG: Was she a virgin? Probably went mad in that house. Was she a virgin?

ELIZABETH: What's that got to do with it?

(*JOHNNY A. continues laughing, rubbing it in.*)

RED DOG: Hell, I was scared to go 'round there. Ain't no telling how she look.

JOHNNY A.: (*Laughing hard.*) Lizzy, give me another beer.

DUCE: Give me one, too, Lizzy. (*She gets beer.*)

JOHNNY A.: (*Laughs as he speaks.*) That's be twenty cents, twenty-five with a cup. You mean you been mailing cash through the mail for seven goddamn years?

RED DOG: Sam Porter that delivered the mail been saying he used to see her sitting up there, crying and carrying on. She had a hole in the door where he pushed the mail through. Sam Porter fall out if he knew what was in that mail.

DUCE: That girl mind was bound to go mad. Shut herself up in that house for seven years, waiting for Johnny B. How old was she when her daddy killed himself?

JOHNNY B.: She was eight. She ain't deserved to be raped. She ain't bothered nobody.

ELIZABETH: She was just a child.

RED DOG: Her daddy stood up over at Good Spirit Catholic Church one Easter morning and slit his throat with a seven-inch butcher knife.

DUCE: Said it was for the blood of the lamb.

JOHNNY A.: Johnny B. always been hardheaded. I told you to stay away from that gull. But you still snuck 'round there. Them people came from deep in them Louisiana swamps, living on the Atchafalaya. Probably put a spell on you, I told you. (Laughs.) I told him.

DUCE: Her mama ain't had all God promised, either. She looked like a witch.

ELIZABETH: She was depressed over her husband's death.

DUCE: You mean, if Johnny A. go and kill himself, you gone put your wedding dress on, pour kerosene on you, and burn yourself up in front of the church?

RED DOG: I say all of 'em witches.

JOHNNY A.: None of this wudna happened if you wudna run away from home.

JOHNNY B.: I didn't run away, I walked. And when I find out who raped her and who got my money, Im'ma keep on walking.

JOHNNY A.: You can walk now. Ain't nobody holding your feet, fool.

ELIZABETH: You left one time too soon. You ain't doing it again, Johnny B. We gone be a family while you here.

JOHNNY B.: I ain't no fool.

JOHNNY A.: Jumped up and sent eight thousand dollars cash in the mail. Probably ain't got nothing for them songs. Is that what you did? Is that what you did, signed away your songs?

JOHNNY B.: They paid me. That's all that counts.

JOHNNY A.: If you'd listen to me, you wudna come back here with nothing but a Cadillac and a conk. Don't own nothing. What you own, Johnny B.?

DUCE: What kind of contract you sign for them three songs?

JOHNNY B.: I don't know. I had them read it to me before I signed.

(JOHNNY A. laughs.)

RED DOG: You understand what you was signing?

JOHNNY B.: I'm tired. Im'ma go back and get in the car.

ELIZABETH: Johnny, you ain't sleeping in no car. You sleeping in the house tonight.

JOHNNY A.: Eight thousand dollars. (*Laughing.*)

DUCE: You gone be getting royalties on them songs? (*JOHNNY B. doesn't understand.*) I be damned, Johnny, you supposed to get royalties.

JOHNNY A.: I bet that boy done sold everything he wrote. I bet them record producers be glad to see him walking with his guitar. Sing a song, nigger. Sing into the mike.

ELIZABETH: Come on, Johnny B., I done made a bed for you.

DUCE: You got them contracts with you? You need an agent, boy.

JOHNNY B.: Yea, they in the trunk.

ELIZABETH: It's getting late.

JOHNNY A.: What they pay you for them records you make? Huh? Fifty dollars? A piece of watermelon? They pat you on your black ass? Eight thousand dollars ain't no money for seven years. What you think that boy Elvis Presley making, running around here, acting colored on stage? Millions. Big Boy Crudup wrote all them songs.

RED DOG: "Rock Me Mama."

DUCE: That bad one he wrote in forty-six, "Hey Mama Everything Gonna Be Alright."

JOHNNY A.: Big Boy Crudup had that big shot Lester Melrose managing him. He jumped up and sold his song "That's Alright" to RCA Victor. Elvis Presley messed it up and made millions. Big Boy sitting right now in Mississippi fifty-five years old with his hand out, looking for royalties. It's a hundred niggers like you leaving home with a guitar waiting for some two-bit record company to buy your songs. I ain't gonna never sell my songs. My daddy told me the only race in the world that sell everything they got is the colored race. He say two things you don't sell—your land and your songs. I still got my daddy's land, got a rent house in New Orleans that help pay these bills, and I got my daddy's songs. You don't see Jews and them Dagos selling their songs. I raised you and Sleepy right. Sleepy too stubborn to learn music. He rather chase the girls. Now look at him. Separated, got a daughter he can't tell half what to do. I sit you down when you was ten years old. I say Johnny B., you gone be great one day. I say you got to stick with the real blues. I say, when I get enough money, we start our own label, press our own records. Do what them Jews do, keep it in the family. The colored man got to keep the blues. The blues ain't for sale.

JOHNNY B.: A colored man can't make no living just crying out blues songs. That was in your time. The blues is changing. The blues got a beat to it. They putting horns in the blues—saxophones, trumpets, people snapping they fingers. The tempo done picked up. I ain't the only one singing it. B. B. King, Junior Parker.

JOHNNY A.: That shit they call R&B ain't nothing but nigger buck dancing music.

JOHNNY B.: We can't all sing the same songs. Music supposed to grow. Little Richard ain't singing the blues.

JOHNNY A.: Little Richard! Boy, Little Richard running round here, screaming and hollering like a naked heathen straight outta Africa.

JOHNNY B.: Fats Domino got his own sound . . .

JOHNNY A.: Fuck Fats Domino. Rufus Perryman could play better drunk with broke fingers.

DUCE: He was bad.

JOHNNY B.: I left here to play my music. That's what I'm gone do.

JOHNNY A.: You think them uppity niggers who left the country, went to the city, now they think blues is slave music.

JOHNNY B.: I don't think blues is no slave music. I ain't gone be no slave to no one kinda music. I ain't gone be no slave to you, too. You drove the blues in my life a rusty spike. You hung a guitar around my neck when I was too young to know what it was. It was too heavy to carry. It was heavy. I was carrying the whole weight of the colored race on my shoulders. I was too young to carry all that on my shoulders. You put the blues inside of me too young. I was a child, singing somebody else's pain. I felt old. I was ashamed to smile. I forgot how to laugh because I used all my tears to sing your songs. Everybody got they own song. That's what Chuck Berry told me. He liked my playing. He said I was the youngest and the best guitar player he ever heard play. Said he liked my name, too. He was going to write a song about me one day. I told him I'm named after my daddy, Johnny A. Goode. He say everybody heard of Johnny A. Goode. But I ain't gone be no slave to Johnny A. Goode. Now that's that.

(JOHNNY A. *is moved by this, but contains it. He looks around at everyone and exits.* SLEEPY *enters in his pajamas, drinking a glass of milk and swapping at his skin where mosquitoes have bitten him.*)

SLEEPY: Daddy done cooled down yet?

ELIZABETH: Johnny, you ain't traveled no thousand miles to sleep in no car.

SLEEPY: You sleep in that car and them mosquitoes gone eat you up. Got me itching and I just walked from the house.

ELIZABETH: Make sho' your brother get in the house. (*Walking out.*) I'll leave a plate of food on the stove for you. (*Exits.*)

SLEEPY: (*Pats Johnny B. on the back.*) Johnny B., everything gone be all right. Daddy been carrying that around on his shoulder ever since he took you to that guitar contest in Dallas. Yawl want a beer?

DUCE/RED DOG: (*Eagerly.*) Yea. Yea.

SLEEPY: I saw it coming. T-Bone Walker was one of the judges. When Johnny B. won first place—(*Hands* DUCE *and* RED DOG *beers.*)—T-Bone Walker told Johnny B. right there on stage, looking at Daddy in the eyes . . . he say, "Johnny B., you ain't but ten years old and you three times better than your daddy." You shoulda seen Daddy's eyes turn red like the devil himself. Daddy jumped out his seat and called T-Bone everything except the child of God. Snatched Johnny's little ass off that stage, drove that night from Dallas to Port Arthur.

JOHNNY B.: I cried from Dallas to Port Arthur.

SLEEPY: I was in the backseat hoping you would just keep your mouth shut.

JOHNNY B.: I was scared.

SLEEPY: Daddy ask Johnny what else T-Bone tell him behind stage? What he do that for? 'cause Johnny B. never could lie. What you tell Daddy?

JOHNNY B.: I told him the truth. T-Bone told me, "If you gone make it in the music business, you can't just be playing that old Mississippi gutbucket blues like your daddy do."

SLEEPY: Shit! Daddy stopped the car, turned it around and headed back to Dallas to kick T-Bone Walker's ass. Only thing changed his mind—was he got two tickets for speeding.

RED DOG: He was just trying to steer you right, that's all.

DUCE: Your daddy ain't never got over what happened to your grandpa back in Mississippi.

SLEEPY: Me and Johnny wudn't even born yet when they hung grandpa from that pecan tree in the front yard.

JOHNNY B.: I still know the story.

DUCE: How old was you, Red Dog, when they hung Amos from that pecan tree?

RED DOG: I was 'round twenty-one; that was 1925. Amos the same age as my uncle. You was twenty and Johnny was twenty. Give me another beer, Sleepy.

(*SLEEPY gets another beer.*)

DUCE: Might well make it two since you up.

(*RED DOG and DUCE simultaneously look toward the door, hoping JOHNNY A. doesn't enter.*)

SLEEPY: You want a beer, Johnny?

JOHNNY B.: You know I don't drink.

(*He picks up his guitar and begins to stroke it as DUCE and RED DOG tell the story.*)

RED DOG: Yea, 1900. White folks that ran them lumber camps, riverboats, and railroads start to listen to the colored workers holler and sing the blues. Your grandfather worked in Luther B. Jackson's lumber camp. Then came home, worked the shit outta Johnny A. in the field. Luther Jackson had a manager named John Skitmore. It was your grand-daddy's boss. He heard Amos singing, told him he ought to be recorded. They called them "race records" back then. Amos told him he don't believe in recording his song 'less he own it. Skitmore saw how he could make money off them niggers singing them work songs and blues. He figured he ain't had to pay 'em much. All 'cept Amos Goode. They had four, five big-time record companies down there on the camp, RCA Victor was the biggest one. Skitmore was getting payoffs from RCA Victor, sticking the money in his pockets.

DUCE: They couldn't work down there without some microphone stuck in they face. None of them signed no contracts. Just singing and grinning. Me, Red Dog, and Johnny A. used to sneak down there and listen. That's the day it happened.

RED DOG: Skitmore knew Amos could sing and play the hell out that banjo. He asked him one more time. Amos said no. Skitmore said to Amos, "A old coon, motherfucker like you ought to be glad to make race records to help your race." 'Bout five seconds later, Skitmore was lay-ing out with six teeth and a broken jaw. The cracker nose was hanging off the bone. They put Amos in jail that night. We all went to see him. He told Johnny don't worry. We stayed at Johnny's house. 'Bout two in the morning, we heard a bunch of shooting outside. They had Amos in the back of a truck with a rope around his neck.

RED DOG: They threw that rope 'round a limb on that old pecan tree, told us if we came out the house, they was gone kill us and burn the house down. Them crackers put that rope round your granddaddy's neck. Old Skitmore told him, since the white man own niggers, they own everything a nigger makes. Your granddaddy told Skitmore, "Well, this is one nigger you ain't gone own." And then kept singing his blues. Johnny sat there and watched his daddy die. Watched him sing the blues. Right before old Skitmore's son drove that truck off, your granddaddy told Johnny A. to carry his name. That made Johnny A. strong. That was his last words—"Carry my name. Carry my name." Then he started singing again. Amos just kept singing. Johnny A. wrote his daddy's name on his guitar. Been on there forty years.

(RED DOG *begins to pat his feet.* DUCE *and* SLEEPY *join him.* JOHNNY *brings in the music on his guitar. They play the old blues song that Amos "Bad Boy" Goode sang that night he was hung. The words should tell the story of a brave black man. This song should also capture the essence of the storyline. FADE TO BLACK.*)

ACT TWO

Scene 1

(*Lights rise on* ELIZABETH *combing* RETHA's *hair with a large comb.* RETHA *is sitting in a chair; she has a white baby doll and is combing its hair.*)

RETHA: Awchee!

ELIZABETH: Hold your head still, Retha. I coulda done this, this morning.

RETHA: I couldn't get up. I was sleepy.

ELIZABETH: You supposed to be up. You be up all night listening to your Uncle Johnny B.'s records.

RETHA: Grandmaw Lizzy, why Grandpaw don't like to listen to Uncle Johnny B.'s records?

ELIZABETH: Hold your head still.

RETHA: Huh, Grandmaw Lizzy? Why Grandpaw don't . . . ?

ELIZABETH: That's grown folks business.

RETHA: They don't say good morning or nothing. Awchee!

ELIZABETH: You don't be bothering your uncle 'bout riding in that car.

RETHA: Why Uncle Johnny look so sad?

ELIZABETH: Retha, keep still now.

RETHA: Uncle Johnny let me keep a picture of Babycake.

ELIZABETH: Hold your head up. (*Pauses.*) That's who you was talking to last night?

RETHA: No.

ELIZABETH: Well, who was you talking to?

RETHA: Babycake.

ELIZABETH: She dead, Retha. She can't talk to you.

RETHA: No, she talk to me, Grandmaw Lizzy.

ELIZABETH: That's who you was talking to last night?

RETHA: I was sleep in my bed. She came through the door.

ELIZABETH: Hold your head down.

RETHA: She just smiled at me.

ELIZABETH: I thought you said she talked to you?

(RETHA *anticipates forthcoming instructions and holds her head down.*)

ELIZABETH: Hold your head down.

(ELIZABETH *laughs, then kisses* RETHA *on the forehead.*)

RETHA: I was sleep in my bed, and she came through my door. Then I got up out of my bed, and I walked over to her, just like normal people.

ELIZABETH: You are normal.

RETHA: (*Sings "Patty Cake" song to her doll as Elizabeth combs her hair.*) Patty cake, patty cake, bake a man; roll 'em, roll 'em, and put 'em in a pan. Grandmaw Lizzy, my daddy say Grandpaw didn't like Uncle Johnny B. running away from home. He say he mad 'cause Johnny B. don't like to sing the blues. I don't like no blues. I like what Elvis Presley sing. He cute.

ELIZABETH: Elvis Presley ain't thinking 'bout you, Retha. Marry you a colored man.

RETHA: Elvis Presley be on television. Why Uncle Johnny B. don't be on television?

ELIZABETH: He will one day.

RETHA: When I get big, I'm gone marry Elvis Presley. He . . .

ELIZABETH: Hold your head still.

RETHA: He . . . (*Stands and struts across the floor, her hands on her hips, walking a sexy walk, flipping her imaginary long hair to one shoulder.* ELIZABETH *laughs.* SLEEPY *walks in on them, wearing long rubber boots and an old hat.* RETHA *doesn't see him.*) . . . Elvis gone see me walking down the screet (*Pronounces street "screet."*) and he gone say . . .

SLEEPY: (*Playfully, mimics Elvis's voice.*) What's your name, little mama?

RETHA: My name Retha. Retha C. Goode.

SLEEPY: (*On his knees, proposing in an Elvis voice.*) You want to marry me, Retha C. Goode?

(*Suddenly* RETHA *begins to cry and runs into the comfort of* ELIZABETH'S *arms.*)

ELIZABETH: Retha, now you stop that crying.

RETHA: (*Crying.*) He gone look at my leg! Elvis Presley gone look at my leg.

SLEEPY: He ain't gone look at your leg. I kick his ass if he do.

RETHA: (*Crying.*) He gone look at my leg.

ELIZABETH: Stop that crying now.

SLEEPY: You ain't gonna have to wear that when you meet him; now, here. (*Goes in pocket.*) Here's a dollar. Go down to Butch's, get you a corn sucker or a lollipop.

(RETHA *stands with a wide smile, snatches the dollar and exits.*)

ELIZABETH: I told you 'bout telling Retha that.

SLEEPY: Ain't no harm.

ELIZABETH: It is harm. Retha born with polio. She gone be wearing that brace 'til she die. Stop telling her that.

SLEEPY: She my daughter, Mama.

ELIZABETH: I know she your daughter. And giving her money for them sweets ain't right. That's why she won't eat half her food.

SLEEPY: (*Hugs her, kisses her jaw.*) Ah, Mama.

ELIZABETH: And where are you going this morning with your daddy's boots on?

SLEEPY: Same place half Port Arthur been going all week. Looking for that eight thousand dollars. (*Goes to the window.*) Look at 'em, mama. Got traffic backed up from Main Street to Lover's Bridge. Boats, hound dogs . . . saw a nigger out there with one leg walking with a shovel as a crutch.

ELIZABETH: If Johnny B. wudna gone there and told them newspaper people nothing, you wouldn't have all those people out there digging along the river.

SLEEPY: They just printed what Johnny B. said, Mama. He told them he went to the place where Babycake mighta hid the money. It wudn't there. He say she probably buried it somewhere by the river before she jumped. I believe him. Johnny B. ain't gone lie 'bout nothing like that.

ELIZABETH: I ain't never said he was lying. I just want us to be a family. It ain't no love in our house. Your daddy get up in the morning, eat breakfast, go over to Duce and hang out there all day. He won't even look Johnny in the eyes. You get up, go to work, come home, shower, then you gone. Johnny B. is out all day, asking questions. We ain't sit down at the dinner table once since he come home. Ain't no love.

SLEEPY: Ain't gone be no love, Mama, 'til daddy and Johnny sit down eye to eye. Both of 'em stubborn than a Mississippi jackass under a shade tree.

ELIZABETH: You sit 'em down together. When I try to talk to him about Johnny B., he won't talk.

SLEEPY: Me? Ain't nothing I can do. Daddy jealous of Johnny B. Jealousy is a hard nut to crack. People get killed over jealousy.

ELIZABETH: I don't know if it's jealousy.

SLEEPY: Mama, the man is jealous. He knew Johnny B. was good, but he ain't expect that boy to leave here and make a living so fast. You seen them pictures he showed us last night. He done been places Daddy can't buy his way in. Been at the Apollo, got record companies after him, got a letter from that big producer up in Houston, Don Robey. The boy was fifteen, playing sideman to Big Mama Thornton. (*Hears* JOHNNY A. *entering and immediately changes the subject.*) Mama, I'm gone. Hey, Daddy.

JOHNNY A.: Tell Johnny B. wherever he is, he got one more week in my house.

ELIZABETH: Why, Johnny?

SLEEPY: He probably down at the police station. I tell him. (*Walks toward door.*)

JOHNNY A.: Where you going in my boots?

SLEEPY: Down to the river.

JOHNNY A.: Go take my boots off.

SLEEPY: I was gonna clean 'em.

JOHNNY A.: Go take my boots off.

SLEEPY: Yes sir. (*Exits.* JOHNNY A. *goes to window.*)

JOHNNY A.: Look at them niggers in trucks, on bicycles, walking like they looking for the Holy Land. You know why that is crazy, Lizzy? 'Cause they want something for nothing. You ask them to come to a meeting to put eight thousand dollars in a colored community fund, I bet you wouldn't find a beating soul.

ELIZABETH: I ask you a question. Why, Johnny?

JOHNNY A.: 'Cause it's my house.

ELIZABETH: It's our house.

JOHNNY A.: You ain't never had to work for nothing. My blues made a easy living for you. Duce and Red Dog running late.

ELIZABETH: For forty years, you been busy singing other people's blues, Johnny A. What about mine? Where is my song?

JOHNNY A.: You ain't never been without a roof over your head, Lizzy. You got a freezer full of steaks over at the house. You got a closet full of nice dresses. We own this place. They got women out there ain't got half of what you got. What blues you talking about? What song?

ELIZABETH: All these things don't mean nothing if you're hurting inside, and I been hurting inside ever since the day you hung that guitar around his neck.

JOHNNY A.: My daddy had a rope hung around his neck.

ELIZABETH: You put your past on his shoulders. This place here is your past. Johnny B. don't want to be a part of your past.

JOHNNY A.: You taking sides with that boy?

ELIZABETH: You got to let go of Johnny B. We gone end up burying this café or burying Johnny B. Which one is it gone be?

JOHNNY A.: This ain't my past, this my life. Blues is my life.

ELIZABETH: I'm your wife, Johnny A. Ain't I?

JOHNNY A.: You took sides with him.

ELIZABETH: Look at me! I'm your life. But when you started to lose business from this place, that's when my life didn't mean shit to you anymore.

JOHNNY A.: That ain't true.

ELIZABETH: When you couldn't come face to face with Johnny B. leaving here without carrying your words on his back. Your words were too heavy. He couldn't carry them. He was too young.

JOHNNY A.: All that I asked that boy to do is to stick with me, play what I taught him. The nigger is shame of me.

ELIZABETH: He shame of what you did to him.

JOHNNY A.: I ain't done nothing to him but sit him down and showed him how to sing words that come out of my daddy's mouth. Words that kept a man's mind from breaking on a chain gang, or on some cracker's lumber camp.

ELIZABETH: Johnny B. ain't on somebody's chain gang. He ain't on no lumber camp. That was your daddy. He don't want to sing your daddy's songs. He got his own. When are you going to face that? You ran him away from you, beating him with a ironing cord 'cause he wudn't play the blues your way. He didn't walk away, you ran him away. Because you didn't leave him room in his own heart to hear his music. A child needs room to find his own road. He needs to know where that road will take him. But every time he took off down that road, there you was, standing in the way. I'm glad he ran away.

JOHNNY A.: Don't you stand there and say that.

ELIZABETH: But hear it now, Johnny A. When my mama and daddy died, I ain't had nothing in the world 'cept myself. I didn't like what I saw when I looked in the mirror 'til you came along. You made me see what I was missing in my life, a good man. You came on me like a mountain, covered me up and made me look in the mirror again. Then I like what I saw. Finally, in my life, I liked being a woman, your woman. But when Johnny B. was born, you broke my mirror, and every time me and Johnny B. Goode looked in that mirror, we didn't see ourself. We saw you. Johnny B. Goode ran 'way from your hands choking his life. You want him to sing your daddy's words, but I'm your life, not the past. And if you don't let Johnny B. go, I swear, you ain't got no wife. (*Storms out the café.*)

RED DOG: (*Enters, passing* ELIZABETH *as she exits.*) Hey Elizabeth. (*She doesn't speak, and he senses friction. Tries to liven* JOHNNY A. *up.*) I know I'm late. I got caught in all that traffic. People going crazy thinking they gone find that money. I don't know why they think they can find somebody else's money and keep it.

JOHNNY A.: Where's Duce?

RED DOG: He told me this morning he was gone close his shop early. I guess he still down there.

JOHNNY A.: Red Dog.

RED DOG: Yea?

JOHNNY A.: Why a man jump up and marry a woman for forty years and she walk up and say she gone leave him?

RED DOG: You can't never figure out a woman, Johnny. The more you try to figure one out, the more you get confused. That's why I ain't married today. I ain't got nobody to figure out, but me.

JOHNNY A.: That boy ain't never brought nothing but hell in my life.

RED DOG: What you talking about, Johnny B.?

JOHNNY A.: Now he got Lizzy turned against me.

RED DOG: Lizzy ain't going nowhere.

JOHNNY A.: I ain't gone let him come home and take everything I done built.

RED DOG: Just don't do nothing crazy.

JOHNNY A.: That boy think he big shit now.

RED DOG: We better start on the songs.

JOHNNY A.: Lizzy think he more important than me. Living in my house, eating my food.

RED DOG: Come on, Johnny A.

JOHNNY A.: I'll kill him. I swear to God. I'll kill him with my bare hands.

RED DOG: Johnny A., you need to get ahold of yourself. Talking 'bout killing somebody.

JOHNNY A.: When Duce get here—(*Walking toward the door.*)—tell him don't leave.

RED DOG: Where you going, Johnny A.?

JOHNNY A.: Talk to Lizzy. (*He exits. DUCE enters.*)

DUCE: Where Johnny A.?

RED DOG: You didn't see him? He just ran outta here, saying he going to talk to Elizabeth 'bout Johnny B. He all mad. I hope he don't do nothing stupid.

DUCE: I tell you what. If Johnny don't come to his senses 'bout that boy, I will.

RED DOG: What you talking about?

DUCE: I'm thinking 'bout being his agent.

RED DOG: You crazy.

DUCE: He passed by the shop. I stopped him, asked him to let me see his record contract.

RED DOG: I say you crazy.

DUCE: Crazy, huh? Johnny B. signed with Savoy Records in fifty-two. That three-year contract is up next month.

RED DOG: You don't know nothing about being no agent.

DUCE: I know how to get that boy some shows. Johnny B. signed away a bunch of songs. Ain't gone get doodly squat.

RED DOG: That boy can't half read.

DUCE: You can't either, nigger.

RED DOG: I say you digging your grave.

DUCE: How I'm digging my grave?

RED DOG: You digging your grave.

DUCE: I ain't saying I'm gone stop playing with you and Johnny A. Shit, ain't nothing wrong with wanting to do better. This rhythm and blues stuff ain't going away.

RED DOG: We been together too long for you to pull some shit like this.

DUCE: What shit?

RED DOG: I'm talking about helping Johnny B. Johnny A. ought to see that.

(*JOHNNY B. enters with his guitar hanging over his shoulder.*)

JOHNNY B.: Evening.

DUCE: Hey, Johnny B.

RED DOG: Johnny B., Duce say you gone let him be your agent.

DUCE: I ain't said that boy gone let me be his agent. I said I'm thinking about it.

JOHNNY B.: Sleepy say my daddy looking for me. He said I got one week in his house. Tell him I be moving out tonight.

RED DOG: You leaving, Johnny B.?

JOHNNY B.: I'm selling my Cadillac to Sleepy, and gettin' me a room at Lola Andrews'.

DUCE: Where you going with your guitar?

JOHNNY B.: Going to Rusty's. People want me to play there tonight.

RED DOG: We got to practice, too. Come on, Duce.

DUCE: Shit! I know you gone pack it.

RED DOG: Where is that song list?

DUCE: What Rusty gone pay you over there?

JOHNNY B.: I don't know. I just feel like playing.

DUCE: You want me to play with you? I can play with you.

RED DOG: We got to practice, Duce.

DUCE: Tell me, Johnny B. Why you end up giving your songs away? Ain't nothing in that contract say you gone get royalties. People gone be singing your songs for the next hundred years, and you and your family don't get shit.

JOHNNY B.: Songs don't belong to nobody. Soon as you sing it, the words latch on to somebody and they take that song with them. Soon as you open your mouth, it's gone. I been singing the blues since I was eight years old. The world got enough blues, and the blues don't die. The singers go, but the blues don't die. I left 'cause I wasn't ready to die. So I took what Daddy taught me and made it what I wanted, not what he wanted. When I die, I want people to say, "There go Johnny B. Goode; he helped to take the blues to another level. He found some new notes. He made other people want to sing his songs." I don't care if they white people singing them. Whenever they sing my songs, they carrying my name, and my daddy's name, and his daddy's name. I live forever in my songs. A contract ain't nothing but a piece of paper. A song lives forever.

DUCE: That's the craziest shit I ever heard. Come on, Red Dog.

(*Suddenly,* SLEEPY *enters, carrying* RETHA *who is kicking and screaming.*)

SLEEPY: Retha, you can't go down there.

RETHA: (*Crying.*) Them other children be there!

SLEEPY: You mess round and fall in that river, then what?

RETHA: I can swim.

SLEEPY: Naw, you stay here with Uncle Johnny B., maybe he sing you a song.

RED DOG: We fixing to practice, Sleepy, we ain't got no time for Retha.

RETHA: I want some moon cookies.

SLEEPY: Okay, here a dollar; you go get a bunch of moon cookies.

RETHA: I changed my mind. I don't want no moon cookies, I want some Sugar Babies.

(*As* RETHA *and* SLEEPY *continue this exchange,* JOHNNY B. *takes out his guitar and begins to strum it softly.*)

SLEEPY: Okay, get you some Sugar Babies.

RETHA: And some Bazooka bubble gum.

SLEEPY: Okay, go on now. Where your manners?

RETHA: (*Stomping her foot.*) I want two dollars.

SLEEPY: (*Reaching in his pocket.*) Okay, another dollar.

RETHA: You go get it. It's hot out there.

SLEEPY: Okay. (*Takes the two dollars from her and heads toward the door.*)

DUCE: You can get me a Tootsie Roll or one or two jawbreakers.

RED DOG: (*Irritated.*) Sleepy, you better take Retha with you. We got to practice.

SLEEPY: You can watch this girl 'til I get back. I'm just going to Butch's.

RED DOG: You know how Retha is.

RETHA: (*Sassily.*) You ain't my daddy.

RED DOG: Don't be sassing me.

DUCE: Where your manners, Retha?

(RETHA *cries more.*)

SLEEPY: I'm gone get you a Baby Ruth, too, and some moon cookies. (*Exits.*)

(JOHNNY B. *suddenly begins an R&B tune he wrote;* RED DOG *comes in on the guitar, and* DUCE *joins him with his harmonica.*)

JOHNNY B.:

    There was a pretty little gal
    Down in Tennessee
    Finest little thing
    You ever did see
    I sung her a song
    And then she said to me
    Take me with you
    Take me with you
    Take me with you
    Johnny B.
    There was a brown-eyed woman
    Down Louisiana way
    Had legs so pretty
    They made me rattle and shake
    I sung her a song
    And then she said to me
    Take me with you
    Take me with you
    Take me with you
    Johnny B.

(RETHA *begins to smile and clap to the beat.* SLEEPY *exits.* JOHNNY B. *does a guitar solo. His fingers accelerate to a light speed across the notes effortlessly. He makes each musical note speak words that are from a higher being. Then he begins to dance sensuously, as if in a trance; then he continues the song.*)

JOHNNY B.:

    There was a sexy little mama
    Down in Galveston
    My she was fine
    She was number one
    I sung her a song
    And then she said to me
    Take me with you
    Take me with you
    Take me with you
    Johnny B.

(JOHNNY *ends the song.*)

JOHNNY B.: You like that song?

RETHA: Yea. Can I play your guitar?

JOHNNY B.: Not right now.

(*ELIZABETH and JOHNNY A. enter.*)

ELIZABETH: Retha, looka your dress. Where your daddy?

RETHA: He at Butch's.

DUCE: He went to get her some moon cookies.

JOHNNY A.: She don't need no moon cookies. Retha, you gone back to the house, get yourself cleaned up.

RETHA: I want to go to the river with my daddy.

JOHNNY A.: Get your butt on to the house.

(*RETHA stubbornly gets up, stomping her feet and mumbling to herself.*)

ELIZABETH: And don't turn on that television.

(*RETHA exits.*)

DUCE: Hey Johnny A. Guess what? I'm thinking about managing your boy.

JOHNNY A.: I ain't got time for no foolish talk, Duce.

JOHNNY B.: I'm moving out tonight after I come from Rusty's.

ELIZABETH: You ain't moving nowhere. We talked. You staying with us.

JOHNNY A.: I say good morning to you, that's all yawl gone git.

JOHNNY B.: You ain't got to say good morning to me; you ain't got to say nothing.

JOHNNY A.: It's my house. I can say good morning if I want to.

JOHNNY B.: It's your house. It's my mouth.

JOHNNY A.: Then I ain't gone say shit to you.

ELIZABETH: (*Scolding him.*) Johnny A.

JOHNNY A.: Don't be playing them records in my house.

JOHNNY B.: Retha be playing them songs.

JOHNNY A.: Don't be tying up my phone with them record managers.

JOHNNY B.: That be friends of mine.

JOHNNY A.: Stay outta my shaving cream.

JOHNNY B.: That be Sleepy.

DUCE: Johnny A., I'm telling you, I could . . .

JOHNNY A.: Don't be parking that Cadillac in front the house blocking my view.

JOHNNY B.: I'm selling it to Sleepy.

ELIZABETH: Where Sleepy get the money to buy a car?

JOHNNY A.: Let me ask you something. Why you ain't recorded the blues?

JOHNNY B.: It's 1955, people wanna dance.

JOHNNY A.: Ain't nothing wrong with dancing.

JOHNNY B.: I can't.

JOHNNY A.: Why? You shame of the blues?

JOHNNY B.: I ain't shame of the blues. I'm shame of you.

JOHNNY A.: I ain't ask you 'bout me, I ask you about the blues, nigger. If you shame of me, I don't give a cripple goddamn.

ELIZABETH: Johnny A., that's enough.

JOHNNY A.: You ain't shame to find your way back to this house.

JOHNNY B.: I'm shame of you. I got whips on my back to show it.

JOHNNY A.: You ain't the only one with whips of your back, boy. My daddy used to whip me with a horse rope. You think I ran away from home? You ever see a man hung? Ever see how they eyes bust out, how they piss in they pants? You ever see a man sing his last song before he die? My daddy saw me standing in the window, crying when they put that rope on his neck. I felt that rope around my neck. It left a scar on me, boy. (*Points to neck.*) I got a scar here. Every nigger who done lived long enough gone carry a scar from the white man. But my daddy passed his song to me that night on the back of that truck. My daddy passed his song to me and you shame of the blues, nigger? (*Exits. Moments later,* SLEEPY *enters with a brown bag of moon cookies.*)

SLEEPY: They found her! They found Babycake body in the river! (*Blackout.*)

Scene 2

(*It's two days later after the small funeral for Babycake. The money has not been found.* SLEEPY *has been sick with a fever and vomiting.* JOHNNY B. *has been playing his guitar in the lounge for two days. The lights rise.* JOHNNY B. *is sitting on the stage, playing his guitar. His playing is hard and intense, as if to kill the demons that caused the death of Babycake. We see* JOHNNY A.'s *name on his guitar. His head and body swivel and rock as if possessed by the spirit of Babycake.* ELIZABETH *enters. He does not hear or see her. She is carrying a plate of food.*)

ELIZABETH: (*Cautiously.*) Johnny B. (*He continues to play.*) Johnny B. (*He continues.*) You been here since the funeral two days ago. You ain't ate nothing. I brought you some fried catfish and . . . (*He begins to move as he plays with a sense of rage in his face.*) Come on, eat this food, then get you some sleep.

JOHNNY B.: (*Still playing.*) Maybe Daddy right, huh, Mama?

ELIZABETH: 'Bout what?

JOHNNY B.: Maybe he right. I shouldna run away from home. God punishing me.

ELIZABETH: God ain't punishing you 'cause you ain't done nothing wrong. If it's anything, he's punishing me.

(JOHNNY B. *stops playing;* ELIZABETH *paces the floor.*)

ELIZABETH: (*Continued.*) Maybe I should have done something to raise you and Sleepy better. Maybe you wouldn't run away, and Sleepy would be still at home.

JOHNNY B.: You raised us good, Mama.

ELIZABETH: I let your daddy do too much of the raising, while I was doing the cooking. I figured he's a man, he supposed to raise the boys. Yawl grew up too fast. I couldn't keep up. Before you know it, you was gone and Sleepy was getting married.

JOHNNY B.: You gave up plenty love, Mama.

ELIZABETH: Come on eat now. (*She goes to him, and he embraces her leg.*)

JOHNNY B.: (*Crying.*) Did you see her eyes, Mama?

ELIZABETH: I saw them.

JOHNNY B.: That river was calm, peaceful, like when they found her. Like it knew she was inside it. Holding her for me. It knew I was coming for her, didn't it, Mama? She gone come for me.

ELIZABETH: Come on, eat your food before it get cold.

JOHNNY B.: That money was for us to get married. I was gonna marry her.

ELIZABETH: Oh, my sweet Jesus.

(JOHNNY B. *begins to sing a down-home blues song, sitting down, with his mother near him.*)

JOHNNY B.:

Oh Babycake

Sweet little Babycake

You said you'd wait for me

Seven year I've been gone.

I wrote you letters

And sent you my love

Cause I knew I'd be coming home.

Oh Babycake

Sweet little Babycake

I wanted to marry you

But somebody came along
And hurt you
And now I got the blues.
Oh Babycake
Sweet little Babycake
Now I got the blues

(RETHA *enters, eating a popsicle, interrupting his song.*)

RETHA: My daddy threw up on the divan.

ELIZABETH: Lord have mercy. (*Walking out the door.*) Johnny B., eat your food.

RETHA: Uncle Johnny B., why you been up here all night playing your guitar?

JOHNNY B.: I ain't been too happy, Retha.

RETHA: About Babycake?

JOHNNY B.: Yea.

RETHA: I saw her.

JOHNNY B.: You saw her?

RETHA: Yea.

JOHNNY B.: When?

RETHA: Grandmaw Lizzy didn't believe me.

JOHNNY B.: When did you see her, Retha? Tell me.

RETHA: I got to go to the store. I'll be back! (*Exits running.*)

JOHNNY B.: Retha! Retha!

(DUCE *enters, looking back at* RETHA.)

DUCE: Johnny B., what's wrong?

JOHNNY B.: Retha said she saw Babycake.

DUCE: You give Retha two moon cookies and a corn sucker, she'll say she saw Jesus in a Cadillac.

JOHNNY B.: She might know something.

DUCE: I know something, too. You look bad.

JOHNNY B.: Thanks for coming to the funeral.

DUCE: Yea, it was nice of Rev. Crowley to get that casket for her and bury her next to her mama and daddy.

JOHNNY B.: You see what happened when I came to the casket and touched her face?

DUCE: Wudn't no tears coming out her eyes.

JOHNNY B.: Rev. Crowley saw it.

DUCE: That wudn't no tears come out that girl's eyes, I tell you.

JOHNNY B.: Well, what was it?

DUCE: Li'ble been anything, embalming fluid, no telling. I stopped by the house to see if you was there. Lizzy say Sleepy been puking for two days. Say he ate one of them catfish out the river. He got a fever of a hundred and twenty. Funny, ain't nobody else got sick from them fish.

JOHNNY B.: I can't worry about Sleepy now.

DUCE: You still gone try to see who got your money?

JOHNNY B.: Whoever got it, paying for it.

DUCE : What you gone do now?

JOHNNY B.: Sleepy gone give me some cash to keep my Cadillac 'til I come back. Im'ma catch me the first Greyhound to Chicago.

DUCE: Must gone be play money. Sleepy can't buy a pair of hobo shoes if they on sale.

JOHNNY B.: I'll make some money and come back and get my car.

DUCE: I'm going with you. I'm tired of Port Arthur. Im'ma be your agent.

JOHNNY B.: Naw Duce, no thank you.

DUCE: Boy, you need a good agent. Look at you—got to rent your Cadillac to get back home. You supposed to be getting royalty checks on them songs they play on the radio.

JOHNNY B.: I ain't worried about it.

DUCE: That's right. You don't have to worry. Let me do the worrying, and you do the playing.

JOHNNY B.: I need to make my own decisions.

DUCE: Johnny B., you supposed to be a millionaire. And you ain't gone never be none long as you sell your songs for pocket change.

JOHNNY B.: I don't sing for money I told you.

DUCE: It take money to make shit, Johnny B. You can't buy no food to eat, you can't shit.

JOHNNY B.: Only thing hurt me is I ain't had money to buy her a casket, no flower or nothing.

DUCE: You ain't gone never have none talking like that.

JOHNNY B.: I shoulda took her with me.

DUCE: You shoulda put that money in a bank. A agent coulda showed you how to do it.

(RED DOG *enters laughing, drinking a Coke.*)

RED DOG: Damnest thing I ever saw. I went up there to see myself.

DUCE: See what?

RED DOG: People driving down the street, telling people to go look at the river. I drove up there to see for myself.

DUCE: What's wrong with it?

RED DOG: It done rose five feet and moving like a hurricane done hit it.

DUCE: Red Dog, how the river gone rise, and it ain't no storm?

RED DOG: All I know, it done raised. I seen it with my eyes, and it's running like crazy.

DUCE: Well, they probably done opened some dam upriver.

RED DOG: Ain't no dam open. You go see.

DUCE: I ain't thinking 'bout no river rising. Me and Johnny B. talking 'bout going to Chicago.

RED DOG: Well, ain't never seen nothing like it.

JOHNNY B.: (*To himself.*) It's rising for a reason.

DUCE: You talking 'bout a damn river rising, I'm trying to get a contract signed.

JOHNNY B.: That's Babycake. She talking.

DUCE: Yea, what she saying is you need a agent, and his name is Duce Carter.

JOHNNY B.: Be quiet!

DUCE: Johnny B., get ahold of yourself.

RED DOG: You all right, Johnny B.?

JOHNNY B.: She mad. She trying to tell me something.

RED DOG: Who she mad at?

DUCE: I ain't done her nothing.

JOHNNY B.: That's why the river gone wild.

RED DOG: Shit, I ain't done nothing neither.

(ELIZABETH *and* JOHNNY A. *enter, troubled and tired.* JOHNNY A. *is carrying a tackle box full of money.*)

JOHNNY A.: Here's your money. Your money in this here tackle box.

ELIZABETH: Sleepy had your money, Johnny B. He had it.

DUCE: Sleepy?

ELIZABETH: Retha found it.

JOHNNY A.: Now you got it, you can keep walking now out that door. And don't come back.

ELIZABETH: Sleepy don't know we found it. I took him down to Dr. Moore's office to get his fever checked. I left him and came back to the house.

RED DOG: I be damned.

JOHNNY B.: Where was it?

ELIZABETH: Retha was under the house looking for her old doll. She found it covered under some papers.

JOHNNY A.: You got your money. There's the door, don't come back here, you hear me? (*Slams the box on the counter.* DUCE *walks over, opens the box, counts the money.* JOHNNY A. *exits.*)

JOHNNY B.: He raped Babycake.

RED DOG: You don't know that, Johnny B. He coulda found that money by the river.

JOHNNY B.: I'm going to find him and talk to him. (*Walks toward the door, and* ELIZABETH *crosses in front of him; he stops.*)

ELIZABETH: Johnny B., he at the doctor's office. He sick. Wait 'til he come home.

RED DOG: She right. That be out all in the street if you go there.

(DUCE *is counting the money; he holds up a stack of twenty-dollar bills, then gives the box to* JOHNNY B., *who puts it behind the counter.*)

DUCE: Hell Johnny B., look like you might got seven thousand dollars there.

RED DOG: Sleepy ate that catfish out the river.

DUCE: (*To* JOHNNY B.) What about me being your manager? All I need is a thousand dollars to start off.

JOHNNY B.: Mama, you and Daddy can have the money. Do what you want with it.

DUCE: Elizabeth, all I need is a . . .

(RETHA *enters, her legs up to the waist of her dress are drenched with dirty river water, her shoes muddy.*)

RETHA: Where my daddy?

ELIZABETH: Retha, you been wading in that river?

RETHA: I can swim.

ELIZABETH: Look at your dress. That's your school dress!

JOHNNY B.: Retha, did you know where your daddy got that money from?

RETHA: Naw, I ain't know.

ELIZABETH: Come on, Retha, you soaking wet.

JOHNNY B.: You telling the truth?

RETHA: The day Babycake died, he bought me a television.

RED DOG: That's where he got the money to buy it.

ELIZABETH: Don't be lying on your daddy, Retha.

RED DOG: You making this up?

RETHA: I'm hungry. I want some moon cookies.

JOHNNY B.: You found that money under the house?

DUCE: You tell us the truth. God gone take that brace off your leg.

ELIZABETH: Don't be telling her that!

(RETHA *begins to cry.*)

JOHNNY B.: Did you see your daddy go in that house?

ELIZABETH: She just a child!

RETHA: (*Crying.*) My daddy say they gone take it off!

ELIZABETH: Retha baby, they can't take it off.

DUCE: You ain't getting nothing outta her.

ELIZABETH: You let her alone. That's between Johnny B. and Sleepy. (*She is about to exit with* RETHA *when* JOHNNY A. *bursts through the door, bleeding on the forehead. His clothes are torn, he is shaking.*)

JOHNNY A.: Sleepy got a knife in the house!

ELIZABETH: You're bleeding!

JOHNNY A.: Hell, I know I'm bleeding, woman.

JOHNNY B.: What happened?

JOHNNY A.: Don't be asking me nothing nigger. This is your fault.

DUCE: Yawl was fighting?

JOHNNY A.: I was eating in the kitchen when he come inside the house screaming and hollering about where his money is. I told him I ain't scared of no knife. I slapped him in the face, and that's when he cut me. I tried to get my shotgun. He hit me again. Now, he over there tearing up the house. (*JOHNNY A. suddenly walks behind the bar, grabs a beer bottle, breaks it;* JOHNNY A. *walks toward the door fast,* ELIZABETH *grabs him.*)

ELIZABETH: Johnny! No!

JOHNNY A.: Move back Elizabeth, nobody cuts me and lives!

RED DOG: Johnny get ahold of yourself.

JOHNNY B.: I'll go over there.

RED DOG: You go over there, that boy gone cut you to pieces.

ELIZABETH: You ain't going over there. Now, we gone call the police.

(RETHA *reaches down and begins to tinker with her brace.* SLEEPY *enters with only jeans on, bare feet, no shirt. He is sweating profusely, breathing hard with a wild look on his face. He has a knife and waves it in everyone's direction. He pukes on the floor first, mucus dribbling from his lips.*)

SLEEPY: Where my money?

ELIZABETH: Sleepy, give me that knife.

JOHNNY A.: (*Walks toward* SLEEPY *with the broken beer bottle.*) You want to cut me boy, now let's do some cuttin'.

(ELIZABETH *comforts* RETHA, *who begins to cry.*)

DUCE: Sleepy you done gone mad eating them catfish.

SLEEPY: I don't want to hurt nobody, where my money?

ELIZABETH: Put that knife down Sleepy.

SLEEPY: I ain't playing Mama.

RETHA: You gone hurt us daddy?

DUCE: This is your family.

SLEEPY: Give me my money.

RED DOG: You sick, Sleepy. Look at you sweating.

JOHNNY A.: Look at you. Look how Retha looking at you. You ain't a daddy, 'cause you never was a man.

JOHNNY B.: You raped her.

SLEEPY: (*Moves to* JOHNNY B., *pointing the knife directly in his face.*) You shut your ass up. You shut your ass up, Mr. Big-Time Singer.

JOHNNY B.: How it feel to rape her?

SLEEPY: Give me my money, Johnny B.

ELIZABETH: Sleepy, you got to stop this!

SLEEPY: Stop what? I ain't doing nothing but asking for my money, then I'm gone. Im'ma take Johnny B. Cadillac and Im'ma drive around Port Arthur, then up to Houston, up Dowling Street, buy me some alligator shoes like Johnny B. Daddy always bought Johnny B. good shoes. Had me in hand-me-downs. Always had Johnny B. hair cut. Mine grew down my neck, couldn't see my neck no more. Them twin girls laughing at me, calling me tar baby.

(JOHNNY A. *steps toward* SLEEPY. SLEEPY *points his knife at him.*)

ELIZABETH: That's your father, Sleepy.

JOHNNY A.: Let me tell you something, boy, I ain't scared of no death. Death ain't nothing but a blues singer without a woman, and you ain't got no woman. (*The SOUND OF THUNDER, which only* SLEEPY *hears;* SLEEPY *makes a stab at anything.*) You done lost your mind, boy.

(SLEEPY *hears* THUNDER *again, and drops to his knees trembling.*)

RED DOG: What's wrong with him?

(SLEEPY *holds his stomach.*)

JOHNNY A.: (*Walking toward* SLEEPY, JOHNNY A. *boldly drops the beer bottle and sticks his chest out.*) Here, cut me.

(SLEEPY *makes a swipe at* JOHNNY A., *purposely missing him.*)

ELIZABETH: Get back Johnny!

RETHA: Don't hurt Grandpa, Daddy.

(JOHNNY A. *turns, nonchalantly goes over to the bar, gets a beer.*)

JOHNNY A.: Don't give him a gotdam penny. It ain't his money. Now Im'ma drink this beer, when I finish, I want you gone.

SLEEPY: Where my money?

JOHNNY B.: Retha say she seen her.

SLEEPY: I said shut your ass up! You shoulda took her with you. It's your fault; you shoulda took her.

ELIZABETH: Did you rape that girl, Sleepy?

JOHNNY B.: He raped her.

SLEEPY: How you know, conk-wearing motherfucker? You up in Chicago, driving a Cadillac, making records, living in hotels where they call a nigger Mister. I'm down in Port Arthur, hauling boxes off of ships. You in the house playing the guitar for Daddy's friends. I'm in the field cutting cane. Sun sitting on top my black head. (*Mimicking* JOHNNY A.'*s friends.*) "Play for us, Johnny B. Goode." Daddy pass the blues on to you. What he pass on to me? A shovel and a mule.

JOHNNY A.: (*Gulps down his beer, then walks over to* SLEEPY.) Now you running my patience boy. Now you put down that knife, and you get out of my place and my house.

SLEEPY: It ain't your place no more. Like Mama said, it's dead; like the blues, it's dying. The white folk done buried the blues with they own voices. They singing it, and it ain't never gone be the same no more. They gone make all the money. Now, I got some money.

JOHNNY B.: I got blues songs.

DUCE: Sleepy this is going too far. Now listen to your daddy.

RED DOG: Then give him the money.

SLEEPY: Where my money?

DUCE: It's blood money Sleepy. It's over somebody's blood.

RED DOG: Give him the money and let him go.

ELIZABETH: Give him the money Johnny.

JOHNNY A.: Don't touch that money, I'm going to get my shotgun and give him a shell. I don't mind going to jail.

DUCE: (DUCE *grabs* JOHNNY A.) You can't kill your own boy Johnny A.

ELIZABETH: You been jealous of Johnny B. all these years?

SLEEPY: Where my money?

ELIZABETH: You kept it inside you like a storm. You kept all that hatred locked up inside you. Instead of finding your own dream, you found jealousy. Yea, jealousy is a hard nut to crack. But you had so much in you, it cracked your soul wide open, and now, you ain't got nothing left but hatred.

JOHNNY A.: I tried to get you to learn the guitar, but that mule had more sense than you. You wanted to get between some girl's legs, just like you got between Babycake's.

(*SLEEPY looks upward, hears loud THUNDER.*)

SLEEPY: (*Crying.*) Tell her to stop.

JOHNNY B.: I got blues songs. I mailed 'em to Babycake. Did you see my blues songs, Sleepy?

SLEEPY: I saw them songs. I found them in the house. I burned them up. I burned all ten of them. Now, you ain't got nothing. Ain't got nothing.

JOHNNY B.: (*Points to his head.*) I got 'em here, Sleepy. They up here. All of them. They inside me.

ELIZABETH: (*Shouting.*) Did you rape that girl?

SLEEPY: (*Begins to cry.*) I just wanted to see how she look. I got up one night, walked down there, looked in her yard. Something told me to go in. Something pulled me. I walked up on the porch, knocked on the door. She ain't say nothing. Then I kicked the door. Kicked it in. She was beautiful. Like one of them angels in the Bible. Sitting there waiting. Waiting for you. Had all kind of candles burning. I figured you was sending her something. She ain't never looked at me when I kicked the door down. She was looking out the window, waiting for you to come up the road with your guitar on your back. But you ain't never come. I came. I came up that road, Johnny B. I reached down to touch her for you. She say, "I'm a virgin; I'm waiting for Johnny B. Goode." That's all she say. "I'm a virgin; I'm waiting for Johnny B. Goode." Daddy make me wait in the back room while he show off Johnny B. Goode to his friends. (*Hears THUNDER again.*) Mama waiting for Johnny B. Goode. She just laid down after I hit her. She was beautiful. I pulled up her dress, pulled her panties to the side, she starting screaming. I never seen so much blood, so I tore her panties off. I got on top of her again, she just looked out the window the whole time. Ain't said a word. Waiting for Johnny B. Goode.

ELIZABETH: That's enough. (*She cries.*)

SLEEPY: I got up. I told her I was sorry. She ain't never looked at me. She say, tell Johnny B. Im'ma meet him on the other side. She walked out the door toward the river singing a song. I went through the house, found that money. (*Screams.*) Where my money?

JOHNNY B.: She sing my song, Sleepy. The one Daddy taught me.

SLEEPY: Give me my money!

(*JOHNNY B. sadly sings a blues ballad that JOHNNY A. taught him. JOHNNY A. attempts to resist the fond memory, but it sinks slowly into his iron pride, as he sings. SLEEPY continues to hear THUNDER, jumping from its tension.*)

JOHNNY A.: Don't be singing my song!

ELIZABETH: Come on, Sleepy.

RED DOG: Come to your senses.

JOHNNY B.: That's the song. (*Continues singing, moving melodically toward SLEEPY. SLEEPY senses his threatening movements and backs away from him, pointing the knife. JOHNNY B. moves behind counter, picks up box of money and throws it at SLEEPY. SLEEPY, with knife in one hand, frantically scoops up the money.*)

JOHNNY A.: That ain't the damn key. It ain't the key! (*JOHNNY B. changes the key.*) You done forgot how to sing the blues. Where the drag? Where the drag? (*JOHNNY B. slows it down, still singing as he moves toward SLEEPY, who is scooping up the money wildly.*) You trying to speed up the bridge! (*JOHNNY A. suddenly grabs SLEEPY and wrestles him down to the floor.*) You don't pull no knife on me, nigger! (*They wrestle. RED DOG moves to help. JOHNNY B. jumps in to take the knife.*)

ELIZABETH: Get the knife.

(*All three wrestle. Someone is stabbed. All three remain still at first. JOHNNY A. moves, then SLEEPY. Both get up stunned. The knife is in SLEEPY's hand. ELIZABETH moves from RETHA who remains standing. JOHNNY B. has a stab wound over his heart.*)

ELIZABETH: (*Kneels down to listen to JOHNNY B.'s heart.*) Johnny B.! Johnny B.!

JOHNNY A.: Call an ambulance, and tell them to send the police too. (*DUCE darts out.*)

SLEEPY: (*Standing with the knife.*) I didn't mean it.

JOHNNY A.: Shut up. You did mean it, and you going to jail. You hear me Sleepy. I coulda took that knife from you and cut your heart out. But

I was thinking you was gone come to your senses. I gave you a chance to come to your senses, like I gave you a chance to play the guitar. Now look where you gone end up. In jail. And when you come out of jail, you better find a road that leads you outta Port Arthur, 'cause if I see you, Jesus is my witness, you dead.

RETHA: (RETHA *runs to* SLEEPY, *hugging him. She cries.*) Uncle Johnny gone die.

SLEEPY: I didn't mean it.

(JOHNNY B. *tries to lift his arm, and he attempts to point a finger.* JOHNNY A. *turns to* JOHNNY B., *looks at him sympathetically.* SLEEPY *stands with knife in one hand and the other hand is wrinkled with dollar bills.*)

ELIZABETH: (*Crying and rocking* JOHNNY B.) Don't move Johnny B.

RED DOG: Listen to her Johnny B. (JOHNNY B. *attempts to point again,* RED DOG *sees that he is pointing at his guitar.*)

ELIZABETH: Johnny B. I said don't move. (JOHNNY B. *points, and* RED DOG *gets his guitar.*) He don't need that, lay still.

(DUCE *enters running.*)

DUCE: I got one coming. Hold on Johnny B. . . . hold on.

(RETHA *goes over to* SLEEPY *and stares at him.* RED DOG *shows the guitar to* JOHNNY B. JOHNNY A. *takes the guitar and looks at it.*)

DUCE: Look there it got your name on it Johnny A.

RED DOG: It's on there Johnny A.

(JOHNNY A. *takes the guitar, looks at it then kneels down to* JOHNNY B., *lays the guitar down, embraces* JOHNNY B.)

JOHNNY B.: I wrote it on there after the funeral Daddy. Ain't nobody noticed it.

ELIZABETH: Your life is more important now Johnny B. Where that ambulance?

(SLEEPY *drops the knife, sits alone in a chair, money still squeezed in one hand.*)

JOHNNY A.: You look at me. You ain't got no time to be dying. We got songs to sing, you hear me Johnny B. Now you keep breathing. (JOHNNY B.'s *eyes slowly close.*) Don't you be closing your eyes on me. (JOHNNY B. *opens his eyes.*) Look at me. We got to carry on the blues. The whole world is waiting out there for Johnny B. Goode and his daddy. Come on Johnny. You keep breathing. (JOHNNY B.'s *eyes slowly close again.*) Johnny look at me. This is your daddy talking. You do what your daddy say. I'm sorry if I ran you away. Now you breathe boy!

(RETHA *looks at the wall, and an image grabs her attention. She walks toward the image, reaches out and touches it, but no one notices her.* RETHA *turns and smiles, and* JOHNNY B. *dies. The SOUND OF THE AMBULANCE is heard.*)

ELIZABETH: He dead Johnny A. Johnny B. is dead.

(ELIZABETH *looks at* JOHNNY A., *as he picks up* JOHNNY B.'s *guitar.* JOHNNY A. *stands alone, looking at his name on the guitar. Suddenly a GUSH OF WIND blows across the room.* RETHA *remains standing in front of the image—which is Babycake's.*)

THE END

A scene from *Killingsworth*. (*Left to right*) Angelo Reid and Lloyd Barnes, Jr.
Photo courtesy of Jubilee Theatre.

Killingsworth

EUGENE LEE

Eugene Lee, an accomplished stage and screen actor, brings a unique actor's perspective to playwriting. Reflecting on his dual roles as actor and playwright, Lee asserts, "I think I'm a better playwright because I'm an actor." Moreover, Lee's insights into the playwright's craft enhance his ability to interpret a script and grasp the author's intent. Born in New Brunswick, New Jersey, Lee moved with his family to Texas when he was an infant. He grew up in Fort Worth, Texas, where he was introduced to theatre in sixth grade via a role in a play at Morningside Elementary. Lee spent summers on a small farm outside of Crockett, Texas, with his grandmother, Big Mama. There he absorbed the culture, language, stories, spirituality, and humor of the people who would become the wellspring of his art. Those summers in East Texas shaped Lee's artistic vision and inspired his commitment to write about blacks in Texas, especially blacks in East Texas. Lee noticed that no one was writing plays about blacks in East Texas, and he set out to fill that void. Lee is a thoughtful, disciplined writer who, whenever possible, arranges public readings of his works in progress to hear the language, evaluate the characters' interactions, and assess audience response.

Lee began writing plays in New York City in the early 1980s, during a three-month period when he was not performing. He has written over half a dozen plays, several of which have been produced by professional theatre companies. Lee's completed plays include *East Texas Hot Links, Fear Itself, Somebody Called: A Tale of Two Preachers, Stones in My Passway, Killingsworth*, and the book for the musical *Twist* (which was never commercially published, but was performed by the Walnut Street Theatre and the George Street Playhouse). His most recent work is *Lyin' Ass*. *East Texas Hot Links*, Lee's critically acclaimed story of self-interest and betrayal, has been produced in several venues, including the Joseph Papp Public Theatre in New York City and the Royal Court Theatre in London.

A Distinguished Alumnus of Texas State University, Lee also serves as artist-in-residence in the university's Department of Theatre and Dance. He is the founder and artistic director of the annual Black and Latino Playwrights Conference, a nationally recognized workshop that offers emerging minority playwrights assistance with play development.

As You Read *Killingsworth*

Killingsworth explores the complicated dynamics of an essentially dysfunctional African American family living in a small town in Texas. Even though members of the family have prospered as a result of the patriarch's hard work and business acumen, they still suffer from the sociopolitical forces that inform race relations. This richly textured, two-act play explores universal themes, including sibling rivalry, father/son conflict, the impact of the past on the present, and the importance of family unity. Symbolically, the play explores the need to bury the hate and mistrust that threaten the family's survival. Like the plays of August Wilson, *Killingsworth* is not plot driven; its meaning resides in the storytelling. A masterful storyteller, Lee possesses a keen ear for the sounds and rhythms of black vernacular English, a gift that allows him to create authentic, memorable characters in *Killingsworth*.

Production History

Jubilee Theatre, Fort Worth, Texas, 1987–1988, 1998, 1999
Hornsby Entertainment, Carver Community Cultural Center, San
Antonio, Texas, 1989

Characters

MORIAH KILLINGSWORTH: Wanderer come home.
ANN EMERSON: His "wife."
JOBETH "SLIM" KILLINGSWORTH: Moriah's sister.
FRANKLIN FONTENOT: Deputy investigator.
LADY KILLINGSWORTH: Mother to Moriah and Jobeth.
BROTHER KILLINGSWORTH: The stepchild.

Setting

Time: 1977
Place: Tyrant County, Texas.

Production Notes

(*Downstage Right is an area of dirt, the land where* MORIAH *will dig his father's grave. As the play progresses, a mound and a hole eventually develop in this area. Upstage in silhouette an oak tree stands. It's big. This is Texas. The action of the play takes place on the land and in minimally furnished settings to suggest the interior of the Killingsworth home. Lights and music serve as segues to shift focus from one setting to another.*)

ACT ONE

(MORIAH'S *sax wails wild dissonant rage, which pierces the darkness. Lights up low and slow Upstage. Three mourning women in silhouette stand near a tree. Lights up to include* BROTHER *alone Downstage in the dirt. He takes note of the women and shakes his head with a slight grin and speaks to the audience.*)

BROTHER: My name is Brother. That's what they call me. Brother Killingsworth. I like that name. Ain't but one family with that name . . . in Tyrant County, Texas. My family. What's left of it. I call 'em family. Truth is, I was adopted, or more or less taken in when I was eight. My real Mama passed on. My Daddy died this mornin'. Kill't. That's who they're grievin'. Shot dead in his own bed.

(*A moment as lights fade out on the women and they move off.* BROTHER *takes a pint bottle from his pocket and turns it up.*)

BROTHER: Texas! If God was to give the world an enema, Texas is where he'd put it. Asshole of the world! No place like it. Nowhere. Lots of everything. Lots of sky. Lotta stars. Lotta light on a full moon night. Lotta land. Lotta love. Lotta hate. Fightin' . . . killin'. Lotta pride. Lotta shit. I guess you find the same thing anywhere else. But like they say, "Everything seem bigger in Texas." Matter of fact, Texas is so big, if you try and leave, you'll get tired befo' you'll get out. And you'll never get Texas outta you. Try what you will or may. If you raised on Texas air and water and sunshine, you can't stay away. If you ever love in Texas, and leave, you come back here lookin' for that love, in time. That's why he's come home.

(*Lights fade out on* BROTHER *as he sneaks off. Later: it's early evening, full moon, Indian summer, 1977. Lights cross fade up on* MORIAH, *agitated and pacing, with* FONTENOT *and* ANN.)

MORIAH: I never figured I'd be asked to do that!

ANN: Be still, Baby.

FONTENOT: It's procedure, Buddy. I'm sorry. I'mo get right on out your way, but gi'me a minute and a half Moriah. It's good to have you back around. Twenty years' a long time. How long you s'pose you'll be around?

MORIAH: I wasn't plannin' on bein' here now. I don't like this place, Frank.

FONTENOT: I'm sorry Mo, and I'm mad too. Mr. K taught both of us a lot growin' up.

MORIAH: Make it make sense Frank!

ANN: Baby, be still.

FONTENOT: I know man. I don't know. People die in this town. But nobody blows nobody away like that.

MORIAH: This is the very stuff about these ignorant ass peckerwoods down here; that's why I couldn't stay here.

FONTENOT: This ain't the same Texas you left Moriah.

MORIAH: This place doesn't change. I know my Daddy didn't kill himself! You've got a badge on your chest now. Go sniff amongst these redneck good ole boys.

FONTENOT: I intend to look wherever I have to. I'll find who did this Buddy. I promise you that.

MORIAH: Can you arrest a White man?

ANN: Of course he can.

FONTENOT: Not just any White man. Not just 'cause he White. Boy, you ain't changed. Moriah we both on the same side. I want the same thing you want. To folks 'round here, Colored and White, Mr. K was a pillar in the county and the community. Folks counted on him. He a businessman and a hard worker, Killingsworth trucks all over everywhere. Even got some city contracts. Cleaning offices and what have you. My first job ever in my life, you should remember, was behind one of your daddy's lawnmowers. Got my first paycheck . . . had his name on it.

MORIAH: What the hell happened, Frank?

FONTENOT: Two gunshots, point blank from a .38. We got no motive. No weapon. No signs of any struggle. Nothing missing that we can tell. Mr. K took one from maybe five, six feet, and one point blank to the head.

ANN: Oh, my God.

FONTENOT: Powder burns on his face. They meant to make sure he was good and dead. This place is pretty tame nowadays. Even the Whites. Ain't too many locked doors. Love and leukemia been the only real killers to pass through of late.

MORIAH: And they get off scot-free, too?

FONTENOT: Hard to handcuff.

MORIAH: That all you got?

FONTENOT: A bathtub full of water. I'm swattin' flies, but I think he talked to whoever shot him. I want to check with his workers, down on the end. See who he's fired lately. People that owed him. People he owed.

(*Lights up low to include* BROTHER *in the dirt.*)

BROTHER: One thing about a death in the family. Brings folks together. The old man built a right nice money-makin' business, moppin' floors and mowing lawns.

MORIAH: He didn't own that anybody who really needed what he had couldn't get it from him by asking, and he wasn't obliged to nobody.

FONTENOT: I'mo talk to Brother . . .

BROTHER: You and yo' mind Deputy Dawg. Boy, if brains was dynamite that man couldn't blow his nose.

FONTENOT: Just a few questions, but I'll come back. I'll find Brother down on the end I'm sure. I want to do an inventory of Mr. K's valuables. You're welcome to come along. More'n likely be some things that you'll want to go through. He moved in up there at your grandad's ole place when Lady put him out. Speakin' on that . . . they ever fight . . . ? To your recollection.

MORIAH: No they were the happiest couple in the world so they got divorced. Of course, they fought.

FONTENOT: What about? Money? Other women?

MORIAH: Down boy! She divorced him. She didn't kill him.

FONTENOT: What about Brother?

MORIAH: What about Brother?

BROTHER: Aw hell. I might have to hurt that boy. People can't be held responsible for what they do when they mind is occupied with losin' a loved one and all the scores ain't been settled.

FONTENOT: Nevermind. You talk much to your daddy lately?

MORIAH: Off and on. Why? What about Brother?

BROTHER: I'm harmless. 'Bout like every other Colored man down on the end. Let the liquor numb the part of ourselves we don't care for.

FONTENOT: Just wondering if your daddy might have said anything to you. If anything or anybody was botherin' him.

MORIAH: Frank, I've gone. You've talked with my family more than I have. You and Jobeth got a child together.

FONTENOT: Yeah, but we don't talk.

MORIAH: 'Cause you married somebody else.

FONTENOT: Aw man, you know. Me and her had split up. I was trying to get on. But I fell for the ole, "one last time" line. You know your sister's got a way of overreacting. She didn't have to get pregnant.

MORIAH: Well, hell she wanted you, Frank?

FONTENOT: I think she learned too much pharmacy in school. It was a moment of weakness. It wasn't like I wanted to spend the rest of my life with her. I know she's your sister, and I hate to be the one to tell you this. But, she's been through some changes since you been gone. She's drinkin', smoking that marijuana and takin' pills. I'm a cop. I couldn't have that. The boy's damn near eight years old, and she'll tell you that I don't care. She sends back any money or gifts I send. Slammed the door in my face a time or two when I come by.

(FONTENOT stops when he realizes MORIAH's not listening.)

MORIAH: He got old.

FONTENOT: I'm just carryin' on. Let me get on. I know you got to get settled. I'll be in touch shortly. You need anything Buddy?

MORIAH: Let me know if you find out anything.

(Lights cross fade out on MORIAH and FONTENOT. Lights up full on BROTHER in dirt, holding a shovel.)

BROTHER: I hated his old ass. Just yesterday he disowned me. For about the umpteen thousandth time. We couldn't never talk. We argued. I was always a kinda embarrassment to him. I guess 'cause we so much alike. The apple don't fall too far from the tree. Even the rotten ones with worms in 'em. Hell, I'm my old man's son. I ain't done much with myself. Forty years old, and I'm known around Tyrant County as being basically unreliable and lazy. I'm what they call a "fuckup." I drinks. Wine mostly. I can give you a honest day's work. I ain't got no "technical" trainin' or book sense. I grew up thinkin' Colored folks, unless they was real intelligent, couldn't do nothin' but the work intelligent people didn't want to do. Didn't nobody never tell me I was intelligent. I didn't want to be no teacher. They have way too many meetings. Plus, I don't care that much for other folks' kids. Preachin' don't appeal to me, and

I doubt I could even touch a corpse, let alone dress one to put it in the ground. And teachin', preachin', and stuffin' caskets was all I saw intelligent Colored end up doin'. Moriah is smart. Yeah, that boy is smart. Too smart for his own good. Don't know what to do wit' hisself. Ain't been home in years. Only left 'cause he was too hardheaded to believe he couldn't leave. A man who ain't made up his mind . . . ain't decided, good and bad, who he is and what he will and will not do . . . shit creek. No paddle.

(*Lights cross fade as* MORIAH *joins* BROTHER *in the dirt and startles him.*)

MORIAH: Who are you talking to?

BROTHER: Hey boy! Just thinkin' out loud. Seed y'all come in. I been waitin' for ole Dudley-Do-Wrong to leave. Just wanted to get a look at you and speak. Welcome home boy!

(*Hands* MORIAH *the shovel.*)

MORIAH: You gon' do it?

BROTHER: Nawh! I better keep movin'. You know how your mama is when it come to me bein' on her property.

MORIAH: You do it. If my memory serves me you are the oldest.

BROTHER: All the more reason for you to dig it.

MORIAH: We should both do it.

BROTHER: You can go 'head. He disowned my ass.

MORIAH: But you showed up with a shovel.

BROTHER: I knew you'd be here.

(MORIAH *takes the shovel and starts to dig.*)

MORIAH: This the spot right?

BROTHER: Right off from the tree there. Lady must not know you doin' this. She put him off this land once already.

MORIAH: She ain't home. He ain't gon' bother her none out here. He didn't look like he could get up and go bother nobody.

BROTHER: You went and saw?

MORIAH: (*Digging.*) The body had to be identified. Where were you?

BROTHER: I don't do that. You all right?

MORIAH: (*Digging.*) Yeah, I guess. You?

BROTHER: I don't think he expects me to mourn for 'im. (MORIAH *digs.*) So Baby Brother, what you and Deputy Dawg was talkin' 'about? If I know he comin' out the side of his mouth I never could understand how you two got to be so tight. Even as kids. He full grown and full of hisself now. You best watch yourself. Damn near had to take your sister over to Rusk and check her in after what he did, marryin' that other gal and leavin' Jobeth with that baby. Any other father would have had his ass lookin' down a gun barrel.

MORIAH: That wouldn't have changed anything.

BROTHER: He wouldn't do it again. He should'a least been made to feel bad about it. She is your sister.

MORIAH: What is she to you?! You were here. Slim was scheming to catch Frank and it backfired on her.

BROTHER: I just don't care for that boy myself. He's dumb. I ain't sayin' I'm smart. But he is dumb. (*Beat.*) Where you been man? What you been doin'? Don't look like you been doin' no hard labor. You still got soft hands. I figured you were somewhere bein' a jigaloo. Why'd you come back? To dig this hole? Lookin' for what your ole man left behind?

MORIAH: (*Digging.*) I am what he left behind. You too. (*He's tired already.*) When did we agree to do this? When did I agree to do this?

BROTHER: He was a hard man to say no to.

(MORIAH *draws the outline in the dirt.*)

MORIAH: This could take a while. Six feet down right? About four feet wide?

BROTHER: That's standard. Who's the fox come in here wit'chall?

MORIAH: My wife, Ann.

BROTHER: Wife!? Damn, boy. She from New York ain't she? I knowed you wouldn't go for none of this homegrown stuff. Actually, truth be told, I figured you to marry a White woman. I did. Figured that was why you left and stayed gone 'cause you had found you a place where you could do that. As mad as you always was at a White man, you sure was crazy 'bout his women.

MORIAH: Yeah, well people change. I'd better let her know where I am and what I'm doing.

(MORIAH *hands* BROTHER *the shovel and starts off.*)

BROTHER: When was the last time you saw him?

MORIAH: The day I left.

BROTHER: My last sight of him was yesterday down the wrong end of the barrel of that twelve gauge of his, with him cussin' me out. That's how I get to remember him. Said some ugly things 'bout my Mama. Said I might not even be his. I told him, "Well shoot me then. If I ain't your blood I'm trespassing," and he slapped me across my head with it.

Didn't hurt none. Hell he old, but I was fend'a slap him back. Had my open hand raised to smite his ancient ass, when his knees buckled and he fell back onto the bed. Talkin' 'bout if I didn't get out his house, he was gon' get up and whip my ass. He was all drunk up. Didn't even try to get up and come after me. I took his shotgun. So he wouldn't hurt hisself. I left. Stood outside on the porch. He was moanin' about bein' all by hisself. I started to tell him he should'a thought about that when he was using and mistreatin' folks all his life. I got in the wind. About a half mile down the road. I stopped and went back just to make sure he didn't do nothin' to hurt hisself, like get up and try to cook and burn the whole house down. I tiptoed up to the window and peeked in, and the damn fool was talkin' on the phone to somebody. Cryin'. I figured his fit had faded. Went on down the road.

MORIAH: Why are you telling me this?

BROTHER: Just so you'll know. (*Beat.*) I been thinking 'bout things. 'Bout this business. How, time was, I would'a starved to death outside there 'side the road before I'd work for him again. I know he left it all to you. Hopin' you'd come on home to stay. Boy, he used to talk about your ass, like you had wings. I know you don't want nothin' to do with no lawn mowers and mops. I can run it. I deserve something. You been gone so, you may need reminding. We both grew up in the same house. Good or bad, he was my father too. I called him daddy when I wasn't callin' 'im a evil old son of a bitch.

MORIAH: Not today Brother.

BROTHER: Why not today!?

MORIAH: 'Cause I don't know where I am just yet.

BROTHER: You back home in East Texas boy.

MORIAH: Things are happening too fast.

BROTHER: You get your bearing. Things been happenin' too slow down here for too long.

(BROTHER *hands him back the shovel and moves off.* MORIAH *stands a moment then drives the shovel home with his foot.*)

MORIAH: Shit, this could kill me, thank God this dirt ain't hard. (*He pushes the blade home with his foot.*) I'll just . . . pull back your covers. Get your spot ready. And once I'm done with that, I'll get my horn and play something for you. Now that I've got your attention. I have to deal with you now. Say all the things I've tried to blow out the end of that horn.

To this hole. To what goes in the hole. I'm talking to you now; you just listen. Damn if this ain't the closest I've come to praying. (*He stabs at the dirt.*)

(MORIAH *digs. Lights cross fade with music segue.* MORIAH *digs in silhouette for a moment.* ANN *joins him.*)

ANN: How's it coming?

MORIAH: It's gettin' deep.

ANN: Why do you have to do it? Somebody must do that for a living.

MORIAH: I said I would.

ANN: How's your spirit baby?

MORIAH: Spirits fine. It's my mind. I keep thinking I should have kept my ass here.

ANN: Why'd you leave?

MORIAH: 'Cause I couldn't stand to stay.

ANN: You might not have met me.

MORIAH: He worked hard.

ANN: I love you. Take a break and talk to me. I love it when you talk. Want your horn?

MORIAH: I needed to talk to him. Never had any idea what I needed to say to him or how to say it.

ANN: You missed him. You loved him. I know you felt him in your life. All the time I've spent listening to you talk about him and this place. I've been looking forward to meeting the place and the people that made you.

MORIAH: I was tired of trying to be somebody else by the time I met you. When you leave home, it's like you take a bucket full of who you are. To keep yourself alive. And everywhere you go, you have to drink some. You use some to wash when you get dirt on you. You give some away. You spill some. After a time some evaporates, or people put their shit in it, try to steal it, and you look down one day to find yourself toting an empty bucket. It was time to come home.

ANN: And now we're here.

MORIAH: For a long time when I'd try to understand why the world wouldn't spin the way I wanted it to . . .

ANN: Baby, you're getting excited.

MORIAH: No, listen to me now so I can say this. You asked me to talk; now you've got to listen. In church, Reverend would preach about "the sin of the father shall be visited on his sons." Brother and I would point at each other. It would scare the hell out of me. He had some sinful ways.

ANN: Everybody's got demons Moriah. Just don't feed 'em.

MORIAH: One of mine just died.

ANN: Then bury it.

(MORIAH *takes the shovel.*)

MORIAH: That's exactly what I'm about to do. Bring my horn. Maybe I'll drop it in this hole too.

ANN: You'd jump in there yourself before you'd do that.

(*Lights cross fade up on* LADY *with* SLIM.)

LADY: I used to all the time tell your daddy about sleepin' in a house with all the windows and doors open. All the crazy people runnin' around loose. 'Course hot as it gets, you can't just close yourself up at night. What time are you supposed to pick up Poochie?

SLIM: Shit! Right now.

LADY: Watch your mouth girl. Here take my keys and hurry up. You want me to call and tell them you on your way? You got to learn to be more responsible. We could have picked him up on the way.

SLIM: No. I'll just go. Is Moriah comin' in?

LADY: Directly. I 'magin'. Frank said he'd fetch 'im from the airport.

SLIM: What you call him for? I could'a done it.

LADY: You don't worry about that and go on and get that child. You be careful in my car. And don't be runnin' all over using up my gas. You ought to get your own car anyway.

(SLIM *leaves.* LADY *starts humming a spiritual. Lights cross fade up on* MORIAH *in the dirt digging.* ANN *sits not far away.*)

MORIAH: A freckle-faced, red-haired, flower child. Becky.

ANN: Becky?

MORIAH: And we had our own little private, passionate rebellion.

ANN: She hated her father?

MORIAH: You may be right. I never thought about it like that before, but I woke up one morning looking down the barrel of the longest gun I had ever seen in my life. And Becky's big-ass redneck daddy said, "Nigger!" And that shotgun pressed against my forehead brought, "Yes sir, please sir" out of my mouth like a reflex. Oh shit I'm glad I lived to laugh about that! I was butt naked, but I was out of bed and on his ass. I got the gun and knocked him into a corner of the room. She ran to him.

ANN: End of rebellion. A woman will do a lot to get her daddy's attention.

MORIAH: I got my clothes and my horn. Joined the army.

(MORIAH *steps back to look at his progress and notices . . .*)

MORIAH: Lights on up at the house. Somebody must be home. Come on and meet the family. Hold on to your hat and fasten your safety belt.

(*Lights cross fade. Music segues.* LADY *sits folding clothes. In time she reaches into her purse, whips out a .38 snubnose, wheels, and aims.*)

LADY: Who is that in here?!!!

MORIAH: (*As they enter.*) Mama! It's me!

LADY: Lord have mercy.

ANN: Please Lord!

(LADY *lowers the gun and eyes* ANN.)

LADY: Boy, never sneak up on old people. Let me look at you. When did you get here?

MORIAH: A couple of hours ago. Was that Slim leavin'?

LADY: She went to get the baby wit her forgetful self. She be back directly. She the reason I was late as it was. I thought you should'a been getting in 'bout now.

(*An awkward moment as the years evaporate between them.*)

MORIAH: You alright, Mama?

LADY: I'm fine. Who is this you got with you?

MORIAH: Mama, this is Ann. My wife.

LADY: What?!

ANN: Pleased to meet you Mrs. Killingsworth.

LADY: Call me Lady. Why didn't you tell somebody? Where she from? Boy! I can't believe this. Ann who?

ANN: Emerson.

LADY: From New York?

ANN: Yes.

LADY: Boy I ought to smack you upside your head!

MORIAH: Mama . . .

LADY: What? You didn't think I might want to know something like that? Excuse me Ann. How long have you been married? I have talked to you on the phone, Moriah and you ain't said one thing not one time 'bout havin' no wife . . .

MORIAH: I'm sorry Mama. But cuss me out about it later, please. What are you doing with this pistol?

LADY: Your daddy give it to me. I have to protect myself. Just me in this house now. He told me to shoot first when I'm by myself too.

ANN: Is it loaded?

LADY: Nothin' but a fool would pull out an empty one.

ANN: That makes sense. I don't feel so good. Where's the bathroom?

(LADY *points the way.*)

ANN: I'll be fine. You two go ahead and get caught up. I'll be fine. Probably that airline food.

(*She's gone. A moment between mother and son.*)

LADY: I'm sorry 'bout your daddy, son.

MORIAH: It ain't your fault Mama.

LADY: No, it's really not.

MORIAH: That ain't no way to die Mama.

LADY: No it really ain't. You mad still? Your daddy did as much to kill himself as anybody did to help him.

MORIAH: I wish I could have seen him to talk to him Mama.

LADY: You could'a done that long before now. I'm sorry. I won't start. He wasn't talkin' 'bout nothin' much, no way.

MORIAH: He didn't look like . . . He looked . . .

LADY: How did he look?

MORIAH: Old.

LADY: He was. His legs givin' out on him. His eyes 'bout gone. But you couldn't melt him and put him in no doctor's office.

(ANN *re-enters.*)

MORIAH: You okay?

ANN: I'm okay.

MORIAH: Do you miss him Mama?

LADY: Your Daddy and me did what we were supposed to do together.

MORIAH: What was that?

LADY: You. Your sister. Brother. We raised you. Kept you out of trouble best we could. Give you things we never had. Both of us working so you could not need for anything. Both of us tryin' to be happy.

ANN: What happened?

LADY: Nothin'. They grew up. Moved out. Moved off. We looked up one day and realized we didn't know each other. We didn't talk. Got to the point where, when I touched him he didn't feel anything. There are better days beyond, according to the Scriptures. We'll meet again. And if it's as nice a place as they say, we'll get to know each other better. "'Til it be 'morrow."

MORIAH: What?

LADY: Nothin'. Just your Mama gettin' old. I've missed him since long before I told him to move out. It hurts a tad knowing he'll never come back, even if I change my mind next week and want him back. Things get easier with time. (*Beat.*) Why don't you go out back and start a fire on the pit, so I can talk to my new daughter-in-law. I ain't gon' bite you Sugar, just get to know you. I've got some nice steaks. And when Jobeth gets back, Moriah, I want you to take my car and get me a carton of my Viceroys.

MORIAH: I'll walk and get them for you.

LADY: You can't walk nowhere 'round here. Jobeth will be back directly. You just got here and tryin' to get out already. Give your mama a minute. Tell me what you've been doin'.

MORIAH: Nothin'.

LADY: I know better than that. Ann don't tell me you the kind of woman let a man get away with doin' nothing.

ANN: No, ma'am, I'm not.

LADY: What do you do?

ANN: I'm an actress.

LADY: A actress!? You famous?

MORIAH: Mama . . .

ANN: No, I'm not famous.

MORIAH: Mama, I been doin' a lot of things. Travelin'. Playin' music. Nothin' to talk about.

LADY: And you been with him for how long, Ann?

ANN: A few years now.

LADY: Well, how do you make a livin'?

MORIAH: I get by. We get by.

LADY: Playin' your music?

MORIAH: I play here and there now and then.

LADY: But what do you do for money? Take odd jobs?

MORIAH: Yeah, been some o' that too.

LADY: You was mad and tied up in knots when you left. Your daddy felt like he was the reason you made yourself so scarce. He lied to folks for a while about you being some kinda spy. Workin' for the government.

MORIAH: You're lyin'?

LADY: My right hand to God. He was old, he was tired, and in a way he was kinda pitiful there towards the end.

MORIAH: What do you mean?

LADY: Just old. Needin' help to . . . get along. Too old to do for himself. I'm happy, knowin' 'bout you Ann and that you're happy. And I hope y'all keep it that way. I don't want my son to die a tired, sad old man.

MORIAH: I don't want that either Mama.

ANN: Me neither.

LADY: Do you still hate it here?

MORIAH: Who?

LADY: Your feet don't fit no limb. You know who. I won't preach. I'm thankful to God you're here. Welcome home. And welcome to the family Ann.

ANN: Thank you.

LADY: Y'all gon' stay?

(*SLIM screams for MORIAH Off Stage.*)

SLIM: Moriah!

LADY: That's your sister.

MORIAH: Mama I started diggin' . . .

(*SLIM bursts in.*)

SLIM: Where is he?! Where's Moriah?! Betty Lou say she saw him at the courthouse.

MORIAH: Here.

SLIM: My brother. My brother!!! You're here! Good God dog it! Skibby weeba! They shot him Moriah! Somebody just took a gun and walked in and . . . I'm tryin' to keep it together.

MORIAH: It'll be all right Slim.

SLIM: No it won't. Shit, I've missed you. I have missed you.

MORIAH: I missed you too. Meet Ann. My wife.

SLIM: For real?! My sister?

ANN: For real.

SLIM: Well, you ain't asked nobody if you could do that.

MORIAH: You had a baby and didn't ask nobody!

SLIM: That's different. And he ain't no baby no more.

LADY: Where is he? You left here to go get him.

SLIM: Up at church playin'. Somebody'll bring him home.

LADY: Run up to Hodge's to get me some Viceroys.

SLIM: You got cancer sticks in your car. I thought you quit. You know those things'll kill you.

LADY: My nerves are bad today. My Viceroys are better for me than that mess you puttin' in your body. You think I don't know nothin'? I'm goin' to lie down for a while.

SLIM: Don't lay up back there smokin' in that bed, Mama.

(LADY *ignores her.*)

LADY: Moriah start a fire out back and fix them steaks if you hungry. And then clean up any mess y'all make in my kitchen.

(LADY *starts out.*)

MORIAH: Mama, somebody's got to see to making some arrangements.

LADY: You go right ahead. That's not my concern. Me and your daddy divorced.

MORIAH: He wanted to be buried out here on this land, Mama. Wanted me to dig . . .

LADY: I know.

MORIAH: Is that alright with you?

LADY: Put 'im on out there. Dig it deep though. You sure are a pretty thing, Ann. Just like his daddy. We'll talk later.

ANN: I'm happy to meet you Lady. My condolences on your loss.

LADY: The Lord moves in mysterious ways, His wonders to perform. He wasn't mine no more anyway.

ANN: I know he was a special man.

LADY: Rare breed child. Just like his son.

ANN: I can see that.

LADY: You'd better. You ever been on TV?

ANN: A couple of commercials . . . in New York.

LADY: I got to tell everybody about my new TV star daughter.

SLIM: Oh, Lord don't let her get started.

ANN: It's nothing to brag about.

LADY: You been on TV. I won't be lyin'.

(LADY *moves off.*)

SLIM: I think she's losin' her mind.

LADY: (*Off Stage.*) I hear you Jobeth!

MORIAH: Talk to me Slim.

SLIM: I don't want to talk. This shit with Daddy didn't sink in yet.

MORIAH: Frank's got it in his head that you might know something.

SLIM: Something like what?

MORIAH: He didn't say. What do you know?

SLIM: (*Pops a pill.*) Nothin'!

MORIAH: You fillin' your own prescriptions?

SLIM: Every now and then. Just for my nerves. Help me get to sleep.

MORIAH: You got a handle on things? Tell the truth now.

SLIM: What was Frank tellin' you?! He wants to take my boy from me Moriah. He puts me down, lies on me. Tells people I'm unfit . . .

MORIAH: He told me he's worried . . .

SLIM: Worried?! Worried?! He don't know worried. You believed him? That's the shit I'm talkin' about . . .

MORIAH: I didn't say I believed him . . .

SLIM: Nawh, he work't his little charm on you. That's why I don't want to be around him. I don't even want to talk about him. The son-of-a-bitch!

LADY: (*Off Stage.*) Jobeth if you don't hush all that cussin' in there . . . you better!

MORIAH: I'd better get this hole dug.

SLIM: Why are you diggin' it?

ANN: That's what I said.

MORIAH: I told him I would.

SLIM: Why out there?

MORIAH: That's what he wanted.

(*Lights cross fade up on* BROTHER *at the tree.*)

BROTHER: It's some sick people in the world. Look at that boy there. I'll bet you he ain't done so much as lift a shovel since he left here. I don't think he's right about White folks doin' this to the old man though. They mean. But they ain't like that.

(*Lights cross fade as* MORIAH *makes his way to the dirt and takes up the shovel.*)

MORIAH: People have called me proud. I always blamed that on you. People called me selfish. You taught me that too.

(BROTHER *joins him.*)

BROTHER: Who you talkin' to?

MORIAH: Him. I used to watch him, one arm out the window, one hand on the steering wheel, one ear taking in Mama, "talkin' crazy." He'd nod a time or two or say something to something she say, but his eyes never left the road in front of him.

BROTHER: That woman talkin' can make you wish you was someplace else.

MORIAH: I still wonder where he went off to in his head.

BROTHER: I never looked at him that close. Wherever it was made him happy.

MORIAH: Is that all we get? What we create for ourselves?

BROTHER: Yeah.

(BROTHER *moves off.* MORIAH *digs a bit. Then . . .*)

MORIAH: I've missed you so hard sometimes, man. I've had good fortune. I never really pointed myself at anything. So I didn't never really hit nothin'. I wake up in the morning sometimes wishing I was someplace else. Somebody else. What were you trying to build?

(MORIAH *digs. Lights fade to black. Music segues to show the passing of time to early morning. Lights up on* ANN *as* MORIAH *joins her.*)

ANN: Where have you been?

MORIAH: With Frank over at Daddy's place. You meet everybody?

ANN: Sure did. People started coming by. A lot of people. Floty Mae, Levayta, and her boy Gussie Joe, and some Watsons and they all brought food. There's enough food here, Moriah, to feed an army. Two huge hams, chicken, fried two or three different ways. I had some potato salad that brought tears to my eyes it was so good. Corn bread. Somebody dropped off some greens. Collard greens and cakes. It's decadent. I had a good time. These people love them some Moriah. Especially one somebody named Wanda. You know Wanda? She's real happy you're back. Can't wait to see you. You want to tell me about Wanda?

MORIAH: Wanda is crazy.

ANN: I know how to act crazy too. If I have to. To save her from herself.

MORIAH: Well, I'm sure you were a big hit.

ANN: Thanks to Lady, I actually signed some autographs.

MORIAH: See, you're a star. You want to stay?

ANN: Do you?

MORIAH: I asked first.

ANN: I've got to be wherever you are.

MORIAH: Ain't no actin' jobs back up here in these woods.

ANN: I know. I didn't leave anything in New York I couldn't live without.

MORIAH: Everything I cared about came on the plane with me. How's the morning sickness?

ANN: I have never felt this sick in my life.

MORIAH: You sure this is where you want to be?

ANN: You're the one.

MORIAH: I need to know who killed him before I can live in these woods again.

ANN: You may never know. You are going to spend the rest of your life

with me and this child and you can teach and guide this baby past the
mistakes you made. I'll make you the happiest man in these woods.
(*A moment.*) We feel you, Honey Baby. I'm here. We're here. (*She puts his
hand on her stomach.*) Frank got any leads?

MORIAH: None that he talked about. Hell, I might as well get back to
diggin'.

ANN: You can't dig in the dark.

MORIAH: He used to get us out of bed before day to go to work. If you're
going to spend the day working outside in Texas, you get your ass up
and get at it before it gets too hot.

ANN: And you hated it.

MORIAH: I just did it. Hell I didn't hate. 'Cause if you could hate, you
could kill. I didn't hate. Except . . . White people. Yes I did. I used to
kill White people . . . in my mind. Just wiped them right off the face
of my thoughts. Walking back and forth in the sun, sweating behind
a mower. I'd cut them down and clean 'em up. Every blade of grass
became a single screaming Caucasoid demon begging for mercy as they
fell, by the hundreds, beneath the front of the mower.

ANN: Hitler had dreams like that.

MORIAH: And when the job was done and mowers were off, I would rake
up the mounds and felt so good; it made all the killing worth it. To this
day, I love the smell of fresh-cut grass. Smells like victory.

ANN: That's sick Moriah.

MORIAH: Yeah. 'Cause that grass got watered everyday and was just as tall
in no time. (*Beat.*) I was scared of Daddy.

ANN: He was scared too.

MORIAH: I know. I loved him.

ANN: You ever tell him that?

MORIAH: No. He never seemed like he could handle it.

ANN: He never seemed like he could handle it?

MORIAH: He didn't ever say it. Made sure we wouldn't expect that kinda
thing from anyone.

ANN: So I don't ever have to tell you that again?

MORIAH: That's not what I said. There's a lot about me that's changed
'cause of you. I need you. I need you to tell me you love me. Yeah, I do.
I've got to go dig a hole.

ANN: Did you make funeral arrangements?

MORIAH: Daddy specified, "Nothing fancy. Not in no church." He didn't go when he was alive. Always said he wouldn't be caught dead in no church. We'll hold a wake at the funeral home tomorrow evening. I want to get this hole dug so as soon as possible, we can lay him in it . . .

ANN: Wake . . . ? What do you do at a wake?

MORIAH: Sit. Eat. Cry. Think. Pull all the wagons into a circle. The first time I went to a wake, Brother told me it was where all the church people got together to pray and hope the dead person would "wake up." I remember thinking that I didn't really want to be around if that happened.

ANN: You alright?

MORIAH: I'm alright. I love you.

ANN: I love you. Go dig. I'll make some breakfast.

(SLIM joins them.)

MORIAH: Good morning.

SLIM: Mornin'. Good mornin' Ann. What'chall doin' up . . . this . . .

MORIAH: I've got digging to do. Ann's going to fix some breakfast.

ANN: You want some?

SLIM: No. How can you eat?

MORIAH: Well, go back to sleep then. Or have some coffee.

SLIM: I hate that mess. It'll stunt your growth.

MORIAH: I don't think you need to worry about that.

(MORIAH moves out. He's gone. A moment between SLIM and ANN.)

SLIM: How long have you known Moriah?

ANN: Three years in January. We've lived together since my divorce, last year.

SLIM: Do you love him?

ANN: Yes.

SLIM: You left your husband for Moriah?

ANN: I like to think he saved me from my marriage. I wasn't expecting this from you.

SLIM: What did you expect? My brother's been gone a long time.

ANN: I don't want to compete with that. I hope there's room in this family for me, Jobeth.

SLIM: Got a fresh vacancy. You can move right in. Seems like this family will forever have holes in it. I'm just stuck in the middle of tryin' to feel something. I want to laugh. I need to cry. To get my brother back, and lose Daddy at the same time freaks me out.

ANN: You never lost Moriah.

SLIM: Yeah we did. He ever talk about home?

ANN: All the time.

SLIM: Good or bad?

ANN: Not all good. Not all bad. I don't feel like a stranger here.

SLIM: Think you could live here?

ANN: I'm not afraid to try. Would you feel better if I weren't here?

SLIM: I think so.

ANN: Do you want me to leave?

SLIM: Not if you're gonna take Moriah with you.

ANN: And I would. I'm pregnant.

SLIM: Get the hell outta here! For real?!

(*MORIAH comes in.*)

SLIM: Moriah!

MORIAH: Don't believe a word of it. I deny everything. What y'all talkin' 'bout?

SLIM: You! You old baby maker you. How come you ain't said nothin' 'bout her bein' pregnant?!

MORIAH: You told her?

ANN: Yep.

SLIM: You should'a told me. You tell Mama?

ANN: No.

SLIM: What's wrong with you boy?! I ought to slap you upside your head.

MORIAH: I didn't say anything because it didn't seem like a good time.

SLIM: Well, when was you thinkin' was gon' be a good time?

MORIAH: I don't know. You want me to go wake her up and tell her now? Damn, forgive me. I've had some other things on my mind.

SLIM: You still should'a made that the first thing you said when you saw me.

ANN: He'll tell her today, right Baby?

MORIAH: Right after you make breakfast. There's plenty of stuff in the fridge. Eggs, bacon, cheese, milk, butter, jelly. No orange juice though.

SLIM: Look in the freezer for concentrated. She bought a shitload of stuff yesterday. They may have used it all last night. Since she's been here by herself, she says no point in cooking a whole lotta food to just go to waste. (*SLIM takes a vial of pills from her robe pocket and pops one.*) I think Mama's lonely. Other than church and her club meetings, she don't go nowhere. And she was so ready to put him out, but didn't want nobody else to have him. She needs a man in her life. (*Beat.*) I didn't mean that. I miss my Daddy. Who could do something like that?

ANN: I don't know.

SLIM: Make me want to get a gun and shoot somebody! Negroes and guns! It's a bad combination.

ANN: You think somebody Black did it?

SLIM: I know somebody Black did it. And the police know it too. They just don't give a damn. My brother, you should'a seen your Mama last night. She was in her glory.

MORIAH: How?

SLIM: Drunk. Her club members from church came by and they drowned her sorrows.

ANN: All the screwdrivers you put in her.

SLIM: She kept askin' for another one. I fixed her *one* screwdriver. The rest were straight orange juice. Love on the rocks.

ANN: Which is probably why there is no orange juice in there now.

SLIM: I don't know how you let them take you through all that Ann. Had the woman signing autographs, Moriah, and ain't but one of 'em got a television, let alone ever seen you on no television.

ANN: They started cryin' and drinkin' and they ended up filin' out of here drunk and singin' spirituals.

SLIM: She put on a show too. Didn't break down weeping and moanin'. Nawh, nawh, nawh, not Lady. She was strong and held her head up and said, "Even though we may be divorced . . . I still wake up and go to sleep with his memory. I always will." She wasn't sayin' nothin' like that while that divorce was goin' on. You missed it. There are stories to make your hair stand on end. Mama's lawyer wanted Daddy's financial statements so they could split up the assets in half. She swore he was hidin' stuff, buyin' property and puttin' it in my name . . .

MORIAH: Was he?

SLIM: He had asked me to sign some papers. I just signed 'em.

MORIAH: You didn't read what they were?

SLIM: They weren't gettin' divorced at the time. You're right though. I should have seen it. They slept in separate bedrooms in this big-ass house and was talking to each other through me. She accused him of chasing every skirt in the county, and he probably was. I swear he was going crazy for a while there, but she should have known he was too old to do any good with these gals out there. She was pissed he was spending money on 'em. He made out like she was naggin' him to an early grave and driving him away. If the truth be told, I was ready for 'em to get divorced and be done with it. If they couldn't spend the rest of their lives together without killin' each other or driving me crazy, then let it go. But don't drag me through it with you. If I came by here, she couldn't wait to let him know. Then he'd call me up, "You can go by and check on ev'body but your old man, huh?"

(SLIM *stops long enough to pop another pill.*)

MORIAH: Break's over! I've got more diggin' to do.

SLIM: I know where the orange juice is and I've got some champagne too. You like mimosa my sister?

MORIAH: You need to keep your wits about you today, Slim. Keep your head up.

SLIM: I know and I need drugs. Moriah, you're gonna take Daddy and put him in the ground and cover him up with dirt, and we won't never see him again. My rock. He used to wonder . . . He'd prob'ly be mad if he knew I told you . . .

MORIAH: I won't tell him you told me.

ANN: Moriah!

MORIAH: What?

SLIM: If you hated him?

MORIAH: I guess I'm not diggin' this hole.

(*Lights cross fade and music segues as* MORIAH *moves back out to the dirt. He starts to dig.*)

MORIAH: What you want me to do with your business? I might have a hard time working for some of these people down here. I've been away a long time. But I've got scars. Real scars. Remember when I was helpin' the Willery boys brand calves, and they held me down, and they put that hot brandin' iron on my ass. Had a good laugh on my ass. Wasn't nothin' you could'a done, and I think that hurt me more than knowin' I couldn't do anything. The White, coward motherfuckers, held me down . . . five of 'em. Willery's three and two others. I don't remember names. I do remember they laughed. I wanted them to die. I couldn't stay here man. You knew your place. I was always mad. I don't want to be mad anymore man. That shit wears on you. How did you keep from killing somebody? I got me a woman now. A good woman. Well so far so good. I guess you the wrong one to ask about how to make something like that last forever.

(*Lights cross fade up on* SLIM *and* ANN. SLIM's *feeling no pain, holding court with a bottle of champagne and a pitcher of orange juice.*)

SLIM: I was tryin' to go to school. And they showed out. Daddy was 'bout to cut Mama's lawyer right in the courthouse. Man called Daddy a liar to his face and in front of God and the judge, Daddy had him by his tie draggin' the little man across the table . . . with his knife out.

ANN: I didn't hear about this.

SLIM: They were like two kids. Two little kids. Couldn't just get divorced and be done with each other. Nooo. That's too much like right. I couldn't concentrate. My phone rang off the wall. "What's she sayin' 'bout me now?" and "You tell your Daddy the judge said he still has to make the house note payment, and be on time with it . . . " I wanted to tell them both to stop callin' me. And he hated payin' on a house he wasn't sleepin' in. Judge or no judge, he wasn't going to do it. She calls him. He won't talk to her. She goes over. He won't come to the door. So she takes out her little pistol and proceeds to shoot out all the windows in the place. Said she wanted to scare him.

ANN: She's lucky he didn't shoot back.

SLIM: He wasn't there. They both went to jail for contempt of court and guess who they both called to get 'em out. I took my time going down there too. They acted like children! Kept me a nervous wreck, thinkin' about what they might try to do to each other. I don't think Mama cares.

ANN: That doesn't make sense.

SLIM: It didn't make sense to me to spend that much of your life with somebody building what they built and just throw it away.

ANN: Sometimes people grow apart. My parents did. They're happier without each other than they ever were together.

SLIM: Not these two. She'd sit here drinkin' some nights and call him up, "talkin' crazy" as he called it. You know I just thought about something. I'd bet she ain't had no sex since the night they made me. That's where the real problem was. Mama's been scared to death Daddy was gon' catch up to one'a them skirts he was chasin' and give away everything she had worked to help him get. She'da kilt him herself 'fore she'd seen that happen.

(SLIM *reaches for the champagne bottle and again fills her glass.*)

SLIM: I wonder if Daddy did a will?

ANN: Moriah talked with the lawyers; I'm sure he knows.

SLIM: Well, hell it can wait. The man ain't even in the ground yet.

(*Lights cross fade up on the dirt.* MORIAH *digs.* FONTENOT *joins him.*)

MORIAH: Frank? You're up and at 'em mighty early.

FONTENOT: Mornin' Buddy. Duty calls. You gon' go ahead and dig that hole huh?

MORIAH: He wanted me and Brother to do it.

FONTENOT: Brother been by here? Nobody's seen him.

MORIAH: I haven't seen him this morning.

FONTENOT: He'll surface. I 'magine everybody was pretty excited to see you.

MORIAH: Yeah. We haven't had much time to get caught up yet.

FONTENOT: You get all the insurance policies and what you have sorted out?

MORIAH: Two of them. Fifty thousand each. One for Slim's boy and for me.

FONTENOT: What about Brother?

MORIAH: Why?

FONTENOT: I've been going over this in my head trying to piece together some kind of a lead to follow. Maybe you can make sense of it. This won't take but a minute. The way I see it. Whoever did this either let theyselves in, or Mr. K must'a let 'em in.

MORIAH: Or the door was unlocked . . .

FONTENOT: . . . and they let theyselves in. Or maybe they were there for a while. He was in the bed. But somebody had run a bath in the tub . . . with some Epsom salts in it.

MORIAH: He could have done that himself.

FONTENOT: True. Somebody called the station house. Said they heard some shootin' in that area. Dispatcher took the message. Said whoever it was hung up on 'im. Out there on that farm road ain't but a coupl'a folks could'a heard. Wasn't but two shots. To the north there, Connell and his wife and all his girls are in Houston. And on the other side, old man Lamb ain't got good hearin'. 'Cross the road from him is all government forest. But the funny thing is your daddy got the only telephone out there. I think your daddy talked to whoever shot him. Somebody he trusted. Somebody he cared enough about to let them in his house, in his bedroom, himself in the bed with his bedclothes on, at that hour of the mornin'. They didn't steal nothin'. They just came in, shot him while he was sleepin' and walked out. I've got to find the somebody who could do that.

MORIAH: That's the somebody you got to find.

FONTENOT: Well, let me get to it.

(FONTENOT *starts off.*)

MORIAH: Everybody's sleeping in there now Frank.

FONTENOT: (*Stops.*) I smelled some bacon (*Sniff.*) . . . a while ago, in the wind; yeah that's bacon. Somebody's up.

MORIAH: That's Ann.

FONTENOT: Can I join you for breakfast?

MORIAH: Frank, Jobeth is in there. She won't want to see you.

FONTENOT: I'mo need to talk to them Buddy. Let me help you with your diggin'.

MORIAH: No. Thank you, but this is something I have to do.

FONTENOT: You're sure? He was like a daddy to me, too.

MORIAH: I appreciate all that Frank; now, will you leave?

FONTENOT: You ought to let somebody help you.

MORIAH: You got enough to keep you busy. I'll be alright.

(MORIAH *digs a moment before taking up his horn and lights fade to black. Music segues the passing of time. Lights up on* SLIM, MORIAH, *and* ANN *in the dirt. Mimosas in hand.*)

SLIM: Frank ask about me and Poochie, Moriah?

MORIAH: No. He wants to talk to you, and Brother and Lady.

SLIM: For what?! I got three words to say to him: Kiss-my-ass.

(BROTHER *enters from the black and scares them.*)

BROTHER: Damn, girl, who you cussin' out this early in the mornin'? Why y'all so jumpy?

SLIM: Don't do that Brother! My nerves is bad enough right now as it is.

BROTHER: How's that hole comin' Baby Brother?

MORIAH: It's deeper than it was.

BROTHER: It's some boys down on the end, for a little bit of nothin', could have that hole dug for you before noon.

MORIAH: We told him we would do it.

BROTHER: Yeah, well he wasn't the best at keepin' his promises either.

SLIM: You ought to help him Brother. Moriah can't dig . . .

MORIAH: That's alright Slim. I can handle it.

SLIM: Why? Put him in the cemetery, with the rest of the dead people.

MORIAH: It's in the will. I've got a hole to dig.

BROTHER: What else did he say in his will?

MORIAH: The lawyer's going to read it next week. I found two life insurance policies. Fifty thousand each. Me and Slim are the beneficiaries.

SLIM: Fifty thousand dollars?!

BROTHER: Anything for me?

MORIAH: No.

BROTHER: That's why you'll be diggin' that hole by your lonesome.

SLIM: That ain't no way to be Brother. I'll give you some of mine.

BROTHER: What about the business? You get that too?

MORIAH: I don't want it Brother.

BROTHER: Then let me run it for you. You can't run it from New York.

SLIM: Daddy will be turning over in that hole.

ANN: Baby remember the smell of fresh-cut grass?

SLIM: Keep it in the family my brother. You got something else in mind?

MORIAH: I hadn't really thought about that.

SLIM: Y'all could work together again. Ann they used to look so pitiful. Both of 'em. I was glad I was a girl. Watchin' y'all go to work. Everybody else playin' ball . . .

BROTHER: Me and you and Bubba Willis would be loading up the truck.

MORIAH: Where is Bubba Willis?

BROTHER: Bubba Willis died. Damn whiskey ate 'is liver.

SLIM: He'd get drunk and call Daddy to get him out of jail. I had to go and get him one time. I will never forget that. A big, black, old baldheaded bastard with blood-red eyes, a beard and bad, bad, bad body odor. Funky man! He got in the car, went to sleep, farted and shit on himself . . . in the car. Loud too, goddamn 'im. (*They laugh.*) That ain't funny. It was the dead of winter. I could have died, closed up in that car with that old man. He didn't wake up either, 'til we got to wherever we were going. He never could look me in my face after that.

MORIAH: Well how would you feel?

SLIM: All my life men keep giving me shit and then they stay away 'cause they're embarrassed about it.

BROTHER: Watch out Ann you don't want to get her started on her man problems.

SLIM: I ain't got no man problems. I still ain't got no man. All I got is what they leave behind. That's why I need a man. They had to cut me open! I got a scar on my body to this day from bringing that monkey into this world. That shit hurt! Hell you try havin' a baby bigger than you are. I told Dr. Alexander to go ahead and tie up my tubes while you're cleaning up in there. No more visitors allowed. Bastard wasn't even around. No time. Work. Plus his lovely wife was having a hard pregnancy at the time herself. They asked me what I wanted to name him, and I just remember being so mad at myself for being myself, and the pain.

ANN: Poochie's going to ask about his father one day.

SLIM: I told him he ain't got one. Should have named him Jesus.

(SLIM *checks the bottle. It's empty.*)

SLIM: To be daddy, you got to be there. Anybody else want more mimosa?

MORIAH: You sure you need any more?

SLIM: Damn skippy, I'm sure. There's some more in the house.

(*She tries to get up but stumbles a bit, and* BROTHER *offers a hand.*)

BROTHER: Hold on there now.

SLIM: Your friend Moriah! Ann, let me tell you something, I wouldn't care if his thang falls off in his hands as he sticks it in his lovely wife tonight and they both drop dead from shock. The boy looks too much like him. So I'm reminded daily. I was gon' put him up for adoption. I didn't want to raise him myself. Period. Have him grow up lookin' like that bastard. Leave me and marry some other woman just like his son-of-a-bitch daddy did. But my daddy was there. He was there . . . and he said he would be daddy to my baby and . . . to me.

MORIAH: Take your drunk ass in the house.

ANN: Moriah!

MORIAH: Well she is drunk . . . !

SLIM: Come on Ann. Leave him to dig his hole. We best clean that kitchen before we have to listen to Mama's mouth. I've got to find my medicine.

BROTHER: You gon' put medicine on top of all that liquor?

SLIM: They both do the same thing.

ANN: I'll take care of the kitchen. You lie down.

SLIM: You sure? I'll help you, you know. I ain't drunk . . . you know.

BROTHER: Yes you are. Go lay down.

SLIM: Yes sir. I'll go lay down. I'mo lay down in Mama's bed.

(SLIM *stumbles off.* MORIAH *goes back to digging.* ANN *gathers the glasses and bottle.*)

BROTHER: I can't stand here and watch you doin' this. You makin' me tired. I'mo get on down to the end. Befo' I go tho', I need to nudge you 'bout this business. I'm the man to . . .

(BROTHER *starts out.* SLIM *screams from Off Stage.*)

SLIM: Mo! Mo! Mama! Mama!

(SLIM *bursts back in hysterical.* MORIAH *intercepts her.*)

SLIM: All my pills are gone! Mo, come look at Mama! She's got all this white mess . . . slobber, . . . all around her mouth and she ain't movin'!

(MORIAH *crosses out.* ANN *takes* SLIM *and tries to calm her down.*)

SLIM: What's wrong with her Moriah! I touched her, and she didn't move, and all my pills are gone! Shit!

(MORIAH *re-enters.* BROTHER *rushes back.*)

MORIAH: Slim, listen to me now. What was in this bottle?

SLIM: Just something to calm my nerves . . . put me to sleep.

MORIAH: How many were in there?

SLIM: I don't remember.

ANN: Is she breathing?

BROTHER: Not that I could tell. What's wrong with her?

MORIAH: She took some pills.

SLIM: It's not my fault!

ANN: It's alright Slim. It's alright. She's going to be alright.

MORIAH: Come on and help me get her to the car Brother.

(BROTHER *and* MORIAH *move off.* ANN *rocks and tries to comfort the whimpering* SLIM, *as the lights fade to black.*)

END OF ACT ONE

ACT TWO

(*Music. Lights up. A few hours later.* BROTHER *is stacking dominoes into a sculpture.* MORIAH *enters and proceeds to set the sculpture in motion. As the dominoes topple . . .*)

BROTHER: Boy! I swear you'd mess up a wet dream. You never did like to leave things like you found 'em. Your Mama's gon' be alright.

MORIAH: Not enough pills in the bottle.

BROTHER: She too 'ornery to die. She just wanted some attention. Ain't nothin' to be gettin' mad about.

MORIAH: This place makes me mad!

BROTHER: What you mad at? She did that to herself!

(MORIAH *moves out to the dirt and takes the shovel. Lights cross fade as* BROTHER *follows.*)

MORIAH: The longer I'm here, the more I remember why I left. I can't live here.

BROTHER: So you gon' just dig that hole and get the hell out of Dodge? Take your fifty thousand dollars and get on with your life?

MORIAH: Ain't no life for me here.

BROTHER: Nothin' but some crazy-ass family. You don't want no parts of that.

MORIAH: I can't live with these White folks.

BROTHER: Ain't but one place you can go if you want to get away from white folks. You don't have to go outside Texas. Go inside yourself. Ain't no White men in there that you can't kick out if you want to.

(MORIAH digs.)

MORIAH: That ain't the easiest thing in the world to do Brother. This shit runs deep with me.

BROTHER: Get over it. I been doin' it all my life. You used to know how.

(MORIAH pauses from his digging a beat.)

MORIAH: No I really didn't. I took a job at the mattress factory the summer before I went to college. I wanted to make my own money. Have my weekends to myself. But I had no idea they could put that many mattresses together in a day. I was on the loading dock with a couple of the older Kolter boys and Henry, the foreman's son. Six square feet of retard with a confederate flag tattooed on his chest and a big-ass chaw of tobacco in his jaw.

BROTHER: I know 'im.

MORIAH: The mattresses came down a conveyor belt and the three of us would wrap them in plastic and cardboard boxes and stack them on pallets so Henry could come along on his forklift and drive the stacks onto the trucks. Everyday, three, four times a day, Henry would slide by with some off-color commentary. "Hey boys! What's the saddest sight you could ever see? A busload of niggers goin' over a cliff with two seats empty." And he'd crack up laughin'. "You boys know why the good Lord invented orgasms? So you niggers would know when to stop fuckin'." And he'd be laughin' louder and harder. Sittin' up on that forklift and wheelin' off another load. Or the one about the old Southern sheriff . . . when they pulled a Black carcass from the bottom of a river wrapped in chains . . . "Just like one'a 'nem Nigras . . . to steal more chains than he could carry." All day long. The Kolter boys would smile, and I tried to smile. I tried to laugh at the shit. And he did it like we had bought tickets. I didn't want to hear that. But I turned the other cheek . . . until Friday of that first week. Just after lunch. I swear mattresses coming off that belt looked like a waterfall. Me and the Kolter boys stacking away. All elbows and ass. Wrap 'em and stack 'em. Wrap 'em and stack 'em. But they were coming so fast we ended up wrappin' 'em and throwing them in the general vicinity of the stack. Henry gets down off his forklift, and runs up in my face. "When you stack dese damn thangs lopsided nigger, they fall over! You stupid ass goddamned . . ." and before he could get another "nigger" out of his mouth, bam, I tried to plant my fist in his brain. Henry went one way and the tobacco flew out his mouth the other.

BROTHER: You lucky you ain't got rope burns on your neck. Did it make you feel any better?

MORIAH: For a minute it did. It was short-lived though. I know the Kolter boys thought I had lost my mind.

BROTHER: And your job.

MORIAH: Henry didn't say anything else to me. He got up, wiped some blood off his lip and walked off. We went back to work. Nobody said a word. Back to wrappin' and stackin'. And Henry didn't come back. So we kept stackin' . . . waitin', but nothing. Until five o'clock when all the work was done. The foreman gave me my check and said I didn't need to come back, 'cause I couldn't handle the job. No discussion. I cried all the way home. Mad.

BROTHER: What'd the old man say?

MORIAH: Nothin'. Early the next morning I was back behind one of his lawn mowers. Mad.

BROTHER: That's exactly how that White man wants you to be. Mad then make mistakes.

MORIAH: You remember when I helped old man Willery and his boys round up some calves to brand them?

BROTHER: And they branded you on the seat of your pants? Yeah, I remember that.

MORIAH: I still got that scar.

BROTHER: It's all behind you . . .

MORIAH: Like a tail and I've got a crook in my mind from tryin' to bite it off. I couldn't let these White folks tell me that's all I could be.

BROTHER: I think it's silly you even hold onto shit like that. All that should be good for is a laugh. So laugh at it. It's niggers that have lived with worse and didn't get to laugh about it. You lucky, like I say. I'mo get on down the road. I'll catch up to you later.

MORIAH: Where are you going?

BROTHER: Just to get off to myself for a minute. Get a change of clothes.

MORIAH: Still don't want to help with this hole?

BROTHER: You doin' alright look like to me. Tell me something. Can you remember anything that you like about this place?

(*BROTHER moves off. MORIAH DIGS.*)

MORIAH: I wasn't no spy man. Government didn't wan' no parts of me. "Unable to adjust to military life." I left the army. Hits the road with music in my head. To Europe. And I was tempted to stay there and never come back to this place where me and that music in my head didn't fit. One time I told this woman in . . . somewhere . . . I . . . it was somewhere in Maine. I told her I didn't have any family. She took me in like a little lost stray cat. Two years later, I was still there, but making more music than money. She got up the courage to ask me to leave. So I left. Some kinda way I found a whole new family every place I spent a bit of time in. I went back and forth across America for about ten years. Spent two years in five different hotels. Working odd hours at different odd jobs and odd clubs in some of the oddest places. New Mexico, Maine, Oregon, Florida, and New York is where I ended up. I have jumped trains. Hitchhiked. Been thrown in jail for being Black and being in the wrong car, with the wrong kinda people. Been calmly handcuffed in a club and led from the bandstand to jail for possession of drugs. That lawyer is still sending me bills. I got robbed on the subway, in New York a time or two, early in the morning, fucked up . . . playin' music all night, shovin' that shit up my nose. My lady helped me. I thank God for that woman. He ought to thank her. I had given up on Him. That's pride talkin'. I got that from you. (*Beat.*) What's wrong with Mama, man? What'd you do to her? Musta been something real bad for her to want to chase you into the hereafter. She was tryin' to get to you. A word of warning wherever you are. She's coming after your ass.

(*MORIAH digs. Organ music segues. Lights cross fade up on SLIM with LADY's snubnose, a drink, and a joint. She is ripped and wearing a house dress and curlers. There is music, "Funky Worm" by the Ohio Players. SLIM dances about and sings entertaining herself. A wreath of flowers is now prominently placed.*)

SLIM: Ladies and gentlemen! Cats and dogs! Cross-eyed mosquitoes and bow-legged frogs! I stand here before you to sit down beside you to tell you a story I don't even know! One bright morning in the middle of the night! Two dead boys got up to fight! Back to back they faced each other! Drew their swords and shot each other! A deaf policeman heard the noise! Came and shot these two dead boys! If you don't believe my tale is true, ask the blind wino . . . he saw it too!

(FONTENOT *steps in.*)

FONTENOT: Jobeth.

(SLIM *downs her drink, pockets the pistol, and* FONTENOT *enters.*)

FONTENOT: Jobeth? You weren't at the funeral home. I just wanted to check in on you. You're not alright.

SLIM: I didn't go. There's shit there that I can't deal with. And I'll be damned if one of the biggest pieces didn't come and track me down.

FONTENOT: Jobeth look at what you're doing to yourself.

SLIM: Must be bloodhound shit.

FONTENOT: That's dope talkin'.

SLIM: How's that pretty little wife of yours?

FONTENOT: She's fine.

SLIM: Y'all still tryin' to have a baby? I know it hurt your heart her losin' the other one. And can't have no mo'? It was prob'ly gon' be a boy too wasn't it? You were going to name him Junior, right? The one that got away. Shame ain't it? Only child like yourself ain't got no kids to raise. But you got the wife you wanted. I didn't give him your name. He's mine. A Killingsworth.

FONTENOT: Jobeth, come on. (*He reaches for her. She moves away.*)

SLIM: Don't put your hands on me.

FONTENOT: (*Reaches again.*) Why don't you lie down?

SLIM: Don't put your hands on me! You just listen! The birth certificate papers say, "Father . . . Unknown." That's you! (*Laughs.*)

FONTENOT: Jobeth, you're talkin' out of your head . . . tryin' to kill yourself. Stop all this nonsense . . .

SLIM: (*Snap!*) Nonsense! (SLIM *pulls the pistol from her pocket.*) This is my house! That's my name on the mailbox. You can't come in here tellin' me 'bout who I'm killin' or how to talk. You know what it's like to kill somebody, don't you! You killed me. You know that? This ain't me. I'm dead. I died. I ain't nobody! Miss Nobody and Mr. Unknown! Your mother didn't never tell you not to go to bed with any woman you wouldn't marry? Huh? Or about a woman scorned? And to always wear clean underwear? In case you have an accident. (*She aims at him.*) Your drawers clean boy?!

FONTENOT: That's enough Jobeth . . . give me the gun.

SLIM: Soooo! You don't have on clean underwear?! What's wrong with that little wife of yours? She can't wash, can't make babies. When I get through, it won't matter if your drawers were clean. I'd like to see you shit on yourself, frankly.

FONTENOT: Jobeth, now you know I've got a gun. Don't make me use it on you.

SLIM: Reach for it! I don't give a shit! I'll take you with me. If you can't hold onto a man in this life meet him in the next one. (*FONTENOT starts to move,* SLIM *cocks the pistol. He stops.*) Don't do that 'til I finish! Fate brought you here today. Know that now. Right here to me. Yeah. I came out of the bathroom here and after what just happened to my Daddy . . . I just started shootin'! Ain't a judge or jury nowhere could convict me. And you won't have much to say about it either.

FONTENOT: You could kill me Jobeth?

SLIM: I do it everyday.

FONTENOT: What's that gon' prove Jobeth?

SLIM: Not a damned thing that I could make you understand. It'll be worth it. Make me feel better.

FONTENOT: You knew I was getting married. I told you. I was honest with you. You lied to me about being protected. It was a little underhanded. Hell, it was a lot underhanded. Your father told me the best thing for me to do was just not come around. That everything would be alright. He knew what you were up to.

SLIM: Leave my daddy out of this!

FONTENOT: I ain't gon' stand here and debate this with you at gunpoint. If you intend to use that pistol, do it. But make sure you hit me in the heart. Right here.

(*FONTENOT starts to back away.*)

SLIM: No mister! I'm gon' blow your brains out! (*He stops.*) Shoot you in your heart?! What? You got an "S" on your chest? A bulletproof vest? You ain't slick. You scared. I might shoot you in your kneecaps first . . . watch you be crippled for a while. Hot damn your asinine ass. I thought you were leavin'. Superman! You scared!? "This crazy bitch just might shoot me!" And you got that right. That much you do. Why did you do that to me?!

FONTENOT: I wasn't doin' it to you. What do you want from me? I'm sorry?
I shouldn't have done it? I offered to help.

SLIM: I didn't need your "help." I needed you. I don't even know what I
meant to you.

(*FONTENOT moves toward her. SLIM raises the pistol. He stops.*)

SLIM: You never gave a shit about me did you?

(*BROTHER enters dressed in a suit and tie. He crosses to her and takes the gun.*)

BROTHER: Girl, you out yo' mind?

FONTENOT: Don't do that Brother!

BROTHER: Gimme this thang! You can't be pointin' guns at people 'cause
you mad at 'em. That's against the law, right Frank?

FONTENOT: Thank you.

BROTHER: It's some evils in the world we got to learn to live with.

SLIM: You stay away from me and my boy.

FONTENOT: Can I talk to him?

BROTHER: Dumb Dudley, dumb.

SLIM: He's not yours. You made your choice.

FONTENOT: He has to know who his father is.

SLIM: When I think it's time, I'll tell him who his daddy is.

BROTHER: The boy looks just like your ugly ass, Frank. How she gon' lie?

FONTENOT: Will you tell him the whole truth?

SLIM: Why? I don't like you. I don't want him to like you either. Just leave
us alone.

(*SLIM starts off. FONTENOT starts to follow. BROTHER stops him.*)

BROTHER: Don't go back there man. She be alright by herself. Whole damn
family's crazy. Boy, you should'a seen your face! Ha!

FONTENOT: I've been tryin' to find you Brother.

BROTHER: I ain't been hidin'.

FONTENOT: You got any ideas who might have shot your dad?

BROTHER: Uh uh. As far as I'm concerned if anybody in this world had
reason to kill him, it was me. And I didn't. So I can't help you. You
were more of a son to him than I was. But I don't harbor no bitterness.
You shouldn't have come by here. Not a good idea. She'll be alright in
time, but she ain't gon' change her mind today. I'll get you a picture of
the boy and bring it to you. You can carry it around in your wallet or
whatever. But don't you tell Jobeth I give it to you.

FONTENOT: That's not funny Brother.

BROTHER: I'd prefer it if you'd laugh about it.

FONTENOT: She pulled a gun on me . . .

BROTHER: Be thankful she didn't shoot your ass.

FONTENOT: This ain't the end of this Brother. Jobeth is not the kind of mother to be bringing up that boy by herself.

BROTHER: She ain't by herself. Ain't you got some investigatin' to do?

(FONTENOT *hesitates then exits. Lights and music segue to later.* ANN *joins* BROTHER.)

ANN: My, don't you look snazzy.

BROTHER: You like this huh?

ANN: You look right handsome. How's Jobeth holding up?

BROTHER: She alright. Layin' down, tryin' to stop the room from spinnin'.

ANN: You going to the wake?

BROTHER: I don't do that.

ANN: You got dressed.

BROTHER: He give me this suit. Seemed like the thing to wear today. Is Lady with y'all?

(MORIAH *enters.*)

MORIAH: Right behind me. You might want to make yourself scarce.

BROTHER: No. I'll wait. I need to talk to her. Before your Buddy gets to her.

ANN: What about?

BROTHER: About why she pulled that stunt.

MORIAH: She told Doc Alexander she was having a hard time getting to sleep.

BROTHER: Nawh, Baby Brother, she was trying to do more than go to sleep. Something ain't right about this bowl of beans.

(BROTHER *takes out the pistol and hands it to* MORIAH.)

BROTHER: That's hers right?

(SLIM *joins them.*)

BROTHER: The old man was shot with a what?

MORIAH: A . . . .38. Aw, hell nawh Brother.

SLIM: Brother, you didn't say nothin' did you?

BROTHER: Two spent shells in the chamber. Jobeth was about to help your buddy Frank put on some weight with the rest of 'em.

SLIM: Brother!

(LADY *enters moving slowly.*)

BROTHER: I'm just tellin' you what I think.

LADY: What are you doing in here? Boy if you don't get out of my house before I send you to meet your maker . . . you better.

(LADY *reaches for her purse.*)

BROTHER: Don't you think He's met enough of this family for one week? That what you lookin' for?

ANN: Brother!

LADY: Where did you get it you roguish bastard?

BROTHER: Why'd you kill 'im Lady? I think you did it with this pistol. The police got some tests they can do. Maybe you ought to get Frank to check it out.

ANN: Brother, now is not the time.

BROTHER: Nawh Miss Ann. I want her to know.

LADY: Boy, you have never been above doin' the devil's work. Don't come in my house pointin' accusin' fingers at me.

MORIAH: Two spent shells in your pistol Mama.

SLIM: What you sayin' Moriah . . . ?

ANN: There's no law against that.

MORIAH: When did you fire these Mama? Did you fire these?

BROTHER: Yestiddy mornin'.

MORIAH: Now shut up Brother! Another wrong won't make any of this right!

BROTHER: I ain't wrong. And who you hollerin' at?

SLIM: Is he tellin' the truth Mama?

BROTHER: You was hard on me Lady 'cause I wasn't yours . . . You was hard and you was wrong.

LADY: I was hard on all'a y'all! You were a child and no you ain't mine, thank the Lord, but you walked in my house wearin' hate like a overcoat.

BROTHER: I didn't hate you. I didn't even know you.

LADY: You hated your father, and you didn't know him either.

ANN: Brother, she's been through enough.

BROTHER: And that's how I know she done it. I tell you women start to think strange once they go through they change. You'll see. She wanted that man 'til death they do part.

LADY: What do *you* want?

BROTHER: Peace of mind. Money. I been broke. No peace there. This business got my name on it. Got some of my sweat in the makin' of it. And it ain't right for him to leave me out here in the world with nothin'. Lady, you turned him against me.

LADY: Damnit to hell, yeah he hurt me. Cut me deep bringin' you in my house. He went out in the streets, walked in shit and brought me his boots to clean.

BROTHER: I ain't had nothin' to do with that! He must not'a been happy at home.

ANN: Brother, be real!

LADY: I was a fool.

SLIM: Did you shoot him Mama?

LADY: By myself here in this house . . .

BROTHER: You hated him more than I did.

LADY: I think about things. I was a stone cold fool. By myself at my age. I wanted to kill him. He wouldn't talk to me; I wanted to kill him.

MORIAH: Did you shoot him Mama?!

LADY: He called me. Said he wanted to see me.

MORIAH: What for?

LADY: I didn't ask. I'd been hopin' I'd hear from 'im. I put on my house-coat, grabbed my purse, and when I got there, the door was open . . . it wasn't locked, so I went on in, and called out to him. He was in the bedroom, and I started in on his ass from the front room, "Wakin' me up at this time of the mornin'! What you want to see me for? You ain't had nothin' to say to me all this time. What you want now?" Oh, I carried on . . . 'til I realized he wasn't talkin'. And y'all know your Daddy could string together some bad things to call if you 'voked 'im. I figured he wanted to come back home, and I couldn't wait to tell him to kiss my behind. Should'a thought about that long time ago. This well done run dry. I wouldn't take you back if you crawled on your knees and begged.

MORIAH: What did he say?

LADY: He told me he couldn't move his legs.

SLIM: What?!

LADY: He couldn't move . . . his legs.

MORIAH: What was wrong with them?

LADY: Can't be sure. He wouldn't go see Doc Alexander. Gout maybe. They used to swell up on him and hurt so bad, he could hardly walk. But he wouldn't stay off 'em.

SLIM: What did you do?

LADY: I called him a stupid, hardheaded, old bastard. Never would listen to nobody with sense. He just sat there lookin' pitiful. Nose all dirty, matters in 'is eyes, and tears runnin' down his face. Part of me left the room not wanting to see 'im so.

ANN: So whoever shot him showed up . . . after you left?

LADY: Didn't nobody else come.

ANN: Oh my God.

LADY: I wiped his face with my handkerchief, and rubbed his legs. I pinched, and stuck my hairpin in both his legs, up and down and on the bottoms of his feet. He started beatin' on his legs with his fists, and grittin' his teeth tryin' to hurt hisself. He couldn't feel none of it.

MORIAH: Why didn't you call for some help?

LADY: He could have done that hisself. He called me. I put my purse on the bed and told him I was goin' to run a hot bath and put some Epsom salts in it and fix him a hot toddy to put him to sleep and I . . . was gon' call Doc Alexander to come look at him to . . . get him up to the hospital. I was puttin' the kettle on to boil in the kitchen when I heard the gun go off. When I got there . . . blood was everywhere. And him sittin' there with half his head runnin' down the pillow. Just layin' there, lookin' at me, half alive, and his eyes beggin' me. He didn't want me to call for no help. I knew what he wanted. Lord, it was so clear, I couldn't argue with it. He was hurtin'. Damn fool couldn't even blow his own brains out. Blood all over his face. All I could make out was the white in his eyes. The pistol was on the floor there by the bed. I bent down and picked it up. I looked right in his face . . . and I couldn't cry . . . I still can't. Nothin' to say to 'im. He wouldn'ta heard me . . . and I felt paralyzed myself. Couldn't move . . . I saw his chest was still heavin', and he made some noises . . . whimperin'. Then he closed his eyes. I aimed the pistol and closed mine. (*Silence.*) I didn't get to talk to him either son. I heard him go. I felt the life come out of what was left of him, like it was my own. I didn't kill 'im. He was dead when I walked in the door. I didn't think I'd miss somebody I hated so much. But I didn't want him to suffer like that. Y'all forgive me if you can. Hate me if you have to. I know it would'a killed him for you to see him crippled like that.

ANN: He shot himself.

LADY: With my pistol.

MORIAH: You called the sheriff?

LADY: I put my pistol back in my purse, shut the door behind me, and came on back to the house and called.

BROTHER: I'm sorry Lady. I didn't know.

LADY: Now you do. Go on . . . call the sheriff and have 'im come get me.

MORIAH: You didn't do anything wrong.

BROTHER: You try explainin' that to Deputy Dawg. Set him to foamin' at the mouth.

ANN: Why do we have to say anything?

BROTHER: Nawh Lady, I'mo take this pistol and . . .

SLIM: What, Brother?!

BROTHER: They got to find a murder weapon, elsewise they can't pin nothin' on nobody. How you comin' with that hole Baby Brother? Won't nobody expect him to have it.

MORIAH: I'm just about halfway done. They're bringing the casket in the morning. I'mo need some help.

BROTHER: Let's go. Now ev'body understand, we got to keep this to ourselves?

(*Nods of agreement all around as* BROTHER *and* MORIAH *start out only to be met by* FONTENOT.)

MORIAH: Frank!

(SLIM *leaves.*)

FONTENOT: Hey Buddy. You boys on your way out?

MORIAH: Back to diggin'.

LADY: Franklin Fontenot! Boy if you don't look more and more like your daddy the older you get. Moriah, Willie James, y'all go on. Franklin will be here 'til you finished. Sit and visit for a while. You want something to eat? Some ice tea or something?

FONTENOT: I wanted to speak. Offer my condolences.

LADY: Well that's mighty kind of you.

FONTENOT: Is Jobeth around? She feelin' any better Brother?

LADY: I didn't know she was sick.

BROTHER: Jobeth don't want to see you Frank. Why you harry-assin' people?

LADY: What you want with my children?

BROTHER: Jobeth run him off with your pistol this mornin' . . .

FONTENOT: That was your pistol she had? Mind if I take a look at it?

BROTHER: I figured you'd seen enough of it already today.

LADY: Give it to him Willie James.

BROTHER: I ain't got it.

MORIAH: (*Lying.*) I had it. I put it . . .

BROTHER: Nawh, I'm the one ended up with it. I took it from Jobeth. Saved yo' ass.

(BROTHER *hands him the pistol.*)

FONTENOT: I know I'm probably barkin' up the wrong tree. But I know how the sheriff thinks. He'll figure somebody in the family did it first off. 'Cause he don't know no better. I know it's crazy, but he's convinced we kill more of ourselves than the Klan ever needed to. I can keep you clear of any suspicion once I clear all your weapons. Brother you got a pistol?

BROTHER: That's Lady's. I don't carry one.

LADY: Do whatever you got to do. Go on and do your job Franklin. I tell you we so glad to have you workin' down there with the sheriff . . . I can't tell you. To have a Colored man workin' like you are is something we didn't have in the old days. Nobody would'a cared one way or another 'bout one of us gettin' killed. Wouldn'ta even been worth lookin' into.

FONTENOT: I'mo do my best. How is the boy?

LADY: Poochie growin' like a weed. You ought to come around sometime and see your boy.

FONTENOT: I'd like that, but Jobeth . . . don't take too kindly to the idea.

LADY: Aw, don't pay no 'tention to that silly. You come on by here when you feel like it and lay your hands on this big ole son of yourn and teach 'im.

MORIAH: That's not what Slim wants Mama.

LADY: Man's got a right to see his child. How's your wife?

FONTENOT: She's fine. Just fine.

LADY: You should bring her by, too.

BROTHER: Yeah, Dudley . . . bring your wife. Ha! Come Baby Brother, we got buryin' to do. These women in here tryin' to start World War Three.

LADY: I'm tryin' to do right by Franklin. This country ain't big enough to harbor no ill feelings. Franklin knows what I mean.

FONTENOT: Yes m'am, I think I do. I 'preciate it.

(FONTENOT *takes the gun and leaves.*)

BROTHER: That boy ain't all dumb. He part stupid.

MORIAH: Brother, I hope you didn't do what I think you did.

LADY: Me too. Jobeth. Get out here!

BROTHER: He said he wanted a pistol, I gave him one. (BROTHER *produces another .38.*) But, I figured I'd better hold onto the family secret.

ANN: What did you give Frank?

BROTHER: I give 'im my old piece of pistol. It ain't been fired since New Year's befo' last.

(SLIM *steps into the room seething.*)

SLIM: I wouldn't give him the news from yesterday's newspaper.

LADY: That's why you laid down and spread your legs for 'im? You got a problem girl.

SLIM: I can't stand him Mama! I still want to hurt him.

LADY: I ain't gon' let you use that child to do that. That man don't want you.

SLIM: I don't want him either. (*She pops a pill.*)

LADY: You got a problem. And it ain't got nothin' to do with nothin' but you and them damn pharmaceuticals.

SLIM: It's not my fault y'all. I need help.

LADY: You got a house full of it wrapped around you right now.

(*LADY crosses to her daughter and embraces her for what is probably the first time in many years. SLIM weeps.*)

BROTHER: Come on Lil' Brother. Let's go. It's gettin' dark.

(*BROTHER and MORIAH move off.*)

LADY: Would somebody make me a sandwich or something? I swear they don't feed you nothin' up at that hospital.

ANN: I can handle that.

SLIM: I'm sorry Mama.

LADY: We gon' all be just fine. One big happy family. We lost your daddy, but I feel like we found each other. You dry up your face. Ain't nothin' wrong with you we can't fix with family.

SLIM: Why did you try to die Mama?

LADY: Why you need to know that? Just you be glad I didn't. Ann when is this baby due?

(*ANN to SLIM, who shakes her head.*)

ANN: Moriah told you I'm pregnant?

LADY: No.

ANN: (*Smiles.*) Seven months.

LADY: Praise the Lord. Another blessing. See the Lord don't close a door without openin' a window.

SLIM: Why did you try to kill yourself Mama?

LADY: That . . . ain't your business. Whatever the reason . . . I changed my mind. Now tell me about this actin' business. I never could be no actress. Gettin' up in front of people. Puttin' on airs. I'm too shy for all that kinda mess.

ANN: They say the whole world is a stage.

SLIM: That's right, and Mama you act every day of your life.

(*Phone rings. The women all look at each other.* LADY *answers in her best "phone" voice.*)

LADY: Uh . . . "Hay low"?

(SLIM *rolls on the floor laughing.*)

SLIM: Uh . . . "haaaay low" . . .

LADY: (*Covers the mouthpiece.*) Girl if you don't hush . . . you'd better. It's the reverend. (*Back to her act.*) Hello. Yes. Oh no Reverend Raven, your prayers have no "bad" time. We thank you. We're all here together doin' just fine Reverend Raven. (LADY *listens.* SLIM *giggles with* ANN.) He wanted something simple so we complied with his wishes. Well thank you. We appreciate it, Reverend Raven, but feel free to say that special prayer with Sunday's sermon. Now is not such a good time to interrupt our family grievin' as it is goin' on. We, uh, we gon' be just fine, as they say in the Bible . . . "in the mornin'." . . . Yes Reverend Raven, "God provides." Good day. (*She hangs up.*) Lord that man can get on a human bein's nerves some time! Wanted to know if any food had been brought by. He wanted to join us for a moment in prayer. Lord knows I don't want to be bothered today.

ANN: You're a much better actress than I ever was.

LADY: You think so?

SLIM: 'Cademy Award . . .

LADY: Hush Jobeth. You ever meet any stars Ann? I always wanted to meet somebody like that. You ever see Billy Dee Williams? Or that woman on Channel Two who wears her hair something like mine . . .

ANN: No.

LADY: Ann, what does Moriah do?

ANN: When?

LADY: For work? Money. How do y'all live? Up there in New York.

ANN: Sometimes hard. Day-to-day. Job-to-job. We hustle.

SLIM: Hustle?

ANN: Not that hustle. Pound the pavement, drive a cab, park cars, tend bar.

LADY: You're an actress.

ANN: I haven't had an acting job in years. Not since I met Moriah.

SLIM: You think maybe Moriah jinxed you . . . ?

ANN: I don't even miss it anymore. I'm pregnant. I've found a new family. And I'm in Texas.

(*Lights fade to black. Music up. Later: Lights up on the following day.* MORIAH *in the dirt. The hole is mostly filled in now.*)

MORIAH: Daddy, I wish you could hear me. I wish you could tell me you're ok. 'Cause you didn't look real good. I love you. I wish I had said it . . . before now. I thought you knew. You never said it. I knew. Who you are . . . that's who I am.

(BROTHER *steps from the shadows with a small bouquet of flowers.*)

BROTHER: Me too. The apple didn't fall too far from the tree. I didn't like him. I know now he didn't care much for hisself. And I know now . . . that's ok.

MORIAH: When Grandad died . . . he cried.

BROTHER: The only time I ever saw him feel anything. I can't cry. Yet. I will in time I reckon.

MORIAH: Everything in life is a prologue.

BROTHER: Good God Almighty what the hell is next?!

MORIAH: I'll be lookin' deep inside myself for you, Daddy. I ran off. I had to do that, but I'm back. You had to call me back in your own way.

BROTHER: Couldn't just pick up the phone.

MORIAH: I'll take care of everything here. (*A moment.*) Me and Brother. I'm home. I'm looking to find where you used to go . . . in my head . . . be so happy I won't need to hate anybody.

(MORIAH *takes up his horn and starts to play. Something serene and dirge-like. The women appear in silhouette at the tree as before. They each in turn take the shovel and pour a shovel full of dirt into the hole.* BROTHER *steps aside and addresses the audience.*)

BROTHER: Suicide is against the law, you know. One thing about a death in the family, it brings folks together. Funny how they all show up looking for something different. But long as they show, I guess that's all that matter. It's good to have family. Havin' secrets not to tell. Sorta made it all worthwhile. I'm lookin' forward to makin' my own livin'. Driving a truck with my name on it. Change my reputation. Workin' with my brother again. I think we'll both like it better this time around. And I'll help 'im with his temper. Help my sister raise that boy right and get her act together. She'll be alright. We'll be alright. Texas! No place like it. Nowhere. Lots of sky. Lotta land. Lotta pride. Forgivin'. Lotta love.

(BROTHER *moves to join the others and hands the flowers to* LADY *with a hug.* MORIAH's *horn segues into something a bit more up tempo as lights fade on the family.*)

THE END

Driving Wheel. (*Left to right*) Bill Southerland, G. A. Johnson, and Cassandra L. Small. Photo courtesy of Jump-Start Performance Company.

Driving Wheel

STERLING HOUSTON

Sterling Houston (1945–2006) was a prolific and innovative African American writer in San Antonio, Texas. During the twenty years he worked with the Jump-Start Performance Company in San Antonio, he received a number of local, regional, and national awards and grants that demonstrate the appreciation of San Antonio, Texas, and the national arts community. He joined Jump-Start as a performer in 1986. Steve Bailey, the founder of the company, recognized his writing talent and encouraged him to develop plays. By 1989 he was elevated to writer-in-residence. His artistic abilities led to leadership responsibilities; by 1990 he was the administrative director, and shortly thereafter the artistic director, a position he held until his death in 2006.

Born and raised in San Antonio, he graduated from Highlands High School in 1963. Shortly after high school he left home for New York to start a career in music and theatre. During his career in professional theatre in San Antonio, New York, and San Francisco, he worked with many celebrated practitioners of modern theatre, including Charles Ludlam, Sam Shepard, and George C. Wolfe. After working on both the East and West Coasts as a performer, technician, and writer, he returned to San Antonio as an experienced theatre professional and found his calling and voice in playwriting.

Houston wrote thirty-three plays and three short novels and edited an anthology. Twenty-four of his plays were first produced by Jump-Start at the theatre renamed in his honor in 2009, the Sterling Houston Theatre. His plays are anthologized in *Myth, Magic, and Farce: Four Multicultural Plays by Sterling Houston* (Denton, TX: University of North Texas Press,

2005) and *High Yello Rose and Other Texas Plays* (San Antonio, TX: Wings Press, 2009), both edited by Sandra M. Mayo. The latter anthology features seven of his thirteen historical plays; those seven feature the Texas milieu and history in legend and fact. Houston's most-produced work, *High Yello Rose*, is a farce that dramatizes the story of the Texas Revolution through the perspective of Emily West Morgan, a mulatto bondswoman who, according to historical accounts and legendary stories, was with Santa Anna at San Jacinto when he was defeated by Sam Houston. *Cameoland*, a multimedia work, showcases the history of a remembered black historical site, the Cameo Theatre, during its most celebrated days in the post–World War II days of the 1940s. Houston also focuses on black San Antonio history in *Miss Bowden's Dream* (1998). Commissioned by St. Philip's College, the play tells the story of Artemesia Bowden, a black woman who was the academic leader at St. Philip's College for close to fifty years, moving the institution from a sewing school for black girls in 1902 to a member of the Alamo Community College District by the 1940s. Houston highlights the stories of several San Antonio icons in his *Living Graves* (2005). Other well-known works from the canon include *Driving Wheel* (1992), *Isis in Nubia* (1993), *Miranda Rites* (1994), and *Black Lily and White Lily* (1996). *Isis in Nubia* reveals Houston's interest in ancient Egyptian and Nubian history. Its retelling of the myth of Isis and Osiris is close to traditional historical narratives, with the exception of his placement of the story south of Egypt with a political assertiveness that reclaims Egyptian myth for black Africa.

Houston's work is quintessentially postmodern in its blend of styles, musical ideas, ritual, documentary, and use of multimedia. His plays encompass elements of melodrama, tragicomedy, farce, and burlesque.

As You Read *Driving Wheel*

Houston develops *Driving Wheel* in one act of seven scenes set in a side yard in San Antonio in the mid-sixties. The action develops with the juxtaposition of the past and the present with several flashbacks in scenes 3 and 4 to earlier periods in the life of the approximately thirty-year-old central character, Joe Jr. This dramaturgical structuring device highlights the work as an autobiographical memory piece. It depicts the events primarily through the mind of Joe Jr., who returns home to confront his past, especially his conflicts with his now-dead father about his homosexuality and desire to learn to drive. The significant memory of his relationship with his father is visually symbolized in the central image of an old American car on stage. Throughout the drama the car throws into relief the driving as a metaphor for the relationship between Joe Jr. and his dead father. The car on stage also gives extra poignancy to the scenes with his father, whose spirit returns to interact with him when he is asleep in the car. Father and son talk about the car, go driving, and discuss driving as a metaphor for life. The image of the car on stage and the focus on the mental anguish of Joe Jr. put this play in the expressionistic tradition of Elmer Rice's *Adding Machine*, with its oversized adding machine on stage. In addition, *Driving Wheel* reflects the tradition of Tennessee Williams' *Glass Menagerie* in its flashbacks and focus on memory and Arthur Miller's *Death of a Salesman* in its focus on the action through the mind of the central character. Finally, the discussions with the spirit of his father are surrealistic scenes that are juxtaposed with realistic scenes, a technique Houston identified as "magical realism." In both the realistic and surrealistic scenes, Houston highlights the African American Texan cultural milieu not only in reference to the Avalon Grill, Wheatley High School, and collard greens but also through music—for example, Junior Parker's blues renditions of "Foxy Devil" and "Driving Wheel"—and the vernacular language of the people of San Antonio's East Side. Maya Angelou encouraged Houston to write the play after he told her about his conflict with his father as a young man. Like many other American playwrights—for instance, Sam Shepard and Eugene O'Neill—Houston confronts his demons by exorcising them in drama. The down-to-earth banter between the characters, the realistic set, and manner of storytelling are in the tradition of realism.

Production History

Jump-Start Performance Company, Carver Cultural Center, San Antonio, Texas, 1992

Characters

CLARICE FERGUSON: Fiftyish widow.
JOE FERGUSON JR.: A failed poet, her son; in his thirties.
JOE FERGUSON SR.: The ghost of a father and husband.
MAUDE ESTHER: Friend and neighbor; fortyish.
CHARLES HAROLD: Maude Esther's brother.
VERONICA: Maude Esther's twelve-year-old.
CAR RADIO ANNOUNCER

Setting

Time: mid-1960s
Place: San Antonio, Texas, the side yard and porches of two modest frame houses.

SCENE 1

(*At center in the middle of a side yard between two houses is an old American car with the hood open. Downstage Right is* MAUDE's *back stoop, and Up Left is the side porch, etc., of the* FERGUSON *house.* JOE JR. *is bent over, leaning into the car engine, tinkering with a wrench.* VERONICA *is jumping rope Downstage,* MAUDE *is in her kitchen area, dialing the wall phone. Music up.*)

CLARICE: Hello? Reverend? How do? This is Mrs. Ferguson. Clarice Ferguson, that's right. I joined your congregation about a year ago, right after I buried my husband . . . well, Greater Mount Calvary is such a big church now; it's hard to remember everybody, I would think. Yes that's right, I work for the Board of Education, same as your wife, I work in the cafeteria at Douglass, where she's assistant principal. Yes, it sure is a small world, isn't it . . . (*Shouts out door.*) Turn it down please, Junior; I'm on the phone! (JOE JR. *turns down car radio.*)

VERONICA: (*Rhyme-singing as she jumps rope.*) Oh Mary Mack, Mack, Mack; all dressed in black, black, black; with forty-four buttons, buttons, buttons; all down her back, back, back.

CLARICE: Beg pardon? Well, yes, I imagine you must be very busy and all, but I was wondering if you had a little time to see me soon, in private. Oh no; it ain't about me! I'm healthy and in my right mind, for the time being anyway. It's my son. My boy, Joseph Ferguson Jr. I'm worried about him. No, he isn't sick, he's . . . he just doesn't have no get-up-and-go about him. Not that he's a trifling kind of person, not at all. Keeps his room neat as a pin, doesn't stay out all night worrying me to death like some boys do. But ever since my husband passed, Junior's been grieving worse than me, though he doesn't think I see it . . .

VERONICA: (*Rhyme-singing.*) . . . She jumped so high, high, high; she touched the sky, sky, sky; and she didn't come back, back, back; 'til the fourth of July, -ly, -ly!

CLARICE: How's that Reverend? Oh, indeed? From who did you hear this? Oh, well, it doesn't really matter about that kind of talk anyway. It doesn't matter to me who he loves so long as he can love somebody. Crosses were sure enough made to bear, that's right. But that's not why I'm concerned about him, no, you see, he's gone and bought himself this old junk car, and my boy don't know nothing about cars. Nothing. I just can't understand it. It's odd when I think about it; his daddy drove a truck for forty years, but he would never teach that child to drive . . .

VERONICA: (*Rhyme-singing.*) I asked my Mamma; for fifteen cents; to see the elephant jump the fence; he jumped so high; he touched the sky; he didn't come back 'til the Fourth of July . . . ! (*She crosses to Center and watches* JOE JR.) What you doin'?

JOE JR.: Nothing. What you doin'?

MAUDE: (*Leans out her door.*) Veronica! Leave that man alone and come in here and eat, girl!

VERONICA: O.K. 'Bye Junior. (*She goes into her house.* MAUDE *comes down to* JOE JR.)

MAUDE: You fixin' it all up, huh?

JOE JR.: Trying to.

MAUDE: Guess it's too late to get your money back . . .

JOE JR.: I'm keeping it. I know it can go again. Sure has a good radio.

MAUDE: You know, Joe Jr., you never did strike me as real, what you call, mechanically inclined, more the artistic type. Don't get me wrong now, ain't nothing wrong with that. Where's your mamma?

JOE JR.: She's in the house. On the phone, I think.

MAUDE: (*Calling out.*) CLARICE! (*To* JOE JR.) Now my older brother, Charles Harold, he was always real mechanical; could fix damn near anything. (*Calling.*) Oh CLARICE! (*To* JOE JR.) He's coming over after while to play bid whist with us.

JOE JR.: Charles Harold?

MAUDE: Unh huh. You want me to ask him to look at it for you?

JOE JR.: O.K., sure.

MAUDE: 'Course, he ain't been inclined to do much of anything since his wife passed.

CLARICE: (*Comes out her door.*) Maude Esther; hi girl. I thought that must be you hollering my name out. I was talking on the phone.

MAUDE: What you got smelling so good, chile?

CLARICE: Mustard greens.

MAUDE: Sister, them greens be sho' nuff talking up the neighborhood.

CLARICE: They're about ready. You want some?

MAUDE: No honey, I came to see if I could borrow your card table. You still got that old card table don't you?

CLARICE: Yeah, sure you can. Come on in. (*MAUDE goes past CLARICE into door.*) There it is, right there 'side the Frigidaire. Junior, don't you want some of these good old greens?

JOE JR.: Yeah, sure; thanks Mamma. I just want to try one more thing here.

CLARICE: Do you know what you're doing in there, son?

JOE JR.: No. But I just might get lucky, you know. Can't have bad luck all the time. It's mathematically impossible.

CLARICE: Lord . . .! I'll bring some on out to you. I know you must be hungry.

MAUDE: (*Enters carrying card table.*) Thanks, sugar pie. See you about eight o'clock then.

CLARICE: Oh, I'll be there.

MAUDE: Don't forget what I said, now. Wear something cute. 'Bye Junior. Don't work too hard.

JOE JR.: 'Bye Maude Esther. (*MAUDE goes into her house.*) What's she talking about, "Wear something cute"? (*Scrapes his hand in engine.*) Oww! Shit. Maybe I ought to take a little break.

CLARICE: Be right back. I'll bring you some greens and corncakes. (*She goes in.*)

JOE JR.: Sounds delightful. Lunch al fresco! (*He crosses Down Right to the water hose, turns it on, and rinses his hands.*)

CAR RADIO ANNOUNCER: Folks, don't forget next Saturday night the Eastwood Country Club will present the fabulous Little Junior Parker, for two dynamic shows at nine and twelve midnight, and cats and kitties, you might want to get there early, cause when Junior Parker's in town the crowds do come 'round. He'll be singing all his hits backed by a twelve-piece orchestra turning it every which-a-way but loose. So get on out to Eastwood, this Saturday, people and check out the one and only Little Junior Parker. It'll make you say "Oh, Yeah!" (*Music: "Foxy Devil."*)

JOE JR.: Bring me a beer, too, would you please!

CLARICE: (*Brings out a tray with two steaming bowls.*) Sometimes food tastes better when you eat it outside. Why is that you think?

JOE JR.: (*Takes food and beer.*) I don't know. Probably reminds us of when we lived in the jungle.

CLARICE: I knew you'd have a answer. Is there anything my child don't know?

JOE JR.: Good greens! (*He gulps food and beer.*) Ain't nothing like this in New York.

CLARICE: They got greens in New York; I know better. Drinking beer in the afternoon, is that a New York thing?

JOE JR.: Don't worry about it. I can deal. What did you do woman, stick your big toe in these?

CLARICE: Quit now! You remind me of your daddy when you talk like that. He used to say I put my whole foot in them. Ha!

JOE JR.: You really miss him, huh.

CLARICE: Like an arm yanked out of its socket. Dreamed about him, again last night.

JOE JR.: Did you?

CLARICE: It was a funny dream. He was all dressed up in a sandy colored lawn suit, spectator shoes, diamond tie pin. He always was a natural sport. For the longest time, he just stared at me, his eyes kinda turned down at the sides, like he was about to cry. Then he reached in his pocket, pulled something out and handed it to me in my hand. It was a little white baby shoe, kinda worn, scuffed on the sides. It felt real heavy in my hand, and when I turned it over, emptying it into the other hand, out poured a shiny little pile of diamonds. It was the funniest thing. Been dead and gone for more than a year, and the man can't rest right for worrying about me. Poor thing.

JOE JR.: You got me to worry about you now.

CLARICE: I know. That's what worries me. I mean, I'm worried about you.

JOE JR.: Me? Don't worry about me.

CLARICE: But what you gonna do? Don't you want to go back to New York?

JOE JR.: No, Mamma. New York has changed, and I have too, boy have I.

CLARICE: You don't have to tell me if you don't want to. I just wish your daddy had lived to . . . I don't mean to talk about him all the time. I hate it when women talk about their dead husbands like they were the weather, or something everybody cared about.

JOE JR.: I like when you talk about him. Seem like I hardly got to know him.

CLARICE: (*Suddenly angry.*) That's because both of you were so damn hard-headed! (*Calm.*) You were his heart, you know. His hope. Know what he said when he first laid eyes on you?

JOE JR.: What?

CLARICE: He said "Oh, here's my little Cadillac driver!" The midwife, old Mrs. Flores, had given you a little bath and was holding you up in her arms when he busted into the room, right off the road, truck motor still running he was so excited. Took one look at you and said "Oh! Oh! Here's my little Cadillac driver! Gonna drive me all the way to California!"

JOE JR.: What did he mean by that? California, huh?

CLARICE: It's the truth from here to heaven.

JOE JR.: Then what happened?

CLARICE: Then you started to laugh. Yes! Laugh out loud. I don't mean no little baby grin, but a pure-dee laugh out loud. Sound like an old man.

JOE JR.: Musta scared ya'll half to death.

CLARICE: Old Miz Flores had been a midwife since horse and buggy days, you know, and she swore up and down she'd never heard no newborn baby laugh like that. Cry yes; but *laugh*? Want some more greens? There's plenty. Help yourself. I've got to git, if I'm gonna make it to the beauty shop on time.

JOE JR.: Getting your hair fixed just to play cards with Maude Esther 'nem? What's she cooking up for you tonight, some kind of blind date?

CLARICE: Nothing formal as that, I guarantee you. I'll be back in a little bit. (*She exits. Music up.*)

JOE JR.: (*Returns to open hood, tinkers for a minute, gives up and takes a swig of his beer.*) So, I'm hardheaded? Was that it, Daddy? What kept you from giving me anything of yourself? You promised so much—then withheld fulfillment. Did you even try to understand? I'm a poet. Images and emotions run in my veins instead of blood. All you saw was softness, weakness. When I went to New York, you put barbed wire on top of the wall that had already grown between us. Maybe I am a fool. But I'm true to my foolishness. I'm sorry you were disappointed in me. But I'm not sorry for myself. Suffering is to the poet like high-octane fuel, allowing him to get to faraway places with great speed and efficiency. (*He drains beer can, opens front door of car and lies down. "Driving Wheel" music up. JOE JR. sleeps as lights change to evening. Light inside car pops on as JOE SR. rises from the backseat. He gets out of the car and smiles at JOE JR. as lights and music fade to OUT.*)

SCENE 2

(Sound of insects and birds singing. Lights up on JOE JR. tinkering with engine as before. JOE SR. stands near him. The light is dreamy and rich with shafts of sun colors.)

JOE SR.: Well, oh well! Went and bought yourself an automobile did you!

JOE JR.: That's right.

JOE SR.: That's good, that's good. A man without an automobile is a piss-poor fella, and that's for damn sure. How much she cost you?

JOE JR.: Hundred dollars. As is.

JOE SR.: Hundred dollars cash? Where'd you get that kind of money, son?

JOE JR.: Wasn't that hard really. Cutting grass, throwing the paper . . . whatever. I gave half to Mamma and saved the other half, till I had enough. No big thing.

JOE SR.: Well ain't you something. Yessir, a fella without a car ain't about much of nothing. Couldn't be. It's a matter of time and distance. If you're walking, you see, you spend all your time getting where you going, and once you get there, if it turns out to be someplace you don't really want to be, you got to wait for the bus driver, or some other driver, to drive you, before you can get the hell on out.

JOE JR.: I guess you're right.

JOE SR.: And shoot! In this town, folks waiting at the bus stop can die of frostbite in the wintertime and sunstroke in the summer. God bless the child that's got his own car! Is it running?

JOE JR.: I drove it over here yesterday, but when I tried to start it up again, nothing happened.

JOE SR.: You mean it wouldn't turn over?

JOE JR.: It wouldn't do nothing, not even click.

JOE SR.: Get in and crank it up.

JOE JR.: *(Gets in car and tries the ignition.)* See? Nothing. And the battery was just recharged. I recharged it myself.

JOE SR.: No, it ain't your battery.

JOE JR.: *(After a pause.)* So what do you think it is? The starter?

JOE SR.: *(Slides under car. He gets back up, dusting off his hands.)* What you have here, son, is a solenoid problem.

JOE JR.: A solenoid problem. You mind telling me what the hell a solenoid is?

JOE SR.: A solenoid, you see, is this little whatchamadoo that fits into the starter. If the solenoid goes out, then the starter don't start, and there you sit.

JOE JR.: So here I sit; so what can I do? Can I fix it?

JOE SR.: It can't be fixed; it's got to be replaced. Don't suppose you got a spare one around here.

JOE JR.: Right.

JOE SR.: Got a little screwdriver? A little one?

JOE JR.: Yeah. (*Gets tool from trunk.*) What's up?

JOE SR.: I think I can make you a temporary adjustment. Till you can get it replaced. (*He slides under car.*) You know Junior, ain't nothing to taking care of no car. Just simple easy things'll add five or ten years to the life of any automobile. Even this old tank.

JOE JR.: Simple like what?

JOE SR.: Well the main thing is to always check your fluid levels. 'Specially your oil. Change it more often than you're supposed to. I'm serious. If you pull out that dipstick and the fluid that drips off looks more like black-strap molasses than cane syrup, then it's time for an oil change. (*He gets back up.*) Get in and try it now.

JOE JR.: (*Car cranks without turning over.*) Sounds like it wants to start.

JOE SR.: It sure wants to, don't it. Try it again. It wouldn't hurt to have these cables replaced. They split in a few places. Means big trouble down the line . . . What it really comes down to is: pretty much you take care of it; it'll take care of you, whether it's a horse, an automobile, or a child for that matter.

JOE JR.: What do you mean by that exactly?

JOE SR.: Don't exactly mean anything by it other than just saying it 'cause it's true.

JOE JR.: Truth has many faces.

JOE SR.: More like different expressions on the same face. Know what I mean?

JOE JR.: It's too late for all that. Why did you come back to haunt me? It's over. I don't need you.

JOE SR.: Yeah. But maybe I need you. You don't seem real surprised to see me.

JOE JR.: The last time you surprised me was when I was fifteen, and one of your friends told you I was "like that"; and you realized that I was one of *them*, that I was "funny" as you called it, not daring to say the word "gay." You slapped me across the face with the back of your hand, remember? As though my queerness was somehow an insult to your fatherhood. That you were the injured party, not me.

JOE SR.: I didn't come back to argue all that up again. I can't change who I am anymore than you can. But now that I'm dead, I found my voice at last. Do you hear me? Do you hear what I'm trying to say to you?

JOE JR.: I'm trying to hear. I'm starting to hear.

JOE SR.: Good. Got any gasoline?

JOE JR.: Half a can in the trunk.

JOE SR.: Bring it here and let me show you something. Now, take a little of that gas and pour it right down the middle of that carburetor, there; not too much, now. Yeah. Alright, go on try to start it now.

JOE JR.: (*Cranks engine and car starts. He guns the motor.*) Alright!

JOE SR.: Ha ha! Come on then let's take it for a drive around the block. There's a couple'a more things I got to tell you. (*They drive off as lights fade to OUT. Music up.*)

SCENE 3

(*Music up. Lights up on* MAUDE, *in her window on telephone.*)

MAUDE: . . . Yes girl, you know I got to go out to Eastwood and see Little Junior Parker. Us married women got to take our thrills when we can get 'em. What you mean "your husband won't let you"? Don't tell him. You gonna be with me, how much trouble can you get into? What? No. I do not think Little Junior Parker is ugly; even if that nose is kinda spread all across his face. Girl, with a voice like that, he can come over here and be ugly on me any time! What you say! Ha! Well, if you can't go, you just *can't*, that's that. Maybe I can get my neighbor to go with me. Clarice. You know Clarice. Used to be Clarice Hawkins. Went to Wheatley with us long years ago. That's the one! Married Joe Ferguson, had a son that went off to New York and got into the Life. What you mean "What life?" The Gay Life, girl. I swear, sometimes you are so country. He's a sweet boy, but he got a hard way to go. His daddy was so hard on him when he was coming up. You know the kind . . .

(*Lights cross fade to Ferguson area—flashback to the past.*)

CLARICE: Don't be so hard on him Joe; he didn't mean nothing! Please!

JOE SR.: Get out of my way! (*JOE SR. pushes JOE JR., and he falls.*)

CLARICE: He's sick. Can't you see he's sick?

JOE SR.: Sick hell! He's drunk! You got the nerve to come in here falling down drunk, as hard as I work to get some respect for this family, and you come disgracing yourself!

JOE JR.: I didn't mean . . . I . . .!

JOE SR.: You had a wreck, didn't you! After I told you not to drive . . . You and that boy Buddy driving around in his daddy's car like a couple of common hoods. You still not too big for me to take my belt off to your ass!

CLARICE: Joseph don't! You got all the neighbors looking out their windows . . . !

JOE SR.: Let 'em look! You think they didn't see the police car pull up and bring this no-account to my front door?

JOE JR.: I don't care let 'em see . . . let 'em see everything . . .!

CLARICE: You only got another month till graduation! You can do what you want! Don't mess it up now, come on in the house and wash your face, son.

(*After a pause* JOE JR. *becomes nauseous, holds his mouth and runs inside.*)

CLARICE: Junior! (*She follows him in.*)

JOE SR.: (*Unfastens his belt, pulling it off during following.*) Don't you vomit on that floor! Goddammit, I'm gone make you lick it up! (*He goes in. Lights cross fade to* MAUDE.)

(*Return to present.*)

MAUDE: . . . Yeah, girl; I don't know why people make problems out of little things that just keep life from being boring. Let me get off this phone, I got company coming directly, and haven't started cleaning this place. See you later, alligator.

SCENE 4

(*Music up as lights cross fade to* CLARICE *getting her hair done.*)

CLARICE: I met Joseph Ferguson when I was twenty years old, and we were married within a year. But Joseph wasn't my first husband, no indeed. When we met, I had been the widow Hawkins for two years, having married old Rev. Hawkins when I wasn't nothing but seventeen. He had a heart attack about a year later, during an exceptionally vigorous usher board meeting. People tried to say I caused his heart attack, you know how people talk, but I wasn't nowhere near him when it happened. Then Joseph Ferguson began to court me, as gently as you please.

(*Continuing.*) CLARICE: We both sang in the choir which was one of the only things I liked about Rev. Hawkins' church. Joe took me out on my first date. We went dancing at the Avalon Grill, to a real live band and everything. We got married at the courthouse, and Junior was born nine months later to the day. Joseph was a good provider. Made a pretty good wage for a colored man back then. Worked for the same people, Larkins Furniture Company, driving a truck for almost thirty years. He was a man who actually liked grocery shopping; knew where all the bargains were. Funny the things you think about. He never cared too much for white folks, his dislike made bitter by fear. "That's how they are," he'd say, after reading about some devilishness done to the colored by the white. "That's just how they are!" Like he could bear their cruelty if it was natural, and not inhuman like it always seems. He wasn't in favor of integration and all that. Him and Junior just argued about it all the time. (*Lights cross fade to Downstage.*)

(*Return to past.*)

JOE SR.: Aw you don't know nothing about white people, nothing! None of you young ones know anything about nothing, but you think you know everything there is to know.

JOE JR.: You all the time worrying about white folks. The hell with them.

JOE SR.: To hell with them? It's fine to talk about to hell with them when hell is where they would like to see us all.

JOE JR.: There's good ones and bad, just like colored.

JOE SR.: But good or bad, he owns the whole pie! How you come talking about getting your piece of the pie, when he owns the whole pie; hell, the whole bakery. White man's only use for the nigger is just that; to use him. Take what you got and give you nothing to show for it. My grandmama was born a slave over in Guadalupe County; it's on the record at the courthouse. Not her birth, mind you, but the fact that she was her master's property.

JOE JR.: Slavery was a long time ago, Daddy. We got Mr. Thurgood Marshall now. *Brown versus Board of Education.*

JOE SR.: You think if he lets you in his schools, he'll let you in his world? All you gonna do is lose your own Negro schools. Colleges. Look at Commerce Street down by the S.R. Station. We got blocks of colored businesses, restaurants, hotels, tailor shops, barbershops, a picture show; it'll all get wiped out; all we worked for, fighting uphill every step, is just gonna get washed away in a wave of "brotherhood"!

JOE JR.: That's why I can't wait to get out of this town! Progress don't mean nothing around here.

JOE SR.: I'll tell you what means something to me. Having you respect what I say to you as much as you do those white teachers at that white school!

(*Lights cross fade to* CLARICE *in present.*)

CLARICE: (*She is dressing to go out.*) He had a bad temper. But worse than his fussing, was his silence. Days might go by and you wouldn't know what had made him mad; just that his mouth was all stuck out again about something. I learned to deal with it, but Junior would take it personally.

(*Cross fade to past.*)

JOE JR.: What? What did I do? I can't say I'm sorry, if I don't know what I did.

JOE SR.: (*After a pause.*) . . . Stay away from that boy Buddy, he's no good and I don't want him coming over here no more. You hear me?

JOE JR.: Why? What did he do to you?

JOE SR.: Don't get smart. You know what you need to know.

(JOE JR. *sighs in frustration as* JOE SR. *exits. Lights cross fade to card-game area. Return to the present.*)

CLARICE: We lived a pretty good life, the three of us. Always paid the rent, kept food in the house. Then Joe Jr. quit college and ran off to New York to find himself, as he put it. Then Joseph took sick and after a few years, died on me; just like Reverend Hawkins had done so many years before. Except I never loved Reverend Hawkins, and I didn't have to watch him die, day by day. Joe was eaten alive by cancer and regret, until the pain of both combined can't even be killed by dope. Then death comes like a mercy. But death isn't really the end of anything; is it? Not the end of anything at all.

MAUDE: (*After a pause.*) Come on, Clarice! It's your play, girl.

CLARICE: Oh, excuse me; I kinda drifted off didn't I. (*She plays a card.*)

MAUDE: No, Sugar; clubs is trumps. Ain't you got no hearts?

CLARICE: I'm sorry. You'd think I never played cards before.

CHARLES HAROLD: That's alright partner; we can still whup 'em.

VERONICA: How come I have to play cards? (*No reply.*) How come Mama?

MAUDE: Because your daddy ticked me off royally, so I had to tell him about himself. He left out of here bookin' knowing that I had invited company to play cards, and went off somewhere in the streets to suck his thumb, I expect.

VERONICA: I still don't see why I have to.

MAUDE: Because I said so. Now be still and play girl. I don't want to have to wear you out in front of company. (*To* CLARICE.) Just getting to be so *fast*. You lucky you never had no little girl.

VERONICA: I got to be fast to keep up with my 1965 *class!*

MAUDE: Girl, I'm going to knock the naps out of your big head, if you don't quit.

CHARLES: Maybe we shouldn't play cards right now, Maude Esther . . .

MAUDE: No indeed! I invited Clarice over here to play cards, and we are going to play!

CLARICE: It's O.K. by me, whatever we do. It's nice to get out of my house, even if it is just next door.

MAUDE: Next Saturday night is Little Junior Parker at Eastwood. Come on go with us, Clarice. All you do is work and go to church. Don't you think that'd be what's happening? You come too, brother-mine . . .

CHARLES: Yeah, if Clarice would be kind enough . . .

CLARICE: Why not? I haven't been out to Eastwood since Junior was little.

VERONICA: Junior is a punk.

MAUDE: Girl, I'm gonna have to kill you. (*Raises her hand as if to strike;* VERONICA *gets up to dodge her.*)

VERONICA: Junior is a sissy punk! Junior is a sissy punk! (VERONICA *runs off as* MAUDE *rises.*)

MAUDE: Veronica! Lord, I swear, I don't know where she gets it. Veronica! Girl, you better answer me when I call you. Ya'll excuse me, please. (*Exits.*)

CLARICE: (*After a pause.*) You have any children, Charles Harold?

CHARLES: Me? Oh yes. Four girls. All married and moved. I've got nine grandbabies. Believe that? A young fella like me?

CLARICE: That's nice.

CHARLES: And you?

CLARICE: What? Oh; just the one. Son. Still not married. He's home with me.

CHARLES: Well, shoot! I got enough grandkids to spare you a couple, till he comes through.

CLARICE: That's mighty nice of you. You seem such a kind person.

CHARLES: Kind enough, when folks let me. But I'm going to have to fuss at my sister, for keeping you a secret for so long . . .

CLARICE: You wouldn't be trying to flirt with me now, would you sir?

CHARLES: I'm surprised I still remember how. It doesn't offend you does it? I know how it is with that grief situation. My wife passed two years ago this April. Sugar diabetes. Suffered with it a long time, you know how it is.

CLARICE: I'm sorry to say I do.

CHARLES: But that grief situation, that mourning thing, it's ongoing, everyday. Some days it'll hit you hard, but most times it's like a low humming noise in the background. It doesn't ever really go away.

CLARICE: I like the way you put that. You have a nice way with words. My son is a poet. Had his poems printed in a book when he was up in New York. I'll show it to you sometime.

CHARLES: I'd like that. We have some mighty great Negro poets in this country you know. Countee Cullen, Langston Hughes . . . Do you like poetry?

CLARICE: I don't know much about it. But I like Junior's. Even if I don't always understand it. When he was in high school, he would stay in his room for hours writing and reading. Come home, eat, and then I might not see him till the next morning. You know, when a child is gifted he's often misunderstood. He'd always be getting his feelings hurt, by some teacher or some jealous classmate. And him and his daddy didn't get along. So he just felt safer in that room with the door closed, playing the radio and writing his poems, long after his daddy and I had gone to bed.

(*Cross fade to* JOE JR. *in the past sitting at desk. Music up.* JOE JR. *is typing the last section of a poem into a portable typewriter. A cigarette curls up from the ashtray. He pulls paper from typewriter, and begins to read.*)

Searching for Bethlehem in the stormy desert
I stumbled upon Mecca in the form of a smooth black tower.
It vibrates at my touch
Reproducing the deep brown cello music
Of my mother's voice.
I bless myself for being blessed in the twisted metal face

Of hope shattered like headlights in head-on crashes.
I declare myself to be a thing as complete as an idea in the mind
Of some unique and cunning ancient god,
Containing all things essential for a journey in this world
Of multiple realities
Of sacred laughter and
Profane tears.

(*Return to present. Lights cross fade to card-game area.* VERONICA *and* MAUDE *enter.*)

MAUDE: Veronica has something to tell ya'll. Go on, now.

VERONICA: I apologize for being so rude and sassy . . .

MAUDE: And what else . . .

VERONICA: . . . And I promise not to do it no more.

MAUDE: *Any* more.

VERONICA: Anymore.

MAUDE: That's fine. Now you may be excused to do your homework, young lady. (VERONICA *exits.*) Lord, I don't know what I'm going to do with that girl.

CLARICE: I know she doesn't mean any harm. She's just a child.

MAUDE: I am so sorry this evening turned out this way. I wanted everything to be so nice . . .

CHARLES: Plans can be like that Sister; don't be worrying about it too much. I got to meet this nice lady, didn't I? And we going to Eastwood Saturday night ain't we?

CLARICE: Sure, we going; a real date, that's right.

CHARLES: Say! How 'bout if I drive us all up to the Dairy Queen for a malted milk! Huh? What do you say?

VERONICA: (*Off Stage.*) Bring me a chocolate!

MAUDE: You better get that lesson. Don't make me come back in there.

CHARLES: How about it, Clarice? Wouldn't a nice malted milk hit the spot?

CLARICE: That would cool me down a bit. So warm this evening . . .

MAUDE: But we don't want you to cool off too much, do we Brother.

CHARLES: Well no; I reckon we don't.

SCENE 5

(*Current time, mid-sixties. Music Up. Lights up as car comes to center.* JOE JR. *and* JOE SR. *are driving through the neighborhood.*)

JOE SR.: Look out! Did you see that jackass!*(Shaking his fist.)* Asshole! Ya see, that's one of many benefits of driving around in traffic; you get to chastise transgressors on the spot.

JOE JR.: I don't think they heard you. I hope not.

JOE SR.: That light's getting ready to change. Get ready to stop now . . .

JOE JR.: Wow, dad are you psychic too? Is that one of the side effects of being dead?

JOE SR.: Shoot! That's nothing, minor stuff. I could fly if I took the notion to do so. Take off and fly right through the air. But I wouldn't want to scare you. You might lose control.

JOE JR.: Thanks. And try not to burst into flames, if you can help it.

JOE SR.: Son, it just wouldn't be right if I didn't tell you something else, something that's not easy for me to say . . .

JOE JR.: Uh oh. Maybe I should pull over.

JOE SR.: There's a price. A price you pay for driving. And the price is always going up. Not down.

JOE JR.: I guess that's fair. Balance in all things, they say.

JOE SR.: For some, having a car is nothing short of a continuous heartache. Just keeping it running right is a constant challenge. No sooner you get your brakes done, buy a new set of tires, then the water pump goes out and the transmission ain't acting right.

JOE JR.: I suppose any old car would be . . .

JOE SR.: That's just it! Not just old ones; the new ones too. And all of them burn gas and eat up insurance money. It's the price you pay, you understand; the *price!*

JOE JR.: Yeah, I hear what you're saying. A car is like a family: great to have around when you need 'em, but always needing something you don't want to give.

JOE SR.: Let me tell you something; there's worse things than being needed. Even by a machine. Look out! Don't you see that stop sign? Don't trust the other driver to see you.

JOE JR.: I see the stop sign. It's a four-way stop sign.

JOE SR.: See, *(Looking out window.)* that's just what I'm talking about. That was a white lady driving, and white ladies don't necessarily believe that stop signs apply to them.

JOE JR.: So, how you handling the white folks on the other side? Don't tell me you got integrated at last!

JOE SR.: It ain't nothing like that. Ain't no white folks over there.

JOE JR.: What?

JOE SR.: No black folks either; not exactly, you see . . . it's kinda hard to explain. Plus, I ain't exactly been over to the other side, not all the way over. Not yet.

JOE JR.: Wow, I hope I remember this when I wake up.

JOE SR.: Turn right here, and we'll be right back home.

JOE JR.: This *is* my dream, isn't it? Not yours.

JOE SR.: All of it's a dream, Joseph, yours, mine, and all the rest of it. That's what makes it so funny. (*Starts to laugh.*) So damn funny.

JOE JR.: What's funny?

JOE SR.: All of it! People crying at funerals! Ha! *Ha!* Saying, "I'll love you forever!" *Ha! Ha! Ha!* Talking about "Peace on Earth!!" "Peace in the Valley!" (*Calming down.*) Peace in the Valley, some day. (*Lights cross fade.*) Home, home again. That's enough driving for me for a while. Enough sightseeing, too . . . Things change so fast. Too fast.

JOE JR.: Has it really changed that much?

JOE SR.: I almost didn't recognize it. Commerce Street used to be so alive! I guess I was too, long years ago.

JOE JR.: How did I do? Driving pretty good huh?

JOE SR.: You did alright, for a beginner.

JOE JR.: It's hard for you to give me a compliment, isn't it? Why you always have to be the hard one?

JOE SR.: Ha! You think I'm hard? Now, my papa, Old Man Wilson, he was a sonofabitch. Always angry about something; with his mouth all stuck out. Couldn't please him if you saved his life. But I forgave him his licks and hurtful words. Even the way he talked to my mamma; I forgave him.

JOE JR.: You want me to say I forgive you?

JOE SR.: Listen, son. The most important thing about driving a car, the one thing above all else; you must always do. Look out for the other fella.

JOE JR.: Look both ways at a stop sign?

JOE SR.: Promise me you will. Every time.

JOE JR.: O.K. I promise.

JOE SR.: 'Cause sure as you're born, no matter how fine your driving is, how razor sharp your responses are, here comes some sucker late for work, or drunk, runs a stop sign and hits you broadside. Next thing you know, you waiting for the bus again.

JOE JR.: Why are you telling me all this now? For ten years you hardly had anything to say to me.

JOE SR.: I wanted to. I wanted to talk. Told myself I'd wait till I saw you again. Wait 'till you came home. But when I finally did see you again, I couldn't concentrate on anything but my pain. There you were. My fine boy. Standing by my hospital bed. If I could have made a sound I wouldn't have known what to say. And when I looked in your eyes, all I could see looking back at me was my own sick pain, magnified by yours. Cancer had been feasting on my insides for months, like every day was Thanksgiving. But it wasn't till I saw you again that I knew I was really going to die.

JOE JR.: I never hated you.

JOE SR.: You didn't even come to my funeral.

JOE JR.: I couldn't bring myself to go. I heard the undertaker stuffed cotton in your cheeks to make you look more natural. I couldn't bear to see it.

JOE SR.: Old Franklin Brothers did a hell of a nice job. Very artistic! You should'a seen it.

JOE JR.: Maybe I should have.

JOE SR.: (*Rooster crows.*) Look, I can't be hanging around here much longer. It's good you stayed around here to help your mamma some, but you got to start thinking about yourself. I know you want to be moving on someday soon.

JOE JR.: I did go to the graveyard though, and I watched them lower you into the ground. Watched the yellow chrysanthemum petals fall onto your coffin lid. Ashes and dust. I wanted to scream. Scream in frustration and rage. But Mamma saw it building up in my throat. She grabbed me by the arm, saying: "No, not here. Don't embarrass us. Be strong. Scream later." But later never came, and neither have the tears.

JOE SR.: (*Pulls stickpin from his tie.*) Here. I want you to have this old horseshoe pin. Ain't but one of the diamonds real. I forget which one. You take it now. It was pretty lucky for me, when all's said and done. Go on, take it. Luck to me now is like water to a drowning man.

JOE JR.: I can't take that. It's part of you. Besides, you already gave me something of yourself. (*He pats car.*)

JOE SR.: I'm glad about that, son, and you've given me a way to get on over. (*JOE SR. vanishes as dogs bark. Lights out.*)

SCENE 6

(*Current time, present, mid-sixties. Lights up.* JOE JR. *is sleeping inside car with his feet out the open car door. It is late evening. Crickets and distant music.* VERONICA *comes out carrying garbage.*)

VERONICA: Here kitty-kitty-kitty. (*She notices* JOE JR.*'s feet out the car window and goes to investigate. She touches his foot. He wakes.*) Mamma! Miss Clarice! Junior done passed out drunk!

(CLARICE *comes out followed by* MAUDE *and* CHARLES.)

CLARICE: Junior?! What in the world? You'll catch your death of cold out here in this night air.

JOE JR.: What . . .? I'm not cold.

MAUDE: (*Picks up beer can.*) Man, you got your head that bad on one can of beer? Well, you know your daddy couldn't hold his liquor neither.

CLARICE: Maude Esther! Don't speak ill of the dead.

JOE JR.: I don't remember falling asleep.

VERONICA: Take me for a ride when you get sober, if this old thing can run.

CHARLES: Is this the old car you wanted me to look at?

MAUDE: Yes! Junior, this is my brother Charles Harold. You believe he paid a hundred dollars for this pile of junk?

CHARLES: How you doin'? (*Looks in car hood.*) Let me take a look. It don't look that bad to me. Give it a crank. (*Car engine starts; motor guns.*) Ain't nothing wrong with that motor.

CLARICE: You fixed it!

JOE JR.: Yeah, how 'bout that. (*Gets out of car.*)

VERONICA: Take us for a ride right now, Junior! (VERONICA *gets in car and bounces on front seat.*) Ouch! Something bit me! Oh look! It's an old pin. Finders keepers, losers weepers! (*She gets out of car and runs around.*)

CLARICE: Let me see that! (VERONICA *gives pin to her.*) That's what I thought; a diamond horseshoe!

CHARLES: Must have been left by a previous driver.

CLARICE: It belongs to Junior now. Doesn't it belong to you now, Junior?

JOE JR.: By rights, I guess it does. (*Lights dim to OUT.*)

SCENE 7: EPILOGUE

(*A few weeks later.* JOE JR. *is polishing the car.* MAUDE *attends the grill, as* VERONICA *sets paper plates.*)

VERONICA: When we gonna eat, Mamma; I'm hungry.

MAUDE: Soon as Charles Harold and Clarice get here. Go get yourself some potato salad out of the ice box if you're hungry. (VERONICA *goes in.*) I wonder what's keeping those two.

JOE JR.: It's good to see them getting along so well; Mamma needs to get out more.

MAUDE: *You* the one needs to get out. How come you didn't go to Eastwood with us? It was fun.

JOE JR.: Mamma said she had a good time.

MAUDE: Honey, yes! Got right into the swing. You know that Little Junior Parker really puts on a show. Had sweat soaking clean through his silver sharkskin suit! Ha! All the women just hollering, and Clarice was right there hollering with 'em!

JOE JR.: Alright!

MAUDE: Hey! I heard you got accepted at college! University of California hey, hey! I hear they a pretty fast bunch out there.

JOE JR.: I can deal with it. I got to.

MAUDE: They really gave you a scholarship for making up poems?

JOE JR.: Somebody must think they're pretty good.

MAUDE: I know Clarice is proud. She's sure gonna be lonesome with you gone.

(CLARICE *and* CHARLES *enter.*)

CHARLES: Hope ya'll saved us some barbecue.

MAUDE: Hey! We been waiting for you.

CLARICE: We lost track of the time walking around downtown.

MAUDE: Veronica, bring out the potato salad and Kool-Aid.

JOE JR.: What's happening downtown?

CLARICE: We just window-shopped. I like looking in Joske's windows at all those nice clothes I can't afford. (VERONICA *comes out with salad, etc.*)

CHARLES: But that's just a temporary situation. Junior's going off to be a famous writer, get rich, and bring it all back home to you. Ain't that right?

JOE JR.: I don't know. Not many poets get rich, Charles.

VERONICA: You gonna drive that old car all the way to California?

JOE JR.: Uh huh. New tires, tuned-up and ready to hit the road . . .

MAUDE: That car ain't no older than you, Miss Smartness; both of ya'll got a few good years left.

CLARICE: Junior, you won't try to drive all night, will you? Pull over side the road and sleep when you get tired. Promise me.

JOE JR.: Oh yeah; I intend to take my time.

CLARICE: Your daddy would be so proud of you; going off on your own. He knew you were born to drive yourself to whatever life holds for you. I knew too; ever since you were little, that day at Playland Park . . .

JOE JR.: I almost forgot about that. Fourth of July, wasn't it?

CLARICE: That's right! Junior wasn't nothing but five or six. Well, bless his heart, he heard this announcement on the radio, where the radio man had said they here having this big old celebration over at Playland Park for the Fourth of July, which it was that day, with fireworks and the army band and all, and everybody was welcome. He stressed that word: Everybody. Now, who was I to tell this child he wasn't some-body? He was bound and determined to go to Playland Park to watch the fireworks along with everybody else who was welcomed that day. Now, remember this was in the late forties. Folks around here still lived pretty much the way they had since emancipation. Still had "Colored only" or "Whites only" signs on everything from restaurants to toilets. Yeah, toilets! Like their shit was too good to go down with ours. Yes Lord, Jim Crow was in full flight, and not too many of us were acting up about it in those days, lynching was not unheard of. So for us to go to Playland Park on a day we were not welcome was more than a notion. But there was no denying that boy. So sure of himself; nothing would do him but to go. So I took a deep breath, talked to God a minute, and we went on over there. It was about a half an hour away on the bus line. He just couldn't stop talking all the way over; he was so excited, and me trying to think who I'd call if we got arrested. We got to the entrance, and I paid the admission. The girl took my money and didn't say anything. We went through the turnstile, and I started to think; maybe Junior was right. Fourth of July. Everybody welcome. Well that boy took off running right over to this merry-go-round of little cars and plopped himself down in the red one. He started jerking the little steering wheel back and forth and smiled up at me. "Look Mamma, I'm drivin'!" But he never got to go 'round. I looked and saw some other little children pulling to get into the kiddie-cars, but their parents, see-ing the dark child in the red car, held them back. Then I heard someone shout at me. "Hey you!" I turned and saw this white fella grinning at me. "What's the matter with you gal?" he said, "This ain't no June-teenth!" He gave me my money back. "Take that kid and go, before you run off all my business." Junior sat very still in that little car watching us. I went over and pulled him out of the car; he said "We not gonna ride today, Mamma?" "No, baby," I said, "not today. We'll come back another time."

CLARICE (*Continued.*): We sat at that bus stop for what seemed like years, watching the little white children come and go with their folks, laughing and carrying balloons and cotton candy like they didn't have a care in the world. The bus finally got there just as the fireworks began to light up the sky. He looked out the bus window at them till we turned the corner and we couldn't see them anymore. Junior looked at me, real serious like, and said; "Don't cry Mamma"; do you remember? "Don't cry. We gonna drive one day. One day we gonna drive, for real."

(*JOE JR. and CLARICE embrace, as lights fade to out.*)

THE END

Br'er Rabbit

....

Adapted by **GEORGE HAWKINS**

George W. Hawkins, founder and first artistic director of Houston's Ensemble Theatre, followed poet Wallace Stevens' example when he maintained his commitment to his work in both business and the arts. Stevens combined a successful career as an attorney and vice president of an insurance company with a brilliant career as a poet, and Hawkins moved freely between the corporate world, where he worked as an accountant, and the arts community, where he honed his acting and directing skills.

In the early days of the Ensemble Theatre, very little money was available for operating expenses, making it difficult to pay actors and royalties for producing well-known plays such as Lorraine Hansberry's *A Raisin in the Sun*. Therefore, Hawkins wrote and directed his own plays to ensure a larger profit margin for his theatre. A versatile writer and gifted director, Hawkins wrote for children and adult audiences. His entertaining and educational adaptations of selected Br'er Rabbit tales from the classic Uncle Remus stories remain favorites with children in grades kindergarten through eighth grade. The centerpiece of the Ensemble Theatre's Touring Education Program, *Br'er Rabbit*, is performed annually in venues around Houston.

Born in Dallas, Texas, in 1947, Hawkins attended the Dallas public schools. After he graduated from high school, he enrolled at Prairie View A&M College, where he pursued an undergraduate degree in business administration. He also earned a degree in accounting from Case Western Reserve University in Cleveland, Ohio. In the early 1970s, a time when many companies were seeking qualified minorities to diversify their workforce, George was hired in the accounting department at Tenneco Oil Company in Houston. Because George enjoyed being on stage, he briefly pursued a career in modeling, which rekindled a latent love of acting and led to the founding of the Black Ensemble Theatre in his home in 1976. Reflecting on his motivation for starting his own theatre company, Hawkins told a reporter, "I was an actor, and I was frustrated because there was no place for me to work." A charismatic, ambitious, and inspirational founder, Hawkins attracted a talented and devoted cadre of ethnically diverse supporters and aspiring actors. Indeed, Hawkins' decision to call his new venture the "Black Ensemble Theatre"—which alludes to its predecessor, New York City's legendary Negro Ensemble Company—signaled his desire to build a professional, rather than a community, theatre. In 1981, Hawkins dropped "Black" from the theatre's name to affirm his rejection of the racial prejudice that had prevented his full participation in Houston's mainstream theatre community.

Hawkins wrote approximately a half dozen plays under his pen name, Carl Anderson. Structurally, his plays generally follow the format of the well-made play. Like the typical well-made play, Hawkins' plays are crafted to appeal to the audience, allow the audience to identify with the characters, and achieve commercial success. His most successful play for adults, *Who Killed Hazel Patton?*, meets all of those expectations. First produced in the 1979–1980 season and staged again in the 1981–1982 season, with Hawkins directing, the play is a parody of a mystery, focusing on the murder of a rich old woman surrounded by relatives and associates who want her money. In 1997, Ensemble staged a revised version of the play directed by Ed Muth, veteran director and friend of George Hawkins. Before Hawkins wrote *Who Killed Hazel Patton?*, he adapted several Br'er Rabbit folktales for his children's touring show. His adaptation combines song and dance.

As You Read *Br'er Rabbit*

An adaptation involves modifying a source, such as a novel, short story, or poem, to another genre, such as a film or stage play. Adapting a literary work to a dramatic form is particularly challenging because playwriting can be extremely difficult. The writer must consider concept, characters, storyline, dialogue, and action. The earliest adaptation of the Br'er Rabbit folktales for the theatre appeared in the 1930s. In the original folktales recorded in the Joel Chandler Harris collections, Uncle Remus recites the tales to entertain a young white boy in a plantation setting. Hawkins eliminates the white character, allowing Uncle Remus to speak directly to the audience. Told in six scenes, the play uses wit, humor, and songs to highlight Br'er Rabbit in the role of the classic trickster figure. The physically weaker rabbit uses his intelligence and cunning to triumph over physically stronger opponents. Because the stories are didactic, like Aesop's fables, children are not only entertained but also taught valuable lessons concerning the consequences of deception, selfishness, and arrogance. Hawkins replaces the heavy, nineteenth-century plantation-era black dialect used in earlier versions of the tales with a stylized dialect that preserves the poetry of black vernacular speech without invoking minstrel stereotypes.

Hawkins' version of the Br'er Rabbit tales highlights the African American oral tradition and calls attention to the Golden Rule: "Do unto others as you would have them do unto you."

Production History

The Houston Public Library, Houston, Texas, 1977–1978
The Ensemble Theatre, Houston, Texas, annually since 1989

Characters

UNCLE REMUS: Narrator of the stories. Old, wise, grandfatherly type.
BR'ER RABBIT: Cunning, conniving rascal of Uncle Remus' tales. Always outsmarting everyone else.
MRS. RABBIT: Br'er Rabbit's wife. Slightly on the dopey side.
BABY RABBIT: Br'er Rabbit's and Mrs. Rabbit's child.
BR'ER FOX: Chief antagonist of Br'er rabbit. Next to Br'er Rabbit, he is just about the slyest in the group.
BR'ER COON: Industrious but always being outsmarted by Br'er Rabbit.
BR'ER BEAR: Very dense and always falling for Br'er Rabbit's tricks.
CHORUS

Setting

Place: Imaginary farm, vegetable garden, etc.

Production Notes

(*The SETTINGS are depicted through the use of boxes in varying sizes. The SCENES are changed artistically and systematically in view of the audience. The COSTUMES are black leotards and black tights accessorized with tails, ears, fur, etc. to help develop the characterizations. The MAKEUP should be a likeness to the animals. The ORCHESTRA can consist of whatever number of instruments desired. However, make every attempt not to use less instrumentation than the score specifies. The LIGHTING EFFECTS should be cheerful and third world-ish.)*

SCENE 1

(The Farm. All actors enter singing "zip pa de do dah . . ." Repeat three times. The scene is preset. BR'ER RABBIT, BR'ER COON, BR'ER BEAR, *and* BR'ER FOX *are frozen in a blackout. The orchestra plays the opening theme.* UNCLE REMUS *picks up the song in the blackout from his stool Downstage of the set. The light slowly comes up on* UNCLE REMUS' *face as he sings. The music underscores the narration.)*

UNCLE REMUS: Hello, my name is Uncle Remus. Remember me? For years and years I been tellin' tales of Br'er Rabbit. Br'er Rabbit dis, Br'er Rabbit dat. Br'er Rabbit, I tell you . . . Humph. I have to give it to him. Dat big-eared rascal is some rabbit! (*Light widens on* UNCLE REMUS *and comes up on the scene as* BR'ER RABBIT, BR'ER COON, BR'ER BEAR, *and* BR'ER FOX *come out of the freeze and begin to put away groceries.*) Did I tell you da time Br'er Bear, Br'er Fox, Br'er Coon, and Br'er Rabbit made a proposition to start farmin'? Well, what dey did was dey bought dis land, you see, built dis farmhouse, and den dey bought lots of groceries for dis year. Dey bought everythin' you could mention, but dis butter was da most important . . . (*Sly laughter*) . . . mostly to Br'er Rabbit. So dey all went out into da field to work dis land. But ol' Br'er Rabbit, he studied a plan to leave Br'er Bear, Br'er Fox, and Br'er Coon in da field doin' all da work and make believe dat someone was callin' him away. (*The light on* UNCLE REMUS *narrows to capture only his face and his reactions to what is happening.*)

BR'ER RABBIT: (*Throws voice towards the farmhouse as if in an echo.*) Uhoo! Uhoo!

BR'ER COON: Whut's dat?

BR'ER BEAR: Whut's whut?

BR'ER COON: You didn't hear dat, Br'er Bear?

BR'ER BEAR: Hear what?

BR'ER RABBIT: I didn't' hear nuthin'.

BR'ER COON: (*Resuming work.*) Well, I coulda swo'.

BR'ER RABBIT: Uhoo!

BR'ER COON: Der it is agin.

BR'ER RABBIT: Oh foot! (*Pointing away from the farmhouse.*) Dat's dem folk over der.

BR'ER COON: Over where?

BR'ER RABBIT: (*Pointing toward farmhouse.*) Over der. I can't work for bein' bothered by folk wantin' me to name der chillum. I guess dey figure I'm 'bout de best chillum namer dis side of da briar patch. (*Dramatically.*) It's my responsibility, I reckon. I gotta go. (*Appeasingly.*) It won't take me long now. (*Exiting.*) Ya'll just keep at it and I'll be back befo' you can say . . . "hippopotamus."

BR'ER FOX: (*Quickly.*) Hippopotamus.

BR'ER RABBIT: (*Daringly.*) Befo' you can spell "hippopotamus."

BR'ER FOX: (*Looks to audience in silence.* BR'ER RABBIT *hops off to farmhouse and eats some of the butter.* BR'ER FOX *looks to* BR'ER BEAR *for help.*) H-I-P . . . hip.

BR'ER BEAR: (*Resuming work.*) I can't help you.

BR'ER FOX: (*Still attempting a spelling,* BR'ER FOX *looks to* BR'ER COON *for help, who shrugs his shoulders and resumes work.*) Po . . . P-O, pa . . . P-A, hippopo . . . ta . . . T-A.

BR'ER BEAR: You gonna blow a fuse, Br'er Fox.

BR'ER FOX: Hip-po-pa-ta . . .

BR'ER RABBIT: (*Entering excitedly.*) Musta been the sweetest baby you ever seen.

BR'ER BEAR: (*Grinning.*) What you name it?

BR'ER RABBIT: Just Begun.

BR'ER COON: Just Begun!

BR'ER FOX: Just Begun!

BR'ER COON: (*Teasing.*) And you da best dis side of da briar patch. Just begun!

BR'ER RABBIT: (*In the midst of the laughter.*) Uhoo! Uhoo!

BR'ER COON: Der it is agin.

BR'ER RABBIT: Ah, dem people just won't let me 'lon. Dey wont me ta name another child. I'm not goin' dis time though. 'Deed I'm not. (BR'ER FOX, BR'ER COON, *and* BR'ER BEAR *take him at his word and return to work.* BR'ER RABBIT *sees he is getting no sympathy and tries again.*) Doggone da luck, dey wanta run a fellow to death.

BR'ER COON: You know best, Br'er Rabbit.

BR'ER RABBIT: I guess you right. I betta go. (*BR'ER RABBIT hops off to farm-house and eats some more butter.*)

BR'ER FOX: Whut you do dat for?

BR'ER COON: All I said was . . .

BR'ER FOX: I know whut you said. I don't trust dat Rabbit.

BR'ER BEAR: You gotta trust somebody.

BR'ER FOX: Yeah, but dat somebody ain't Br'er Rabbit.

BR'ER BEAR: What you got 'gainst Br'er Rabbit, Br'er Fox?

BR'ER COON: I'm not too sure about that Rabbit, give 'im an inch and he'll take two weeks vacation on ya.

BR'ER BEAR: Open your heart, Br'er Fox.

BR'ER FOX: I do every time you open your face.

BR'ER BEAR: (*To BR'ER COON.*) What dat mean?

BR'ER RABBIT: (*Entering.*) Well here I is!

BR'ER BEAR: Whatcha name da little darling?

BR'ER RABBIT: Half Gone.

BR'ER BEAR: What kinda name is dat?

BR'ER RABBIT: It's a . . . And a . . .

BR'ER BEAR: Oh-h-h-h.

BR'ER RABBIT: (*Seeing that not much work has been done.*) How's things co-min' along Br'er Fox. (*BR'ER FOX gives BR'ER RABBIT an evil look. They all go back to work and BR'ER RABBIT begins to hum the "Work Song" a cappella until he is able to sneak in his call.*) Uhoo! Uhoo! (*Disgustedly.*) Now you know dat's rotten. Now wouldn't you think a rabbit like me would have more to do dan think about baby rabbits.

BR'ER FOX: Like workin'.

BR'ER RABBIT: Dat's whut I mean. But you know, we rabbits . . . we sorta . . . stick together. When da other one needs de one, da other one is naturally gonna be da one who is der to hold da other one up. It's dat animal nature in us, I guess. (*Dramatically.*) I must go. I can't turn my back. (*He hops off to the farmhouse to eat some more butter. BR'ER COON and BR'ER FOX look at each other. BR'ER BEAR stands smiling approvingly.*)

BR'ER BEAR: Ain't dat just wonderful?

BR'ER FOX: Br'er Bear, you mean you fell for dat macaroni? (*Recalling in jest.*) Da other one and da one is da one or da other. I'm gonna see what dat . . . (*BR'ER FOX turns and bumps into BR'ER RABBIT as he is entering from farmhouse.*)

BR'ER RABBIT: (*Shaking* BR'ER FOX'S *hand.*) Rabbit's da name. Yearns?
(BR'ER FOX *jerks his hand away.*)

BR'ER COON: Ya'll gon' play around or can we get some work done around here?

BR'ER RABBIT: At your service, my good Coon, at your service. (*They all return to work.* BR'ER RABBIT *works to the beat of the flute playing the work song.* BR'ER RABBIT *begins to sing.* BR'ER FOX, BR'ER BEAR, *and* BR'ER COON *join in. The* CHORUS *sings from Off Stage.*)

BR'ER RABBIT:
Jump down, turn around, pick a peck of peas
Gonna jump down, turn around, pick a cob of corn
Jump down, turn around, pick a peck of peas
Gonna jump down, turn around, pick a cob of corn

CHORUS:
Yang, yang ya yang yang
Yang, yang ya yang yang
Yang, yang ya yang yang
Yang, yang ya yang yang

BR'ER FOX:
Corn, peas, cabbage
Beans, squash, yams

BR'ER COON AND BR'ER BEAR:
Jump down, turn around, pick a peck of peas
Jump down, turn around, pick a cob of corn

BR'ER RABBIT: (*In the midst of the singing and working with movements to the beat,* BR'ER RABBIT *soon finds it convenient to call himself again.*) Uhoo! Uhoo! (*Singing and music fade.*) Did you hear whut I heard?

BR'ER FOX: (*Suspiciously.*) No! And you can't be sure. Let's wait and see if dey call you agin. (BR'ER FOX *watches* BR'ER RABBIT *intensely.*)

BR'ER RABBIT: (*Nervously to* BR'ER FOX.) I really think dey too proud to beg, Br'er Coon. (*Appealing to* BR'ER COON.) My folk are darn proud people, Br'er Coon. (*As a last resort, he appeals to* BR'ER BEAR.) Dey figure once dey call, you done heard 'em.

BR'ER BEAR: (*To* BR'ER FOX.) Dat's somethin' to think about, Br'er Fox.
(BR'ER FOX *turns his attention to* BR'ER BEAR.) If you's called once . . .

BR'ER RABBIT: Uhoo! Uhoo!

BR'ER FOX: Dad-blasted Bear!

BR'ER RABBIT: (*Relieved.*) Dis time it must be twins. I better run. (*BR'ER RABBIT exits to eat some more butter. BR'ER FOX is furious.*)

BR'ER FOX: I hope you satisfied, you grizzly, hairy . . .

BR'ER COON: (*Thinking to himself.*) I'm beginning to believe what you say is a fact, or else somebody is having a rabbit a minute, Br'er Fox.

BR'ER FOX: Not so unusual for dem creatures. (*Conceiving that rational thought.*) What I figure is, I figure Br'er Rabbit is up to somethin' else. I figure dat Rabbit is pullin' a trick on us. I figure Br'er Rabbit done took us for fools. I figure Br'er Rabbit say, "Dem fools, I'll play a game on dem fools." (*To BR'ER COON.*) You a fool? (*BR'ER COON shakes his head.*) I ain't no fool. (*To BR'ER BEAR.*) You a fool? (*Thinking twice.*) Never mind. (*Looking over the work they have done.*) Look, we done all da work and he ain't done nuthin'.

BR'ER RABBIT: (*Entering.*) Well, I named another child.

BR'ER BEAR: Whut you name 'im?

BR'ER RABBIT: All Gone. (*They all look at BR'ER RABBIT curiously then freeze as light widens on UNCLE REMUS.*)

UNCLE REMUS: (*Laughing.*) Now, about da middle of June . . . (*Everybody makes a complete turn clockwise as lights change to depict a change in season, and they go immediately to the farmhouse*) . . . dey all was gonna open da keg of butter. But when dey opened da keg, da butter was all gone . . . (*light narrows on UNCLE REMUS' face.*)

ALL: Who stole da butter?

BR'ER COON: (*Sharply to BR'ER FOX.*) I don't know.

BR'ER FOX: (*To BR'ER BEAR.*) I don't know.

BR'ER BEAR: (*Sharply to BR'ER RABBIT.*) I don't know.

BR'ER RABBIT: (*All eyes on him as he turns sharply to no one and then back again to them staring at him.*) Don't look at me. (*BR'ER COON and BR'ER FOX go into conference while BR'ER RABBIT takes BR'ER BEAR aside.*) I tell you, Br'er Bear, Br'er Fox, he been laying around dat farmhouse all da time talking 'bout "Ooooo, I wish I had some butter . . . Oooo, I wish I had some butter." Dat makes me believe he done it.

BR'ER BEAR: (*Innocently.*) Done whut?

BR'ER RABBIT: Ate the butter dummy . . . I mean . . . dat dummy Br'er Fox ate the butter.

BR'ER BEAR: You kiddin'. (*BR'ER RABBIT nods.*) Well, let's get 'im!

BR'ER RABBIT: No! No! You gotta prove it first. (*Master plan.*) I tell you

what let's do. Let's build a fire. And lay down around da fire after supper . . .

BR'ER BEAR: As hot as it is out der?

BR'ER RABBIT: Good for ya! (*Continuing*) . . . and whoever ate da butter
well, da grease will come out on his belly. Okey. (BR'ER BEAR *nods.*)
Okey! Now you build da fire and I'll get Coon over near da fire. (BR'ER
BEAR *proceeds to the field to build the fire as told, and* BR'ER RABBIT *con-
fronts* BR'ER COON *and* BR'ER FOX *with his plan.*) Uh . . . Br'er Coon, Br'er
Fox . . . I think I know who ate the butter.

BR'ER COON and BR'ER FOX: Who?

BR'ER RABBIT: Br'er Bear.

BR'ER FOX: How do you know?

BR'ER RABBIT: Well-l-l-l . . . I can't really prove it. Tell you what let's do.
Let's build a fire and lay down around da fire after supper. (*They get into
a huddle and* BR'ER RABBIT *continues his plan in mimes. Then they go to the
field and sit around the fire with* BR'ER BEAR *who has already begun eating.
They eat then they fall asleep.* BR'ER RABBIT *sneaks away to the farmhouse
and gets a handful of scrapings from the butter keg. He returns and rubs
grease on everybody's bellies (accented by flutes) and then plays 'possum.*
BR'ER COON *wakes up first and spots the grease on* BR'ER BEAR's *belly.*)

BR'ER COON: (*Waking up* BR'ER FOX *and* BR'ER RABBIT.) Bear did it. Bear did
it. (BR'ER COON *and* BR'ER FOX *merge on* BR'ER BEAR *and then start chasing
him as* BR'ER RABBIT *stands back laughing and musing. The chase song is
played.*)

BR'ER RABBIT: Uh . . . what's dat on Br'er Coon's belly dar, Br'er Bear? (*They
stop chasing* BR'ER BEAR *and start chasing* BR'ER COON.) Uh what's that I
see on your belly dere Br'er Fox? (BR'ER COON *and* BR'ER BEAR *start chasing* BR'ER FOX *until they embarrassingly realize that* BR'ER RABBIT *must
have been the one. They then start chasing* BR'ER RABBIT. *During the chase,*
BR'ER RABBIT *disappears Off Set as* BR'ER FOX, BR'ER COON, *and* BR'ER
BEAR *chase each other into a freeze. The lights dim and the scene changes as
the orchestra continues playing the chase song.*)

SCENE 2

(*Roadside No. 1. The lights slowly come up on the roadside.* BR'ER FOX *is frozen
Downstage in a thoughtful pose, coming to life as the lights become full.*)

UNCLE REMUS: Br'er Fox reckoned he'd had all he could take of dat Br'er Rabbit and so he 'cided he was gonna have him some plump, tender rabbit. (*BR'ER FOX moves to a tall stump and sneakily lays a noose across the road, then disappears behind the stump.*) Well by and by Br'er Fox started doin' everythin' he could to catch Br'er Rabbit. (*BR'ER RABBIT comes briskly down the road and neatly sidesteps the noose and continues Off Set.*) And Br'er Rabbit had done everythin' he could to keep from bein' caught. So Br'er Fox sat down to think about his next move. (*BR'ER FOX sits on tip of tall stump in thoughtful pose.*) Well, he thought and he thought, and he thought, and finally he said to himself:

BR'ER FOX: (*With an air of inspiration.*) Self, you is gonna run a game on Br'er Rabbit. (*BR'ER RABBIT comes quickly up the road.*)

UNCLE REMUS: Well, no sooner was da words out of his mouth, when here come Br'er Rabbit hoppin' up da road.

BR'ER FOX: (*Vacating the stump.*) Hold on a second, Br'er Rabbit.

BR'ER RABBIT: (*Without stopping.*) Sorry, ain't got the time.

BR'ER FOX: (*Frantically.*) Wait a minute, Br'er Rabbit. I need to talk to you.

BR'ER RABBIT: (*Scratching.*) All right Br'er Fox but you betta holler from where you standin'. I'm monstrous full of fleas dis mo'ning.

BR'ER FOX: (*Cautiously.*) Well then, you stay where you is 'cause I don't need no fleas on me. Whut it is Br'er Rabbit is I was talkin' to Br'er Bear yesterday and he really got on my case 'bout how you and me have been neighbors so long and still don't live too neighborly and don't make friends. And I seen he was right so I told him I'd see you today and try to be a little more neighborly. (*BR'ER FOX looks at BR'ER RABBIT curiously to see if he will fall for it.*)

BR'ER RABBIT: You all right, Br'er Fox. (*BR'ER FOX nods.*) You wants to be neighborly. (*BR'ER FOX nods.*) You wants to make friends? (*BR'ER FOX nods. BR'ER RABBIT points to his itching back.*) Then scratch me right there. Come on. (*BR'ER FOX hesitantly scratches BR'ER RABBIT'S back accented by the music. Then as fleas get on BR'ER FOX, they both start scratching and go into a scratch dance, which ends in a fit of laughter. Music stops.*) I guess you right, Br'er Fox. Tell you whut, suppose you drop by da house tomorrow and have a bite of supper wit' me and da family. We may not have no big feast, but we can scramble up somethin' dat'll stick to your ribs.

BR'ER FOX: (*In an attempt not to let his plan backfire.*) Well, I was thinkin' 'bout havin' you for dinner . . . I mean . . . *over* for dinner, Br'er Rabbit.

BR'ER RABBIT: No dinners on me . . . I mean . . . No! Dinner's on me.

BR'ER FOX: (*Plotting.*) Oh well . . . I'm agreeable, Br'er Rabbit.

BR'ER RABBIT: In dat case, we'll be 'xpecting you.

(*They say goodbye; BR'ER RABBIT continues Off Set. BR'ER FOX looks very pleased with himself as he waves goodbye to BR'ER RABBIT. Then he turns and exits into a freeze. The light dims, the music begins, and the scene is changed.*)

SCENE 3

(BR'ER COON's *Garden. The lights rise slowly to bright morning as a rooster crow is heard, which should be vocalized by a cast member. BR'ER RABBIT and MRS. RABBIT are frozen behind the hill, entering* BR'ER COON's *Garden. As the narration begins, they come to life and enter to pick vegetables.*)

UNCLE REMUS: Bright and early da next mo'ning, Br'er Rabbit went out to a beautiful little garden across the hill aways. It was just full of ripe vegetables. He saw old Br'er Bear and they picked some of everythin' dey liked. And dey picked and dey picked. (*Big yawn.*) And dey picked . . .

BR'ER RABBIT: (*Hushed voice.*) We got everythin' we need?

BR'ER BEAR: Let's see . . . tomatoes?

BR'ER RABBIT: (*Looking around.*) Sh-h-h-h!

BR'ER BEAR: Carrots?

BR'ER RABBIT: Check—

BR'ER BEAR: Cabbage?

BR'ER RABBIT: Check—

BR'ER BEAR: Roasting ears?

BR'ER RABBIT: Check—

BR'ER BEAR: Asparagus?

BR'ER RABBIT: Check—Asparagus??

BR'ER BEAR: I like asparagus.

BR'ER RABBIT: Check. Check. Check. It looks to me I got everythin' I like. Whut does a fox eat?

BR'ER BEAR: He *wants* to eat rabbit.

BR'ER RABBIT: Der ain't no rabbit in dis here garden.

BR'ER BEAR: Whut you think you is—raccoon?

BR'ER RABBIT: He wants to eat me?

MRS. RABBIT: Oh no! (*In one breath.*) He can't do dat! I got a house to

take care of and chillum to feed and socks to mend and Thursday I'm gonna have des teeth pulled in da front and look at me, I'm all dried and wrinkled, ain't a tender spot nowhere. And besides, I'm a fightin' rabbit.

BR'ER BEAR: (*Taking her in his arm.*) Calm down. Calm down. I won't let no fox eat you. I'll protect you.

BR'ER RABBIT: An who's gon protect you?

BR'ER BEAR: (*To audience.*) Will you protect me?

SCENE 4

(*Fox's House. The lights come up on BR'ER RABBIT frozen peeking in BR'ER FOX's door and BR'ER FOX frozen at the table in great pain.*)

UNCLE REMUS: When Br'er Rabbit got der, he found Br'er Fox groanin' and lookin' mighty weak. On the table was no food. But close by on the stove was this pot of boilin' water and a carvin' knife. So Br'er Rabbit, he say "Humph."

BR'ER RABBIT: Humph!

BR'ER FOX: O-o-o-oh!

BR'ER RABBIT: Looks like you gonna have chicken for dinner, Br'er Fox.

BR'ER FOX: (*Moving towards BR'ER RABBIT over the table.*) No. Turkey. A nice, fresh, tender . . .

BR'ER RABBIT: (*Quickly.*) Have you got any calamus root?

BR'ER FOX: What?

BR'ER RABBIT: I done got so now dat I can't eat no bird 'ceppin' she's seasoned up with calamus root. I'll go get some! (*BR'ER RABBIT hops off outside. BR'ER FOX realizing that BR'ER RABBIT has tricked him again, attempts to chase after BR'ER RABBIT but burns his hand on the stove. Meanwhile, BR'ER RABBIT has gotten the calamus root and shouts to BR'ER FOX inside.*) Oh, Br'er Fox! I'll just put your calamus root out here on dis stump. (*Echoing as he hops off home.*) Better come git it while it's nice . . . fresh . . . and tender.

(*BR'ER FOX is still struggling to get out of the house and go after BR'ER RABBIT. They freeze. The lights dim as the scene is changed. UNCLE REMUS laughs with great energy during the scene change.*)

SCENE 5

(BR'ER COON's *Garden. Lights rise on* BR'ER RABBIT *as he is going home. He spots* BR'ER COON *in his garden fussing to himself over all the damage that* BR'ER RABBIT *has done.* BR'ER RABBIT *comes over the hill.*)

BR'ER RABBIT: Hold der, Br'er Coon.

BR'ER COON: Not now, Br'er Rabbit.

BR'ER RABBIT: (*Seated on the hill looking at the mess they made.*) Gollee, whut a mess!

BR'ER COON: My tomatoes, my carrots, my cabbage, my roasting ears, my asparagus . . .

BR'ER RABBIT: (*To audience.*) Check.

BR'ER COON: Whut's dat, Br'er Rabbit?

BR'ER RABBIT: I said, dis is outrageous!

BR'ER COON: Look-a der. Ain't a cabbage leaf left!

BR'ER RABBIT: (*Rubbing his stomach, mouth watering.*) Yeah. (BR'ER COON *gives him a curious look.* BR'ER RABBIT *agrees more sympathetically.*) Yeah!

BR'ER COON: I'm out-right, in-right, up-right, down-right mad cause of dis. I'll do just about anything to find out who did dis out-right, in-right, up-right . . .

BR'ER RABBIT: (*Unbelieving.*) Sure yeah, I know. You'll do anythin'.

BR'ER COON: I'll do anythin'.

BR'ER RABBIT: (*Plotting.*) Anythin'?

BR'ER COON: Anythin'! I'll even teach him my prize-winnin' hambone act.

BR'ER RABBIT: You can't hambone, Br'er Coon.

BR'ER COON: (*Ego takes over.*) Oh no? Humph! I can't hambone. (BR'ER COON *begins to hambone. Fascinated,* BR'ER RABBIT *watches intently.* BR'ER COON *hamboning,* BR'ER BEAR *passes by . . . sees* BR'ER COON *and joins him in hamboning, passing* BR'ER RABBIT *without seeing him. Suddenly,* BR'ER COON *remembers about the garden and loses his rhythm and starts off the hill.*)

BR'ER RABBIT: Where you goin', Br'er Coon?

BR'ER COON: To find out who done dis unneighborly act.

BR'ER RABBIT: (*Calling after him.*) Yeah! I'm gonna try to find out who done dis unneighborly act. (*Plotting as he watches* BR'ER BEAR *hamboning . . . too.*)

UNCLE REMUS: (*Warning.*) Dat Br'er Rabbit is up to somethin'.

BR'ER RABBIT: Oh, Br'er Bear!

BR'ER BEAR: (*Suddenly seeing* BR'ER RABBIT *for the first time.*) Well, it's Br'er Rabbit.

BR'ER RABBIT: (*Quickly and in one breath.*) Good to see you der, Br'er Bear. Br'er Bear, I was just a-thinkin' today about whut a wonderful voice you have and how der's some ladies down der and dey givin' a social and since you have dis wonderful voice, dey want you to sing a bass solo.

BR'ER BEAR: (*Stunned by how fast* BR'ER RABBIT *has said everything.*) Could you run dat by me agin?

BR'ER RABBIT: Good to see you, Br'er Bear. Br'er Bear . . .

BR'ER BEAR: Not dat!

BR'ER RABBIT: . . . Some ladies want you to sing a bass solo at der social.

BR'ER BEAR: Me? (*Quickly and proudly.*) All right.

BR'ER RABBIT: Good! Den I'm gonna try to train your voice. Now you listen to me and do everythin' I tell you.

BR'ER BEAR: All right.

BR'ER RABBIT: Now I'm gonna sing a song. Listen to me. When I say dese lines. (*Speaks lines to song.*)

Who stole ol' Br'er Coon's greens?
Who stole Br'er Coon's greens?
Who stole ol' Br'er Coon's greens?

You just sing back . . .(*Sings* BR'ER BEAR's *line*) "Nobody but me!" Okey? (BR'ER BEAR *nods.*) Okey. (BR'ER RABBIT *begins singing.*)

Who stole ol' Br'er Coon's greens?
Who stole Br'er Coon's greens?
Who stole ol' Br'er Coon's greens?

BR'ER BEAR: (*Sings with style.*) Nobody but me!

BR'ER RABBIT: Dat's right, Br'er Bear. Dat's fine. My, but you got one fine voice.

BR'ER BEAR: (*Singing endlessly with obvious pride in himself.*) Nobody but me!

BR'ER RABBIT: Yeah!

BR'ER BEAR: (*Begins to dance while singing.*) Nobody but me!

BR'ER RABBIT: Dat's it!

Who stole ol' Br'er Coon's greens?
Who stole Br'er Coon's greens?
Who stole ol' Br'er Coon's greens?

BR'ER BEAR: Nobody but me!

(BR'ER RABBIT *and* BR'ER BEAR *sing another stanza alone. Chorus joins in for two stanzas.* BR'ER RABBIT *and* BR'ER BEAR *sing another stanza alone.* BR'ER COON *returns to the garden and takes up song and dance until he realizes what they are singing.*)

BR'ER COON: (*To* BR'ER BEAR.) What? So you da one!!

(BR'ER COON *chases* BR'ER BEAR *over the hill hitting and scratching while* BR'ER RABBIT *laughs at having tricked them again. They freeze. The lights dim as the orchestra continues playing until scene is changed.*)

SCENE 6

(*The Well. The lights come up on scene.* BR'ER RABBIT *and* BR'ER FOX *are frozen on set until lights are full.*)

UNCLE REMUS: Well by and by, his time was a-comin'. Der Br'er Rabbit was a-sittin' in da shade on one of da hottest days he could recollect. And that little rabbit brain of his was turnin' faster dan a locomotive.

BR'ER RABBIT: (*Conceiving a beautiful plan.*) Dig a well!!

UNCLE REMUS: So, he saw Br'er Fox sunbathing on da other side of da road, and he went to tell Br'er Fox his plan.

BR'ER RABBIT: (*Wiping sweat.*) Gee whiz, Br'er Fox. It's getting dry here, and we can't git any water; we get a little in da mo'ning but dat ain't enough. You know what we need? We need a well.

BR'ER FOX: (*Wiping sweat.*) A well?

BR'ER RABBIT: A well. We need a well.

BR'ER FOX: (*Thinking.*) Hmmmmmmm . . . Okey. (*Getting up.*) Let's get to diggin'.

BR'ER RABBIT: Uh-h-h . . .yeah . . . right . . . but round up the others. (*Yelling to* BR'ER FOX *as* BR'ER FOX *is exiting.*) Coon! Bear! Git 'em here in a hurry 'cause we need a well!

BR'ER FOX: (*Shouting to* BR'ER RABBIT.) A well! (*Exits.*)

BR'ER RABBIT: (*Shouts back.*) A well! (BR'ER RABBIT *giggles and rests himself near a tall stump. Soon he hears singing coming up the road.* BR'ER COON, BR'ER FOX, *and* BR'ER BEAR *enter singing.*)

BR'ER COON, BR'ER FOX, and BR'ER BEAR:
A well, a well
We need a well
Just wait and see

Our well will be
A cool, clean well.

(*They end in a barbershop quartet style but vary off-key.*)

BR'ER FOX: (*Calling to* BR'ER RABBIT.) Hey, Br'er Rabbit, let's go.

BR'ER RABBIT: (*Repositioning himself.*) Go where?

BR'ER BEAR: (*Usual smiling personality.*) To dig a well.

BR'ER RABBIT: Not me.

BR'ER FOX: (*Demanding.*) Help dig dis well, Rabbit. We all need water. An' besides, it was you idea.

BR'ER RABBIT: Oh, da devil! I don't need no water. I can drink dew.

BR'ER FOX: Dew it is den. Come on, ya'll. (BR'ER COON, BR'ER FOX, *and* BR'ER BEAR *proceed to the site of the well singing as the orchestra accompanies them.*)

BR'ER COON, BR'ER FOX, and BR'ER BEAR:
A well, a well
We need a well
Just wait and see
Our well will be
A cool, clean well.

(*They sing throughout the construction of the well. After the construction, they exit singing and dancing. The music fades slowly.* BR'ER RABBIT *waits until they are out of sight and sneaks to the well, with music dramatizing his footsteps, and draws water. He runs away as* BR'ER FOX, BR'ER BEAR, *and* BR'ER COON *are heard entering, singing a capella. Their singing fades as they approach the well and see that* BR'ER RABBIT *has stolen their water.*)

BR'ER COON: Well! Whose tracks are dose?

BR'ER FOX and BR'ER BEAR: Br'er Rabbit's!

BR'ER BEAR: Who stole our water?

BR'ER FOX and BR'ER BEAR: Br'er Rabbit!

BR'ER FOX: Who can drink dew?

BR'ER FOX and BR'ER BEAR: Br'er Rabbit!

BR'ER COON: Let's git him! (BR'ER COON *and* BR'ER FOX *start after* BR'ER RABBIT. BR'ER BEAR *stops them.*)

BR'ER BEAR: Wait! I tell you whut. I'll lay here and wait for him and when he comes, I'll grab him!

BR'ER COON and BR'ER FOX: (*Looking at each other, then to* BR'ER BEAR.) Okey!

(BR'ER FOX *and* BR'ER COON *exit.* BR'ER BEAR *lies at the foot of the well and*

sleeps. While BR'ER BEAR *sleeps,* BR'ER RABBIT *enters and drinks from the well.*
BR'ER RABBIT *then teases* BR'ER BEAR *by waking him up, then running off
before* BR'ER BEAR *can grab him.* BR'ER FOX *and* BR'ER COON *enter.*)
BR'ER BEAR: (*Looking pitiful.*) He was too fast for da kid.
BR'ER COON: We got to do somethin'. I'll go find him and whop him one
with my paw.
BR'ER FOX: I tell you whut! Let's make a tar baby and put him up by da
well.
BR'ER COON: For whut?
BR'ER FOX: (*Sly laughter.*) You'll see. Come on.
(*They move to behind the well and in commotion come out with the tar baby and
set him up in front of the well and then run off to hide behind the tall stump.*)
UNCLE REMUS: Br'er Fox had finally come up with a good trick. Br'er Rab-
bit was sho' to fall for dis one, dontcha see? (BR'ER RABBIT *enters and goes
up to Tar Baby, meddling.*) But as soon as Br'er Rabbit comes up to da well
and see da tar baby . . .
BR'ER RABBIT: (*To Tar Baby.*) Mo'ning!
UNCLE REMUS: Tar Baby didn't say nuthin'.
BR'ER RABBIT: Nice weather dis mo'ning.
UNCLE REMUS: Tar Baby didn't move.
BR'ER RABBIT: Woo-o-o-o-o-o!!!
UNCLE REMUS: Tar Baby ain't budged.
BR'ER RABBIT: Boo!
UNCLE REMUS: Tar Baby ignores him still.
BR'ER RABBIT: How you? Come on. Is you deaf? Cause if you is, I can holler
louder. (BR'ER RABBIT *screams.*) You stuck up, dat's whut you is, and I'm
gonna learn you how to talk to respectable folks, if it's da las' act. (*He
paces around Tar Baby.*) If you don't take off dat hat and tell me howdy,
I'm gonna bust you wide open! (*Furiously.*) Don't you hear me talkin'
to you? I'll slap you into next week. (*He hits Tar Baby, and his paw gets
stuck.*) If you don't let me loose, I'll knock you again right upside your
big head. (BR'ER RABBIT *hits Tar Baby with his other paw, and it gets stuck
also.*) Turn me loose befo' I kick da natural stuffing out of you. Oh! Don't
believe me huh? (BR'ER RABBIT *kicks Tar Baby, and his foot gets stuck.*)
Turn me loose, you big ugly devil! (*He kicks Tar Baby with his other
foot and gets stuck again.*) I know if I butt you one, I'll hurt you. (BR'ER
RABBIT *butts Tar Baby and his head gets stuck.* BR'ER FOX, BR'ER BEAR, *and*
BR'ER COON *enter with excitement and victory.*)

BR'ER FOX: Howdy, Br'er Rabbit. You look sorta stuck up this mo'ning. Well, I 'xpect I got you dis time Br'er Rabbit. You been runnin' round here sassin' after me and dem a mighty long time. But I 'xpect you done come to da end a da road. And der you is and der you'll stay until I fix up a fresh pile and fires her up. I'm gonna barbeque you dis day. (BR'ER FOX *proceeds to build a fire.*)

BR'ER RABBIT: I don't care whut you do with me Br'er Fox, so long as you don't fling me in dat briar patch. Roast me, Br'er Fox, but don't you throw me in dat briar patch.

BR'ER BEAR: No, roastin' him is too good for him, we can't let him off dat easy. Hang him.

BR'ER RABBIT: Hang me jes as high as you please, Br'er Fox, but, for da Lord's sake, don't fling me in dat briar patch.

BR'ER FOX: No, we can't hang him. He's too light. He wouldn't break his own neck. Drown him.

BR'ER RABBIT: (*Singing the old familiar spiritual.*) Deeeeeeeeeeep River, Lord.

BR'ER COON: Shut up, Br'er Rabbit.

BR'ER RABBIT: Drown me jes as deep as you please, Br'er Fox, but don't fling me in dat briar patch.

BR'ER COON: Da water ain't high enough. Skin him.

BR'ER RABBIT: Skin me, Br'er Fox. Snatch out my eyeballs, tear off my ears by da roots, chop off my legs. Make rabbit soup out of me, but please Br'er Fox, don't fling me in dat briar patch.

BR'ER FOX: (*A bong sounds.*) Rabbit soup?

BR'ER COON, BR'ER FOX, and BR'ER BEAR: (*The bong sounds again.*) Rabbit soup?

ALL: (*Singing the rabbit soup song.*)
Rabbit soup, Rabbit soup
Rabbits are my turnip top.
Rabbit hop, Rabbit jump,
Rabbit hide behind dat stump.

BR'ER BEAR: Rabbit's honey is full of bees.

BR'ER COON and BR'ER FOX: Yeah!

BR'ER BEAR: Now, let's see you scratch dem fleas.

BR'ER COON: I can drink dew.

BR'ER BEAR: You can drink dew.

BR'ER FOX: All God's chillum drink dew.

BR'ER COON, BR'ER FOX and BR'ER BEAR: Hallelujah!

BR'ER RABBIT: Oh, please don't eat me!

BR'ER COON, BR'ER FOX, and BR'ER BEAR: Hallelujah!

BR'ER RABBIT: Oh, please don't eat me!

BR'ER COON, BR'ER FOX, BR'ER BEAR:

> Eat 'im all up!
> Eat 'im all up!
> Eat 'im all, Eat 'im all
> Eat 'im all up!
> Uhoo! Rabbit's mine.
> Uhoo! Rabbit's skint.
> Clean him off and put him in!

ALL: We got the rabbit (*Repeat.*)

BR'ER FOX: (*With an air of disdain.*) This old rabbit is too tough to eat. Let's throw him in the briar patch to teach him a lesson!

BR'ER BEAR: (*With great anticipation.*) Yeah! That's it! Toss him in that briar patch! That'll teach him not to mess with us!

(BR'ER FOX *and* BR'ER BEAR *take* BR'ER RABBIT *by the arms and escort him to the edge of the briar patch.* BR'ER RABBIT *is squirming as he tries to free himself from their grip. He begs them not to throw him in the briar patch.*)

BR'ER FOX: Don't pay him no mind Br'er Bear. He gonna be crying like a baby when we throw him in da briar patch. Okay, on the count of three, let's chunk him way over in the briar patch!

BR'ER FOX: One! Two! Three! There he goes!

BR'ER RABBIT: Ya'll ain't got the rabbit. The briar patch is my home. My friends live in the briar patch.

UNCLE REMUS: As the story goes, Br'er Rabbit is at home in the briar patch. Br'er Fox, Br'er Coon, Br'er Bear sure ain't going in the briar patch. I'm sorry ya'll, that's all the time we got for ya'll today, but if you want to learn more about Uncle Remus and all his friends, ya'll go to the neighborhood library, Okey? Bye Ya'll.

(*Back into zip pa de do dah song.*)

THE END

When the Ancestors Call. (Left to right) Stacie Doublin, J. J. McCormick, and Carolyn Nelson. Photo by Kenneth Simmons.

When the Ancestors Call

ELIZABETH BROWN-GUILLORY

Elizabeth Brown-Guillory is Distinguished Professor of Theatre and associate provost/associate vice president for academic affairs at Texas Southern University. She holds a PhD from Florida State University. She is a theatre scholar, playwright, and performing artist. Before joining the faculty of Texas Southern University, she was professor of English at the University of Houston, where she was employed for twenty-one years and where she won the university's Cooper Teaching Excellence Award, the College of Liberal Arts and Social Sciences Teaching Excellence Award, and (two-time winner of) the English Honor Society's Sigma Tau Delta Distinguished Professor Award. The University of Houston Alumni Organization selected her in 2007 as one of four "Phenomenal Professors" at the University of Houston. Brown-Guillory's areas of expertise include dramatic literature, playwriting, African/Diaspora literatures, theatre history, women writers, and American ethnic literatures. On September 1, 2009, Brown-Guillory joined Texas Southern University, marking a new chapter in her career.

Brown-Guillory's books include *Their Place on the Stage: Black Women Playwrights in America* (New York: Greenwood Press, 1988); *Wines in the Wilderness: Plays by African American Women from the Harlem Renaissance to the Present* (New York: Greenwood Press, 1990); *Women of Color: Mother-Daughter Relationships in Twentieth-Century Literature* (Austin: University of Texas Press, 1996); and *Middle Passages and the Healing Place of History:*

Migration and Identity in Black Women's Literature (Columbus: Ohio State University Press, 2006). She frequently publishes scholarly articles, book chapters, reviews, and interviews in major refereed journals and critical anthologies.

Brown-Guillory served as founder and faculty advisor/mentor to the Houston Suitcase Theater, a faculty, staff, and student troupe committed to enhancing diversity in the arts at the University of Houston. For seventeen years, she wrote, directed, and produced plays for the campus and the Houston metropolitan area as well as arranged for nationally and internationally recognized playwrights and scholars to visit the university. She also was the founder and director of Erzulie, an African Dance Troupe at the University of Houston. She won the University of Houston Council of Ethnic Organizations' Outstanding Service Award for her dedication to students.

Brown-Guillory has had twelve plays produced across the country, in cities including Washington, DC, New York City, Los Angeles, Denver, New Orleans, Houston, Cleveland, and Chicago. The plays in her canon include *Bayou Relics, Snapshots of Broken Dolls, Mam Phyllis, La Bakair, When the Ancestors Call,* and *The Break of Day.* Ten of her plays have been published in *Black Drama: 1850 to Present,* an online collection of twelve hundred plays by black writers. The plays have won for her a series of honors and awards, including residencies in Illinois, Wisconsin, and New York. She was among the Texas playwrights showcased in Houston at the Ensemble Theatre's "Heart of the Theatre" series.

Brown-Guillory's plays are most often traditionally structured dramas centered around a realistic domestic entanglement. However, the supernatural intervenes in the dramatization of characters, influenced by forces in the form of their ancestors, who give them inspiration and strength. She depicts upwardly mobile middle-class families in recognizable dysfunctional patterns—sibling rivalry, betrayal, and father-son conflicts. She hints at black color consciousness, that is, characters commenting on the lightness or darkness of others in pejorative ways. She also comments in her work on the stigma of rape, the search for manhood, and homophobia. Repressed traumatic events often influence her characters' interactions and sense of self.

As You Read *When the Ancestors Call*

Brown-Guillory takes us to Louisiana with *When the Ancestors Call,* a two-act domestic drama. This time it is in Bayou St. Claude, a town in the southwestern region of the state. She focuses on the black middle class. The play highlights sibling rivalry, child abuse, psychoanalysis, dysfunctional families, and the quest for love. It takes its place among the plays (and movies) analyzing the effects of child abuse—for example, Paula Vogel's play *How I Learned to Drive* (1997) and the movie *Precious* (2010), an adaptation by Geoffrey S. Fletcher of the 1996 novel *Push* by Sapphire. Two sisters, Caroline and Jackie, on the surface are in conflict about what is the best home for their aging grandfather; however, this conflict overlays a more serious break that propels the drama to its startling revelation and denouement. The loss of the matriarch, causing a loss of cohesion, is a reoccurring motif in Brown-Guillory's work. The play juxtaposes realism with surrealism as a force from the other side takes shape and influences the forward thrust of the action. Some of the themes that come to the fore are the damage secrets can have on relationships, the significance of the past on the success of the present and future, and the role of examination and redefinition in saving a family after devastating events.

Production History

Originally titled *Just a Little Mark*, the play has been retitled twice, as *Wango! Oh, Me Papa* and, finally, *When the Ancestors Call*.

As *Just a Little Mark*:

    Cullen Performance Hall, University of Houston, Houston, Texas, November 5–8, 1992

    St. Peter's Catholic School, Houston, Texas, November 6–7, 1992; directed by Elizabeth Brown-Guillory

    Frank Haydon Hall, Southern University, Baton Rouge, Louisiana, 1996

As *Wango! Oh Me, Papa*:

    Shwayder Theater, Denver, Colorado, September 1997

As *When the Ancestors Call*:

    eta Creative Arts Foundation, Chicago, Illinois, May 1–June 15, 2003

Characters

CAROLINE: A woman in her mid-thirties, Caroline is an MD, specializing in oncology.

BILL: A psychologist in his mid-thirties who specializes in hypnotherapy.

POP: A walker-bound man in his early seventies, Pop (Ernest) is the grandfather of Caroline and the husband of the deceased Granny Vi; also a retired sharecropper.

GRANNY VI: An ancestral epiphany, Granny Vi (Viola) is the grandmother of Caroline. She is a spunky woman in her early seventies.

JACKIE: A forty-year-old secretary, Jackie is the sister of Caroline.

Setting

Time: The Present
Place: Bayou St. Claude, a town in southwestern Louisiana

ACT ONE

Scene 1

(*Early morning at* BILL's *office.*)

(AT RISE: *The scene opens in* BILL's *office with* BILL *taking notes.* CAROLINE *enters and interrupts him. She is wearing her medical paraphernalia, lab coat, stethoscope, etc.* BILL *is wearing khaki slacks, a sky-blue shirt, tie, and a navy blue sleeveless pullover sweater vest. During hypnosis,* CAROLINE *becomes increasingly fidgety, alternating between shaking her legs, twisting her hair, and holding her shoulders.*)

CAROLINE: (*Poking her head in the door.*) Bill, may I have a few minutes? One of my patients didn't show up, and I thought I'd run downstairs to see if you had a cancellation.

BILL: (*Scribbling notes.*) Actually, I do. I was just finishing up this report. Give me a second.

CAROLINE: I know I'm on your calendar for later today, but I'd rather meet with you this morning.

BILL: That'll work for me.

CAROLINE: Great. (*Taking a deep breath.*) I'm so grateful we work in the same building. (*Pause.*) I hope you don't think I'm taking advantage of our friendship.

BILL: Of course I do. That's what friends do. They take advantage of each other.

CAROLINE: I'm serious. Let me know if I'm taking too many liberties by popping in to see you.

BILL: Don't sweat it, Caroline. You and I go back a long ways. We've been friends for what, ten years now? I'd let you know if you were misusing me. (*Chuckling.*)

CAROLINE: Are you sure you don't mind?

BILL: It's fine.

CAROLINE: I know there's chemistry between us. We can't deny that.

BILL: But we don't want to go there, right?

CAROLINE: It would never work. Besides, we can't cross those lines.

BILL: Not while I'm your therapist.

CAROLINE: Absolutely! Let's just stick to being friends.

BILL: You know I care about you.

CAROLINE: You're my best bud, Bill. There's not another soul I'd let put me under hypnosis. And that's a fact.

BILL: That's called trust. (*Finishing up his report.*) So, what's up?

CAROLINE: More of the same. I think I put something together since the last time I talked to you.

BILL: What's that?

CAROLINE: I've been anxious for a long time, you know that. But, I think my level of anxiety increased when my Granny Vi died.

BILL: I've told you before, that's a normal part of grieving. She raised you. She's gone and now you feel a sense of loss, right?

CAROLINE: It's deeper than that. The loss, I mean. I miss my granny a lot, but there's something else going on. (*Looking down at her hands.*) Look at my hands, they're shaking. I sense there's something inside of me that I can't get to, and that's why I need your help.

BILL: Have you been going to the gym like I suggested?

CAROLINE: Yes. Four or five times a week. I can't sleep. I'm eating five and six Snickers a day. I'm really tense about something.

BILL: We'll keep working through this. It takes time to figure these things out. Let's have a session.

CAROLINE: I don't think hypnotherapy is working. Three months of digging around in my past, and we've come up with nothing.

BILL: I disagree. We've made good progress.

CAROLINE: I'm just as uptight as I was when we started these sessions. Yesterday, I snapped at the director of the clinic. Can you believe that? He's my immediate supervisor. I really lost it.

BILL: What happened?

CAROLINE: He's a flirt. I know he's harmless, but it makes me uncomfortable.

BILL: Do you feel he's crossing boundaries?

CAROLINE: Yes, and I don't like it. It's not just him, though. Seems like I've been getting into it with everybody at the clinic. Most of my colleagues

are men and . . . well . . . they seem to cross the line often. Maybe, it's
me, but . . .

BILL: But things are getting out of control.

CAROLINE: Right. I'm tense. I need to see some progress soon.

BILL: Listen, we were finally able to talk about your father last time.
That's progress.

CAROLINE: Really?

BILL: (*Changing the subject.*) I think we're getting closer to finding out why
you can't remember blocks of time from your childhood.

CAROLINE: I'm starting to feel anxious right now. Just the mention of
those lost blocks of time makes me feel tense. I know there's something
inside of me that's begging to come out, but it scares me.

BILL: Maybe we should consider . . .

CAROLINE: (*Interrupting* BILL.) I don't want an antidepressant. I discussed
it with my primary-care physician. She says it might help. Maybe I do
need something. I don't know . . .

BILL: You're a wonderful woman. You have to allow yourself to see how
wonderful you are.

CAROLINE: You're biased. Everybody thinks I have it together. There goes
Dr. Caroline Mark. She's on a fast track in her profession—was named
oncologist of the year for the entire state of Louisiana.

BILL: You should be proud.

CAROLINE: But I'm not. There's this brick wall and I can't get around it. I'm
jammed up. It takes all my energy to pretend I have it together. What
would my cancer patients think if they knew I was a fraud?

BILL: You're not a fraud.

CAROLINE: Don't you understand? I'm strapped with something that keeps
me up most nights. I'm scared, Bill.

BILL: We'll work through this.

CAROLINE: Will you listen to me? I am spinning out of control. I'm afraid
of everything. Afraid of loving . . . I can't live like this anymore.

BILL: Let's get you to relax.

CAROLINE: And, I just found out today that Jackie is trying to take Pop.

BILL: Take him where?

CAROLINE: To live with her. Granny Vi's only been dead six months and
Jackie is itching to make changes. She thinks Pop shouldn't live in the
house anymore.

BILL: But you're there with him.

CAROLINE: It doesn't matter. She says I'm never home and Pop needs better care.

BILL: Does he?

CAROLINE: He gets around on a walker without any problems, same as always. He's grieving, but that's natural.

BILL: Then what's the real issue?

CAROLINE: The real issue is . . . Jackie wants to get her hands on Pop's Social Security check. Maybe she just wants to control everything. She called before I left for work and we had a big argument about Pop. I'm not letting her take Pop away from our home. It's his home, and when he says he wants to leave, he'll leave. Jackie is not having her way with me, not this time.

BILL: I'm happy to see you so assertive. This is progress. The more you prevent people from walking all over you, the better you'll feel about yourself.

CAROLINE: I don't feel good about arguing with Jackie. We go around and around until she wears me out. We start on one point, and she brings up ten things from before the Civil War. Old grudges. Things I have no control over and can't do anything about.

BILL: Close your eyes and relax.

CAROLINE: I'm on the edge . . . Do you think I'm losing it, Bill?

BILL: Look, we've been through some pretty sensitive stuff in the past few months. I didn't think you were ready for the asylum when you began obsessing.

CAROLINE: Don't remind me. I paired every sock and found covers for every plastic container in the kitchen cabinets.

BILL: We worked through all of that, Caroline.

CAROLINE: And of course, there was the AIDS scare. I just knew I had AIDS. Remember the report in *Newsweek* about those dentists who don't sterilize properly? I had an allergy attack and blamed it on AIDS. I vowed I'd never get my teeth cleaned again.

BILL: Then you started obsessing about your hair. You were sure that you were going to be bald in a matter of days. You started counting the strands in your comb.

CAROLINE: I couldn't go past a mirror without looking at my thin spots and wondering how long until I was completely bald. I really was out of control.

BILL: You were trying to adjust to what's disturbing you.

CAROLINE: I need to know what's making me so anxious, and I'm not going through twenty years of therapy to find out. I've wasted too much of my life already.

BILL: Let's get started.

CAROLINE: (*Attempting to get up from the chair.*) Wait . . .

BILL: Caroline. (*Gesturing for her to sit.*) Sit back. (*Dimming the lights.*) Take a deep breath. Close your eyes. This time keep them closed. Drift away. Go all the way down. Good. Keep breathing deeply. I think we're making real progress. Let's talk about your father. In our last session, you mentioned firecrackers. Go all the way down. You know the cue. At the count of three, I want you to tell me what you see. One, two, three. (*Calling to her.*) Caroline.

(CAROLINE *is terrified; she shrieks and lifts both feet into the chair.*)

BILL: Caroline, what are you remembering?

CAROLINE: (*Resisting what she's remembering.*) The snakes. The snakes are all around me. They're biting me. Make them stop. Get away. Get away from me. Get away. They're biting me. (*Out of breath.*) They're all over me. I can't make them stop biting me.

BILL: Take deep breaths, Caroline. Drift away. Go all the way down. Take long, slow, deep breaths. Open your eyes now, Caroline, but you will remain in a deep hypnotic state. The snakes are gone now. Are they gone?

CAROLINE: Yeah, they're gone. (*Putting her feet back on the floor.*)

BILL: Tell me about your father and the firecrackers.

CAROLINE: (*In a daze.*) It was Christmas. My brother, Ben, and I were fighting over firecrackers.

BILL: Ben was killed in a car accident, wasn't he?

CAROLINE: Yeah. I miss him.

BILL: I bet you do. So, tell me about that Christmas and the firecrackers.

CAROLINE: Daddy was drunk . . . totally out of his mind. (*Pleading in a boy child's hot-tempered voice.*) "Daddy, Caroline won't give me no firecrackers."

BILL: What happened then?

CAROLINE: (*Straining not to tell.*) He just came from nowhere, talking out of his head, and snatched me up. I was ten . . . but I remember. His eyes were on fire. He threw me up against the bedroom wall . . . like I was a basketball. He punched me in the stomach two or three times. I remember the punches most of all. (*Leaning forward and cupping her mouth like she's going to regurgitate; speaking in a child's voice.*) "Mommy, Mommy, make him stop. Make him stop, Mommy. Daddy, please . . . please. Mommy . . . Mommy." (*Speaking in her own voice.*) I remember Mama . . . she came running . . . swinging a baseball bat. (*Speaking in a powerful woman's voice.*) "You gonna hurt that child. Don't beat that child in the belly. She ain't gonna be able to have no babies. Leave her alone, you hear me? Stop hurting my child."

BILL: What do you want to tell your father?

CAROLINE: (*Adamant.*) Nothing.

BILL: Sure you do.

CAROLINE: (*Less sure of herself.*) Nothing.

BILL: Talk to me, then. It's ok. I'm right here. I'll listen.

CAROLINE: (*Voice cracking.*) He took away my confidence . . . (*Pause.*) He was always getting drunk and hurting one of us. (*Pause.*) I never forgot about the time he tied Jackie's braids to the iron bed and banged her head every time she tried to get away. I saw it and I ran . . . I ran into the closet. My little feet just ran.

BILL: Where was your mother?

CAROLINE: I don't know.

BILL: Of course you do. Where was she?

CAROLINE: She left us behind.

BILL: Where did she go?

CAROLINE: To Detroit. With her new boyfriend. She left us with Daddy.

BILL: Who drank too much.

CAROLINE: (*To herself.*) He drank more after Mama left. He ruined his liver.

BILL: Is that when you went to live with your grandparents?

CAROLINE: Yeah, after Daddy died. Pop and Granny Vi raised me and Jackie.

BILL: Back to your father . . . and the abuse. Do you believe he felt sorry for hurting you?

CAROLINE: He hurt me. Why does it matter if he was sorry?

BILL: It matters. Sometimes it's easier to forgive and move on when we know the abuser is sorry. Do you think your father was burdened by his actions?

CAROLINE: I don't think he remembered. He drank so much of the time. He was a big bully.

BILL: Did you ever talk to him about the abuse?

CAROLINE: I was too scared of him. We used to stop breathing when he walked into a room. I remember holding my breath whenever I was around him.

BILL: Caroline, I want you to find your father. Look for him. Can you see him? Go way back.

(CAROLINE *turns her head in a semicircular motion each time she regresses or progresses under hypnosis.*)

CAROLINE: (*In a six-year-old child's voice.*) I can see him.

BILL: How old are you?

CAROLINE: I'm six.

BILL: Talk to your daddy.

CAROLINE: (*Hesitant.*) Noooooooooo.

BILL: Try.

CAROLINE: (*Fearful.*) Daddy . . . Daddy, you hurt me. You're a bad, bad man, Daddy. I don't like you . . . because you keep hurting me. I remember you made me kneel on a bed of gravel behind the house in the hot sun. I was just a little girl, Daddy, doing and saying little girl things. How come you hurt me?

BILL: What's he saying, Caroline?

CAROLINE: My daddy's crying. (*Speaking in her father's voice.*) "I did the best I could. I made a whole bunch of mistakes, and I'm sorry. I love you, child. I love all my children." (*Pause, then in a six-year-old child's voice.*) But you hurt me. (*Pause.*) What? (*Pause.*) I didn't hear you. (*Speaking in her father's voice.*) "We didn't have a crust a bread and I took it out on your mama and y'all. (*His voice cracking.*) I'm sorry . . . so, so sorry. If I could, I'd do things different. I didn't mean to hurt you, child. I wish I could take it all back and keep you safe. Protect you instead of . . . hurting you.

BILL: Do you have anything to tell him? Let it go, Caroline. It's time to let it go.

CAROLINE: No. I can't. (*Shaking her head to indicate that she can't let go of the pain.*) Daddy, you hurt me. (*Thrashing intensifies.*) No, no, stop it, please don't touch me, you're hurting me. (*Screaming.*) Granny Vi, make him stop it. Granny Vi, please make him stop it.

BILL: Just relax. Come on back. You're not quite ready to remember yet. Find your way back to the present. I'm going to count backward. You know the cue. At the count of one, open your eyes. Three, two, one.

(*Lights fade to black.*)

Scene 2

(*Mid-morning of the same day at* POP'S HOME.)

(AT RISE: POP *is sitting at the dining room table with his walker next to him. He is wearing khaki pants and a plaid work shirt.* CAROLINE *enters from the kitchen carrying a tray, a pitcher of iced tea, and two glasses.* POP *and* GRANNY VI *always pronounce* CAROLINE'S *name* CARRY-LINE *and* JACKIE'S *name* JACKLEEN.)

POP: Carry-line, what were you and Jackleen arguing about early this morning?

CAROLINE: Just stuff, Pop. You know how we are. Oil and water.

POP: Are you keeping something from me, Carry-line?

CAROLINE: Why do you ask that?

POP: It's not like you to take off in the middle of the day. You should be doing your work.

CAROLINE: I just felt like coming home, Pop. It feels good to be in here.

POP: Another bad day at the clinic? Are those white folks messing with you again?

CAROLINE: Pop, I feel alienated. There's me and then there's them.

POP: (*Rolling up his sleeves to show he's readying for a fight.*) Let me know if I need to go over there and put a whipping on those white boys. I won't stand for nobody misusing my grandbaby. And that's a fact.

CAROLINE: I'm fine. Don't you love this old house, Pop?

POP: (*Unrolling his sleeves and chuckling.*) Of course, I do.

CAROLINE: This is the only place I've ever felt safe.

POP: It's your home, Sugar.

CAROLINE: You and Granny Vi made this house a home for me and Jackie. I can feel Granny Vi's presence. She's in the walls. I can still smell her cabbage and ham hocks. Her sausage jambalaya. Her gumbo. All of it. Right here in these walls.

POP: Oh, she's here, all right. There are a lot of memories in these walls. Your grandmother and I lived in this same spot for forty-five years. And before that, Mom and Papa called this place home. Someday, it'll be yours and Jackleen's.

CAROLINE: Did I mention Jackie's coming over to make gumbo? She said you need tending to.

POP: Is that why you came home? Are you and Jackleen having some little meeting? Don't y'all be talking about me behind my back.

CAROLINE: No, I just needed to be in a safe space right now. Jackie has her own agenda.

POP: That girl acts like I'm helpless. I just let her do. It's easier than arguing with her. Don't let Jackleen get to you, Sugar.

CAROLINE: I try not to, but she has a way of knocking me off balance.

POP: Just look past it. Her little drinking problem gets the best of her sometimes. She means well.

CAROLINE: I'm not putting all the blame on Jackie. I'm a bit on edge myself. To tell you the truth, Pop, I've been lost without Granny Vi.

POP: Nobody's been the same, Sugar. Every little thing in the house reminds me of her. She's in everything I touch around here.

CAROLINE: I miss her, Pop.

POP: Lord knows I sure do. I just wish I had done right by Viola.

CAROLINE: You did the best you could, day in and day out, while she was sick. I don't know another man with a walker who could have taken care of his wife like you did.

POP: But it wasn't enough. I should have made my peace.

CAROLINE: What do you mean, Pop?

(*A knock is heard at the door.* JACKIE *enters wearing jeans and a sweatshirt. She has a can of beer in one hand and a shiny container in the other. She approaches the table and pours the beer into her favorite drinking vessel which she carries around in every scene.*)

JACKIE: What are you doing here in the middle of the day? Don't you have a job?

CAROLINE: I need some down time. I decided to take the rest of the day off.

JACKIE: Why? Are your white folks giving you the blues, too? I'm not surprised.

POP: Come on in, Jackleen.

JACKIE: Hey, Pop. (*Kissing him on the forehead and then hugging him.*)

POP: How you today?

JACKIE: I can't complain. It wouldn't do any good anyway.

POP: Ain't that the truth? How's Malcolm?

JACKIE: He's fine.

POP: And little Tim and Jessica?

JACKIE: Hardheaded—you know how kids are. How are you feeling today, Pop?

POP: (*Grabbing his walker and heading toward the exit.*) Old Arthur is giving

me the blues, but I can't complain too much. Jesus woke me up this
morning in my righteous mind. (*Chuckling.*)

JACKIE: Did you take your Advil?

POP: I'm on my way to get some now.

JACKIE: (*Rolling her eyes at* CAROLINE.) I'll get it. Caroline, why didn't you
get Pop his Advil?

POP: I can get it, Jackleen. I'm not helpless yet. And don't be blaming
Carry-line. I didn't tell her Old Arthur was bothering me today.

JACKIE: Well, she should have asked. She's the doctor of the family, right?

POP: Now settle down, Jackleen. It's too early in the day to start your
foolishness. (*Exits.*)

JACKIE: (*Calling to* POP.) Ok, Pop. I'm just trying to help out.

CAROLINE: Are you still making gumbo?

JACKIE: (*Signifying on* CAROLINE.) Somebody's got to cook around here. I
hate to see Pop eating four-day-old leftovers.

CAROLINE: (*Frustrated.*) Don't act like I'm not taking care of Pop. I cook
every chance I get, and when I don't, I pick up something.

JACKIE: Some of that stuff in the fridge has hair growing on it. Are you
growing penicillin in there?

CAROLINE: I just haven't had the time to clean the refrigerator. But don't
accuse me of not taking care of Pop.

JACKIE: Humph! You have answers for everything, don't you? But I'm still
taking Pop to live with me, Malcolm, and the kids.

CAROLINE: Shhhhhhh. Let's not talk while Pop's up. (*Wanting to change the
subject.*) Soooooo, you didn't have to work today?

JACKIE: I can take off just like you. Anyway, they're giving me the blues
at the office. (*Noticing* CAROLINE'*s nervousness and distraction.*) What's
wrong with you?

CAROLINE: I've been putting in a lot of hours. I'm really tired and stressed.

JACKIE: You've always been wound up pretty tight. Even when we were
little, you used to get so nervous you'd pee in the bed. (*Laughing.*) Are
you still peeing in the bed?

CAROLINE: How many beers have you had today?

JACKIE: None of your business, little sister. Don't try to change the subject. Are you still peeing in the bed?

CAROLINE: Jackie, you need to go take a nap.

JACKIE: Why, because the little baby can't remember wetting the bed?

CAROLIE: I don't remember, Jackie. And I wish you wouldn't tease me.

JACKIE: I'm not teasing you. I'm just trying to help you remember things. Peeing in the bed is one of those things. I hated having to clean up behind you. When Mama went off to Detroit, you peed in the bed a couple times a week, child. Daddy used to get you up to use the bathroom, but you'd still pee in the bed. Don't you remember that?

CAROLINE: I don't! And why is it so important to you?

JACKIE: It's not that important. I was just thinking . . . you were getting ready to go to high school before you stopped wetting the bed. (*Laughing.*) I used to call you "Polecat"—because you were always spraying the bed sheets just like a nasty little polecat. I thought you'd want to take that to your shrink-friend, Bill. Ask him why you wet the bed so much.

CAROLINE: Who told you I was in therapy?

JACKIE: Pop told me, but I had already figured it out.

CAROLINE: Really?

JACKIE: Girl, you've been hanging around with Bill for years. I know you tell him all your business.

CAROLINE: I feel safe with him.

JACKIE: You've got the hots for him.

CAROLINE: We're just friends.

JACKIE: I can see sparks between y'all, but you're both ducking and dodging and dipping and acting like white folks.

CAROLINE: How did white folks get into this conversation?

JACKIE: White women don't date their therapists. Everybody knows that. But I do know that it would take more than a little therapy to keep a sistah and brotha from dancing the dance. Especially if there were sparks flying between them like I've seen between you and Mr. Freud. (*Laughing.*)

CAROLINE: I don't see anything funny, and please lower your voice.

JACKIE: If you got your own place, you wouldn't have to worry about Pop hearing us.

CAROLINE: Granny Vi's only been dead six months and you're trying to uproot Pop. That'll kill him to make a big change like that.

JACKIE: (*Burping.*) He'll get used to it.

CAROLINE: No, he won't. Leave him alone. You just want to get your hands on Pop's check.

JACKIE: That's a lie.

CAROLINE: If you need money, I'll lend you some.

JACKIE: I'm not after Pop's money . . . and I don't want a dime from you.

CAROLINE: So what is it you're after? Control? You want to control Pop, me, the house? What?

JACKIE: Shut up! Just shut up!

CAROLINE: I think you've had more than one drink this morning. I think you should take a nap, and then we'll talk about what's best for Pop. (*Trying to make conversation.*) Did you call in sick today?

JACKIE: (*Irreverently stressing "Dr. Caroline" each time she says it.*) Yes, Dr. Caroline, I did.

CAROLINE: I know you don't want to lose your job.

JACKIE: Now look at you, who's pointing the finger now? I know it's the third one I've had in two years.

CAROLINE: (*Softly.*) You've got to try to make it work out.

JACKIE: Look at the pot calling the skillet black. Pop told me you're not getting along with some of the doctors at your clinic. You'd better watch out before you get fired, Missy.

CAROLINE: I wish Pop wouldn't tell my business.

JACKIE: I wish you'd stay out of mine. Look, let's cut the small talk. I got the letter you wrote me.

CAROLINE: I was wondering . . .

JACKIE: I felt like bringing it here and stuffing it down your throat.

CAROLINE: If you're going to talk like this . . .

JACKIE: Don't tell me how to talk. I said to myself, "Well, I know I'm just a secretary. I'm not some big fancy cancer specialist like her, but she could have called me on the phone and talked to me like I'm people, too."

CAROLINE: We always wind up fighting. I didn't know what else to do.

JACKIE: So you wrote me a letter and told me I've got ugly ways.

CAROLINE: I asked you to stop criticizing me.

JACKIE: I bent over backwards to help you through medical school. Sent money to you off the top, before I paid my own bills. And you didn't appreciate any of it.

CAROLINE: That's not true.

JACKIE: Well, you have a terrific way of showing it, Dr. Caroline.

CAROLINE: I want you to stop treating me like I'm an idiot, that's all.

JACKIE: If I'm always hurting your feelings you should stay out of my way.

CAROLINE: You should watch what you say.

JACKIE: You need to get a thick skin, Baby Girl.

CAROLINE: No, you need to know that you're hurting me. Seems like telling you would be enough, but you keep right on with the insults. (*Mimicking* JACKIE.) "You don't live in the real world." . . . "You can't cook dry beans." . . . "You know medicine but you don't know anything else." . . . "Where did you get your MD . . . from Harvard or from A&P?"

JACKIE: (*Mimicking* CAROLINE'S *blocked memory.*) "I don't remember. I can't remember any of that. Big chunks of time are gone—just slipped away from me." You're a nut!

CAROLINE: See, there you go again. You're mocking me. You think it's funny I can't remember.

JACKIE: Get over yourself, will you? Whatever was in the past, let it be. Quit acting like it's the end of the world. Lots of people don't remember things.

CAROLINE: But I need to . . .

JACKIE: The walls are closing in on me. (*Exiting.*) I need to get out of here.

CAROLINE: You're running because you're scared, aren't you? I'm getting too close.

JACKIE: (*Re-entering.*) Too close to what?

CAROLINE: I'm getting to you. Any minute I might ask you something . . . like . . . does it still hurt that Daddy beat you with a tree branch that time and Granny Vi took a sugar cane to him?

JACKIE: (*Stammering.*) I don't remember any such thing. And don't be running Daddy down. He's not here to defend himself.

CAROLINE: He beat you, Jackie. I do remember that!

JACKIE: You don't know the first thing about Daddy. He was tired of owing his soul . . . breaking his back on land that didn't belong to him.

CAROLINE: So he took it out on us. I remember that like it was yesterday. Granny Vi made him back away with her cane.

JACKIE: Granny Vi was a meddlesome old woman. And she never did get to Daddy with that cane. (*Laughing.*) She tripped and those big white bloomers nearly scared him to death. (*Laughing.*) Whoosh! (*Laughing.*)

CAROLINE: Everything that comes out of your mouth has to be a joke. Why is that? Nobody can be that happy and that funny all the time. What are you hiding behind all that laughter?

JACKIE: Go to hell! That Harvard MD has gone to your head.

CAROLINE: You know what, I don't think my degree has a thing to do with your taking potshots at me all the time.

JACKIE: What are you talking about now, Dr. Caroline?

CAROLINE: You don't want me to be close to you. I scare you for some reason. Maybe you're afraid I'll make you remember those years when we were too scared to breathe. When we thought Daddy would beat Mama and then turn around and beat us.

JACKIE: How you gonna make me remember anything and you can't remember squat yourself? The blind leading the blind. You got jokes, Baby Girl.

CAROLINE: There are lots of things I don't remember, but what I do remember, I wish I could forget!

JACKIE: You need to move on.

CAROLINE: I can't; I'm stuck. You're mad because you think I'm ok . . . that I survived those beatings without scars . . . That I've made it and you haven't. That's what you think, don't you?

JACKIE: Girl, sometimes you act like you crawled out from under a shell. And you better watch out because you're dripping slime all over my happy day.

CAROLINE: What happened to us? We can't keep dancing this dance.

JACKIE: You're making me tired. (*Burping again, this time louder.*)

CAROLINE: It's not even noon and you're drunk.

JACKIE: (*Rushing over to slap* CAROLINE *but holding her fist in midair.*) Shut your stupid mouth up.

CAROLINE: You put your fist up every time I come near you. If Granny Vi were here, you know she wouldn't let us fight like this.

JACKIE: Even Granny Vi let me down. She hurt my feelings really bad.

CAROLINE: How's that?

JACKIE: I did everything I could for Granny Vi while you were off jump-starting your career in New Orleans; I was right here in Bayou St. Claude. I cooked, cleaned, did laundry, drove her everywhere she needed to go. And I don't regret a bit of it. I'm just saying . . . aw . . . forget about it.

CAROLINE: Saying what?

JACKIE: I never saw her eyes light up for me the way they did for you when you walked into the room. I loved Granny Vi, but her eyes never lit up for me. I don't think she ever told me thank you.

CAROLINE: She loved you, Jackie. You know she did, in her own way. Don't talk like she didn't love us both.

JACKIE: I'll say what the hell I want to say. You're the one who wanted to talk. Let's talk, Baby Girl. I worked my butt off to take care of Granny Vi and Pop, and you'd blow in for the weekend and get all the praise.

CAROLINE: I tried my best to praise you for all the things you did for Pop and Granny Vi.

JACKIE: I felt like a field hand. (*Pause.*) And then when Granny Vi got sick, you moved back home to Bayou St. Claude and into this old rattrap. By then, you were the big cancer specialist. And nobody else was worth anything in Granny Vi's eyes.

CAROLINE: (*Awkward.*) She talked about you all the time. She could depend on you. She loved you, too, Jackie.

JACKIE: Not like she loved you, though, and there wasn't very much left for me.

CAROLINE: How can we make things better between us now?

JACKIE: You can help me get Pop ready to move over to my house. He needs somebody to look after him all day long.

CAROLINE: How is he going to get that at your house? You work all day, just like me.

JACKIE: I can quit this little nickel-and-dime job tomorrow and take care of Pop.

CAROLINE: And why move him?

JACKIE: Because I'm tired of coming over here to clean up behind him and you.

CAROLINE: You're not taking care of me, Jackie. You haven't in a long time. No, there's something more going on here. What's really up?

JACKIE: I am so tired of you; let me get out of here. Tell Pop I'm going to get some shrimp for the gumbo. (*Exiting.*)

CAROLINE: (*Calling after JACKIE.*) I'm not letting you take Pop.

JACKIE: (*Off Stage.*) Yeah, right!

(CAROLINE *removes the tea from the table, slamming the tray on the buffet.* POP *enters with his walker carrying in his shirt pocket* GRANNY VI's *white lace handkerchief.*)

POP: What were you and Jackleen carrying on about?

CAROLINE: Same old thing, Pop.

POP: (*Stopping to smell the handkerchief.*) I took a little catnap. When I woke up, I found Viola's handkerchief in the bed with me. I must have put it there before I fell asleep.

CAROLINE: Oh, look at it. She loved that handkerchief.

POP: She sure did.

CAROLINE: Did you have a good nap?

POP: I wish you'd woke me up. Lord, I was having the worst nightmare.

CAROLINE: About Granny Vi again?

POP: Yes, Lord. She came to me in a dream. I've been dreaming about her a lot lately. She talks to me, you know. Oh, Viola, I wish you were here.

(GRANNY VI *appears. She is wearing a Sunday-go-to-meeting two-piece white suit, white shoes, a small white hat, and white gloves. She has in her hand a white lace handkerchief that matches the one* POP *has in his hand.*)

CAROLINE: I've been dreaming about her, too.

POP: Sometimes I feel like she's right here with me.

CAROLINE: I feel that way, too. Sometimes I feel her brushing my hair or rubbing my back. Sometimes I feel her kissing me on the forehead. And sometimes, I feel a breeze and then I'll smell her Estée Lauder perfume. It all feels so real. But, she's on the other side, Pop.

POP: Lord, if I could just have my Viola back. I could make things right with her.

CAROLINE: What do you need to make right, Pop?

POP: Viola was the sugar in my coffee, but I didn't do right by her, I tell you.

CAROLINE: What didn't you do, Pop?

POP: Take care of Viola like I should have.

CAROLINE: Granny Vi was blessed to have you.

POP: She wasn't always blessed. I did a terrible thing long years back.

CAROLINE: What did you do, Pop?

POP: I don't know if I can tell you . . . been so many years back . . . but I want to tell you. Because Lord knows I don't want to leave this world without begging Viola's pardon. I'm asking you to sit in Viola's place and let me beg your pardon. I need to unburden myself, Sugar.

CAROLINE: You know you can talk to me about anything, Pop.

POP: I know it. That's why I'm coming to you. I woke up . . . and I couldn't get Viola's face out of my mind. I thought my heart would give up on me. I thought maybe it was my time. Seems like Viola was in the room with me. I got to tell you something that chills my bones.

CAROLINE: Tell me, Pop, it's ok. Whatever it is . . .

POP: I'm talking about the day Viola got caught in the barn.

CAROLINE: Who caught her? What are you saying, Pop?

POP: I ain't never told nobody. You hear me . . . nobody. But I saw.

CAROLINE: What did you see, Pop?

POP: I saw Old Man Broussard catch Viola . . . (*Pausing with fists clinched.*) that piece of poor white trash. (*Pausing.*) He took her right there in the barn. I saw it with my own eyes.

CAROLINE: (*Moving toward her grandfather midway between him and* GRANNY VI.) Oh, my Lord, Pop.

POP: He took her. That's what he was used to doing—taking colored women when he wanted them.

CAROLINE: She never told me she had been pinned down like that. Who was this piece of trash?

POP: He owned the land we worked. We worked from can't see to can't see for Old Man Broussard. That wasn't enough for him. He wanted my Viola. It was a sickness, I think. He took her and I saw it with my own eyes. One day I was coming from breaking corn . . . and that's when I saw it. I remember I wanted to crawl into the ground. I almost stopped breathing. Old Man Broussard had pinned her down in the barn . . . like Jesus on the cross. I can still see it. And he was drunk. Had a big bottle of vodka laying on the ground right next to my Viola. Yes, Lord, he forced himself on my Viola. White men could do that back then and get away with it.

CAROLINE: I don't know how she survived it. And it must have been horrible for you.

POP: Well I declare, I watched him take her, and I couldn't move. My mind started playing tricks on me. One second I was in the barn with my feet glued to the ground, and the next I was on some big ship packed together like sardines in a can . . . packed so tight . . . no light . . . no air . . . dry heat that burns your flesh. (*Covering his eyes with* VIOLA's *handkerchief.*) Then Viola screamed and I was back in the barn. I couldn't breathe. I threw up. I emptied myself right there in the barn.

CAROLINE: (*On the verge of hyperventilating.*) She must have been so afraid . . .

POP: I know I was. Child, I looked down and saw my feet running. My feet was running, and I wasn't moving. I think I lost my mind that day. My feet was just a running.

CAROLINE: Your feet were running, but you weren't moving.

POP: That's right, Sugar. I was stuck. But after awhile, I commenced to running. I ran . . . ran . . . ran, I tell you. Long as I live . . . I'll never forget that I ran off and left Old Man Broussard taking what he wanted.

(*Simulating the act.*) He was just laughing and grunting and laughing and grunting. I saw it and I ran. I beg your pardon, Viola, the sugar in my coffee. And . . . I beg your pardon, Carry-line, for running off and leaving your grandmother.

CAROLINE: I love you, Pop.

POP: Viola thought I had run off with some little finger-popping woman. That's what I told her when I came back some months later. The truth is I left her because I couldn't stop seeing the hurt in her eyes. I didn't help that pain by running off and leaving her to fend for herself. Oh, in time we patched things up. We never talked about that day in the barn. She never brought it up, and I was too coward. We acted like it never happened.

CAROLINE: I bet she was ashamed.

POP: I know for a fact she was, but I couldn't talk about it. Never could. Now, it's too late to tell Viola what a coward I was, so I'm telling it to you. I needed to tell you I was a coward. I don't want you to be like me. Sugar, if somebody pins you down, get back up. That's what Viola did. I was a coward, and I'm sorry. Don't you be a coward, Carry-line. Don't you run away from your troubles like I did. Viola told me in the dream this afternoon to talk to you. She said, "Tell Carry-line . . ."

GRANNY VI AND POP: (*Simultaneously.*) ". . . When somebody pins you down, you got to find a way to get back up."

POP: Yep, that's what she said. Oh, Lord, I feel better already. Took a load off my feet, yes Lord.

(CAROLINE *begins massaging* POP's *neck.*)

GRANNY VI: (*Singing.*) "We've got the power to heal ourselves. We've got the power to heal ourselves. Oh, we've got the power to heal ourselves." (*Exiting into the kitchen.*)

CAROLINE: (*Singing and massaging her grandfather's neck and back.*) "We've got the power to heal ourselves."

POP: That was Viola's favorite song.

CAROLINE: I remember, Pop. "We've got the power to heal ourselves. Oh, we've got the power to heal ourselves."

(JACKIE *enters.*)

JACKIE: (*To* CAROLINE.) What are you doing singing to Pop? You sound like a pig stuck under a fence.

POP: Now, Jackie, leave her alone.

CAROLINE: I thought you were going to get shrimp.

JACKIE: (*To* POP.) I made it all the way to the store and forgot my coupon. There's a special on shrimp, Pop.

POP: I know how you like your coupons.

CAROLINE: (*Exiting through the kitchen door.*) I'll go start the water for the gumbo.

POP: (*Indicating* GRANNY VI'*s handkerchief.*) Jackleen, look what I found when I woke up from my nap.

JACKIE: (*Taking the handkerchief.*) Granny Vi's favorite handkerchief. Lord, she loved this one, with all that lace.

(GRANNY VI *emerges from the kitchen with the mention of her handkerchief.*)

POP: Jackleen, what's going on between you and Carry-line?

JACKIE: Nothing, Pop. You know how sisters are. One likes red beans; the other likes black-eyed peas.

POP: I can't stand to see the two of you carrying on. Viola didn't like it neither. Y'all try to get along.

JACKIE: Don't worry about us, Pop.

POP: I'm going out to get a little fresh air in the back yard. Let me know when the gumbo is ready.

JACKIE: I'm putting shrimp, crab, and oysters in the gumbo. I know how much you love seafood, Pop.

POP: I can taste it already. (*Exiting singing.*) "We've got the power to heal ourselves. Oh, we've got that power to heal ourselves."

JACKIE: (*Still holding onto the handkerchief and talking to it.*) Well, Granny Vi, I wonder what mess you're stirring up in heaven? You sure gave me the blues. Always praising "Carry-line." Like she was your only grandchild. I was here, too, Granny Vi. I washed your old butt plenty days, and you didn't even say thank you.

(*Ringing of cymbals or dimming of lights when* GRANNY VI *speaks.*)

GRANNY VI: Thank you, Jackleen, you silly child.

JACKIE: (*Terrified.*) Lord, have mercy. (*Collecting herself.*) That beer is getting to me.

(JACKIE *is terror-stricken as she looks straight ahead while* GRANNY VI *speaks.*)

GRANNY VI: You better straighten up, Child. I know I raised you better than that. Here you are carrying on like the world owes you something. Well, it doesn't. And if you keep waiting for somebody to come around and hand you a good life, you're going to wake up and find you've missed out, Child. I know you think I'm meddlesome, but that's because I won't let you get away with foolishness. And as for talk about me not loving you, . . . Child, I loved you with everything inside of me. You see only what you want to see. You like being miserable, and you want to make everybody around you feel your misery. That's not right, Child. You better stop that foolishness, and I mean right now. I am here to set you straight—shake some sense into you, before it's too late.

JACKIE: (*Dropping the handkerchief on the table and running out of the house.*) Oh Lord, let me out of here!

(*Lights fade to black.*)

Scene 3

(*One day later in* BILL'*s office.*)

(AT RISE: CAROLINE *is pacing the floor while* BILL *sits at his desk taking notes.* CAROLINE *is fidgeting with* GRANNY VI'*s lace handkerchief.*)

CAROLINE: Something strange is going on with Jackie.

BILL: Like what?

CAROLINE: She was supposed to make gumbo for Pop last night. She went out to get shrimp and didn't come back. I called over to her house and Malcolm told me she was asleep. That's not like her. Pop was waiting for his gumbo.

BILL: Has she been drinking again?

CAROLINE: Pretty hard. She needs help. I'm trying to get her back into AA.

BILL: What about you? How are you doing?

CAROLINE: I'm pretty shaken up about Jackie wanting to take Pop to live with her. I can't figure her out. She's got her hands full with her kids. We had it out about Pop yesterday. It was ugly.

BILL: What does your grandfather think of Jackie's plan?

CAROLINE: He doesn't know yet. I'm hoping Jackie will forget about it. Maybe it was just the beer talking. Hey, guess what, Pop told me a story yesterday that blew me away. The man he worked for raped Granny Vi in the barn . . . right next to the pigs and the chickens . . . and Pop ran. He told me he ran.

BILL: (*Writing notes on his pad.*) Why did he tell you? Why now?

CAROLINE: He told me Granny Vi came to him in a dream and told him he needed to talk to me. He asked me to take my grandmother's place and forgive him. It was so hard for me to hear that somebody raped my Granny Vi. It was like I was there. Like it was happening to me, and my little feet just started running, too.

BILL: Did he say why he ran?

CAROLINE: He said he was scared. He knows I'm dealing with something, and he knows I'm scared, too. He wants me to stop running. He's a wise old man. Last night he told me a bunch of stories about people in our family who had been pinned down, but who got up.

BILL: Oh, yeah?

CAROLINE: Yeah, he's full of stories about our ancestors. He told me about my great-uncle Paul who was tied to a barrel in Opelousas and whipped for stealing corn to feed his hungry children. A group of white men whipped him in the "for whites only" park and then put salt in his wounds. Pop said Uncle Paul almost died, but he wouldn't give the white men who beat him the satisfaction.

BILL: That was a horrible hate crime.

CAROLINE: But Pop didn't focus on the lynch mob. He focused on Uncle Paul's will to live. Pop said Uncle Paul was pinned down, but he got up and raised his family. He didn't run away. He told me he doesn't want my feet to keep running, Bill.

BILL: He's right, you know. You don't have to stay pinned down.

CAROLINE: You know what else Pop told me last night?

BILL: What?

CAROLINE: He said, "When you're feeling whipped, Caroline, call on your ancestors."

BILL: Sounds like good advice to live by.

CAROLINE: (*Beginning to rub her chest.*) My chest is hurting. Jackie's stressing me out.

BILL: Let's get you to relax. See if we can get that pain to go away.

CAROLINE: (*Suddenly sad.*) Bill, do you know what's wrong with me?

BILL: (*Jokingly.*) You're neurotic, psychotic, and mentally disturbed.

CAROLINE: (*Jokingly.*) I know that, but what's wrong with me?

BILL: That's it, Caroline, you keep that sense of humor.

CAROLINE: Granny Vi used to say, "You gotta have a sense of humor, Tootsie. It'll help you bounce back from the blows of life. Then life won't owe you nothing."

BILL: She was a wise woman. Now close your eyes, Caroline. Take a deep breath, hold it to the count of four, and let it go slowly. Exhale every obstacle to your relaxation. That's it. Drift away. Let go. Now, let your breathing settle down. You know the cue. I'm going to count to three. One . . . two . . . three. Raise your right hand if you can hear me.

(CAROLINE *raises her right hand.*)

BILL: Put it down. Open your eyes slowly. But you will remain in a deep hypnotic state. In one of our sessions recently, you said you often felt ugly and ashamed when you were a child.

CAROLINE: I did. Sometimes I still do. I feel different and alone.

BILL: Can you tell me about a particular moment when you first felt different?

CAROLINE: (*Fidgeting with the handkerchief.*) I don't know—maybe when I was nine or ten.

BILL: Find your way back to when you were nine. Tell me what happened back when you were nine.

CAROLINE: (*Giggling and speaking in a nine-year-old child's voice.*) Granny Vi happened.

(GRANNY VI *appears.*)

CAROLINE: She'd never admit it, but she didn't like dark skin . . . and don't you know . . . she was sundown brown. Well, one day she wormed and squirmed her way to our house and was looking at all the pictures on the wall. She started with my oldest sister and moved on down the line to my cousins' pictures. She said:

GRANNY VI: Ooooooooh child, look at that Jackie. She got such pretty hair . . . good hair . . . straight hair . . . just like white folks. And look at Betty, such high cheekbones and teeny-weeny lips . . . pretty child. Don't have much Africa in her, no sir. And look at Linda . . . with that smooth high-yellow skin . . . child most can pass for white, yes sir. And oh, look at Marie . . . that child is prettier than all the rest . . . hair most blonde and eyes gray as a cat.

CAROLINE: Then she moved to my picture and said:

GRANNY VI: But Carry-line . . . boy that's a ugly child. I don't know where y'all got that little ugly black Buckwheat. Look at those two big teeth in the front. And that little nappy hair brushed to one side. And, ooooooooohhhhhh child, that little thing got big feet and a big belly. She looks like a poor starving child in Africa, yes she do.

CAROLINE: And then, she must have seen the light go out of my eyes because she shouted:

GRANNY VI: But Carry-line, she makes four thousand points in school, yes she do. That's a smart child. She might be president some day. She's our Moses.

CAROLINE and GRANNY VI: (*Simultaneously extending their hands to suggest generations.*) She's gonna carry us through. She's gonna carry the line through to the next generation.

GRANNY VI: Yeah, she's the one.

CAROLINE: She said I was the one.

(GRANNY VI *makes conjuring motions around* CAROLINE *while* BILL *delivers his next line.*)

BILL: Find your way back to the present, Caroline. I want you to close your eyes again. This time I want you to go still deeper. Drift away. Caroline, you are to relax and begin seeing yourself the way the world sees you. You are smart, beautiful, sensitive, and sensuous. Don't let the snakes get to you. And you don't have to stay pinned down. Starting today, whenever you hear negative things that eat at your confidence, merely say to yourself, "Cancel, Cancel!" Do you understand me?

CAROLINE: I do. I'm to say, "Cancel! Cancel!"

(GRANNY VI *exits.*)

BILL: Let's move to a new topic. I want you to go still deeper. Drift away. Feel every muscle in your body loosening up and freeing you to relax. Go all the way down. Feel the clouds beneath you as you imagine your body floating peacefully. Are you totally and completely relaxed?

CAROLINE: (*With a heavy tongue.*) Absolutely.

BILL: Let's talk about your past romantic relationships.

CAROLINE: They've been short-lived.

BILL: Why?

CAROLINE: Jackie says it's because I'm frigid.

BILL: What do you say?

CAROLINE: (*Hesitant.*) I get uptight in romantic relationships.

BILL: Do you know why you get uptight?

CAROLINE: No. I just can't respond the way a woman should.

BILL: How do you mean?

CAROLINE: I don't feel anything. There's no passion. I'm not in it. I don't even want it. I like to be held close, but I can't give anything more.

BILL: Why?

CAROLINE: I'm afraid.

BILL: What are you afraid of?

CAROLINE: I don't know.

BILL: Are you afraid of loving someone?

CAROLINE: Maybe. Who could love me without hurting me? I can't take that risk.

BILL: You have to be open to it, Caroline.

CAROLINE: I've had at least a dozen men friends. They'd get close. Want too much. I'd find something wrong and then push them away. Frank was a classic case.

BILL: Who's Frank?

CAROLINE: Somebody I thought I was going to marry.

BILL: What happened?

CAROLINE: He dumped me.

BILL: Why?

CAROLINE: He said I was just a tease. All talk and no show. One night, we were making out and I freaked. Just for a minute, I thought he was raping me. I started fighting him. (*She recalls the scene with much animation. Note:* CAROLINE *can't separate one abuse from another, even under hypnosis, at this stage of her recovery. She links Frank's aggression with her father's abuse.*) Stop it. Stop hurting me. Get away from me. The snakes are biting me. Make him stop, Mommy. The snakes are all over me. They're all around me. Get your hands off of me. Make them stop, pleaseeeeeeeeee. Oh, God, make it stop. Mommy. Mommy. Mommy. (*Lights fade to black.*)

INTERMISSION

ACT TWO

Scene 1

(*Two weeks later at* POP's *home on a Friday early afternoon.*)
(AT RISE: JACKIE *enters and goes to buffet, holds up an eight-by-ten-inch photo of* GRANNY VI, *and pours a glass of vodka. She's already had too much to drink. She picks up* GRANNY VI's *handkerchief from the buffet.*)

JACKIE: (*Fingering the handkerchief.*) I ran out of here a couple of weeks ago because I thought I saw you, Granny Vi. I have to cut back on some of this vodka. It's making me nutty. I'm back, and I've got news for Dr. Caroline. Today is the day I tell Pop I'm taking him to live with me. I don't care what Caroline says. Pop shouldn't be staying here all by himself every day. We need to sell this old rattrap of a house. Something is not right in this house anymore. I can feel it in the walls. This house has got to go. Caroline will have to find herself another place to hide from herself. Scaredy-cat. (*To* GRANNY VI's *handkerchief.*) Your Carry-line makes me sick, with her uptight self. She acts like she's the only one with problems. Like she's the only one with a past filled with the blues.

(GRANNY VI *materializes, and* JACKIE *looks straight ahead in fright.*)

GRANNY VI: Lot's of folks get bruised and knocked around, Jackleen. You ain't lived unless you been pinned to the ground at least once. Some get up and wash the bruises and keep moving . . . and some . . . well some just get mad and mean, like you, Jackleen.

JACKIE: (*Waving her hands.*) Get out of my face, Granny Vi. Go back to where you came from and leave me alone, you old bat! I did everything I could for you, but I couldn't do anything to make you happy like your precious (*Sneering.*) Carry-line. Get out of my sight.

(GRANNY VI *disappears into kitchen.*)

JACKIE: What am I doing talking to myself? I do not believe in spirits, (*Chuckling.*) except the kind I'm drinking. (*Chuckling.*) I wonder where Pop is? He's probably visiting one of the neighbors, maybe Mr. Jacob or Mr. Mansy. (*Picking up the handkerchief again.*) You let me down, Granny Vi. I just wanted you to love me. What did I ever do to make you not love me? What did I do that was so horrible that you couldn't forgive me? I needed you to love me. Was it the drinking? I went to AA for you. You never gave me one word of encouragement. I stopped going after you died. What's the point? Huh, Caroline is seeing a shrink to try to remember, and I'm drinking to try to forget. What a pair we are. Just lovely.

(GRANNY VI *reappears.*)

GRANNY VI: You're carrying around a secret, and it's eating you up, Child. You got to give it to God. You hear me, you got to give it to God.

JACKIE: Get out of my head, Granny Vi. Stop messing with me.

GRANNY VI: You have to find a way to get that bitter taste out of your mouth. Bitterness will break your back, Child. You have to come to Jesus. Jesus will heal you. He'll help you carry the load. But, first, you got to come to Jesus.

JACKIE: (*Screaming.*) Stop it. (*Holding her ears.*) Get out of my head!

GRANNY VI: Your feet can't keep running. What you do in the dark will come out in the light of day. You got to make things right, Jackleen.

JACKIE: What are you talking about, Old Woman? Why are you bothering me? You're talking nonsense.

GRANNY VI: Just say you're sorry, and Jesus will wash away your sins.

JACKIE: Go away. I don't want you here. You're talking in riddles. I don't know what you want from me. So, just get out of my head.

(GRANNY VI *disappears into the kitchen again.* CAROLINE *enters in her lab coat, etc.*)

CAROLINE: What's wrong, Jackie? Who are you screaming at?

JACKIE: Don't you see Granny Vi? She's messing with me.

CAROLINE: You've had too much to drink, Jackie.

JACKIE: So, are you calling me a drunk?

CAROLINE: I am too tired to argue.

JACKIE: Girl, you're tense. You need to loosen up. You need to get yourself a man. That's all you need. That's why you're so uptight. You ain't never had a real man to help you relax. I know just the man. There's this guy I work with who lost his wife about six months ago, so you know he's carrying a load. He is some fine. I bet he could ring your bell.

CAROLINE: Thanks, but no thanks.

JACKIE: See, you don't listen to anything I tell you. That's why you're all messed up. You're just a candle waiting to be burned, Baby Girl.

CAROLINE: (*To herself.*) Cancel! Cancel! (*To* JACKIE.) I don't have time for nonsense. I had a hard day.

JACKIE: Hey, we all got to go sometimes.

CAROLINE: Jackie, this black woman, this single mother of three children, is only forty-five years old.

JACKIE: Oh, a sistah?

CAROLINE: Yes, and she's going to die.

JACKIE: I'm sorry about the sistah, but life ain't fair, Caroline, so you better deal with it.

CAROLINE: Listen at you, you're sounding like Granny Vi.

(GRANNY VI *appears.*)

CAROLINE: She used to say:

GRANNY VI: Sugar, life ain't always fair, and if you keep on waiting for life to be fair, somebody's gonna come along and pin you down and you won't be able to get back up.

CAROLINE: She told us so many stories about the ancestors. Can't you hear them sometimes? She used to say:

GRANNY VI: When the ancestors call, you better listen, Child.

JACKIE: I never liked hearing those old stories. What was the point? I never got the point.

CAROLINE: The point was that she was telling us about ourselves; we just couldn't see it then. Lately, I've been trying to remember all those stories. Pop's been telling me lots of stories at night. He gets all fired up. Do you remember the story about Granny Vi's sister, Cleotha?

JACKIE: I heard it at least a hundred times.

GRANNY VI: My sister Cleotha didn't let her husband run her crazy. When his outside woman came to Cleotha's house, she pitched him and his little no-necked woman out the door.

CAROLINE: And do you remember the one about Doublehead?

JACKIE: How could I forget it?

GRANNY VI: Doublehead tried to violate my cousin, Marguerite. He came scratching through her bedroom window, and she put birdshots in his backside. He came to try to fill her up with his shotgun, but she got him with hers first.

JACKIE: Oh, yeah, sorry to say, I remember all those old stories she used to tell.

CAROLINE: Remember the one about Cousin Lutie Mae Johnson?

GRANNY VI: When Lutie Mae Johnson married that little white fellow, the church members ate into her like she was red beans and rice. When she started having all those babies, everybody thought it was a disgrace. They called her all kinds of dirty names . . . "hussy this" . . . "heifer that." Lutie Mae didn't let nobody break up her home, and she didn't walk around with a sour taste in her mouth because folks was acting mean and nasty. She kept on smiling and having those babies. Yes, Lord, honey. She had thirteen little yellow babies, and she named them after every pastor, deacon, head mother, usher, and Sunday School teacher she could think of. (*Laughing.*)

JACKIE: But what was the point of all of those old stories?

CAROLINE: The point is somebody just like us went through tough times, and it wasn't the end of the world.

JACKIE: I still don't get the point. Granny Vi lived too much in the past for me. All those old stories just made me tired.

CAROLINE: You weren't listening.

JACKIE: Those old stories were boring. They put me to sleep, (*Talking to an imaginary GRANNY VI.*) with all due respect to you, Granny Vi.

CAROLINE: Granny Vi had courage. And I want to be like her.

GRANNY VI: Yes, Lord, life don't owe me nothing!

JACKIE: (*Picking up the handkerchief.*) I got to give it to her; she was a tough old hen.

GRANNY VI: (*Exiting to the kitchen.*) Jackleen, a secret will eat you up. You have to give it to Jesus, and don't take it back.

CAROLINE: I miss her. Did I tell you she's been coming to me in my dreams? Just as clear as day.

JACKIE: (*Still a bit bewildered.*) Listen, Caroline, I don't have all night to hang around. I just want us to come to some agreement about Pop. Will you help me talk to him about moving in with me?

(POP *enters with his walker.*)

JACKIE: I thought you were up the block, Pop.

POP: I was. I came through here thirty minutes ago and you were snoring so loud I thought you were sawing logs. So, I took a little nap, too.

CAROLINE: How was your day, Pop?

POP: I was having a good day until I heard Jackleen in here talking about selling my house.

JACKIE: I want you to come live with me.

POP: I heard you. I'd rather go to the nursing home.

JACKIE: Pop!

POP: (*Becoming angrier with each succeeding line.*) I mean it. What makes you think you can walk in my house and just take over? Like I'm senile and can't make my own decisions?

CAROLINE: She didn't mean . . .

POP: Stay out of this, Carry-line.

JACKIE: I'm trying to look out for you.

POP: No, you're not. If you were, you would have asked me what I wanted to do, instead of coming in here talking about me like I'm a child. I'm a grown man, and you had better mind what you say.

CAROLINE: (*To* JACKIE.) Didn't I tell you this would upset Pop?

JACKIE: Pop, you didn't hear all of my plans.

POP: I don't want to hear nothing more about your plans.

JACKIE: My house has two spare bedrooms, Pop. There's plenty of room for your stuff.

POP: Jackleen, didn't you hear me? I am not thinking about leaving my home. I don't think I could sleep in another house. Lord, I'd have to leave all these stories in the walls behind. And, Lord knows the walls in your house are empty . . . nothing but sheetrock and two-by-fours.

JACKIE: Now why you want to talk about my house like that? It's better than this termite-infested place.

POP: (*Shouting.*) This termite-infested house kept a roof over your head. Kept you safe . . .

JACKIE: I didn't mean to upset you, Pop. I just thought you'd be better off with me.

POP: How could I be better off? My friends live up and down the block. I've talked to Cousin Laura across the fence nearly every day for forty years. I've hung around nearly every day with Mansy and Jacob for the past fifteen years.

JACKIE: They could come visit you.

POP: Child, Mansy and Jacob haven't crossed the bayou in thirty years. Do you think they'll cross it to come over to your house? They don't even drive anymore.

JACKIE: You could make new friends.

CAROLINE: Jackie . . .

POP: I don't want new friends. I like the ones I have now. I like everything just the way it is. My doctor is just a few blocks away. My church is just three blocks . . . But more than anything, I won't leave Viola.

JACKIE: What?

POP: You heard me. She's in these walls. So, go on back there and get yourself a little nap. Sleep off some of that vodka. I don't want you driving until you've had a nap.

JACKIE: I'm all right.

CAROLINE: Go on, Jackie.

JACKIE: But, Pop . . .

POP: I don't want to hear it.

JACKIE: Ok, Pop. I was just trying to help. (*Exiting.*)

POP: Thank you, just the same. (*To* CAROLINE.) I'm going up the street to meet Mansy. I'll be back before dark.

CAROLINE: I'm proud of you.

POP: This is my house, and I'll sell it when I get good and ready, and not a minute before.

(*Lights fade to black.*)

Scene 2

(Mid-morning, one month later in BILL'S *office.)*

(AT RISE: CAROLINE *is being prepped for a hypnosis session. She is wearing her lab coat on top of slacks and a blouse. She is holding her grandmother's lace handkerchief.* BILL *is wearing dark slacks and a turtleneck shirt.)*

BILL: Ok, Caroline. You are as relaxed as you can possibly get. More relaxed than you have ever been. You are strong enough now to handle what it is time for you to remember. So go all the way down. Imagine you are a brick wall and the bullet that is about to come your way cannot destroy you. Do you see yourself as a brick wall?

CAROLINE: Yes, I am a brick wall.

BILL: Can you handle the bullet that's coming?

CAROLINE: *(Fidgeting with the handkerchief.)* I can. I'm ready—me and the ancestors. *(Touching her heart.)* I have them all stored right here. They won't fail me. Granny Vi is with me.

*(*GRANNY VI *appears and hovers.)*

BILL: I won't fail you, either. Go back now. Go back to when you were between the ages of five and seven. Go back to the time you blocked from your memory. You have repressed something and only you can name it. I can't name it for you, but I am fully confident that you are ready to name it. Go back, Caroline. Go back now. You're a little girl again. Go back. Are you there yet?

*(*CAROLINE *recalls her molestation in a little girl's voice.)*

CAROLINE: *(Whimpering a bit.)* Yes. *(More whimpering.)* It's dark. I'm scared.

BILL: Don't be afraid. I am right here with you. I will not abandon you. I will be here, no matter what. I promise. Tell me, Caroline, what's happening in that dark space?

CAROLINE: I'm scared. I'm trembling. *(Beginning to exhibit nervous leg movement.)* I can't make my leg stop shaking.

BILL: It's ok, let it shake. Don't try to stop it.

CAROLINE: Ok.

BILL: What do you hear in this space?

(Sound effects—a fan.)

CAROLINE: There's a fan and it's making noise. Like it needs to be oiled.

BILL: Any other sounds?

(Sound effects—laughter on television.)

CAROLINE: There's a television on in Daddy's room. Jackie's watching television. She's watching *The Brady Bunch*. I can hear Marsha laughing in the background because Jan is complaining, "Marsha, Marsha, Marsha. It's always about Marsha."

BILL: Can you smell anything in this space?

CAROLINE: It smells like liquor. Smells like somebody's been drinking.

BILL: What else, Caroline? What else do you smell?

CAROLINE: (*Pausing a second.*) Urine. I smell urine. Somebody's wet the bed. I can feel the wet spot. It's cold. A cold, wet bed sheet.

BILL: Can you see anything in the dark?

CAROLINE: I see somebody. I'm scared.

BILL: Who is it?

CAROLINE: I can't see. It's too dark. Wait, I see someone covered in a blanket.

BILL: Ok, let's skip back a bit. What happened in that dark space where you are right now?

CAROLINE: (*Hesitant.*) Somebody hurt me. (*Whimpering and thrashing around.*) No, stop it. Please don't hurt me again. Stop it, please. Stop touching me. (*Screaming.*) Mama, make it stop. (*Hyperventilating.*) I'm going to tell Mama. Yes, I will. I'm going to tell. I don't care if you beat me. Get away. You're hurting me. Ouchhhhhh. Mommy, Mommy, Mommy. (*Fighting with her fist.*) Get away. Get away. Get away.

BILL: Caroline, settle down. Take a deep breath. It's ok.

CAROLINE: No, it's not. I'm a bad girl. I'm a bad little girl. I'm so ugly; I can't stand to look at myself. I hate myself. I'm dirty. I can't get the dirt off me. I don't want it there. Make it go away.

BILL: Ok, Caroline, let's go forward again. Can you see the blanket?

CAROLINE: Yes, I see it.

BILL: You must pull off the covers.

CAROLINE: Noooooooooooooo. I don't want to get beaten anymore. No, no, noooooo.

BILL: Don't be afraid, Caroline. You have to pull off the covers so you won't be afraid anymore. He can't hurt you anymore.

CAROLINE: I can't. I'm too tired. My hands can't move. I can't move. I'm just lying in this cold, wet spot on the bed sheet. I wet on myself.

BILL: Get up, Caroline. Get up from that wet spot and go pull off the covers.

CAROLINE: I can't.

BILL: Let's get Jackie to come help you. Ok, that's good. Yes, let's get Jackie.

CAROLINE: No, don't get Jackie. Jackie is tired, too.

BILL: (*Surprised.*) What? Did somebody . . . ?

CAROLINE: Somebody hurt Jackie, too. (*Whimpering again.*)

BILL: Is it the same person who hurt you?

CAROLINE: (*Shaking her head.*) No. Don't make me look at that. I don't want to see it. Please don't make me see this.

BILL: You cannot resist my instructions, Caroline. You have to comply. Go all the way down. Let's get back to Jackie. Can you tell me who hurt Jackie?

CAROLINE: I'm not sure.

BILL: Ok, let's take it slowly. Can you see Jackie anywhere?

CAROLINE: She's in Daddy's bedroom. And she's crying.

BILL: Why is she crying?

CAROLINE: Because somebody hurt her.

BILL: Did you see what happened to her?

CAROLINE: Yes.

BILL: I want you to identify him.

CAROLINE: (*Hyperventilating.*) I can't stand to look at him. (*Hiding her eyes.*) He's the devil. He's been drinking vodka. There's a big bottle of vodka on the floor.

BILL: Name him.

CAROLINE: It's Uncle Syrus.

BILL: (*Stunned again.*) Uncle Syrus?

CAROLINE: Yeah, Daddy's baby brother. He's sleeping in Daddy's bed. Wrapped in Daddy's blanket. He hurt Jackie.

BILL: What's he doing in your father's bed?

CAROLINE: He's our sitter. Daddy went out to the club. Uncle Syrus always sleeps in Daddy's bed when Daddy goes out. He hurt Jackie in her private. (*Trembling and crying.*)

BILL: Did you see him hurt Jackie?

CAROLINE: Yes. I was playing with my doll in the closet. I don't think he saw me. I saw him hurt her. I kept quiet. I couldn't move. I was so afraid. My little feet started running but I wasn't moving. I was stuck.

BILL: Focus on the blanket. Is he under the blanket in the bed?

CAROLINE: No. He's not there now. Uncle Syrus isn't there with me in that cold wet spot. It's not Uncle Syrus.

BILL: Are you sure, Caroline?

CAROLINE: I'm sure.

BILL: Just relax. Keep on relaxing. Who is under the blanket?

CAROLINE: I don't know.

BILL: I believe you do. You have to pull off the cover and name him. Tell me who hurt you. Who took away your innocence?

CAROLINE: I can't do it.

BILL: You have to do it now, while you still have the courage. You told me the other day Granny Vi gives you courage. Call on her now.

CAROLINE: Granny Vi. I need you.

(GRANNY VI *moves closer to* CAROLINE *and begins conjuring, a ritualistic healing.*)

BILL: Ask your Granny Vi to help you pull off the covers. I know you can do this, Caroline. Go to the blanket and pull off the covers now.

CAROLINE: I'm getting scared again. I don't think I can.

BILL: It's time now! You have to do this now. Pull off the covers right now. Right now, Caroline.

CAROLINE: Please don't make me do it. I'm afraid.

BILL: You'll always be afraid if you can't name him and see that what he did was wrong. The little girl in you needs to know that she didn't do anything wrong. You can't grow into the woman you need to become until the little girl in you is healed.

CAROLINE: (*Crying.*) I'm so afraid. Can you come with me?

BILL: I'm right beside you. But, you have to do it. I can't do it for you.

CAROLINE: Ok, I can do it. If you're with me, I can do it.

(GRANNY VI *simulates pulling off the covers and* CAROLINE *follows with the same motion.*)

CAROLINE: (*Pulling off the imaginary covers and gasping.*) Oh God! Oh God! Oh God!

BILL: Who is it?

CAROLINE: (*Her breath is taken away.*) Oh, my God.

BILL: Who do you see? Name him!

CAROLINE: It's Jackie.

BILL: What?

CAROLINE: Jackie touched me in my private.

BILL: Are you sure?

CAROLINE: I'm sure.

BILL: Are you absolutely sure?

CAROLINE: (*Crying.*) I can see her. It's Jackie.

BILL: Ok, Caroline, we've made a breakthrough. We did it. I want you to start your journey forward. Come on back. Find your way back to the present where you will remember everything you just saw. You can handle this now. There are people around you who will continue to help you. You can now name the thing that has kept you running your whole life. You will be able to deal with this new information. I'll help you. I will not abandon you. I'm going to start counting backward. You know the cue. At the count of one, you will regain full awakening consciousness. Three, two, one. Open your eyes, Caroline.

(*After a second or two,* CAROLINE *becomes aware of what she has remembered. She puts her hands up to her mouth and begins to cry.* BILL *takes her in his arms and lets her empty herself.* GRANNY VI *encircles* CAROLINE.)

(*Lights fade to black.*)

Scene 3

(*Mid-afternoon one week later at* POP's *house.*)

(AT RISE: GRANNY VI *emerges and walks around the kitchen touching the chairs, picking up a picture of herself, and savoring the moment.* JACKIE *emerges from the bedroom yawning. She's been napping. She sits at the table and picks up* GRANNY VI's *handkerchief.*)

GRANNY VI: What's done in the dark, comes out in the light of day. That secret is eating you alive. (*Exiting into the kitchen.*)

JACKIE: (*Shaking her head as if to shake* GRANNY VI *away.*) This hangover is doing me in.

(CAROLINE *enters.*)

CAROLINE: (*Very restrained.*) I didn't know you were here.

JACKIE: I quit my job today.

CAROLINE: What happened?

JACKIE: White people. They give me the blues. I called and told them, "I'm out of here."

(CAROLINE *walks around the table but says nothing.*)

JACKIE: I came over here to see what Pop was up to. We've been on bad terms since he told me he didn't want to come live with me.

CAROLINE: I told you.

JACKIE: Yeah, but he didn't have to hurt my feelings like he did. (*Mimicking* POP.) "I'd rather go to a nursing home." That old fool.

CAROLINE: (*Angry.*) Stop it! He's not the fool. You're the fool.

JACKIE: Who are you calling a fool?

CAROLINE: You. For thinking your dirty little secret would never come out.

JACKIE: What's wrong with you?

CAROLIINE: Where's Pop?

JACKIE: He's down the block at Mr. Mansy's house.

CAROLINE: Good. Because I want to talk to you, and I don't want Pop to hear this. This is between us, you and me.

JACKIE: So what's on your mind?

CAROLINE: The secret is out, Jackie.

JACKIE: (*Stunned.*) What secret?

CAROLINE: I know what Uncle Syrus did to you, and I know what you did to me.

(*JACKIE turns away from* CAROLINE.)

JACKIE: Don't come here with a lot of noise. My head hurts. I told you I'm not having a good day. Didn't I just tell you I got fired?

CAROLINE: Fired? You just said you quit. Look, I don't care about your job. I don't even care about you right now.

JACKIE: Baby Girl, you better get a grip.

CAROLINE: Cut it out, Jackie. I had a session with Bill last week, and I remember everything. I've been trying to digest all I remembered but I am still so angry I could explode.

JACKIE: I don't know what you think you remember. But you better stop shouting at me and tell me what you're talking about.

CAROLINE: Uncle Syrus raped you. I was playing in the closet with my little doll with the red ruffles and white lace.

JACKIE: Oh, you remember playing with dolls now, huh? (*An exaggerated whine.*) "Jackie, why don't I remember any dolls? Everybody tells me I had dolls, but I don't remember one. Not one." So, now you remember that scraggly haired doll. I hated it. You always wanted me to comb that doll's hair.

CAROLINE: Jackie, I didn't remember that doll until last week. Bill put me under hypnosis and helped me to remember.

JACKIE: Bill is a freak, if that's what he helped you to remember.

CAROLINE: Uncle Syrus didn't know I was in the closet. I was just playing with Ruby. Yeah, that was my dolly's name. He came into the bedroom. He pinned you down. You were fighting him. Biting him and scratching him. He had his hand over your mouth, but you kept clawing at him. I didn't know why he was fighting you, but I was scared. I was so afraid. I couldn't move I was so scared. Then after he left, you started crying. When I tried to come sit next to you, you pushed me away. You were so angry. You hit me on the head. Do you remember?

JACKIE: I don't know what you're talking about.

CAROLINE: Don't lie to me, Jackie. You were always crying after that. Every time I looked for you, you were somewhere off crying.

JACKIE: That shrink has filled your head full of nonsense.

CAROLINE: Do you think I'm lying? Do you think I would make up something as horrible as this?

JACKIE: (*Pouring herself a glass of vodka.*) I think you made up something in your head to explain why you've always been a little bit off.

CAROLINE: What was I thinking? I thought I could talk woman to woman with you. Tell you what I remember.

JACKIE: Uncle Syrus never touched me and I certainly never touched you. Oh, my God, what do you think I am? A pervert?

CAROLINE: You know, Jackie, what you did may have only lasted a couple of minutes, but it has hung over me a whole lifetime. And now you're standing here telling me I'm lying.

JACKIE: I'm saying it's all in your head. You've been obsessing too much. Every day, you're digging and digging and digging.

CAROLINE: And that's why you kept teasing me about seeing a psychologist. You didn't want me to remember. You were hoping this would just go away. That I would stop walking around here like I'm about to pee in my pants. (*Realizing the connection to molestation.*) Oh, Lord!

JACKIE: I know where you're about to go, but don't even try it.

CAROLINE: Polecat. You've been calling me "Polecat" for years. I started wetting the bed because of what you did, and you called me "Polecat." I am this close to strangling you, Jackie. And the only reason I'm not is because I've spent years learning restraint. That's what children who've been molested do. They spend all their energy trying not to spin out of control.

JACKIE: You're pretty out of control now.

CAROLINE: (*With clinched teeth.*) You had better pray that I can keep it together, because you haven't seen me out of control.

JACKIE: You don't scare me, Caroline.

CAROLINE: I should. You're the reason I've been scared of everything. You know how you're always teasing me about my night-light? (*Mimick-*

ing Jackie.) "Oh, look at that little stinky pus; she has to sleep with a night light. Are you scared of a boogey man?" Well, yes, Jackie, I'm still sleeping with my night-light because I'm afraid of the dark. I'm afraid somebody is going to touch me in places no little girl should be touched and make me feel dirty. I felt dirty. I thought it was my fault. So dirty, that I had to block it out. That's how I survived, Jackie. I had to block it out.

JACKIE: I can see you're going through something, and I don't know what to do.

CAROLINE: You can own up to what you did.

JACKIE: I didn't do it, Caroline.

CAROLINE: Yes, you did. I can see it in your eyes. You're afraid. Just like I was. I know fear when I see it. I've lived with it my whole life. I thought it was because Daddy whipped us. I think I've been confusing the whippings with molestation. I guess after a while, one bad thing feels like another. It's all the same thing. But I'm not confused anymore.

JACKIE: It doesn't matter what I say; you've made up your mind that I did some dirty little thing to you and you're all messed up because of me.

CAROLINE: That's right, except that it wasn't a little thing.

JACKIE: How many times do I have to tell you that all this mess is in your head, girl? And this is the thanks I get for helping you through medical school.

CAROLINE: I appreciate all that you did, Jackie.

JACKIE: Well, thank God for that.

CAROLINE: But it was guilt money. I remember thinking how nice it was for you to send me so much cash. I didn't expect it. I knew things were tight for you, but you wouldn't let me give it back. You said I'd be insulting you. I think in the back of your mind, you wanted me to succeed.

JACKIE: Not in the back of my mind. In the front of my mind. You wanted to be a doctor, and I was your big sister. I was supposed to help.

CAROLINE: And when I became an MD, you never let an opportunity pass to call me (*Sneering.*) "Dr. Caroline."

JACKIE: That's who you are, isn't it?

CAROLINE: Don't play with me, Jackie. You were jealous. You helped me and then you couldn't stand that I was becoming successful. You wanted me to go get an education, and then come back exactly like I left. Well, I couldn't. Education changes people. But you always tried to make out like I was acting like I was better than you. That was your projection of your own sense of inadequacy.

JACKIE: There is nothing inadequate about me. And if you want to talk about jealousy. Let's come clean. You've always been jealous of me and my relationship with Malcolm and the kids. You have your MD, but you're all alone and hiding out in this old house, scared of men.

CAROLINE: (*Raising her voice.*) You got that right. I was hiding, but I'm not any more. I am out of the closet, if you know what I mean.

JACKIE: You've always been frigid. You're thirty-five and still a virgin.

CAROLINE: Am I? I don't feel like one. I feel like no man could love me because I'm so dirty inside. Remember Frank? I loved Frank.

JACKIE: Yeah, I remember him.

CAROLINE: I wouldn't let him touch me. I was thirty, and he couldn't understand why he couldn't touch me. That's not normal, Jackie.

JACKIE: I told you to get that fixed.

CAROLINE: You're so cavalier. Well, I got it fixed. (*Moving toward exit.*) And I'm going to tell Malcolm and Pop.

JACKIE: Tell them what?

CAROLINE: Tell them about what happened to you and then tell them about me.

JACKIE: Why would you want to tell them? What can they do about anything?

CAROLINE: They can help convince you to go into therapy, and they can support me while I continue with mine.

JACKIE: I don't see why we have to tell.

CAROLINE: (*Picking up GRANNY VI's handkerchief from the table.*) You don't want to admit what's happened, and I don't think I can convince you of anything by myself.

(GRANNY VI *appears.*)

GRANNY VI: (*To JACKIE.*) Don't stand there holding onto a lie. Let it go. It's eating you up. Syrus was a rattlesnake. He bit you, and you turned around and bit your sister. Lord, help us. Those snakes she's been dreaming about . . . that's you, Jackie. Carry-line's been walking around here struggling with snakes, and you've been acting like it's all in her head. Well, enough is enough. You can lie to Carry-line, but you can't lie to yourself and you sure can't lie to me. No more secrets. No more lies. No more blaming somebody for your troubles. Carry-line took this first step; the next one is yours. You can keep on lying or you can put your foot on that snake's neck. Say to that snake, "I won't let you claim another minute of my sister's life, and I won't let you control mine not one more day." Talk to your sister, Jackleen. Meet her halfway, that's what you have to do. It's never too late to say you're sorry and start again, child. You can do it. I'll help you. But, if you don't make things right, I will be in your face for the rest of your life. You can count on me.

(GRANNY VI *exits into the kitchen.*)

JACKIE: (*Moving toward conciliation.*) I'm not saying I didn't do anything, I'm just saying I don't remember it the way you did.

CAROLINE: You don't remember Uncle Syrus forcing himself on you?

JACKIE: Of course, I remember, but I've tried to put that out of my mind and move forward.

CAROLINE: Really? Do you think that maybe all that drinking might have something to do with Uncle Syrus?

JACKIE: (*Wanting to bargain.*) Maybe. Maybe. I'm going to go back to AA. That's something I've been promising myself I would do. Yeah, yeah, that's one thing I can do. I'll go to a meeting when I leave here. Is that good, Caroline?

CAROLINE: Of course, it's a good thing. You need help, Jackie. You've been needing help.

JACKIE: I said I would go back to AA.

CAROLINE: I think you need to get into therapy.

JACKIE: Oh, nooooooo. That's not for me.

CAROLINE: That's your choice. You do what you have to and I'll do what I have to.

JACKIE: I feel like I'm being railroaded and you're driving the train.

CAROLINE: I'm not responsible for how you feel about me anymore. You don't think you need help, but everything I know about what's happened to us tells me that we have to break the cycle.

JACKIE: What cycle?

CAROLINE: As hard as it may be to look this thing straight in the eye, the truth is that Uncle Syrus molested you and you molested me. That's the way the cycle runs.

JACKIE: You make it sound like that's the worst thing in the world.

CAROLINE: How can you not think it's the worst thing in the world? That tells me how sick you are, Jackie. And I don't want the cycle to continue. I don't want any part of it.

JACKIE: What are you talking about?

CAROLINE: I want to make sure that little Timothy and Jessica will be all right.

JACKIE: (*Crying now.*) Oh, Caroline! How could you think that of me? I would never hurt my babies.

CAROLINE: You hurt me.

JACKIE: I'm not altogether sure I did what you said. I remember trying to comfort you. I used to hold you close. I used to rub your back.

CAROLINE: You did more than that. And you can't blame it on liquor. That was before you started with the vodka.

JACKIE: I don't know. It was a crazy time. Daddy was mean as a snake. Uncle Syrus was taking what he wanted, when he wanted it. Maybe I crossed the line with you.

CAROLINE: And how would you feel if someone did that to Timothy and Jessica?

JACKIE: I'd break their legs and make them dance.

CAROLINE: Well then, you understand my concern that nothing happens to my niece and nephew.

JACKIE: So, what are you going to do?

CAROLINE: The question is, What are you going to do?

JACKIE: The first thing I'm going to do is say I'm sorry, Caroline. I don't know how I could have done this to you and then turned my back and think it wouldn't matter. I'm sorry. I am so sorry. You have to believe me.

CAROLINE: (*Crying.*) I believe you, Jackie. And I forgive you. Everything in my heart tells me to forgive you. Everything Granny Vi and Pop taught me tells me to forgive you. But I can't sweep this under the rug. Because tomorrow, I'll wake up angry. So I know it's going to take a long time for us to work through this. Maybe the rest of my life. But I am not going to be evil and mean to you. That's not what Granny Vi would want.

JACKIE: Thank you, Caroline.

CAROLINE: Let me finish. You're going go back to AA and you're going to go every night, just like you used to until the counselors tell you it's ok to cut back.

JACKIE: Ok, I said I would and I will.

CAROLINE: And you're going to find a psychologist and start therapy.

JACKIE: (*Sighing.*) Ok, Caroline. You win.

CAROLINE: No, you win. And there'll be no more talk of moving Pop or selling this house. We'll take care of him here. It's nonnegotiable.

JACKIE: Ok.

CAROLINE: And finally, you're going to pray.

JACKIE: What, like five Our Fathers and five Hail Marys a day, like we did when we went to confession in grade school?

CAROLINE: I don't care how many you say. I'll let you be the judge, but it had better be enough to keep me from telling Pop and Malcolm.

JACKIE: That's blackmail.

CAROLINE: It's better than the alternative.

JACKIE: You're so cold, Caroline.

CAROLINE: Actually, I'm thawing out from the big freeze.

JACKIE: Do you think we'll be able to get through this?

CAROLINE: I hope so, for both of us. Granny Vi won't rest in peace if we can't get past this.

JACKIE: What else can I do? What do you want from me?

CAROLINE: I told you, I want you to get help. And then I want to learn to trust you again. I want to be able to love you without looking over my shoulders. I want to get to a place where we aren't hurting each other every time we're in the same room. Mostly, I want you to love me and know I would never hurt you deliberately. I hope someday soon we can begin again . . . start over. That's what hope is . . . the possibility of a new beginning.

JACKIE: Thank God for hope.

CAROLINE: Didn't you see the hope in all the stories Pop and Granny Vi told us? We have something to grab hold of when everything around us is falling apart. Well, I'm grabbing hold now, and I'm moving on, Jackie.

JACKIE: And you're willing to take me with you?

CAROLINE: I'm certainly not willing to leave you behind. You're my sister.

JACKIE: I'm going to get help. I promise.

CAROLINE: I'll go with you to the AA meetings sometimes, if you want me to.

JACKIE: I'd like that.

CAROLINE: You know what else I'd like?

JACKIE: What?

CAROLINE: I'd like a life, and I think I'd like it with Bill.

JACKIE: (Pointing a finger.) Girl, I told you he'd be the one to ring your bell.

CAROLINE: Yeah, I guess you did. That Bill is one fine man, and I want him. I really want him.

JACKIE: Go get him.

CAROLINE: I intend to. As of this minute, he is no longer my therapist. I'll choose another psychologist. Tonight I am going out with Bill, the man who makes my heart skip a beat.

JACKIE: The man who burns your candle.

CAROLINE: And tomorrow when I wake up . . .

JACKIE: With Bill?

CAROLINE: I'm going out there . . . and this time I won't be afraid.

JACKIE: You're going to kick butt!

CAROLINE: I'm going to take a deep breath and move forward. I'm ready to move ahead. My feet aren't running anymore. I'm not stuck. I am free, finally free.

(*A knock is heard at the door.*)

CAROLINE: That's Bill. He told me he was coming over later. I'm going out to get pizza with him. (*Heading to the exit.*) Tell Pop I'll be in late.

JACKIE: I'll stay with him tonight.

CAROLINE: Good, but don't wait up. And don't make a big fuss over Pop. He's all right. Granny Vi's been coming to him, too, in his dreams. And his feet aren't stuck anymore, either. I had to see it in him before I could see it in myself. We can run, now. You, too, Jackie.

JACKIE: (*Nodding affirmatively.*) Caroline, I do love you.

CAROLINE: I know you do.

JACKIE: I'm sorry. I'm really sorry. I wish I could . . .

CAROLINE: I know. Stop wishing, Jackie. Just make the change.

(*JACKIE and CAROLINE embrace briefly. CAROLINE exits. JACKIE picks up the handkerchief and cries into it.*)

(*GRANNY VI appears.*)

GRANNY VI: It'll be all right, Jackleen. Carry-line is going to carry you through. (*Singing.*) We've got the power to heal ourselves. We've got the power to heal ourselves. Oh, we've got the power to heal ourselves.

JACKIE: (*Making the sign of the cross and singing.*) "We've got the power to heal ourselves. Oh, we've got the power to heal ourselves."

(*Lights fade to black.*)

THE END

Ancestors

Theodis "Ted" Shine, the dean of black playwrights in Texas, has written over thirty plays, including comedies and serious dramas. He is also a highly regarded teacher, screenwriter, director, and editor. Shine was awarded the Brooks-Hines Award for playwriting in 1970, and he was honored in the Ensemble Theatre's "Salute to Black Texas Playwrights" in 2007. Although he retired from his post as professor of theatre at Prairie View A&M University in 1998, he continued to teach part-time in the Prairie View theatre department until the spring of 2010.

Shine was born in Baton Rouge, Louisiana, but by the age of three, he was living with his family in Dallas, where he grew up. He credits his father, a theatre buff, with introducing him to amateur and professional theatre. Shine's interest in writing plays dates back to elementary school, where he wrote skits that were performed by his classmates. After graduating from high school, Shine enrolled in Howard University in Washington, DC, where several of his early plays were staged. At Howard, he was influenced by Professor Owen Dodson, playwright, who became his mentor.

Shine received additional training while working with the Karamu Repertory Theatre in Cleveland, Ohio. After completing his studies at Howard University, Shine was accepted into the graduate program at the University of Iowa where he earned an MA degree in 1958. At Iowa, Shine's mentors were the noted theatre historians Oscar Brockett and William Reardon. His experiences at Iowa influenced his decision to pursue a career in higher education. He enrolled in the PhD program at the University of California, Santa Barbara, where he received his degree in 1973. He has taught at Howard University, Dillard University, and Prairie View A&M University. In each of his college appointments, he has taught English and theatre courses, and he has directed theatre troupes, such as Prairie View's Charles Gilpin Players.

Noted for his mastery of the playwright's craft, Shine consistently delivers realistic, cleverly constructed plots, finely articulated dialogue, and well-developed characters, as well as insightful commentary on the human condition in general.

Thematically, Shine's plays explore thought-provoking topics such as racism in American society and the African American's struggle to construct a viable identity. As a measure of his status as an American playwright, his papers will be archived in the prestigious Hatch-Billops Collection in New York City. A strong voice in the Black Arts Movement, Shine is also co-editor (with James Hatch) of one of the best-known anthologies of plays by black playwrights, *Black Theatre U.S.A.* (New York: Free Press, 1996). Ted Shine's legacy as a black Texas playwright is a tremendous gift to Texas and the nation.

As You Read *Ancestors*

Centered on the 1836 Battle of San Jacinto, *Ancestors* is a compelling historical drama that gives voice to individuals whose contributions to Texas history have been omitted from the official historical record. Although blacks and Mexicans fought in support of Texas during the Texas Revolution, their courage and sacrifices are rarely acknowledged. In spite of broken promises and sociopolitical betrayal, free blacks remained true to their strong family values, extraordinary work ethic, and their unwavering quest for human dignity. For example, in the play Mary Logan demonstrates individual courage and a strong sense of self-worth when she boldly confronts Jimmy Fox, the white racist preacher. Greenbury Logan and his wife Mary call attention to the plight of economically and politically powerless blacks confronting racism and injustice. Shine enriches the historical context of the play by referencing pertinent historical details, such as the Navasota slave revolt and the 1840 legislative order forcing free blacks to leave Texas. Commissioned for the Texas Sesquicentennial Celebration, *Ancestors* reinterprets one of the most important events in Texas history, challenging readers and theatre audiences to embrace a more inclusive view of the Lone Star State's past.

Production History

The New Arts Theatre and Stage One Theatre, Dallas, Texas, 1986

Characters

BOSE IKHART: A black man, slave to Joseph Rankin.
FRANK KIRKPATRICK: A white Southerner.
GREENBURY LOGAN: A former slave, freed by his dying master.
LUIS ORTEGA: A man of Mexican descent.
MARY LOGAN: A former slave, wife of Greenbury.
TITUS WEBB: A slave, scout for the Texas Army.
JIMMY FOX: White preacher.
JOSEPH RANKIN: A white southerner.
MARIO ORTEGA: Son of Luis.
JIMMY FOX'S COMPANION: A white man.
EXTRA TEXAS AND MEXICAN SOLDIERS, as feasible

Setting

Time: The play begins on the day of the Battle of San Jacinto, April 21,
    1836, and moves backward and forward in time, from 1836 to 1841.
Place: San Jacinto, Logan's cabin and property, and Austin

SCENE 1

(*April 21, 1836. San Jacinto. Darkness. Drums roll. Four circles of light with men in each circle: BOSE, LUIS, LOGAN, and KIRKPATRICK. They are marching slowly in place: Marching into battle.*)

BOSE: Hup! Two . . . Three. Hup! Two . . . three . . .
    Right foot, Kirk! Right foot, Kirk!
KIRKPATRICK: Listen, horse's ass—Listen, horse's ass—
BOSE: Hup! Three . . . four. Hup! Three . . . four . . . Keep in step, Lu. Keep
    in step, Lu. Hup! Hup! Hey, Kirk, tell your heart to stop beating so loud,
    they can hear you all the way to Corpus Christi!
KIRKPATRICK: That's your teeth, you rascal!
LOGAN: Don't slow down, Luis, too late for second thoughts now.
LUIS: Right beside you, Logan!
BOSE: Why don't yawl keep up with me?

LOGAN: This is supposed to be a straight line!

BOSE: You're too slow.

LUIS: Right now I do wish I had stayed home.

LOGAN: If the truth were known, I suspect that's how we all feel.

BOSE: Hey, Kirk, since I'm in front, don't that make me leader?

KIRKPATRICK: No. Just makes you the closest target to the enemy.

BOSE: Since I'm leading yawl into battle, henceforth call me "Captain."

LUIS: Annamaria, Jorge, Mario, and little Lupe—take care of them all,
Blessed Mother.

BOSE: Luis, you act like you're dead before the fight's even started!

LOGAN: Have some respect, Bose!

BOSE: I'm only kidding.

LOGAN: No time to kid!

LUIS: They say that I would be ashamed fighting against my own people.

LOGAN: You live in Texas, Luis, and you're a Texan now. Everything that
you love—that you own—is here.

LUIS: And I fight to protect and keep it. That's what I keep telling myself.
If I don't fight, Santa Ana will tax me to death.

BOSE: I fight for the best reason of all—*freedom.* Yes, sir, when I fight this
battle, marse promised me my freedom.

LUIS: Suppose we lose?

BOSE: That's a chance I take.

KIRKPATRICK: And if you die?

BOSE: My soul will be free.

KIRKPATRICK: (*To* LOGAN, *who rubs his neck.*) What's the matter, Logan, you
sweating around the collar?

LOGAN: Maybe I shouldn't have let you talk me into joining this army.

KIRKPATRICK: Me? When Houston said "Free land for serving," who could
have stopped you? You're here because of your greed, Logan.

LOGAN: Patterned myself after you, Frank Kirkpatrick.

KIRKPATRICK: Couldn't have picked a better model.

BOSE: Hup! Two . . . Three. Hup! Two . . . three . . . Left foot, Lu! Left foot,
Lu!

KIRKPATRICK: Here we go again. Here we go again.

BOSE: Hup! Three . . . Four . . . Hup! Three . . . Four . . . Hup! Hup!

(*The circles of light fade as the men march off in darkness. Blackout.*)

SCENE 2

(*Six days earlier, April 15, 1836.* LOGAN's *cabin.* MARY, *with a pot of food, crosses to* LOGAN *and* KIRKPATRICK *and serves them.*)

MARY: Never thought I'd see the day when a white man would come to one of our cabins and eat.

LOGAN: This is Texas, Mary.

MARY: Still ain't like this all over.

KIRKPATRICK: Logan and I ate together when we were back in the States.

MARY: (*Grunts.*) When nobody was looking.

LOGAN: Frank was what a lot of folks would call an abolitionist, at least he had abolitionist leanings.

KIRKPATRICK: I was a Southerner just like the rest.

MARY: Not the rest I know!

KIRKPATRICK: Sit down and join us, Mary.

MARY: I'll sit when I get ready Massa Kirkpatrick.

KIRKPATRICK: (*To* LOGAN.) I think she believes I'm poison.

MARY: (*Mumbling.*) Don't believe nothin' of the sort!

KIRKPATRICK: If not that, then she's just out and out scared of me.

LOGAN: Well, remember she was a slave until recently.

MARY: You was a slave too, Greenbury Logan.

LOGAN: But I've been free for many a year now, and freedom's not frightening to me anymore.

MARY: Who's scared? Huh! I just don't want to develop no habits that can get us in trouble. I learn to be familiar with Massa Kirkpatrick, next thing you know I'm familiar with some other white person who don't like it. Texas still got slaves with more coming.

LOGAN: If Texas wins independence, what about the slave issue then?

KIRKPATRICK: At best it could only be the same—

LOGAN: And at worse?

KIRKPATRICK: I don't want to think about it.

MARY: I do 'cause I ain't gon be a slave no more. This man sold his land to buy me my freedom—to marry me, and I ain't gon be nobody's slave no more—never!

KIRKPATRICK: Then act like the free person that you are and sit down here and eat your vittles.

MARY: Massa Kirkpatrick, you trying me! (*She sits abruptly in a huff.*)
(*LOGAN and KIRKPATRICK are amused.*)

KIRKPATRICK: You know why your owners let Logan purchase your freedom, Mary? Because you're too high-spirited.

LOGAN: Got a mind of her own.

KIRKPATRICK: And that's not good in a slave. Slaves are not supposed to think—

MARY: Ones I know got minds.

KIRKPATRICK: Owners didn't know, I'll bet.

MARY: Most all we think about was freedom.

KIRKPATRICK: See, thinking like that will get you into trouble.

MARY: Wonder you didn't get yourself into trouble—

KIRKPATRICK: How's that?

MARY: Abolitionist and all. When you teach Logan to read and write—

KIRKPATRICK: Many a year ago.

MARY: —You broke the law!

KIRKPATRICK: My law is the law of God. (*To LOGAN.*) How much you pay for this lady, Logan?

LOGAN: Fifteen hundred dollars.

KIRKPATRICK: Bargain.

LOGAN: I was lucky. Her master had recently died and the mistress was having trouble keeping her spread.

MARY: She was deep in debt.

LOGAN: So when I asked to buy Mary, she sold her to me. We got married that very afternoon.

MARY: In a church with a priest.

LOGAN: I can't tell you how happy I've been.

KIRKPATRICK: I'm happy for you both.

LOGAN: You know when Stephen Austin invited me to Texas I didn't figure I'd stay, but I liked it here and bought my land cheap like everybody else and I swore I would never leave this place. If I hadn't stayed I'd never have met Mary.

MARY: I begged this man not to sell his property.

LOGAN: There's only one you, Mary, but there's a hell of a lot of land out here that can be bought. Hell, I won't even have to buy it! When we run the Mexicans outta here, I'll get a bonus of free land. I've already picked out my spread, Frank.

MARY: Men and their armies and wars!

KIRKPATRICK: I've got mine picked out too—near Nacogdoches, but more than the land, I want to make a name for myself so that after the war I can establish myself as a politician. Who knows, I may even become governor one day.

LOGAN: Wouldn't that be something!

MARY: Would you free the slaves?

KIRKPATRICK: If it were in my power.

MARY: Then I reckon it's a pleasure sitting here beside you.

KIRKPATRICK: I appreciate that, Mary. (*To* LOGAN.) I'll be heading out to join General Houston at daybreak.

LOGAN: I'll meet you at the crossroad beyond Rockwell Creek.

KIRKPATRICK: See you there. Fine vittles, Miss Mary. Look forward to more when I return from the war.

MARY: You'll be welcome.

KIRKPATRICK: (*Exiting.*) Rest easy.

LOGAN: Same to you.

MARY: Bless you.

(*They watch him leave.*)

MARY: Seems like just as we starting to get on our feet something always happens. Your business is going good, and my garden is the best it's ever been. We just at the point where we can save us some money and buy us a spread—

LOGAN: The army will give me land free for serving, Mary.

MARY: What good is free land if you're dead?

LOGAN: I don't intend to die, sugar. We're gonna spend the rest of our lives together.

MARY: Don't go, Logan! We can save and buy land.

LOGAN: Most of the money that we have saved, the Mexicans take from us for taxes. We'll never get enough to buy land or anything else with taxes getting higher and higher. Besides, we can't lose. We live here, the Mexicans don't. We'll be fighting to protect everything that we love; everything that's precious to us, they'll be fighting because they've been commanded to—

(BOSE *enters abruptly, frightening both* MARY *and* LOGAN.)

BOSE: And I *command* you to salute me, the next captain of the Texas army!

LOGAN: (*Who has drawn and aims his pistol.*) BOSE! Don't you know better than to bust in here without knocking?

BOSE: Thought I'd give you a surprise.

LOGAN: What if I had returned the surprise with a bullet?

BOSE: You couldn't shoot Brother Bose, now could you? How're you, Miss Mary?

MARY: 'Bout the same as my husband right now, Bose Ikhart, you honery slave. What you doin' out after dark anyway? You got a pass?

BOSE: My, my, we sure did get white after we got our freedom, didn't we, Miss Mary?

MARY: What?

BOSE: Wantin' to check my papers 'n all, knowing full well that the Bose goes and comes as he pleases. I may be a slave, but I play slavery like it's a game.

LOGAN: A very dangerous game! Now what's this noise about you being a captain?

BOSE: My good man, I have convinced marse to let me join the army along with him—to be his servant and protector.

MARY: *He* let *you* join the army?

BOSE: Why not? We cut trails to the north and to the west; we fought Indians together, why can't we fight the Mexicans together?

LOGAN: What's in this for you, Bose? I don't suspect the army's gonna give a slave land for fighting.

MARY: Maybe that's how come he let you join, so that he can get some extra acres for your fighting.

BOSE: Listen good people! Number one: I said, "Marse, you be sleepin' in the cold marsh when the rooster crows at the crack of dawn, you need to wake up to the smell of boiling coffee and some fatback frying and biscuits baking. Number two: you need hot water at hand for a shave. Number three: you need an expert shot like me to guard over you when nature comes a'calling and you have to excuse yourself behind a clump of trees." When I got through giving him the facts, he not only allowed me to join, but I showed him that my service was so valuable that I should be free once I win this war—

LOGAN: And he agreed?

BOSE: (*Removing a paper.*) He wrote me this paper which I brought for you to read to me.

LOGAN: (*Reading.*) "I, Joseph H. Rankin do, in sound mind and body, agree to grant my faithful servant and slave, one Bose Ikhart, his freedom upon completion of his service in the Texas Army." And it's dated and signed.

MARY: Lordy! Your massa must be crazy.

LOGAN: How'd you pull this one off?

BOSE: Oh, I just gave him a little more toddy in his tea than he's 'customed to. We leaving in the morning.

LOGAN: So are me and Kirkpatrick.

(*There is a sudden knock on the door. Again* LOGAN *has his pistol at ready. He nods to* MARY.)

MARY: Who's there?

TITUS: (*Softly.*) Titus Webb, scout for Texas Army.

LOGAN: Speak up, man!

TITUS: Scout for army.

LOGAN: Let him in, Bose.

(BOSE *opens the door, and a slave scout enters. He is an imposing man in his twenties.*)

TITUS: Titus Webb, Aldridge Plantation, Navasota. Scouting with massa for the army now.

LOGAN: Where is your master?

TITUS: He took the east fork and told me to take the west, we'll meet up at the Brazos.

BOSE: What's a soldier doing without a rifle or pistol?

TITUS: Massa says slaves don't need weapons.

MARY: Not even when you're fighting a war?! You hear that, Bose?

BOSE: (*Revealing his pistol.*) I've been carrying this since I was twelve years old. Can shoot a fly off a horse's back at a thousand yards.

LOGAN: (*To* TITUS.) Can we get you some grub?

TITUS: It would be appreciated, but I've got to take it and run. Got other stops to make before I meet massa.

(MARY *prepares his food.*)

TITUS: You Greenbury Logan, the free Negro?

LOGAN: Yes, and this is my wife, Mary, and my friend, Bose Ikhart.

TITUS: I'm please to meet you all. (*Looking at* BOSE.) I come to bring a message to Logan.

BOSE: You want me to git?

LOGAN: No, what you have to say to me you can say before my friend.

TITUS: Can he be trusted?

LOGAN: (*Nods.*) I trust him.

TITUS: Slaves up Navasota way planning to revolt.

MARY: What?!

TITUS: They planning to free themselves!

MARY: Lordy! I used to hear talk like that years ago, but nothing came of it.

TITUS: The time is ripe now. Texas in confusion and we feel we got a chance.

BOSE: We? You in this too? You supposed to be in the army.

TITUS: I deserted with the rest.

LOGAN: The rest?

TITUS: Massa and the men from our community. The army a mess of confusion. Everybody get disgusted and leave; say they concerned about their wives and families.

BOSE: They know the slaves back home planning to welcome them back with a revolt?

TITUS: They don't know nothing!

MARY: What you here for, Titus Webb? How come you telling us this?

TITUS: 'Cause your skin is the same color as mine; 'cause our problems the same as you got, even though you are so-called free. We calling all the sons of Africa together to join us. We got weapons and we intend to form our own army—

LOGAN: And if things don't work out?

TITUS: We scatter. Join the Mexican army or maybe one of the Indian tribes. We can escape west or maybe to Mexico. Important thing is to strike now while the country's all confused. What do you say?

MARY: About what? (*She gives him the food.*)

TITUS: Joining us.

LOGAN: There's no way that you can win—

TITUS: Then we die in the name of freedom rather than continue to live in shame.

BOSE: I'm gonna fight for my freedom. Marse free me after the war.

TITUS: Well, my massa won't free me! Think about what I said. If you change your mind set a fire to that brush on the hill yonder. Someone will contact you with the details. Gotta be going now. Things got to look normal for the time being. No word of this to nobody.

(*LOGAN nods. TITUS dashes out into the darkness.*)

MARY: Lordy!

LOGAN: "We die in the name of freedom rather than continue to live in shame."

MARY: What are you mumbling, Logan?

LOGAN: Something that fellow said reminded me of—! "Gbogbo àwa omo Yorùbá l'a mò pé ikú yá jù èsín lo."

BOSE: What kinda talk is that?

LOGAN: African. Words I was taught back home when I was a boy by my ancestors.

MARY: What do they mean, Logan?

LOGAN: "All of us Yoruba people, Yoruba sons, know that death is preferable to disgrace." Strange I remember that after all these years.

BOSE: Slave uprising! Dog! If I wasn't joining the army, I'd be right there with them.

LOGAN: I thought you were partial to your master?

BOSE: I am, but I'd be there for the thrill of the battle.

MARY: Men and their fighting! And it's us women who're left behind to grieve and suffer, and raise another generation of men to do the same thing all over again.

(*The lights fade. Blackout.*)

SCENE 3

(*Back to the day of the Battle of San Jacinto, April 21, 1836. A lull in the battle. BOSE, LOGAN, KIRKPATRICK, and LUIS sit. LOGAN is writing a letter. The others are cleaning their weapons.*)

BOSE: That little skirmish wasn't so bad, was it, Luis?

LUIS: Oddly enough it wasn't. I was too busy to be afraid. Loading, firing, loading again. Advancing. It was like time stood still and I acted automatically not knowing where I was or why. Like I was suspended in space, and then it was over almost as suddenly as it began.

BOSE: Over for the moment. They'll be prepared next time. (*To LOGAN.*) What you thinking about, good friend?

LOGAN: If you were me, what would you be thinking about?

BOSE: Miss Mary, I reckon.

LOGAN: You're right there. Formation was called so quickly I didn't have a chance to write her a letter.

BOSE: You let a white man see you write?

LOGAN: I'm free, Bose.

BOSE: Still don't matter. White men don't like to see a man your color doing something he can't do himself, ain't that right, Marse Kirkpatrick?

KIRKPATRICK: But I can write, Bose.

BOSE: What about you, Luis?

LUIS: Yes, in Spanish.

BOSE: (*Looking over* LOGAN's *shoulder.*) What does that say?

LOGAN: This letter is personal.

BOSE: It's okay, we're friends. What're you saying to her?

LOGAN: I'm telling her how much I love and miss her.

BOSE: That's exactly what I'd say, if I had someone to say it to.

LUIS: Your master won't allow you to take a wife?

BOSE: No slave woman on our ranch.

LUIS: This is Texas, my friend, you're free to marry who you want to here. Negroes have married Mexican women, native American white women, Indians—

BOSE: Free Negroes, but I'm a slave, Luis.

LUIS: Americans and their slavery! How can you stand it?

LOGAN: He has no choice—now.

BOSE: But after we win this war, I'll have my freedom and I'll get free land like the rest of you. I'll own myself a ranch. Break horses, raise cattle, and cut new trails taking 'em to market.

LOGAN: (*To* KIRKPATRICK.) And when you get to be a representative are you gonna press to get voting rights for free Negroes?

KIRKPATRICK: All in good time, Logan, all in good time.

LOGAN: Seems like I've heard that line before.

KIRKPATRICK: It takes time for change to come, but it eventually will come.

BOSE: We may not be here "eventually."

KIRKPATRICK: You've got all kinds of personalities to deal with in politics—tough old coots. I sure don't envy Austin. It took all he could do to keep these colonies together and the Mexicans at bay.

LOGAN: And still there's confusion and unrest. Disorder. Hundreds of soldiers deserted.

LUIS: If it wasn't for pride, I might have been one of them, but had I deserted, I could never have lived with myself or looked my sons in the eye knowing what I had done.

BOSE: Man was made to fight. This is *adventure*.

LOGAN: People fight for causes, Bose. We're Texans and we're fighting to hold on to this land. You're fighting for your freedom, and once you're free you'd fight to keep it. I'm fighting so that I can have property of my own and be respected as a man when all of this is over.

(*Gunfire in the distance. Shouts. The men rise gathering their weapons. A trumpet sounds in the distance. An Off Stage shout: "Company, fall in!"*)

LOGAN: Looks like this is it, men!

BOSE: Fight like wildcats!

VOICE: (*Off Stage.*) Tennnn-hut! Forward march!

LUIS: (*Crossing himself.*) Protect us, Blessed Mother.

(*The men are marching in place now as they were in the first sequence, their weapons drawn and aimed. Shouts and gunfire get louder. Drums roll. Music.*)

LOGAN: Advance you scalawags!

BOSE: Fight like cornered bears!

LUIS: Like alligators!

KIRKPATRICK: Go, Texans!

BOSE: *Adventure!*

(*The lights dim. Blackout.*)

SCENE 4

(LOGAN's *spread, two years earlier, 1834. The garden.* MARY *is on her knees weeding her crop, humming as she works. An itinerant preacher, white, enters and observes her for a moment. He is an ancient little man, bearded, and carries a bible.*)

FOX: You there, slave gal.

MARY: No, massa, I'm free woman. I got papers.

FOX: (*Grunts.*) I'm the Right Reverend Doctor Jimmy Fox.

MARY: Obliged to meet you, Reverend Fox.

FOX: Ministering to heathens and otherwise up and down the highways and byways of Texas. Is there sickness in your household? Is there a child with the croup? An adult with arthritis? Is there a sinner drawn to tobac-kee and spirits? A sinner who cusses and stands in the need of prayer? (*He kneels beside* MARY.) Look into the heart of this poor gal, Father, and teach her to love, honor, and obey her master; to be humble in her service. Teach her that Second Timothy says "as a slave she needeth not be ashamed . . . but to shun profane and vain babblings for they will increase unto more ungodliness." The Lord wants you to serve your masters here on earth. Know that in the great house there are not only vessels of gold and silver, but also of wood and earth! *Do not steal!* Remember "the steward of the Lord must not strive, but be gentle . . . for then the Lord rewardeth the proud doer—in heaven." Now say "Amen!"

MARY: Amen.

FOX: (*Rising.*) That'll cost you one quarter.

MARY: I didn't ask for your prayer, Mister!

FOX: You got it and you'll pay—one way t'other.

MARY: I'm giving you this 'cause I don't want trouble. (*Gives him a coin.*)

FOX: (*Bites the coin.*) Now that's good sense. (*Puts coin in his pocket.*) Y'know, a nigger's got no business being free. You're like children and don't know what to do with yourselves. You need white people to look out for you—a good person like me. I'd feed and clothe you, give you shelter. No worries 'bout nothing.

MARY: You get away from me 'cause I'm a free woman now!

FOX: Freedom teach you to talk to your betters like that, nigger?

MARY: (*Mumbling.*) No, sir, massa.

FOX: I've whipped many a nigger for less sass than that.

MARY: Yes, sir. (*He takes a step toward her but stops when she removes a pistol from her skirt.*) Is that a field mouse way over yonder, massa? (*She aims and fires.*) Sure was. (*She blows the barrel of the pistol.*) Probably the one that's been eatin' my corn.

FOX: (*Amazed at her accuracy with the pistol.*) I . . . suppose I'd better be gittin'.

MARY: Yes, sir, I suppose you better.

FOX: And may the Lord bless you. (*He exits quickly . . . .*)

MARY: I don't need your kinda blessin'! (*She spits in the dirt . . . .*)

(*LOGAN and LUIS enter.*)

LOGAN: What's wrong honey? We heard that shot.

MARY: I just had to shoot a mouse in order to get rid of a rat.

LOGAN: Huh?

MARY: A so-called preacher was here. Charged me a quarter for a prayer.

LOGAN: That get you riled?

MARY: Sure did. Said I was dumb and needed to be taken care of by white folks—namely him.

LUIS: And you Americans complain about *our* religion.

LOGAN: It's not the religion, it's the person preaching it.

MARY: He was one of them old plantation preachers we used to have to listen to—"Love and honor massa; work hard for massa and get your reward in heaven." How come massa rewarded here on earth and I got to wait to get to heaven to get mine?

LOGAN: Maybe master won't be in heaven.

MARY: If the Lord's fair he won't be.

LUIS: I've heard about such church services where slaves are taught what the master wants them taught. That's not religion, it's blasphemy!

LOGAN: That's why a lot of slaves steal away deep in the night and gather around a fire out in the middle of nowhere and hold their own services. When I was a slave that's what we used to do. We had a slave preacher who could read a little bit, and he would read to us from the Bible. We knew all about Moses leading the children of Israel from bondage because no man was born to be a slave. We made up songs from the Bible stories and passed them down from one generation to the next. Passed down to us from our ancestors, and we'll pass them on to the next generation, and they to the next.

MARY: Logan used to tell me stories from the Bible, Señor Luis, and he made me have faith. He told me that I was gonna be free and I just laugh, but he taught me faith, and sure enough it happened. I listen to this man talk, and it's like he lifts a burden off my heart. It's been like that since I first saw him, walking tall down the road in the evening sun. I had never seen a colored man carry hisself like that before—he walked like a man 'mongst men instead of a slave. There's something about the way a slave walks that lets you know he's a slave, but I knew Logan wasn't one the minute I saw him. I was working the field, and he nodded and tipped his hat to me like a gentleman to a lady.

LOGAN: You are a lady, Miss Mary. A beautiful one.

LUIS: I agree with that.

MARY: Yawl flatter me!

LOGAN: It's true.

MARY: Next time I saw this man he spoke to me; asked me to meet him a few days later after sunset. I said, "You know slaves can't be out after dark," but I knew in my heart I would be there, and I was. He was the first free colored man I ever met, and he taught me so much. This man is ordained by God to be His spiritual leader I do believe—like Moses, to lead His children out of the grips of slavery. I know it, Señor Luis. I can feel it in my bones.

LOGAN: I'm a far cry from a preacher, honey, best I can do is blacksmith.

MARY: One day the Lord's gonna call you, Logan, and you'll have to obey.

LOGAN: If I'm called to do anything it's to honor my ancestors, to never forget them. To let you know and all the other slaves know that we're from a proud and heroic people. Descendents of kings and queens and brave warriors. My duty is to you, honey, and to the family that we'll have one day. I want us to be proud of who we are and where we came from, to be prosperous and respected—honest, noble, men among men. That's what I want to be and what I want our children and their children to be.

LUIS: Perhaps you will lead people one day.

MARY: Sure he will.

LOGAN: (*Amused.*) The best I can do, Luis, is get your horse shoed. Come along.

(*MARY watches as they exit. The lights dim.*)

(*Blackout.*)

SCENE 5

(*Back to the Battle of San Jacinto, April 21, 1836. Gunfire. Screaming, shouting. An encounter between an American and a Mexican soldier in a circle of light. The circle fades and we pick up BOSE in another circle in combat with a Mexican soldier. A second Mexican soldier appears, and BOSE, enjoying the encounter, is able to subdue both men. He yells victoriously, then stops suddenly as he sees something Off Stage. He screams, "LOOOOOGGGAAAAAAAAN!" He rushes off as the lights fade. Blackout.*)

SCENE 6

(*A little later, a circle of light picks up a makeshift hospital at the battleground. LOGAN lies unconscious. LUIS and BOSE are with him. Gunfire, shouts in the distance.*)

BOSE: The bleeding's stopped, that's a good sign.

LUIS: He fought even after he was wounded.

BOSE: And he'll be alright. Logan's a tough old coot. The medics will take care of him now, we'd better get back to the battle.

LUIS: You go on, I'll join you in a minute.

BOSE: (*Removing his pistol.*) The next one's for you, good friend. (*He exits toward the battle.*)

LUIS: I'm still shaking, Señor. I dread going back, but I must go. My honor is at stake. Oh, Señor, why did this have to happen to you and not me? You are the brave one and I am merely a coward.

LOGAN: (*Stirring.*) No . . . coward . . .

LUIS: Don't try to talk. Save your strength. You faced death like a man, and I shall do likewise, and when this is over I get my land and open a business—a business that I can pass on to my sons. You shall be alright, the medic is coming. (*He prays.*) Blessed Mother, comfort and keep thee. (*He crosses himself and exits.*)

(*The lights fade. Blackout.*)

SCENE 7

(*The battle. BOSE's master is in combat with a Mexican soldier, who is getting the better of him. During the scuffle the Mexican is able to disarm the Texan, then aims his pistol to his head. BOSE enters but his pistol is not loaded. He jumps the Mexican and during the scuffle is able to turn the weapon so that the Mexican soldier shoots himself.*)

BOSE: You alright, marse?

RANKIN: Thanks to you, Bose.

BOSE: (*Assisting his master up.*) Weren't nothing, sir.

RANKIN: I've seen you fighting like a tiger. I'm proud of you, Bose; indebted to you.

BOSE: (*Loading his pistol.*) Come on! We'll talk about that when this battle's won! (*Rushing off.*) Remember the Alamo!

RANKIN: Remember Goliad!

(*The lights fade as they rush back into battle. Another circle of light picks up LUIS. He stands firing in all directions. Suddenly there is a shot from Off Stage. LUIS is struck. Muffled drum sounds. LUIS, in slow motion, falls in agony to the ground, dead. Blackout.*)

SCENE 8

(*May 10, 1836. Army hospital.* LOGAN, *using a crutch and with his arm in a sling, is up and about now, ready to leave for home.* MARY, *dressed in her finest outfit, has come to fetch him.*)

MARY: You look fit as a fiddle. When they said you were wounded, I thought the worse.

LOGAN: What could be worse than being a cripple with a useless arm?

MARY: You've been blessed with your life.

LOGAN: (*Nods in agreement.*) And you. I've missed you so much.

MARY: And I've missed you.

LOGAN: (*Holding her.*) If your mistress hadn't sold you to me, I would have indentured myself to her—given myself to her, just to be with you.

MARY: Don't say that.

LOGAN: It's true. When I first looked at you when you were working in that field, I knew then that I had to have you. You were on my mind day and night. I couldn't get your smile out of my mind. You were like a rose in that parched field. I tried to find a word to describe you and all I could come up with was "sweet." And you are sweet, Miss Mary.

MARY: Why thank you, Mr. Logan.

LOGAN: I thought about you all during the fighting. I was worried that you wouldn't be alright.

MARY: I was perfectly fine. Scared a little but—

LOGAN: Well you don't have to be scared no more.

MARY: Logan, the slaves up around Navasota did revolt.

LOGAN: What?!

MARY: White folks ain't said much about it 'cause they don't want to stir up slaves on other plantations, but they did revolt. They killed some whites, took horses and cattle, and had gathered the cotton crops and was planning to ship it to New Orleans for sale. They took over some of the plantation big houses and intended to become massa with white folks as slaves. White mens formed a posse and drove 'em from the plantations. Caught up with 'em somewhere on the Brazos, and there was a big shootout before it was all over. More than a hundred slaves captured and whipped, some hanged. They hanged that Titus who came by our place. Folks whisper 'bout it, and all colored folks suspect now. They come by our place.

LOGAN: Who?

MARY: White men. Said that free niggers encouraged slaves to rebel. They asked for you and I told 'em you was serving in the Texas army and they left.

LOGAN: I told that man they didn't have a chance—

MARY: Don't say nothing 'bout it, Logan, 'less they accuse you of being a part of it. (*LOGAN nods.*) Attitudes changed back home. White folks look at coloreds, slaves and free, with snarls on their faces, and slaves walkin' round like zombies. There's a silence there that I ain't never witnessed before.

LOGAN: Well, there won't be silence on our new spread. There's gonna be joy and happiness and the sound of me pounding iron on my old anvil. (*He tries to lift his arm as in work, but can't. He cries in pain.*) Ahhhh! (*He gathers his few belongings.*) Let's get out of here, honey, and head for home.

(*MARY tries to assist him but he pulls away.*)

LOGAN: I can do it myself!

MARY: You're still weak, honey, not completely healed.

LOGAN: I can do it myself.

(*MARY nods and they start to exit as the lights dim, but not completely out. MARY and LOGAN move outside. Off Stage: the sound of military music. The couple begins a slow circle around the stage area. They stop to observe a military ceremony that is ending Off Stage.*)

VOICE: (*Off Stage.*) Company, 'tenhut! Dismissed!

LOGAN: They're honoring the heroes of the battle today.

MARY: You're a hero—

LOGAN: There are other soldiers more important than me.

BOSE: (*Off Stage.*) Hey, good friend! (*He enters running.*) I hoped I wouldn't miss you.

(*KIRKPATRICK enters behind BOSE.*)

KIRKPATRICK: You look better than you did before the battle!

BOSE: How're you, Miss Mary?

MARY: Fine, Bose.

BOSE: Captain Kirkpatrick here got himself three citations today for bravery in combat.

KIRKPATRICK: You and Logan deserve them more than I do, but this sure will be a feather in my cap with the voters I hope.

LOGAN: You're really serious about this politics, aren't you?

KIRKPATRICK: Sure am. You're always talking about pride and respect, I want the same thing for myself. We're no different in that regard, only our methods are different. You want property and security, I want land and *wealth*. You want to be a man among men, I want to be a man *above* men—and I'm going to be.

LOGAN: I've known you practically all of my life, Frank, and I've loved you like a brother because you've treated me like a brother. You've always been a good, kind person. I just pray that this dream of yours won't change you.

KIRKPATRICK: Will your dream of prosperity change you?

LOGAN: I don't intend it to.

KIRKPATRICK: Neither do I. So long, pal. We'll keep in touch. (*They embrace and* KIRKPATRICK *exits.*) Bye, Miss Mary, Bose.

MARY: Bye.

BOSE: Take care.

LOGAN: (*After a moment.*) Bose saved his master from death and they didn't give him a citation or even a thank you from the commander.

BOSE: That don't bother me.

LOGAN: It bothers me! Slave or not, you deserve to be honored—more so than Kirkpatrick. He even said so himself.

MARY: What you planning to do now that you gonna be free?

BOSE: Work my land, Miss Mary, and purchase me some cattle and some more and some more 'til all the eye can see is Bose Ikhart's land and cattle.

LOGAN: He may do it too, Mary, if somebody can keep him from "adventure."

BOSE: My adventure'll be cuttin' new trails.

MARY: Well, you come visit us now.

BOSE: Soon's I get home, Miss Mary. Bye, good friend.

LOGAN: Goodbye, Bose.

(LOGAN *and* MARY *exit. After a moment* BOSE's *master,* RANKIN, *enters.*)

RANKIN: Bose.

BOSE: Yes, sir, I was just coming to look for you.

RANKIN: I think we need a little talk.

BOSE: Yes, sir.

RANKIN: Reports I get from home indicate that things aren't going too well. Mrs. Rankin just can't manage the ranch properly. Crop failed, a lotta the cattle died. Things have just gone to pieces without us men there.

BOSE: Yes, sir.

RANKIN: What I mean is—We've been together for a long time.

BOSE: Since I was six, marse.

RANKIN: And I raised you like my own son, didn't I? (BOSE *nods in agreement.*)

RANKIN: You're the best hand that I have on the place. Nobody there— white or black—can break horses or herd cattle like you. You've always been my right hand—if you had been a white man, Bose, you would have been my foreman years ago. (BOSE *is startled and angered by this.*) This war has been costly to all of us. The ranch just couldn't function properly with us away and it's just gone to rot. Take a lot of work to get it back in shape. A lot of work.

BOSE: What you tryin' to say, marse?

RANKIN: Bose, I pride myself as a man of my word so this is difficult for me—that paper I signed agreeing to free you after this war—

BOSE: Yes, sir?

RANKIN: Damnit, I'm gonna have to postpone it, Bose!

BOSE: No, sir, marse—

RANKIN: You're needed on the ranch and I just can't let you go at this time.

BOSE: No, sir, marse, please—

RANKIN: Once we get things back into shape; once the place starts making money again—

BOSE: Please, marse, that can take years—

RANKIN: I'm sorry, Bose, I just can't let you go.

BOSE: Oh, marse, please, you promise—

RANKIN: You're a valuable nigger and I'm not gonna let you go!

(*Pause. They look at each other for a moment.* BOSE *with disbelief and hurt,* RANKIN *with embarrassment.*)

RANKIN: Pack your gear and meet me over at the mess tent.

(RANKIN *exits.* BOSE *stands for a moment, then falls to his knees sobbing softly to himself. Drums and music in and continues through the fadeout. Blackout.*)

SCENE 9

(LOGAN's *cabin, 1840.* LOGAN *is alone On Stage washing up after a hot day of blacksmithing.* MARY *enters, tired after spending the day in the field. She rests her hoe against a wall, then wipes her brow. Both* LOGAN *and* MARY's *expressions and attitudes indicate that life has been exceedingly hard for them. Music and drums underscore the dialogue.*)

LOGAN: Never wanted to see my wife spend her life working in a field.

MARY: Least it ain't a cotton field. How'd it go with you today?

LOGAN: Hot and slow.

MARY: Old man Griffin pay you?

LOGAN: Only person paid was Ross. Two bits for sharping some knives.

MARY: We sure won't get rich off that.

LOGAN: Seem like the harder we work the worse things get.

(*There is a knock at the door.* LOGAN *crosses and answers it; it is* KIRKPATRICK. *He is dressed in a suit, wears polished boots and a hat. He looks prosperous.*)

LOGAN: Frank Kirkpatrick—!

KIRKPATRICK: How are you, Logan? Mary?

MARY: Look at you.

KIRKPATRICK: Take a good look. I'm the newest representative to the congress of the independent Republic of Texas, Nacogdoches County.

MARY: My, my!

LOGAN: So you were able to sway the voters with your charm, huh?

KIRKPATRICK: Let's make that "dedication."

LOGAN: I hope the first thing you do is tell the legislature that we can't afford these high taxes. They're higher than when the Mexicans were here. Folks can hardly live.

KIRKPATRICK: Texas is deep in debt. Now, how've you two being doing?

LOGAN: Fine, other than for taxes.

KIRKPATRICK: I'm on my way to the capitol, and since I was this close I thought I'd stop and say hello.

MARY: Well, it sure is good to see you. Sit down and let me fix you something to eat.

KIRKPATRICK: No, thanks, Mary, perhaps next time.

LOGAN: What kind of work you doing back there in Nacogdoches?

KIRKPATRICK: I have a plantation, the largest one in the county. Came into a little inheritance and invested it in land.

LOGAN: A plantation?

KIRKPATRICK: A little sugarcane, but mainly cotton.

MARY: And slaves?

KIRKPATRICK: Yes, Mary, slaves.

LOGAN: You, a slaveowner, Frank? (KIRKPATRICK *shrugs.*) I never thought I'd live to see the day—

KIRKPATRICK: Neither did I, but things change—

LOGAN: So do people.

KIRKPATRICK: My feelings about Negroes and slavery hasn't changed.

LOGAN: Then how do you justify being a slaveholder?

KIRKPATRICK: Slavery is going to be sanctioned in the Republic, Logan, whether we like it or not. We've got a lot of slaveowners here and more coming each day. They are not about to disband slavery. Cheer up. I'm a good master. Slaves are much better off with me than with many other white men.

LOGAN: How many do you have?

KIRKPATRICK: Thirty at the moment. My wife brought her slaves with her into the marriage. Rest assured, Logan, that they are quite content; they're treated quite humanely.

MARY: Will you teach 'em to read?

KIRKPATRICK: (*Amused.*) My constituents keep me so busy, I don't even have time for reading anymore.

LOGAN: There are a lot of white men who'd like to see free Negroes enslaved again.

KIRKPATRICK: I'm not one of them and you know it.

LOGAN: The legislature did agree to deport all free Negroes from Texas.

KIRKPATRICK: But that law hasn't been enforced. Look, Logan, as a representative I don't speak or vote for myself. I represent the people of my district. Why are we getting philosophical? Why can't we just talk as friends like we used to do? Where's that Bose—Bose Ikhart?

MARY: We ain't seen Bose since San Jacinto.

KIRKPATRICK: Four years? Doesn't he live around here?

LOGAN: If he did he would've come by. I suspect he's got his ranch as far west as possible, he loved the wilderness.

KIRKPATRICK: I meant to tell you, Mary, that was mighty brave of you coming to fetch Logan like you did after the war.

MARY: No more than any wife should do.

LOGAN: Where'd you meet your wife, Frank?

KIRKPATRICK: Her papa owns the general store in town where I get my supplies. He invited me out to his farm and that's where I met her. We have a son, Logan. If you and Mary ever get up my way you must—

MARY: Come by? Now how would missus like that? Can't you see us sitting in your parlor drinking coffee?

KIRKPATRICK: Well . . .

MARY: I told you years ago not to treat me too familiar, Massa Kirkpatrick, 'cause I just may get familiar with the wrong white person.

LOGAN: She's only kidding, Frank, we know . . . our place.

KIRKPATRICK: Hey, you've got no "place" with me. It's like it has always been, and that's the way it's gonna be.

LOGAN: Sure.

KIRKPATRICK: Next time I'm in the vicinity, I'll call on you.

MARY: You do that.

KIRKPATRICK: Take care.

LOGAN: God bless you.

(*KIRKPATRICK exits. LOGAN and MARY stand in the doorway watching. After a moment.*)

MARY: Say something, Logan.

LOGAN: What is there to say?

MARY: He told you he's rich.

LOGAN: He didn't say that.

MARY: A big plantation! Slaves! You could have asked him to help.

LOGAN: I can't beg, Mary.

MARY: It's not begging. It would be a loan. Honey, we owe creditors and they want their money.

LOGAN: I've given credit and I'm not paid.

MARY: Deliberately not paid! The folks who owe you have money to pay but they won't. If Kirkpatrick is your friend like he says he is, if things are still the same, get him to testify on your behalf in court. Get him to tell the court who owes you and for how long. That's the only way you gonna get your money.

LOGAN: I couldn't ask him to do that.

MARY: You scared he wouldn't?

LOGAN: I believe that he would, and if he did it would spell his ruin as a politician. What white man would vote for another white man who sided with a Negro? Who spoke up for a Negro in court?

MARY: So we just sit here and let things crumble? You can't do all the blacksmithing jobs you usta do before you lost use of your arm, you can't work the fields. We ain't got money to hire help, so what we gonna do? Can't borrow no more, and what crops we got, we need.

LOGAN: (*Knows that she is right. Sighs.*) Someone riding this way.

MARY: If it's Kirkpatrick come back, ask him, Logan.

LOGAN: No! It's not Kirkpatrick.

(*The sound of a horse trotting closer. It stops. A voice with a Mexican accent is heard Off Stage. It is* MARIO, LUIS' *son. He is played by the actor who portrays* LUIS.)

MARIO: Señor Greenbury Logan?

LOGAN: That's me.

MARIO: (*Entering.*) I am Mario Ortega, son of Luis Ortega. You and my father were friends.

LOGAN: Luis' son! Welcome to our house.

MARIO: My father often spoke of the free Negro who lived in this area. He was very fond of you.

LOGAN: And I of him. This is my wife, Mary.

MARIO: Pleased to meet you, ma'am. I am on my way to Goliad on business for my mother. She told me that you would give me food if I stopped by.

LOGAN: Sure we will.

(*Without being asked* MARY *prepares food for* MARIO *to take with him.*)

MARIO: My brothers and I have taken over my father's responsibilities now. We are hoping to establish a business one day like he always wanted to do. He was a kind and gentle man.

LOGAN: He was a brave and honorable man—a hero. When I was wounded, he risked his life getting me to medical aid. You should be very proud of him.

MARIO: I am, Señor.

MARY: Here you are, son.

MARIO: Thank you, ma'am. Señor Logan, I shall tell my mother of your kindness.

LOGAN: Tell her that Luis' thoughts were of her and his family until the end.

MARIO: I will.

LOGAN: (*Removing a coin.*) And take this, son, you may need it on the way.

MARIO: Thank you, Señor. (*He exits.*)

MARY: Lordy, lordy! We can't buy a dime worth of flour and this man's giving our last two bits away.

LOGAN: It's no more than you would do, Mrs. Logan.

MARY: (*She nods in agreement.*) Somehow the Lord'll provide . . . He's got to! (LOGAN *looks at her.*) Logan, we're gonna have a child.

(LOGAN *is silent and expressionless for a moment. He embraces her as the lights fade. Blackout.*)

SCENE 10

(*A road leading from town, 1841.* LOGAN *and* MARY, *carrying their baby, enter. They are tired from the long way.*)

LOGAN: Let's sit and catch our breath for a minute.

MARY: Two days worth of walkin' for nothing. (*Sits.*)

LOGAN: (*Pulling the baby's blanket aside.*) How're you doing, little fellow? He's a real good traveler. Better'n me.

MARY: Men at the bank wouldn't even see us!

LOGAN: (*Talking down to the child.*) Say, Mama, least I got a chance to see the town.

MARY: That baby ain't big enough to recognize a town, Logan.

LOGAN: It sure has grown since we were there last. So many people.

MARY: And the fields covered with slaves.

(*Two white men enter. One is* JIMMY FOX, *the minister. They discover* MARY *and* LOGAN.)

FOX: Well, well, well, look-a-here. Sambo and Mammy.

FOX'S COMPANION: Say, nigger, don't you know how to stand up in the presence of a white man?

LOGAN: (*Rising.*) Yes, sir.

FOX: What are you doing in these parts?

LOGAN: I'm a free Negro, sir.

FOX: You trying to sass me, boy?

LOGAN: No, sir.

FOX'S COMPANION: First time I ever seen a free nigger. Don't look no different from the rest of 'em.

FOX: Who says you're free?

MARY: We got papers!

FOX'S COMPANION: Who asked you anything?

FOX: I don't suppose yawls heard about the new regulations regarding niggers, huh?

LOGAN: What regulations, sir?

FOX: That you cross to the other side of the road and stay there when you see a white man coming. Don't move or look in his direction until he passes.

FOX'S COMPANION: Keep your head bowed in his presence.

FOX: Didn't you hear what he just said? Bow your head, nigger! Bow it!

MARY: Listen to him, Logan. Do what he say!

FOX: Smart one, huh? Know what we usta do with your kind back home? Tear up them papers you carrying and sell your ass right back into slavery. All of you—including that baby! Now since you obviously don't have respect for white gentlemen, I think you ought to apologize to Mr. Livingston here and myself—

LOGAN: I apologize, sir.

FOX'S COMPANION: Get on your knees, nigger. (*LOGAN kneels with difficulty. The man lifts his foot, spits on his boot, then extends it toward LOGAN.*) Wipe it off! (*LOGAN wipes the boot with the cuff of his shirt.*) Now back off. (*LOGAN rises and begins to walk backward.*)

FOX: I don't think I heard Mr. Livingston tell you to get up, nigger. Get back on your knees and back off! (*LOGAN kneels again on his hands and knees and backs away from the men.*)

FOX'S COMPANION: Reverend, you gonna say a prayer for these niggers?

FOX: They ain't worth the breath.

(*Amused, the men laugh as they exit. MARY crosses to LOGAN and assists him up.*)

FOX'S COMPANION: (*Exiting.*) Don't let us catch either of you out after dark. If we do, it's back into slavery you go!

LOGAN: (*Picks up the baby.*) Mary, I don't want this child to ever forget about slavery. I want him to know how it was for you and how it was for me. I want him to know that, even though my master freed me upon his death, I hated having my childhood taken from me; hated being snatched from my parents and brought to a land that I didn't know anything about and where I didn't want to be. I hated being forced to do anything that a master asked. I want this child to remember this day, Mary, and to know that this is the last time that any man—*any man* will *ever* humiliate me or my family—so help me God!

(*She nods, takes his arm, and they start their exit, LOGAN carrying his son. Blackout.*)

SCENE 11

(*LOGAN's blacksmith shed. Winter, 1841. LOGAN holds his hammer in his good hand and is struggling to hold a large clamp in his useless hand. He cannot bend the arm, nor can he manipulate the clamp properly. After a few futile attempts to use the clamp, he gives up in disgust.*)

LOGAN: If I just had some use in this arm!

(MARIO, *a bit more mature now, enters. He is wearing a coat.*)

MARIO: Señor Logan?

LOGAN: Yes?

MARIO: I'm here from Rancher's Bank.

LOGAN: Yes?

MARIO: I work there now, sir.

LOGAN: Don't I know you, son?

MARIO: I'm Mario Ortega.

LOGAN: Luis' son! It's good to see you again. How's your mother?

MARIO: She's doing well, and you?

LOGAN: Things could be a lot better or a lot worse, I suppose. So you've moved to town and gotten yourself a job at the bank, huh?

MARIO: I was lucky.

LOGAN: What about that family business?

MARIO: That's still our dream, Señor. I save my money with that purpose in mind.

LOGAN: How come the bank send you way out here? To tell me that I owe them money? I already know that.

MARIO: It's more than that, Señor.

LOGAN: Well, what is it?

MARIO: They sent this letter. (*Gives letter to* LOGAN.) They're going to confiscate your farm.

LOGAN: (*Reading.*) Foreclosure . . . December 23rd . . . If all debts are not paid on or before December 22, 1841, Rancher's Bank of Goliad in the Independent Republic of Texas will seize all lands and properties belonging to one Greenbury Logan of Goliad County for debts incurred.

MARIO: I'm sorry, sir.

LOGAN: They can't take my land like this! This land was given to me for services rendered in the war. I gave an arm and a leg for this land and no bank has the right to take it from me. It's not fair. They know that when I manage to get a little work, folks don't pay me.

MARIO: I wish I could help, Señor.

LOGAN: Why is it that the people I owe are allowed to sell their debts due to the bank and not me? I've got a wife and child to care for, if they take my land, what are we going to do?

MARIO: I hate to be the one to bring you such news, Señor.

LOGAN: It's not your fault, Mario, it's those heartless bankers that you work for.

MARIO: There are foreclosures everywhere. Some for debts even smaller than yours. They only foreclose on the best land.

LOGAN: This land is some of the best in the county.

MARIO: They know that, Señor.

LOGAN: And they get it for practically nothing! Well, I won't let them take my property without a fight!

MARIO: If there is anything that I can do—

LOGAN: Thanks, Mario, that's kind of you, but I've got to handle this myself. My regards to your family.

MARIO: Sí, Señor. (*He exits.*)

(*MARY enters with LOGAN's lunch.*)

MARY: Who was that leaving?

LOGAN: Luis Ortega's son, Mario.

MARY: What was he doing here?

LOGAN: He was here to tell me that the bank's gonna take our property—

MARY: But we didn't borrow that much—

LOGAN: They consolidated our debts—bought our debts from people that we owe. That plus the tax money that we borrowed comes to three hundred fifty dollars including interest.

MARY: Where we get that kind of money?

LOGAN: If the law would force people to pay me or if the bank would buy my debts due—

MARY: They ain't gonna do that.

(*Sound of a child crying Off Stage.*)

LOGAN: This is a disgusting shame—

MARY: I'd better go see about the baby. (*She starts off.*)

LOGAN: Mary?

MARY: Yeah?

LOGAN: I'm going to Austin to see Kirkpatrick. Don't worry, hon, everything's gonna be alright.

MARY: I'll pack four days worth of grub in your knapsack. (*He nods as she exits.*)

(*Blackout.*)

SCENE 12

(*Austin, Texas. Several days later. The capitol building.* LOGAN, *cold and tired, enters the capitol building, where he encounters the minister,* JIMMY FOX. LOGAN *coughs from time to time.*)

FOX: Don't you know you're not allowed in here? What's your business anyway?

LOGAN: I'm here to see Representative Frank Kirkpatrick, sir. It's urgent.

FOX: Mr. Kirkpatrick's in session now, you have to wait—outside.

(FOX *exits.* LOGAN *moves outside and stands in the cold restlessly. After a moment there is the sound of conversation Off Stage that gets closer and closer.* KIRKPATRICK *enters with two other white men,* RANKIN *and* FOX.)

KIRKPATRICK: We've got to appropriate more money to the military. How else do you expect our forces to keep the Mexican army out of our territory?

RANKIN: And there're the Indian uprisings—

KIRKPATRICK: The only way our citizens will feel secure and safe is with a large, well-equipped, and ready army. Now you vote with me on this issue.

(*The men mumble among themselves.* RANKIN *and* FOX *exit.* KIRKPATRICK *moves outside.* LOGAN *sees him.*)

LOGAN: Frank! Er . . . Mr. Kirkpatrick, sir?

KIRKPATRICK: Logan? What in hell are you doing here?

LOGAN: I came to see you. It's important. I've been waiting since noon.

KIRKPATRICK: We had a long session, but—what's this all about? Why're you in Austin?

LOGAN: The bank's foreclosing on my property. The owners are speculators, buying up people's debts and foreclosing in order to get land.

KIRKPATRICK: I have no money here, Logan, but—

LOGAN: I'm not here for money.

KIRKPATRICK: Then what do you want?

LOGAN: I came to Texas in 1831 invited by Colonel Austin. He gave me letters of citizenship and a quarter league of land. I felt more of a freeman here than in the states so I decided to stay. I love Texas. You know that I lifted my rifle in every fight with the Mexicans during the campaign of '35 until San Jacinto, where I was the third man that fell. My discharge shows the manner in which I served as a freeman and a soldier, but now look at my situation. Every privilege dear to me as a freeman is taken away, and I'm liable to be imposed upon by anyone that chooses to do it. I can't collect a debt without a witness, I have no vote or say in any way, yet I'm liable for taxes like any other person.

KIRKPATRICK: I know and I'm sorry, Logan.

LOGAN: You're the first man that I've ever come to for help, sir, and as a gentleman, I hope you see the injustice—

KIRKPATRICK: I do see it, Logan, and this isn't right, but the law—

LOGAN: Then will you petition Congress to exempt my lands from taxation and to restore those rights taken from me?

KIRKPATRICK: I understand how you feel—

LOGAN: Then you'll help?

KIRKPATRICK: No. I can't, Logan. If I ask Congress to exempt you, then why shouldn't they exempt other veterans with disabilities?

LOGAN: Maybe they should! Maybe they're not in the situation I'm in.

KIRKPATRICK: I sympathize but I can't be partial.

LOGAN: They'll sell everything that we've got—cow, mule, my tools, all that we'll have left will be the clothes on our backs. Mr. Kirkpatrick, sir, Texas owes me something.

KIRKPATRICK: You received land like we all did!

LOGAN: But it's being taken away! I fought believing that things would continue to get better for me and my people, but things have only gotten worse. More and more slaves are being brought into Texas each day. Mary and I are afraid to stray too far from our spread or each other for fear of being captured and sold back into slavery despite our papers. This has happened, you know? (*Pause.*) Mr. Kirkpatrick—

KIRKPATRICK: Why're you so formal, Logan? We're still friends.

LOGAN: I don't want to embarrass you in public by being too familiar.

KIRKPATRICK: Oh, Logan, please—!

LOGAN: I'm not asking you to do this for me, but for my son's sake.

KIRKPATRICK: You've got a son! How wonderful.

LOGAN: I humbly bow my head to you for his sake.

KIRKPATRICK: You'll do nothing of the sort! You have an earnest request, I just regret that I'm not the person to fulfill it. Nobody is, Logan. I'm sorry. Try to see it from my point of view—as a politician. My duty above all is to the state.

LOGAN: Suppose this were happening to your wife and your son, would you petition if your situation were like mine?

KIRKPATRICK: You know that isn't a fair question. (*Pause.*) You look tired, you'd better get in out of the cold. (*LOGAN nods.*) I'll try to stop by to see Mary and your son when Congress recesses.

LOGAN: If it's after December 23rd, I don't know where we'll be.

KIRKPATRICK: Have faith, Logan. Things have a way of working themselves out for the better. Regards to Mary. (*He exits.*)

(*LOGAN stands for a moment as the lights dim but not completely out. He is cold and shivering. He takes his long journey home by circling the stage.*)

LOGAN: "Get out of the cold, Logan." Get where? (*Coughs. Continues to walk until he is exhausted. He lies down, tries to cover himself as best as he can and, coughing and shivering, he tries to sleep.*) Forward you sons of Texas ... Aim straight ... shoot fast ... Fire! Fire! Advance!

(*As LOGAN tosses, turns, coughs, the lights fade to blackness, but the sounds continue. Gunfire. Screaming and shouting. A circle of light picks up LOGAN in combat. He fires then senses that someone is behind him, but before he completes his turn he is fired upon several times. Before he falls he is able to return the fire, subduing the Off-Stage perpetrator. LUIS enters, sees LOGAN and rushes to him as LOGAN begins to fall. At the same time we hear BOSE's scream "LOOOOOGAAAAAAAN!" BOSE enters in the midst of the scream, rushing to LOGAN and LUIS, who kneels holding LOGAN in his arms. Muffled drum sounds as the lights fade to black. The drum sounds continue in the dark.*)

LOGAN: Mary ...? Where ... are you?! ... Behind you, Frank! ... Got ... him! Forward! Fire ... fire ... fire ... sooooo hot! Burning ... inside ... Can't ... stop ... Advance, men! Remember ... Alamo ... fire ...

(*The lights come up, but not completely, as LOGAN mumbles, hallucinating about the battle. The lights brighten and we find LOGAN ill but in his own cabin with MARY and BOSE with him. MARY applies a cold towel to his forehead.*)

MARY: It'll be alright, honey. Rest ... rest ... sleep. (*To BOSE.*) He's burning up with fever one minute, then chillin' the next. All I can do is cool his brow and keep vigil.

BOSE: Watch and pray, Miss Mary, watch and pray.

LOGAN: My land ... mine! For ... my ... son.

MARY: Hush. Hush. They gonna come in four day, Bose, to take his land and property. Sometimes I pray he don't live to see it. He tried so hard to get us established after the war and things were pretty good at first, then everything just seemed to crumble. But it must be worse for you, being promised something you want so bad and not getting it.

BOSE: I'm gonna get what's mine, Miss Mary, one way or another. Just as sure as I'm standing here, I'm gonna be free.

MARY: (*Nods.*) Sometimes he speaks African words—

BOSE: "Gbogbo àwa omo Yorùbá l'a mò pé ikú yá jù èsín lo."—"All of us Yoruba people, Yoruba sons know that death is preferable to disgrace." He taught me that, Miss Mary.

MARY: He tells our child how honorable and proud his ancestors were.

LOGAN: Faith . . . things . . . better . . .

MARY: This man don't believe it, but God is in his heart. Logan told me that the first thing he ever bought after he was freed and working for pay was a Bible. He was seventeen years old, Bose, and he read that Bible through and through, wore out the pages, but he still got it—to pass on to his son.

BOSE: Logan's a good man.

MARY: First thing he wanted us to have after we marry was a family Bible, and he saved 'til we got one. This is Logan and my precious possession and I'm gonna hide it. (*She shows him a rather new Bible.*) They ain't gonna sell our Bible, Bose. They can sell everything else, but not this.

BOSE: Hide it well, Miss Mary, 'cause nothing ain't safe nowadays. Once when a man told you something, you could believe in his honesty, but times've changed. It's hard to trust the folks you believe in most 'cause you don't know what their position is nowadays.

MARY: Your massa ain't treatin' you bad, is he, Bose?

BOSE: No, he don't treat me bad, but he act like he don't trust me either. He's always got somebody watching me now. That's how come I can't go nowhere!

MARY: You sure used to do your share of slippin' off.

BOSE: Can't no more. But I still get to go places. He takes me to help him cut new trails through unknown wilderness gettin' cattle to market. Discoverin' and explorin' new territories.

MARY: I suspect you doin' most of the exploring and once you've explored and found, he's the one who suddenly "discovered."

BOSE: We work together, Miss Mary—

MARY: Then how come you ain't foreman like you oughta be? How come you ain't *free*?

BOSE: Marse changed. He ain't like he used to be before he learned of that slave uprising in '36. Now he don't trust no Negro, me or nobody else.

MARY: So he goes back on his word and takes your freedom papers.

BOSE: He goes back on his word, but I still got my papers.

(LOGAN *moans softly. He twists about for a moment as* MARY *and* BOSE *observe him. He appears to calm down, then slowly his eyes open.*)

LOGAN: Mary?

MARY: (*Removing the towel and feeling his forehead.*) Yes, honey? (*To* BOSE.) I think his fever's broken!

LOGAN: Mary, I'm so thirsty . . .

BOSE: I'll fetch some water! (*He crosses to get a dipper of water.*)

LOGAN: Who's that with you, honey? Bose?

MARY: Yes, it's Bose. Him and his massa found you passed out on the road from Austin and brought you home . . . over a week ago.

LOGAN: Bose's master?

MARY: He ain't free, Logan.

BOSE: Come on, good friend, drink this cool water.

LOGAN: (*Drinks.*) You're not free? (BOSE *shakes his head, no.*) After all these years he didn't set you free like he promised? (BOSE *does not answer.*) Damn! (*He turns to* MARY.) Kirkpatrick wouldn't help us.

MARY: It's alright now, honey, even if we got the money the bank's found a way to keep this land whether we like it or not. We got to be out of here in four days.

BOSE: Where're you goin'?

LOGAN: I . . . don't know . . .

MARY: You got no need to think about that now, honey. Let me get you some vittles to get your strength back. (*She exits to another side of the room.*)

LOGAN: Bose, everything we ever had, everything that we ever hoped for is gone now. I'm . . . embarrassed, ashamed! I came to Texas an honorable man. I at least wanted to leave, if I had to leave, that way. One thing I do know, I won't take my family back to the States. If we got to leave maybe we'll go to Mexico or further west. We could join up with an Indian tribe—

BOSE: That's adventure, brother, and that ain't you. You've always been a one-place man, and now you've got a family—

LOGAN: Yeah, I know.

BOSE: I'm a free spirit—

LOGAN: You always have been.

BOSE: That's how come I slipped off and come here today. Marse know you and me friends, yet he wouldn't let me come visit, so I—

LOGAN: Just took off at sunset like you've always done?

BOSE: No, good friend, his eyes don't let me go nowhere—never.

LOGAN: That's why we didn't hear from you for . . . years since the war?

BOSE: Marse got tighter reins than I'da thought.

LOGAN: Bose, don't you get yourself in trouble for me. You got many a mile to go to get home. I hope you still riding a fast horse.

BOSE: Yeah, I guess you right, but I'll come again as soon as I can, good friend.

LOGAN: Or else we'll come see you. (*They look at each other, each knowing that this is impossible.*)

BOSE: Bye, Miss Mary.

MARY: Bye, Bose.

(*BOSE exits. MARY sits beside LOGAN and begins to feed him. The lights dim. Blackout.*)

SCENE 13

(*Four days later. The edge of LOGAN's property. He stands with MARY, watching the last of their things being carted off from his home in the distance. MARY holds their family Bible. LOGAN carries a knapsack. After a moment there is a hiss from Off Stage, then BOSE appears cautiously. He is hurt and in obvious pain.*)

MARY: Bose—!

LOGAN: What happened?

BOSE: Marse found out I slipped off. He was waiting when I got back. Said he was gonna teach me how to mind.

MARY: He beat you?

BOSE: (*Shakes his head, no.*) He had his foreman, Hancock, do it. He tied me to a stake, made another nigger hold my head down with my mouth in the dirt and he beat me with a big bullwhip 'til the blood ran out and reddened up the ground. He sent one of the churren to get some salt from Jane, sprinkled it in the cut places until I could feel my skin jerk and quiver. All I could do was slobber and puke.

LOGAN: Jesus! (*He gently pulls back BOSE's coat to examine his back.*) Jesus!

MARY: This man's back still raw and bloody.

LOGAN: You don't need to be out like this, Bose.

BOSE: I've run off. If I go back now, they'll kill me.

LOGAN: You're too valuable.

BOSE: Marse changed, Logan. He'd kill me just to teach the other slaves a lesson.

MARY: I seen a massa beat a woman once. Beat her with a handsaw with the teeth on her back. When she died she still had the marks on her, the teeth holes going crosswise on her back.

BOSE: I'm going to New Mexico . . .

MARY: Indians there, Bose!

BOSE: Indians here, too, and I ain't had no trouble. They can't be no worse'n the white man. Maybe I settle with them.

LOGAN: Your master must be looking for you.

BOSE: I know he is, but I know this territory pretty well. I hide out in the day and travel in the darkness. Yawl look like you traveling, why don't you come and go with me? I got a good horse and know how to live off the land.

LOGAN: No, Bose, we got a child to care for.

BOSE: You gonna try to get to Mexico?

MARY: We don't know where we're going, Bose.

LOGAN: Yes we do, honey.

(MARY *looks at him surprised by his sudden decision, but before she can reply there is the sound of a horse approaching.*)

BOSE: Shhhhhhhh! Someone's coming. (*He ducks out of sight.*)

(*The horse stops.*)

KIRKPATRICK: (*Off Stage.*) Whoooooa . . .

MARY: It's Massa Kirkpatrick!

KIRKPATRICK: (*Entering.*) Logan, I hoped I'd see you before you left. Hello, Mary. (*She nods.*) I'm . . . sorry about this, Logan. I really am.

LOGAN: Thank you.

KIRKPATRICK: This foreclosure of land for debts has been on my mind since I talked to you. I . . . I know what I have in mind is too late to do you any good, but I thought you might like to know . . .

LOGAN: Yes, sir?

KIRKPATRICK: I'm going to introduce a homestead law when Congress resumes next year. I've talked to some of the representatives about it and they seemed pretty interested.

LOGAN: What will this law do?

KIRKPATRICK: It will make sure that no homestead will be taken for debts other than those contracted for that homestead.

LOGAN: That'll be nice, I reckon.

KIRKPATRICK: Have you decided where you'll go?

LOGAN: Yes, sir, I've decided, Mr. Kirkpatrick. I'm staying right here in Texas. I fought for me a piece of this territory and I'm intending to keep on fighting until me and my people have freedom and rights by constitutional law.

KIRKPATRICK: That may be pretty difficult.

LOGAN: Settling Texas has been difficult.

KIRKPATRICK: You're sounding like that abolitionist that you used to accuse me of being.

(BOSE *suddenly appears.*)

BOSE: Captain Kirkpatrick!

KIRKPATRICK: (*Surprised to see him.*) Bose! I thought you were out west somewhere—

BOSE: I will be soon.

KIRKPATRICK: Where's that son of yours, Logan?

LOGAN: Sleeping peacefully yonder under that tree.

KIRKPATRICK: (*Looking in the distance at the child.*) Strong little fellow.

MARY: Sure is.

KIRKPATRICK: Good seeing you again, Bose.

BOSE: Good seeing you. Logan, you and Mary keep in touch.

LOGAN: I intend to, sir. I'll be in Austin a lot from now on letting you representatives know about injustices—

KIRKPATRICK: Serving as our moral conscience, huh?

LOGAN: That's right, sir.

KIRKPATRICK: Take care, Mary.

MARY: I will.

(KIRKPATRICK *exits.*)

MARY: (*To* BOSE.) How come you show your face?

BOSE: I realized he don't know I'm a runaway.

MARY: How do you know what he knows?

LOGAN: Even if he does, he won't tell.

MARY: How do you know?

LOGAN: I know Frank.

BOSE: I'm sure gonna miss you both.

MARY: We gonna miss you, Bose.

BOSE: (*To* LOGAN.) You my best friend. We been through a lot together.

LOGAN: I know, and I'm not ever going to forget you.

BOSE: That boy of yourn looks just like you.

MARY: He's named after Logan, but Logan calls him "Bose."

BOSE: (*Pleased.*) He's gonna be a tough and wild one then!

LOGAN: And he's always gonna be free.

MARY: I dreamed once that this little man would do important things for his people, Bose; that he was gonna be like Moses and start our people on the long march to the promise land—

LOGAN: Here on *earth*. And if he's not able to do it, then his son will.

MARY: Gbogbo àwa omo Yorùbá l'a mò pé ikú yá jù èsín lo.

BOSE: " . . . death is preferable to disgrace."

LOGAN: We've got a lot of fights ahead of us, you in new territory, Bose, and us—here.

BOSE: But we're tough soldiers, right? (*The others smile.*) Company, 'ten-hut! (MARY *and* LOGAN *stand at attention as does* BOSE.) Forward . . . march!

(*The three of them begin to march in place. Cross fade leaving the three of them in circles of light, just as the actors were in the first scene of the play.*)

BOSE: Hup! Two . . . Three. Hup! Two . . . Three . . .
Right foot, Mary! Right foot, Mary!

MARY: Knock it off, Bose—Knock it off, Bose—

BOSE: Hup! Three . . . four. Hup! Three . . . four. Keep in step, Lo. Keep in step, Lo. Hup! Hup!

LOGAN: Here we go again. Here we go again.

BOSE: Hup! Three . . . four. Hup! Three . . . four. Hup! Hup!

(*During the above sequence the other actors appear in circles of light. Drums. Music. Blackout.*)

THE END

....

Chronology

This chronology highlights a sampling of representative events in black theatre in Texas and in the United States, guided by Mikell Pinkney's periods of development in black intellectual thought and aesthetics ("The Development of African American Dramatic Theory: W. E. B. DuBois to August Wilson," in *August Wilson and Black Aesthetics*, ed. Dana Williams and Sandra Shannon [New York: Palgrave Macmillan, 2004]). It also showcases a few significant black history events.

Black Theatre in Texas (Emphasis on Theatre Companies)	Black Theatre in the United States (Emphasis on Theatre Companies and Major Playwrights)	U.S. History (Emphasis on Key Figures, Historically Black Colleges, Salient Events in Black Life and Culture)
1. Plantation or Slave Era (1600s through the Civil War)		
	1830s–early 1900s: The first blackface minstrel companies form. They were popular until the turn of the century and formed the basis of vaudeville and the American musical. Whites in blackface imitated singing and dancing blacks; blacks joined minstrel troupes after the Civil War. Black troupes that dominated in the late 1860s and 1870s were Brooker and Clayton's Georgia Minstrels and Sam Hague's Slave Troupe of Georgia Minstrels. 1821: African Grove Theatre, founded by William Archer Brown in New York City. 1856: *Escape, or A Leap for Freedom*, written by William Wells Brown.	

Black Theatre in Texas (Emphasis on Theatre Companies)	Black Theatre in the United States (Emphasis on Theatre Companies and Major Playwrights)	U.S. History (Emphasis on Key Figures, Historically Black Colleges, Salient Events in Black Life and Culture)
2. American Minstrel Era (1860s through the turn of the century)		
		1865: Civil War ends. The Thirteenth Amendment to Constitution abolishes slavery.
		1867: Howard University is founded by Union General Oliver O. Howard as an institute for preachers and teachers.
		1868: The Fourteenth Amendment to the Constitution grants citizenship to former slaves.
		1870: The Fifteenth Amendment to the Constitution prohibits states from denying the right to vote because of race.
		1873: Wiley College is founded.
		1876: Prairie View A&M University is founded.
		1876: Samuel Huston College is founded.
		1877: Tillotson College is founded.
		1881: Tuskegee Institute is founded.
		1894: Texas College is founded.

Black Theatre in Texas (Emphasis on Theatre Companies)	Black Theatre in the United States (Emphasis on Theatre Companies and Major Playwrights)	U.S. History (Emphasis on Key Figures, Historically Black Colleges, Salient Events in Black Life and Culture)
1890s: Texarkana Minstrel Company; Scott Joplin is a member in 1897.	1895–1908: The Williams and Walker musical theatre comedy team tours the country.	1896: The *Plessy vs. Ferguson* Supreme Court decision makes segregation legal.
1890s: Dudley Georgia Minstrels, led by minstrel and producer Sherman Dudley.		1898: St. Philip's Normal and Industrial School is founded.
1896: *Smart Set*, a musical written and first produced by Sherman Dudley.		1909: The NAACP (National Association for the Advancement of Colored People) is founded.
1900s: Black-oriented vaudeville theatres in Texas that booked Chitlin Circuit plays include the Pastime Theatre and American Theatre in Houston, the Pastime Theatre in Greenville, and the Ruby Theatre in Galveston.		1919: W. E. B. Du Bois organizes the first Pan-African Congress in Paris, France, and he is elected executive secretary.
1919: The Colored Community House, San Antonio, opens; it is renamed the Colored Library Auditorium in 1930 and renamed the Carver Library Auditorium, after George Washington Carver, in 1938. After renovation in 1976, it is reopened as the Carver Community Cultural Center.		

Black Theatre in Texas (Emphasis on Theatre Companies)	Black Theatre in the United States (Emphasis on Theatre Companies and Major Playwrights)	U.S. History (Emphasis on Key Figures, Historically Black Colleges, Salient Events in Black Life and Culture)
3. New Negro Renaissance Era, or Harlem Renaissance (1917 through 1920s)		
1920s: Myra Hemmings establishes the Phyllis [sic] Wheatley Dramatic Guild Players at Phillis Wheatley High School. Post–World War I: The Coleridge Taylor Glee Club and Drama Group, founded by E. O. Smith, starts in Houston. 1920s: J. W. Hemmings (with George Webster, Cliff Richardson, Emil Farnsworth, and Edna Griffith) presents Broadway shows in Houston. 1925: The Log Cabin Players at Wiley College is founded by Melvin B. Tolson. 1929: The Charles Gilpin Players, the oldest consistently performing minority theatre troupe in Texas, is founded at Prairie View A&M College.	1920: *Appearances* by Garland Anderson is produced on Broadway. 1920: The musical *Shuffle Along*, by Aubrey Lyles and Noble Sissle. 1920: Charles Gilpin stars in *Emperor Jones*, by Eugene O'Neill. 1923: *The Chip Woman's Fortune*, by Willis Richardson, is produced on Broadway. 1928: The Harlem Experimental Theatre is founded. 1929: The Krigwa Players are founded by W. E. B. Du Bois.	1920s: The Harlem Renaissance begins, a period of almost fifteen years when some of the most important and prolific writers, artists, and musicians—such as Zora Neale Hurston and Langston Hughes—emerge in the African American community, taking up residence in New York's Harlem district. 1920s: Marcus Garvey, entrepreneur, journalist, and proponent of black nationalism, starts the UNIA (Universal Negro Improvement Association). He encourages black Americans to return to their African homeland, establishing the Black Star Line, a fleet of black-owned steamships. 1925–1927: Wiley College Extension is founded. 1927: St. Philip's Normal and Industrial School becomes a junior college for the black community in San Antonio; its name is later changed to St. Philip's College.
4. Assimilationist Era (1930s through 1950s)		
1931–World War II: The Houston Negro Little Theatre is founded and operated by Robert Holland. 1936: The black intercollegiate Southern Association of Dramatic and Speech Arts is founded by Melvin B. Tolson at Wiley College.	1935: Langston Hughes' *Mulatto* is produced on Broadway.	1930s: The Great Depression. 1930s: The Nation of Islam is founded in the United States. Its members are commonly known as Black Muslims. 1935–1947: Houston Colored Junior College becomes the Houston College for Negroes.

Black Theatre in Texas (Emphasis on Theatre Companies)	Black Theatre in the United States (Emphasis on Theatre Companies and Major Playwrights)	U.S. History (Emphasis on Key Figures, Historically Black Colleges, Salient Events in Black Life and Culture)
1940s: The Tillotson College Players, in Austin, an academic theatre troupe, is active during the early years of the decade. The group performs *Craig's Wife* and other standard plays. Tillotson College is later renamed Huston-Tillotson College. 1947: Ollington Smith is hired as the first theatre instructor and director in the English Department at Texas State University for Negroes; he founds the University Players.	1940s: The ANT (American Negro Theatre) Company is founded. 1940s: The Negro Playwrights Company is founded.	1947–1951: Houston College for Negroes changes its name to Texas State University for Negroes.
1950: The Southern Association of Dramatic and Speech Arts becomes the National Association of Dramatic and Speech Arts.	1955: Alice Childress' *Trouble in Mind* wins an Obie Award for best off-Broadway play of the year.	1951-present: Texas State University for Negroes becomes Texas Southern University. 1952: Malcolm X begins his ascent as the chief spokesperson for the Nation of Islam. He leaves the Nation in 1964. 1952: Tillotson College and Samuel Huston College merge, forming Huston-Tillotson College. 1954: *Brown vs. Board of Education.*
	1959: *A Raisin in the Sun*, by Lorraine Hansberry, is produced on Broadway; it wins the New York Drama Critics' Circle Award for best play of 1959. *A Raisin in the Sun* was the first play written by a black woman to be produced on Broadway, as well as the first play to have a black director (Lloyd Richards) on Broadway.	1960: The Student Nonviolent Coordinating Committee (SNCC) is founded; freedom riders began their work.

5. Black Revolutionary Era (mid-1960s to mid-1970s)

	1960s to 1970s: Over six hundred community and university black theatre organizations flourish. 1961: The comedy *Purlie Victorious*, by Ossie Davis, opens on Broadway. 1961: *Black Nativity*, by Langston Hughes. opens on Broadway; it becomes a Christmas holiday classic.	1963: Rev. Martin Luther King, Jr., delivers his "I Have a Dream" speech before a crowd of two hundred thousand during the Civil Rights March on Washington, DC.

Black Theatre in Texas (Emphasis on Theatre Companies)	Black Theatre in the United States (Emphasis on Theatre Companies and Major Playwrights)	U.S. History (Emphasis on Key Figures, Historically Black Colleges, Salient Events in Black Life and Culture)
	1964: *Dutchman*, by LeRoi Jones (later Amiri Baraka), opens off-Broadway, heralding the beginning of Black Revolutionary Theatre. 1965–1975: The Black Arts Movement is launched by LeRoi Jones (Amiri Baraka). It inspires black people to establish their own publishing houses, magazines, journals, and art institutions and inspires the establishment of African American Studies programs within universities.	1964: President Johnson signs the Civil Rights Act, which prohibits discrimination based on race, color, religion, or gender; Dr. King is awarded the Nobel Peace Prize. 1965: President Johnson signs the Voting Rights Act, which prohibits discriminatory voting practices. 1965: In six days of rioting in Watts, a black section of Los Angeles, 35 people are killed, and 883 are injured. 1965: Malcolm X, Black Muslim leader, is assassinated.
1966–1967: St. Philip's College starts offering speech courses "designed [for] such vocations as the theatre."	1967: The Negro Ensemble Company is founded in New York City by Douglass Turner Ward, Robert Hooks, and Gerald Krone.	1966: In Oakland California, Huey Newton and Bobby Seale found the Black Panther Party for Self-Defense.
1968: The Myra D. Hemmings Memorial Theatre Guild evolves from the Dramatic Theatre Guild at the Second Baptist Church in San Antonio. 1968–1969: St. Philip's College bulletin lists a Speech and Drama Department.	1968: The New Lafayette Theatre is founded by Robert Macbeth in Harlem, New York; Ed Bullins is established as playwright-in-residence.	1968: Rev. Martin Luther King, Jr., is assassinated in Memphis.
1969: The Urban Theatre is established by Barbara Marshall in Houston. 1969: The Mary G. Campbell Players at Tyler College produce *The Irregular Verb to Love*. 1969: While serving as a professor at Prairie View A&M University in Texas, Ted Shine writes his most-produced play, *Contribution*. The Negro Ensemble Company produces it that same year off-Broadway with thirty-two performances.		

Black Theatre in Texas (Emphasis on Theatre Companies)	Black Theatre in the United States (Emphasis on Theatre Companies and Major Playwrights)	U.S. History (Emphasis on Key Figures, Historically Black Colleges, Salient Events in Black Life and Culture)
6. Afrocentric Era (mid-1970s through 1980s)		
1970s: The Black Arts Alliance is founded by Elouise Burrell in Austin. 1970: The Repertory Theatre is founded by Rev. Earl Allen in Houston. 1972–1981: The Sojourner Truth Players are founded by Erma Duffy Lewis and five others in Fort Worth.	1970s: Numerous black musicals triumph on Broadway: *Purlie* (book by Ossie Davis, Philip Rose, and Peter Udell), *Ain't Supposed to Die a Natural Death* (book by Melvin van Peebles), *Don't Bother Me, I Can't Cope* (book by Micki Grant), *The Wiz* (book adaptation from *The Wizard of Oz* by William F. Brown), *Bubbling Brown Sugar* (book by Loften Mitchell and Rosetta LeNoire), *Ain't Misbehavin'* (book by Murray Horwitz and Richard Maltby), and *Eubie!* (revue, music by Eubie Blake). 1970: Charles Gordone wins the Pulitzer Prize for his play *No Place to Be Somebody*.	
1973–ca. 1979: The Dallas Minority Repertory Theatre is founded by Irma P. Hall and Reginald Montgomery. 1973: The Afro-American Players are founded by GloDean Baker and Freddie Gardner in Austin. 1974: Texas Southern University begins offering a bachelor of arts degree in theatre.	1974: *The River Niger*, by Joseph A. Walker, receives the Tony Award for drama.	
1976: The Black Ensemble Theatre is founded by George Hawkins in Houston; its name is later changed to the Ensemble Theatre. 1977: The Junior Black Academy of Arts and Letters is founded by Curtis King in Dallas; its name is changed to the Black Academy of Arts and Letters in 1997.	1977: *for colored girls who have considered suicide when the rainbow is enuf*, by Ntozake Shange, opens on Broadway; it wins the Outer Critics Circle Award, a Grammy, an Emmy, and three Obie Awards.	
1981: The Jubilee Theatre is founded by Rudy and Marian Eastman in Fort Worth. 1981–1982: St. Philip's College changes the department name from Speech and Drama to Speech and Theatre.	1982: Charles Fuller receives the Pulitzer Prize for *A Soldier's Play*. 1984: August Wilson makes his Broadway debut with *Ma Rainey's Black Bottom*.	1980: Robert Johnson launches BET (the Black Entertainment Network).

Black Theatre in Texas (Emphasis on Theatre Companies)	Black Theatre in the United States (Emphasis on Theatre Companies and Major Playwrights)	U.S. History (Emphasis on Key Figures, Historically Black Colleges, Salient Events in Black Life and Culture)
1985–1995: The Dallas Drama Company is led by Dianne Tucker.		
1986–2006: Sterling Houston joins the Jump-Start Performance Co. as an actor, later becoming writer-in-residence and artistic director. Jump-Start produces twenty of his thirty-three plays. 1986: The Austin Theatre Project is founded by Boyd Vance.	1986: George Wolfe's *The Colored Museum* opens at the New York Shakespeare Festival/Public Theatre in New York City.	1986: Oprah Winfrey makes her debut; she becomes a successful talk-show host and entrepreneur.
1987: The first production of Celeste Bedford Walker's *Camp Logan* at Kuumba House in Houston, Texas. The play has toured to theatres in Texas as well as coast to coast between New York and California since then.	1987: August Wilson wins the Pulitzer Prize for *Fences*. 1988: August Wilson's *Joe Turner's Come and Gone* wins the Drama Critics Circle Award. 1989: Larry Leon Hamlin organizes the National Black Theatre Festival in Winston-Salem, North Carolina.	

7. New Age Post-revolutionary Era (1990s to Present)

Black Theatre in Texas (Emphasis on Theatre Companies)	Black Theatre in the United States (Emphasis on Theatre Companies and Major Playwrights)	U.S. History
1990–1995: The Vivid Theatre Ensemble is founded by Akin Babatunde and Christopher Long in Dallas. 1992: The Progressive-Arts (Pro-Arts) Collective theatre group is established in Austin by Boyd Vance, Dewy Brooks, and Trina Scott. 1992: St. Philip's College opens a state-of-the-art theatre complex.	1990: August Wilson wins a second Pulitzer Prize, for *The Piano Lesson*. 1991: August Wilson's *Two Trains Running* wins the American Critics/Steinberg New Play Award.	
1993: The Hornsby Entertainment Theatre Company is established under the leadership of Kathy Hornsby; the company started in 1987 as the Christian Players.	1993: George Wolfe is appointed director of Joseph Papp's New York Shakespeare Festival/Public Theatre in New York City. 1993: Anna Deveare Smith, best known for her "documentary theatre" style in plays such as *Fires in the Mirror* and *Twilight: Los Angeles*, both of which featured Smith as the sole performer of multiple and diverse characters, wins the Drama Desk Award for Outstanding One-Person Show two years in a row.	

Black Theatre in Texas (Emphasis on Theatre Companies)	Black Theatre in the United States (Emphasis on Theatre Companies and Major Playwrights)	U.S. History (Emphasis on Key Figures, Historically Black Colleges, Salient Events in Black Life and Culture)
1994: The first production of *East Texas Hot Links* by Eugene Lee; productions of the work have appeared in several other venues around the United States and also at the Royal Court Theatre in London.		
1995: Encore Theatre founded by Harold Haynes in Houston. 1995–2002: Soul Nation is founded by Guinea Bennett-Price, Tisha Crear, and others; it becomes the Soul Repertory Theatre Company. 2001: The Renaissance Guild is founded by Raul Riddle, Latrelle Bright, and Danielle King in San Antonio.	2000: Tyler Perry, in drag as Medea in *Woman, Thou Art Loosed*, begins renting theatres in the Urban Circuit (formerly the Chitlin' Circuit); he becomes a multimillionaire actor and producer and owner of his own movie studio. 2001: Suzan-Lori Parks receives a MacArthur Foundation "Genius" Grant in 2001 and the Pulitzer Prize for Drama for her play *Topdog/ Underdog* in 2002. 2002: August Wilson's *Jitney* wins the New York Drama Critics' Circle Award.	
	2005: Lloyd Richards, director of the 1959 production of *Raisin in the Sun*, dies. 2005: August Wilson dies, and the Virginia Theatre on Broadway is renamed the August Wilson Theatre. 2005: Lynn Nottage receives a Guggenheim Fellowship; she later receives a MacArthur Foundation "Genius" Grant in 2007 and wins the Pulitzer Prize for Drama in 2009 for *Ruined*.	
2006–2008: The Ebony Emeralds Classic Theatre Company is founded by Akin Babatunde in Dallas.	2006: The Signature Theatre in New York City produces a season of August Wilson's plays.	
2008: The African American Repertory Company in Dallas is established by Irma P. Hall, Vince McGill, and Regina Washington.	2007: August Wilson's *Radio Gulf*, the final play in his ten-play cycle, opens on Broadway and is nominated for four Tony Awards.	2008: Barack Obama becomes the first African American to be elected president.

....

Playwrights' Canon

This is a list of playwrights who have lived and written in Texas or who are currently living and working in Texas.

Note: p = date first produced; w = date written; * = published.

BABATUNDE, AKIN

Zig-Zag (p: 1985)
What If? (p: 1991)
Before the Second Set: A Visit with Satchmo (p: 1997)
Of Ebony Embers: Vignettes of the Harlem Renaissance (p: 1998)
Shakespeare . . . Midnight Echoes (p: 2003)
Blind Lemon Blues (co-writer) (p: 2007)
God's Leading Ladies (p: 2007)
Obituary (p: 2007)
Songs in the Key of Glee (p: 2007)

BROWN-GUILLORY, ELIZABETH

*Bayou Relics (p: 1981)
*Mam Phyllis (p: 1981)
*Somebody Almost Walked Off with All of My Stuff (p: 1982)
*Marry Me, Again (p: 1984)
*Snapshots of Broken Dolls (p: 1986)
*Saving Grace (p: 1993)
*Missing Sister (p: 1996)
*La Bakair (p: 2001)
Ten Years in a Suitcase (p: 2002)
*When the Ancestors Call (p: 2003)
*The Break of Day (p: 2005)
A Little Diversion (p: 2005)

CARRIER, NAOMI MITCHELL

*Slav'ry Chain Done Broke at Las' (p: 1994)
*Arcy Attempts Escape (p: 1995)
*Arcy Makes Room for Judith Martin: The Breakup of a Slave Family (p: 1996)
*Christmas at Varner-Hogg: Patton Plantation (p: 1998)
*Hello or High Water: Brit Bailey Heads Off Stephen F. Austin (p: 1998)
*Jumpin' Juba: Uncle Bubba and Mammy Bell Jump de Broom (p: 1998)
*Juneteenth at the George Ranch (p: 1998)
*Social Politics in Victorian Texas: A Living History Interpretation of African
     Americans and Their Responsibilities (p: 1998)
*A Little Slave for Sale—Cheap! (p: 1999)
*Fugitives of Passion: On the Texas Underground Railroad to Mexico (p: 1999)
*Sweet By and By: Barrington Farm Chronicle (p: 2000)
*Cane Cutter Country: The Saga of the Lake Jackson Plantation (p: 2000)
*Still Am A'Risin': The Battle of Velasco and the Vigil at Bolivar (p: 2002)
*Plantation Liendo: Civil War Reenactment (unknown)

CAYWOOD, MARK

Go Tell It on the Mountain: The Second Greatest Story Ever Told (with Joe Rogers)
     (p: 1991)
Black Orpheus (with Joe Rogers) (p: 1995)
The Book of Job (with Douglas Balentine) (p: 1996)
The Ballad of Isom Dart (with Joe Rogers) (p: 1997)

DUDLEY, SHERMAN

The Smart Set (p: 1896)
The Black Politician (with S. B. Cassion) (p: 1908)
His Honor, the Barber (p: 1909-1911)
Dr. Beans from Boston (with Henry Troy) (p: 1911-1912)

EASTMAN, RUDY

Blues Ain't Nothin' but a Good Man Feeling Bad (p: 1982)
Dunbar Is Not Just a High School (p: 1982)
It Ain't Grease, It's Dixie Peach (with Darwin Mendoza and Joe Rogers) (p: 1984)
Prodigal (with Robert Sanders) (p: 1984)
Drums (with Betty Green and Quincy Johnson) (p: 1986)
Negroes in Space (with Doug Balentine) (p: 1986)
Class of '62 (p: 1988)
Dreamin' on a Hot Summer Night (with Doug Balentine) (p: 1989)
Empress of the Blues (p: 1989)

On the Corner (with Robert Sanders and Darwin Mendoza) (p: 1989)
Imaginary Invalid (p: 1989)
A Joyful Noise (p: 1990)
Dem Birds (p: 1990)
Midnight Walker (with Joe Rogers) (p: 1990)
Kate and Petruchio (Or You Ain't No Street Walker . . .) (p: 1991)
The Tarzan Movie (with Douglas Balentine) (p: 1991)
Harlem Blues (p: 1992)
Black Diva (with New Arts Six) (p: 1992)
Back on the Corner (with Joe Rogers) (p: 1992)
Blacula: Brother of the Night (p: 1993)
Brother Mac (with Michelle Baker) (p: 1993)
Straight, No Chaser (with Joe Rogers) (p: 1994)
Caesar and Cleopatra (p: 1995)
Book of Job (with Joe Rogers) (p: 1996)
Lysistrata Please (with Joe Rogers) (p: 1996)
Dirty Laundry (under the alias C. C. Cole-Eastman) (p: 1997)
The Sho-Nuf Blues: A Musical Tribute to W.C. Handy (p: 1998)
Spirits of the Passage (p: 1998)
Zimwe and the Drum (p: 1998)
I Too Sing (with Joe Rogers) (p: 1999)
Travelin' Shoes (with Joe Rogers) (p: 1999)
Coop DeVille: Time Traveling Brother (with Joe Rogers) (p: 2001)
The Tempest (with Joe Rogers) (p: 2000)
The Low Down Man/Woman Dirty Blues (with Joe Rogers) (p: 2002)
Alice Wonder (with Joe Rogers) (p: 2002)
Romeo (under the alias Charles C. Cole-Eastman) (p: 2002)
Auntee Explains Xmas (with Joe Rogers) (p: 2003)
Rhythm: A Musical Myth (with Joe Rogers) (p: 2004)
The Odyssey (unfinished when deceased; completed by Sheran Goodspeed
    Keyton with Joe Rogers) (p: 2006)

EDMUND, REGINALD

The City of the Bayou Collection (a nine-play series, in progress):

- *Juneteenth Street* (w: 2006)
- *Redemption of Allah Black* (w: 2006)
- *The Ordained Smile of Saint Sadie May Jenkins* (w: 2008)
- *Last Cadillac* (w: 2010)
- *Blood Moon* (w: 2010)

- *White America* (w: 2010)
- *Southbridge* (p: 2013)

A Love Story (p: 2004)
Southpark (p: 2005)
Nat Turner: A Prophet's Sorrow (p: 2006)
Black Theatre: Our Story (p: 2006)
Picnics (w: 2008)
Everybody Respects Big E (w: 2009)
Apartment 2301 (p: 2010)
Racing the Blue Lights (w: 2010)

GLENN, DON WILSON

American Menu (p: 2009)

HALL, IRMA P.

From Excellence to Exploitation (p: 1974)
Black Girl (p: 1974)
Gentle Fires (p: 1975)

HAWKINS, GEORGE

Br'er Rabbit (p: 1977)
Surprise, Surprise . . . A Love Story (p: 1979)
Who Killed Hazel Patton? (under the alias Carl Anderson) (p: 1980)

HAYNES, HAROLD

*Schezelle (p: 1983)
Three Little Pigs (adaptation) (p: 1984)
Rulers, Riches and Rainbows (p: 1985)
*Alleyways (p: 1987)
*I Just Wanna Tell Somebody (p: 1987)
Cinderella (p: 1990)
*Behind Closed Doors (p: 1991)
Isolation (p: 1993)
*Incarceration (p: 1995)
Shout! Hallelujah! (p: 1996)
*It Ain't Over 'til the Fat Lady Sing (p: 1997)
*Rage (p: 1998)
Romeo and Juliet (adaptation) (p: 1999)
Othello (adaptation) (p: 2000)
*Samson and Delilah (p: 2002)

Three Blind Mice (p: 2002)
*God's Mad Clown (p: 2004)
*Women in Prison (p: 2005)
Stand (p: 2006)
Black on Broadway (adaptation) (p: 2007)
Divas and Daredevils (adaptation) (p: 2007)
*Jezebel (p: 2008)
Love on the Rocks (w: 2008)
The Greatest Story Ever Told (adaptation) (p: 2009)
Driven (w: 2010)
Jack and the Beanstalk (adaptation) (p: 2010)

HOLMES, WILLIE

The Wounded (p: 1999)
The Corporate Plantation (p: 1999)
Rhaka's Redemption (p: 2000)
Daddy's Girl (p: 2001)
Love Doesn't Hurt (p: 2002)
Saturday (p: 2002)
America vs. Racism (p: 2002)
Suspects in America (p: 2003)
Eve's Garden (p: 2003)
A Heaven for a Gee (p: 2006)

HOUSTON, STERLING

Harlem: A Renaissance Remembered (p: 1986)
A Brief History of American Song (p: 1988)
The Modernization of Sainthood (p: 1988)
The Late Late Show at the Gilded Cage (p: 1989)
Relationships: Good and Not So Good (p: 1989)
A'lelia (p: 1990)
Kool Jams (p: 1990)
Travels of the Time-Train (p: 1990)
Cheap Talk (p: 1992)
*Driving Wheel (p: 1992)
*High Yello Rose (p: 1992)
*Womandingo (p: 1992)
*La Frontera (p: 1993)
*Isis in Nubia (p: 1993)
*Miranda Rites (p: 1994)

Snow White and the Seven Deadly Sins (p: 1994)
On the Pulse of Morning (adapted for the stage from the poem by Maya
 Angelou) (p: 1995)
Santo Negro (p: 1995)
*Black Lily and White Lily (p: 1996)
*Miss Bowden's Dream (p: 1998)
The Alien Show: Kool Jams (p: 1999)
Le Griffon (p: 2000)
Message Sent (p: 2000)
*Cameoland (p: 2002)
El Calor de Amor (p: 2003)
Black and Blue, Four Centuries of Struggle and Transcendence (p: 2003)
*The Living Graves (p: 2005)
The Last of the Tennessee Waltz (p: 2006)
Leche de Luna (p: 2006)
Millie and Christina (p: 2006)
Hollywood and Time (p: 2007)
Miz Johnson and Mr. Jones (undated)
The Ballad of Box Brown (undated)

KEYTON, SHERAN GOODSPEED

Diaries of a Barefoot Diva (p: 2006)
The Odyssey (p: 2006)
Uncle Duz Christmas (p: 2008)
I'm Every Woman: A Tribute to Great Women in Music (p: 2009)
The Man I Love (p: 2010)

LEE, EUGENE

Killingsworth (p: 1988)
*East Texas Hot Links (p: 1990)
Twist (w: 1993)
Stones in My Passway (w: 1994)
Fear Itself (p: 1996)
Somebody Called (w: 2003)
The Rest of Me (w: 2010)

MAYO, SANDRA

Frederick Douglass: Reflections on a Struggle for Freedom (w: 1982)

MELONCON, THOMAS

    The Death of O. D. Walker (p: 1975)
    From Africa to Third Ward (p: 1980)
    The Diary of Black Men (p: 1982)
    Where Were You in '65 (p: 1984)
    Guess Who Is Pregnant (p: 1988)
    Poetry in E Minor (collection of poetry) (p: 1991)
    Their Berries Are Sweeter (p: 1991)
    Mrs. Cavender's Class (p: 1992)
    A Matter of Manhood (p: 1993)
    A Storm in the Church (p: 1993)
    Our Feet Can Tell a Story (p: 1993)
    The Colored Section (p: 1994)
    The Melting Pot (p: 1994)
    Before Time Runs Out (p: 1995)
    If Beds Could Talk (p: 1997)
    The Drums of Sweetwater (p: 1997)
    Stop the Noise (p: 1997)
    The Tree That Grew Human (p: 1997)
    When Love Is Not Enough (p: 1997)
    Ain't Nothin' Wrong with a Gizzard Sandwich (p: 1998)
    Johnny B. Goode (p: 1998)
    Whatever Happened to Black Love? (p: 1998)
    The Dream of Doors (p: 1999)
    A Song of Abstinence (p: 2000)
    Four Songs in the Key of Love (p: 2000)
    The Rainbow Celebration (p: 2001)
    The Tobacco Road (p: 2001)
    Young Mandela (p: 2002)
    The Laws of Storms (p: 2002)
    Let Yesterday Go (p: 2002)
    Jump the Broom (p: 2003)
    Restricted Area (p: 2003)
    The Grass Ain't Always Greener (p: 2003)
    A Hip Hop Wedding (p: 2004)
    Father in the House (p: 2004)
    The Robeson Family Chronicles, A Radio Drama Series (p: 2006)
    What Shall We Teach the Children (p: 2006)
    Sarah and Joshua: A Juneteenth Musical (p: 2008)

The Marriage Test (p: 2008)
Carlton's Closet (p: 2009)
Christmas with Great Aunt (p: 2009)
Dreams and Decisions (p: 2009)
The Man Who Saved New Orleans (p: 2009)
The Gospel According to Hip Hop (undated)

MONTGOMERY, REGINALD

When the Last One Goes (p: 1974)

SANDERS, BOB RAY

Blues on 125th Street (p: 1978)

SHINE, TED

Cold Day in August (p: 1950)
Sho Is Hot in the Cotton Patch; Miss Weaver (p: 1951)
Dry August (p: 1952)
The Bats Out of Hell (p: 1955)
Entourage Royale (p: 1958)
Epitaph for a Bluebird (p: 1958)
A Rat's Revolt (p: 1959)
Morning Noon and Night (p: 1964)
Miss Victoria (p: 1965)
Pontiac (p: 1967)
Jeanne West (p: 1968)
Revolution (p: 1968)
Come Back after the Fire (p: 1969)
Contributions (p: 1969)
Flora's Kisses (p: 1969)
Hamburgers at Hamburger Heaven Are Impersonal (p: 1969)
Idabel's Fortune (p: 1969)
Shoes (p: 1969)
Waiting Room (p: 1969)
Plantation (p: 1970)
Packard (p: 1971)
Herbert III (p: 1974)
The Night of Baker's End (p: 1974)
The Woman Who Was Tampered with in Youth (p: 1981)
Ancestors (p: 1986)

TUCKER, DIANNE (diannetucker)

Shoes (p: 1986)
Cat Cross (p: 1988)
The Christmas Secret (p: 1988)
When Effie Burke Passed (p: 1989)
The Gamesmen (p: 1990)
Mahalia Speaks (p: 1991)
Profiles in Faith (p: 1992)
Hershey with Almonds (p: 1995)
Daddy's Maybe (p: 1996)
Madam Queen (p: 1998)
Attitude, Girlfriend, Attitude (with Joe Rogers) (p: 1999)
Fat Freddy (with Joe Rogers) (p: 2001)
Road Show (p: 2003)

WALKER, CELESTE BEDFORD

Once in a Wife Time (formerly *Sister, Sister*) (p: 1978)
Smokes Bayou (w: 1979; p: 1979)
The Wreckin' Ball (p: 1980)
Spirits (w: 1980; p: 1981)
Adam and Eve, Revisited (p: 1981)
Reunion in Bartersville (p: 1983)
Camp Logan (w: 1987; p: 1987)
Over Forty (p: 1989)
Brothers, Sisters, Husbands and Wives (p: 1993)
Noble Lofton, Buffalo Soldier (p: 1994)
Praise the Lord, and Raise the Roof (p: 1996)
Jack Yates (p: 1996)
Distant Voices (p: 1997)
The Boule (p: 1997)
Blacks in the Methodist Church (p: 1998)
The History of Wheeler Baptist Church (p: 1998)
The African Talking Drum (p: 1999)
Where My Girls At? (p: 1999)
Fabulous African Fables (p: 2001)
Reparations Day (p: 2001)
Freedom Trail (p: 2002)
Harlem after Hours (p: 2003)
Sassafras Girls (w: 2003)

Giants in the Land (p: 2004)
Hip Hoppin' the Dream! (p: 2006)
Sassy Mamas (p: 2007)
I, Barbara Jordan (p: 2008)

WINSTEAD, ANTOINETTE

Too Long Coming (p: 2003)
The Interrogation (p: 2004)
Blues before Sunrise (p: 2005)
For the Love of Man (w: 2005)
Somebody Else's Life (p: 2005)
The Birthday Surprise (p: 2007)
The Gift (p: 2008)
A Lifetime of Lifetimes (p: 2009)
Common Ground (p: 2009)

Publications by Black Texas Playwrights

Black Drama: African, African American, and Diaspora, 1850 to Present. 2nd ed. Alexandria, VA: Alexander Street Press, 2013. Database. Available through Alexander Street Press, http://solomon.bld2.alexanderstreet.com/, or through university libraries. (Includes ten plays by Elizabeth Brown-Guillory.)

Brasmer, William, ed. *Black Drama: An Anthology.* Columbus, OH: C. E. Merrill, 1970. (Includes *Contribution*, by Ted Shine.)

Carrier, Naomi Mitchell. *Go Down Old Hannah: The Living History of African American Texans.* Austin: University of Texas, 2010.

Hatch, James V., and Ted Shine, eds. *Black Theater U.S.A.: Forty-Five Plays by Black Americans, 1847–1974.* New York: Free Press, 1974. (Includes *Herbert III* by Ted Shine.)

———. *Black Theatre U.S.A.: Plays by African Americans: The Recent Period, 1935–Today.* New York: Free Press, 1996. (Includes *Contribution*, by Ted Shine.)

Haynes, Harold. *Darker Faces: A Collecting of Works for the Theatre.* Xlibris Corporation, 2011. E-book.

Haynes, Harold. *I Just Want to Tell Somebody.* Schulenburg, TX: I. E. Clark Publishing, 1987.

Houston, Sterling. *High Yello Rose and Other Texas Plays by Sterling Houston.* Edited by Sandra M. Mayo. San Antonio, TX: Wings Press, 2009.

———, ed. *Jump-Start Play Work: A Collection of Multicultural Plays and Solo Performance Works from Jump-Start Performance Co.* San Antonio, TX: Wings Press, 2004. (Includes *Womandingo*, by Sterling Houston.)

———. *Myth, Magic and Farce: Four Multicultural Plays by Sterling Houston.* Edited by Sandra M. Mayo. Denton: University of North Texas Press, 2005.

Lee, Eugene. *East Texas Hot Links.* New York: Samuel French, 1994.

Richard, Stanley, ed. *The Best Short Plays.* Philadelphia: Chilton Book Co., 1972. (Includes *Contribution*, by Ted Shine.)

Shine, Ted. *Contributions.* New York: Dramatists Play Service, 1970.